Global Technology Management 4.0

Pratim Milton Datta

Global Technology Management 4.0

Concepts and Cases for Managing
in the 4th Industrial Revolution

Pratim Milton Datta
Ambassador Crawford College
of Business and Entrepreneurship
Kent State University
Kent, OH, USA

University of Johannesburg
Johannesburg, South Africa

IT University of Copenhagen
Copenhagen, Denmark

This work contains media enhancements, which are displayed with a "play" icon. Material in the print book can be viewed on a mobile device by downloading the Springer Nature "More Media" app available in the major app stores. The media enhancements in the online version of the work can be accessed directly by authorized users.

ISBN 978-3-030-96928-8   ISBN 978-3-030-96929-5   (eBook)
https://doi.org/10.1007/978-3-030-96929-5

© PiaDura LTD 2022
This work is subject to copyright. All rights are solely and exclusively licensed by the Publisher, whether the whole or part of the material is concerned, specifically the rights of translation, reprinting, reuse of illustrations, recitation, broadcasting, reproduction on microfilms or in any other physical way, and transmission or information storage and retrieval, electronic adaptation, computer software, or by similar or dissimilar methodology now known or hereafter developed. The use of general descriptive names, registered names, trademarks, service marks, etc. in this publication does not imply, even in the absence of a specific statement, that such names are exempt from the relevant protective laws and regulations and therefore free for general use.
The publisher, the authors and the editors are safe to assume that the advice and information in this book are believed to be true and accurate at the date of publication. Neither the publisher nor the authors or the editors give a warranty, expressed or implied, with respect to the material contained herein or for any errors or omissions that may have been made. The publisher remains neutral with regard to jurisdictional claims in published maps and institutional affiliations.

Cover illustration: adventtr

This Palgrave Macmillan imprint is published by the registered company Springer Nature Switzerland AG
The registered company address is: Gewerbestrasse 11, 6330 Cham, Switzerland

For last year's words belong to last year's language
And next year's words await another voice.

T.S. Eliot, Four Quartets

Dedicated to

Milton
my Guardian Angel!

Freya Milou
my Inspiration!

Papillon
my Muse!

&

Curiosity

Preface

We live in a 4th Industrial Revolution (4IR) world with two essential truths. First, we are residents in a globalized marketplace. Second, technologies define our work and life! Whether we are globetrotters or couch-potatoes, technophiles, or luddites, we are expected and manage in a globalized, technological landscape.

The book helps students learn how to navigate the global digital and technological order driven by culture, politics, cybersecurity, economics, and operations. From using strategy models and data mining to understanding AI, cybersecurity, projects, and 4IR digital transformation, this book helps students fathom and manage technology across geopolitical cultures and economics that define today's and tomorrow's business and technological trends.

Technology is pervasive in today's globalized world, often its largest investment, exceeding 70% of capital expenditure. But Technology simply serves the company enabling other services and processes in the global world. From IBM's Artificial Intelligence (AI) threatening primary care physicians and salespeople, Apple moving all data under Chinese control, Equifax and SolarWinds cybersecurity breaches, Google sued for antitrust, Russia's cyber-meddling in elections, Uber changing taxis and ambulances, Facebook becoming our health profile generator, we are truly in the cusp of massive innovations.

This course is a course on decision-making using technology as a reference frame. We will deal with the messy and unstructured world of decisions. We will delve into the grey areas of overlapping facets in Finance, Economics, Accounting, HR, Ethics, Marketing, and Branding knit by the fabric of technology.

This book uses technology management as the central theme to cover multiple business and social facets, including digital transformation, cybersecurity, international operations, marketing, finance, culture, human capital, and political economics. I particularly emphasize on a changing future driven by AI, autonomous vehicles, new business models, operational automation, robotics, cyberthreats, blockchains, ethics, etc.

Given that technology and globalization are predominant curricular themes, the book can be used at various levels. The book can be used to serve as a global business and technology management primer for Freshmen and Sophomore students. The book can also be used as a capstone course for reconnecting various business threads using a technology-perspective. Finally, this book serves as a useful M.B.A. text to guide learning on technology management and decision-making in a global world!

Hudson, Ohio, USA   Pratim Milton Datta

About This Book

The book covers all aspects of AACSB recommended global management and technology management education recommendations.

The book is divided into four modules or sections:

1. Understanding the Emerging World Order, business and 4IR Concepts.
2. Using Analytical, Statistical, and Strategy models for driving performance.
3. Managing Cybersecurity in a Global Context.
4. Offshoring, Sustainability, Global Supply Chains, and Digital Transformation.

Learning Outcomes

The book will help students:

1. Understand technological evolution from the 1st Industrial Revolution to the 4th Industrial Revolution.
2. Appreciate and Grasp the socio-politics and culture of globalization.
3. Critically assess how globalization, existing, and emerging technologies influence the heart of a corporation's global technology strategy and operations.
4. Connect multiple facets of global operations across areas of finance, economics, technology, HR, branding, and operations.
5. Understand and explain relevant nuances of culture and global projects, operation, and digital transformation.
6. Evaluate issues of effective technology management of technology innovations such as AI, Autonomous Driving, and Blockchains.
7. Recognize Cybersecurity threats to plan and manage Cybersecurity in a global context.
8. Understand the use and application of Statistical, Analytical, and Strategic Models to solve business problems.
9. Understand how to harness the power of emerging technologies to make better decisions for more effective management in a competitive global environment.

Introduction

We shall not cease from exploration.
And the end of all our exploring
Will be to arrive where we started
And know the place for the first time.

T. S. Eliot, *Little Gidding*

This is how the story goes- a country's railway minister was presiding over a panel of statisticians analyzing data on train crash reports. After covering various statistics from mining millions of historical data points, the panel chair summed up the most pronounced pattern.

The panel chair pensively remarked, "the most worrisome fact that surfaced was the growing casualties- interestingly, about 65 percent of casualties in our train crashes were concentrated in a single carriage compartment!"

"Pray tell, which carriage compartment?" the railway minister asked in anticipation.

"The last carriage compartment"

"Well, that's an easy fix" the railway minister observed, profusely, "remove the last carriage compartment- problem solved!"

"Je ne pense pas, je ne comprend pas, donc je suis"
(I don't think, I don't understand, therefore I am)

There are hundreds of rulebooks on decision-making. They are opinion pieces pontificating heuristics. This book is not about that. This book is about the wonderful yet messy grey zone of decision-making. *This book is about paradoxes, mostly without the puns.*

The job of the decision-maker is not meant to be easy. Yet, paralyzed by analyses, companies stop being mindful of their environment and sink into obscurity. Companies get too focused on their traditional routines and fail to understand the ramifications of global events.

So why is decision-making so intractably elusive? Why do leaders spend years and years planning and plotting only to realize that "the best-laid plans of mice and men, often go askew"? Perhaps it is because decisions are often thought of as shots in the dark—especially for a landscape teetering on the brink of competitive flux. A flux that ushers in the dawn for some and dusk for others. We are furtive weavers on a tapestry whose final pattern we are yet to decipher. King Lear's exasperation rings true—"as flies are to wanton boys, are we to the Gods- they kill us for their sport." God, in this case, is the environment with a gingerly-sprinkled providence. Truly, it is the environment-in-flux that often spells the demise of long-range enveloping decisions. It is a dismal landscape. The fog is heavy, the mist is deep, the coast is unclear, yet we stand at the wheel and have two choices—ponder the absurdity of it all or rebel to clear the fog and mist. "Do not go silently into the good night...rage, rage against the dying of the light," wrote Dylan Thomas. It takes more than a torch and a beacon to fathom the depth and seek the shore. It takes our understanding of both the inter-connections and the paradoxes. But *c'est la vie*! It is a test of the human intellectual mettle- social, managerial, political, or otherwise.

TS Eliot, in his poem, Prufrock, elegantly emits his stream of conscious-ness—*"let us go, then, you and I"...to..."streets that follow like a tedious argument, of insidious intent, leading you to an overwhelming question. Do not ask "what is it?", instead let us go and make our visit."* "Making a visit" requires you to know the road and connect them from origin to destination. The quintessential decision-maker is a skeptic and a renaissance person.

A decision-maker is not a slave to a preset path. Instead, a decision-maker is an evolved sceptic that never wavers from deciding but seldom assumes that a decision cannot be improved.

Decision-makers face a blurry landscape littered with options yet choked by constraints. It is up to them to connect the dots to reveal the landscape. What may seem good from far may be far from good. So, intellectual curiosity must lie at the core of decision-making; making decisions is a preamble to action. Possibly pressing yet pressingly possible. They who fail to trace interconnections fail to see the rich tapestry of the decisional landscape. Without understanding interconnections, we succumb to myopia.

In a globalized world connected by technology, **butterfly effects** abound. A butterfly may flap its tiny wings by the Mediterranean Sea. Its tiny wing-flaps will resonate with the grass, the grass with the trees, the trees with the forests, the forests with the clouds, the clouds with the waves, and a Tsunami may rage in the Pacific.

A single event has far-flung effects in today's world. Here's a hypothetical scenario. The Fukushima reactor meltdown causes a production freeze; Nuclear fears bring anti-nuclear protests to the streets; Crude gas gains popularity; Crude supply chains get stretched; Energy prices rise; Production costs increase; European exports suffer; Greece defaults; Italy and Portugal stand on the brink; Japan devalues its Yen to boost exports; China reacts by refusing to float its currency; Austerity measures beckon cheap imports; US and western European labor wages seem unsustainable. Massive layoffs occur followed by protests in the streets of Paris, Berlin, DC, and Shanghai; China cracks down heavy-handedly on protestors and its factories lose production. Chinese imports drop further and consumer prices (inflation) increase. Markets go for a tailspin, and YOU stand in the middle of it—figuring a way out.

Here, we discuss the key, basic facets of the geopolitical landscape and key business rules that govern the game reset by technology. We will discuss the economic, innovative, and strategic thinking and solutions that envelop organizational practices and actions.

So, the path of decision-making is a quest for the truth, not a fact. That is why no decision is immutable, etched in stone, marked with a timestamp. If decisions were immutable, they would become laws, axioms, and truths. And decision-making would, quoting Oscar Wilde, "lose all its intellectual curiosity."

The French Philosopher Voltaire once said, "*Le mieux est l'ennemi du bien!*" (Best is the enemy of Good), symbolizing how waiting for perfection can halt progress. We will never have perfect information and we cannot get paralyzed from analysis. Decision-making cannot stop. So, what matters is the logic behind decisions rather than the perfection of decisions.

Decision-making is an attempt to provide a grounded solution to a pressing question. It is the process of seeking the truth through meandering and overwhelming paths. It cannot be evaded, only explored, discovered, faced, and rediscovered. Our decisions must change with the landscape.

This book is all about building the mindfulness and business acumen needed to make decisions and manage under ambiguity in a 4IR (4th Industrial Revolution) world!

Contents

About the Author

Dr. Pratim Milton Datta, Ph.D., M.S., M.B.A. is a Professor of Information Systems in the College of Business at Kent State University.

Pratim also serves as a Senior Research Associate at the University of Johannesburg, South Africa, and as a visiting faculty with ITU, Copenhagen, Denmark.

Pratim specializes in Cybersecurity, Digital Transformation, Corporate Analytics, and 4IR global ICT strategy. Ranked among the top 100 researchers internationally, Pratim has more than 75 journal articles and conference proceedings with multiple best paper nominations and awards. He has published in multiple A and A+ journals such as *European Journal of Information Systems*, *Journal of the AIS*, *Information Systems Journal*, *Journal of Knowledge Management*, *ACM Transactions*, and *IEEE*.

He served as the Ph.D. Director for the College of Business from 2012 to 2018. He also served as the College's AACSB accreditation Assurance of Learning (AoL) lead from 2010 to 2012.

Prior to academia, Pratim worked for global technology consulting firms. He actively consults, teaches, and presents his research internationally.

Pratim received the Farris Family Research Innovation Award twice (2009, 2010). He was the 2014 University Scholar of the Month and received the prestigious University President's Faculty Excellence Award in 2017.

With multiple sole-inventions and patent applications, Pratim enjoys designing engineering and technological solutions. His E-Voting process invention was featured on FOX8 news and has been cited in multiple business articles. He is an avid traveler and photographer.

List of Figures

List of Tables

This part begins with an overview of technological evolutions from 1IR to 4IR. The part then discusses various business concepts that connect the dots to gain a better perspective on how countries and economies compete in technological and global landscape.

Learning Outcomes

By the end of this part, students will be able to:

- Investigate and discuss the role of society, politics, and technology in globalization.
- Assess the existing global order across countries and regions.
- Evaluate the use of various business concepts and their applications in achieving business goals and objectives.
- Evaluate the application of business performance measures such a Break Even Point Analysis.
- Examine global labor, labor costs, and innovation.
- Explore global challenges from various economic crises.
- Investigate and report on the intersection of globalization and technology.

Globalization—The New World Order: Technology—The New NormalTechnology is pervasive in today's world and is no longer a backend operation. Instead, technology drives global strategy. **This is the 4th Industrial Revolution (4IR).**

From E-Commerce giants such as Amazon and Alibaba, FinTech such as M-Pesa, Robinhood, and Betterment, Artificial Intelligence such as IBM's Watson and Google's DeepMind, Smartphones and Wearable Tech such as Apple Watches and iPhones, Electric Cars such as Tesla and Otto, Delivery Drones from Amazon, Movie Streaming with Netflix, Smart Homes (Internet of Things), Virtual Reality, and Social Media, our lives are immersed in technology. Social Media technology has become the spark to kindle revolutions as well as spread misinformation and fake news.

In this technology-driven 4IR (4th Industrial Revolution) age, how do we "strategically" harness and manage the power of technological innovation and manage technological change across countries and societies around the globe?

This book helps you navigate the global digital and technological order driven by cultures, politics, economics, and operations. The book helps you fathom and manage across geopolitical cultures and economics that define today's and tomorrow's business and technological trends.

The 4th Industrial Revolution is upon us but not many students understand its evolution or impact. This teaching case looks at socio-technical evolution from 1 to 4IR. A mini-case follows, exemplifying how 4IR quietly helped the COVID-19 vaccine development. This section ends by highlighting the dark sides of 4IR.

The confluence of globalization and technology is being rewritten as a post-COVID-19 twenty-first-century story. But the story begins more than three centuries ago. A tale of an incredible mix of innovation and upheaval.

We live today in this age of something called the Fourth Industrial Revolution (4IR). Well, it's called 4IR because we've gone through four specific punctuated industrial revolution phases (Fig. 1.1).

The 1st IR (1760–1830): The Coming of Machines Over Men

The **First Industrial Revolution** (1IR), of course, was the steam revolution. This was the coming of age of what we think of as industrial economies as societies tore away from handmade goods and agrarian livelihoods. The politics and technologies that were laid in a place defined 1IR, just the way the politics and technologies that define today are defining and will define the 4IR.

1IR began around the time that the US was gaining its independence in the 1770s. The whole world was changing rapidly and dramatically.

1. The 1IR period saw the Baroque age of aristocracy and intricate manual labor wane and the modern age rise.

The 1st IR (1760–1830): In 1760, James Watt's Steam Engine started the 1st Industrial Revolution. Instead of using horses and humans to move things, suddenly coal and water could "automatically" generate power that would run factories and various machines. Suddenly, machines emerged that started to replace horses and manual labor.

The famous Scotsman James Watt's steam engine could use coal to convert water into steam. The steam pressure would be released to rotate a machine wheel that could print, press, mold, dig, cut, and do many other things. Suddenly, production was revolutionized.

In a few years, George Stevenson, a brilliant, self-taught engineer, came up with the steam engine locomotive that could pull carriages of heavy coal faster than horses. At a galloping speed of 36 mph, Stevenson's steam engine, Rocket, would go on to be the speediest engine-powered vehicle in the world, showing how using machines could be more efficient and more humane than using animals. The First industrial had begun in earnest.

© PiaDura LTD 2022
P. Datta, *Global Technology Management 4.0*,
https://doi.org/10.1007/978-3-030-96929-5_1

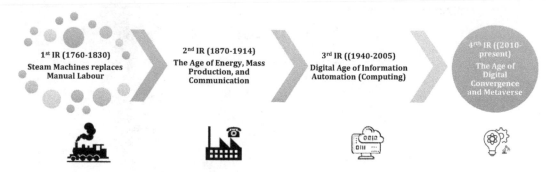

Fig. 1.1 1IR to 4IR timeline

Did You Know That?

Around 1830, Ada Lovelace, Lord Byron's brilliant daughter, worked with Charles Babbage, the father of the first computing engine, to write the first algorithm! Every 2nd Tuesday in October is called the Ada Lovelace Day!

2. The **age of Enlightenment** fueled the 1st IR. The 1st IR had become the talk of the town, led by famous mathematicians and philosophers such as Newton, Descartes, Kant, Hobbes, Locke, Rousseau, Voltaire, and Adam Smith. It was the age of reason, independent thinking, and innovation.

   a. Newton redefined the universe as a fragile but stable system where gravity holds us together, where actions create reactions, and where certain forces cause us to move or stay in place.

   b. Descartes, the French philosopher, and mathematician redefined the need for thinking over obeying commands with his famous phrase *"cogito ergo sum"* (I think, therefore, I am).

   c. The German philosopher Immanuel Kant's *Sapere Aude* (dare to know) challenged tradition with curiosity.

      • Locke challenged tradition, superstition, and the divine authority of kings with the need for reason, democracy, and human dignity. To Locke, a government had to be just and representative of the people it governed—the same idea that ignited the 1776 American revolutionary war based on "taxation without representation." 1IR saw the waxing of Republicanism over Monarchism and the need for human dignity and quality of life.

   d. The French revolution was overthrowing French aristocrats and being led by Voltaire's "enlightenment" thinking that became the revolutionary theme of liberty, equality, and fraternity (brotherhood/sisterhood). According to Voltaire, "Those who can make you believe absurdities can make you commit atrocities"—something that we still need to understand, especially in an age of misinformation and fake news.

   e. Rousseau's *Social Contract* defended human freedoms and individual rights. Rousseau's social contract was a contract between the government and the people, where people would trade some of their liberties for stability, safety, and laws.

   f. Hobbes' *Leviathan* inched the social contract further by saying that people needed a government to protect them but needed to create checks and balances so that the government would not become so powerful or large as to become a monster or a *Leviathan*. These principles also became the central pieces for the US constitution based on term limits, separation of the executive, legislative, and judiciary, and their checks and balances.

g. The Scottish Economist Adam Smith's book "Wealth of Nations, Theory of Moral Sentiments, Capitalism, and Liberal Economies," was laying the groundwork for capitalism. In capitalism, the money needed to flow freely, allowing people to borrow and innovate. Here, prosperity depended upon clever, innovative thinking and hard work, creating specialized "divisions of labor." Adam Smith believed that becoming specialized and good at something would make people prosperous and prosperity would benefit society.

The 1st IR came up with a social sea change of revolutions and the industrial sea-change of mechanical power generation. Then came the 2nd IR.

The 2nd IR (1870–1914): The Age of Energy, Mass Production, and Communication Technologies

A century later, the **Second Industrial Revolution (2IR)** arrived. Steam engine railroad networks were cross-crossing countries like motorways and interstate highways via rail.

Steam was a good start, but steam power took a lot of water, a lot of coal, and a lot of space to build pressure that would boil water to create steam that would turn the turbine. 2IR replaced steam power with other modes of power generation, mainly petroleum and electricity. Gasoline, from petroleum, was extremely combustible. The internal combustion engine (ICE), the type we generally have in our cars, could produce much more energy within a space a fraction of the size of a steam generator. Gasoline mixed with oxygen and ignited created an internal explosion powerful enough to move pistons to turn the turbine. Suddenly smaller engines with tremendous power dominated the economy, from automobiles and tanks to aircraft.

Electricity was the other 2IR game-changing invention. Electricity could be generated by a small dynamo that could turn mechanical/physical work into energy that could be distributed over wires at the speed of light. Of course, we know of the two behemoth inventors, Edison and Tesla, each promoting different types of electricity generation. While Edison promoted direct current (DC), the type of electricity that makes batteries, Tesla promoted alternating current (AC) that runs our household appliances and our electricity grids.

Gasoline is difficult and environmentally dirty to extract from petroleum but easy to store and refill. Electricity generation is clean and easy to distribute but difficult and expensive to store in batteries. Have you seen how quickly batteries die?

The telegraph's arrival was an additional 2IR game-changer and paved the path to information and communication networks—connecting the world. In 1844, Samuel Morse, in the US, invented the telegraph with the first message "What hath God wrought?" 1844. Around the same time, private companies such as the British East India Company were become the first global brands by stretching their businesses across the world. To maintain communications.

To support private businesses, the UK started controlling telegraph communications by laying the telegraph lines across the world. With electricity powering telegraph communications passing quietly under the seas and oceans, the first trans-Atlantic telegraph message read:

"Directors of Atlantic Telegraph Company, Great Britain, to Directors in America:—Europe and America are united by telegraph. Glory to God in the highest; on earth peace, good will towards men!" followed by a text from Queen Victoria to US President Buchanan to congratulate his election victory.

Bell's Telephone invention in 1876 quickly followed the telegraph, allowing voice, not just text to travel around the world.

In 1897, another technological innovation changed communication. Marconi, an Italian inventor in the UK, invented wireless communication, called Radio.

With wired and wireless communications, the UK and the US knew that building and controlling networks and communication would give them a global advantage.

International communications using technology had begun.

So, armed with petroleum and electricity, the 2nd IR (1870–1914) became the age of mechanization and mass production.

1. Suddenly, machines started getting automated. Interchangeable parts and reduced costs (Bessemer Steel process) brought mass production (with rail networks for mass distribution), sewage networks (to build communities), electric lines to supply energy, and telegraph networks for mass communication.
   a. There was a rapid shift from steam power to petroleum and the coming of the ICE (Internal Combustion Engine).
   b. Steel could be produced faster, oil could be extracted from the ground in millions of barrels, and electricity could be generated in megawatts to power entire cities.

2. Society became more organized. With rail and communication networks, cities, and countries started building electricity, water, and sewage networks. Life was becoming cleaner and more convenient. With fewer diseases and better quality of life, society became more mechanized and urbanized. Factories were arriving, replacing farming.

3. The confluence of communication, electricity, and petroleum brought about an innovation: better, faster, and cheaper ways of producing things! The Bessemer Steel making process pushed manufacturing forward. Europe was experiencing its *belle epoque* (beautiful age) and the US focused on massive industrialization and growth. Henry Ford had come up with a brilliant process innovation called an assembly line. An assembly line used interchangeable parts to build things faster and cheaper. Henry Ford's assembly line churned out the mass-produced Ford Model T in the early 1900s. Suddenly inventions became accessible across industry and society and life changed for good.

4. Like wireless radio, the Wright brothers' airplane proved human ability to take flight with a mechanized engine and wings, untethered to the ground.

5. But with some much faster and cheaper mechanization came a lot of social and political turmoil. People left farms and started overcrowding cities. Colonial powers were fighting for resource control in South Africa (Boer War between the British and the Dutch), India, and China (Opium Wars). In Europe, the seeds of hatred were being sown. Napoleon's conquests across Europe, from Austria and Italy to Portugal, had left a bitter taste in every mouth. European countries wanted to unify into nation-states, often paying a price in blood. The warring Italian states unified in 1861. In 1871, the Prussian general Bismarck led the Franco-Prussian war to unify Germany and Prussia against France's Napoleon III and annexed Alsace, France's industrial heartland. Thus, began Germany's rise as an industrial power.

This heightened sense of fragile European nation-states simmered long-lasting suspicions. The pressure pot burst into flames in 1914 with World War I, consuming all of Europe, from the Balkans to Britain, laying the stage for the US to gain industrial supremacy by supplying its allies with its industrial productive might. The same mechanizations that defined 2IR were now being turned into machine guns, tanks, and military aircraft to unleash terror, leading to 40 million deaths.

Did You Know That?

Young DIYers used Marconi's radio invention to build amateur "ham" radios that created the first virtual community. Ham radio networks worked like a radio internet and were also used to spread fake news such confusion about Titanic's sinking!

The 3rd IR (1940–2005): The Digital Age of Information Automation (Computing)

The 1940s opened with war in the air. World War I, meant to be "the war that ended all wars," rather became the linchpin for World War II. The

1920s and 1930s had seen stock market madness and its 1929 "black Tuesday" collapse, followed by a dreadful financial depression. In the middle of a worldwide economic downturn arrived World War II, with Germany invading Poland, marching their jackboots across Europe, and systematically planning a Jewish holocaust. Several **Third Industrial Revolution (3IR)** military events and innovations followed:

1. To counter Germany to the West and Japan to the east, countries ramped up their 2IR mass production infrastructure to build for war. Countries started inventing faster and deadlier solutions to wreak havoc on the enemy, from Germany's V2 rockets to the US' atomic bomb. But information was becoming the hallmark of the times.

   a. In 1940, when Nazi Germany's air force, the *Luftwaffe*, began bombing Great Britain, the only country left fighting against the Nazi *blitzkrieg* (lightning warfare), the British realized that information was key to preempting Luftwaffe bombardments. So, Radar was invented. Radar could echo-locate aircraft from far away and allowed the British to prepare offensive and defensive solutions slightly ahead of time. Not only did the radar save Britain but also brought RAF (Royal Air Force) victory over the Luftwaffe in the Battle of Britain.

   b. In addition to the Radar, Britain needed to crack German military encryptions in the early 1940s. Nazi Germany was using a sophisticated encryption machine called Enigma. Even when the essential Enigma encryption process was discovered, processing the complicated cipher encryptions. Alan Turing, a brilliant scientist, built the first commercial computer called the Turing machine that could run thousands of computations to break the Enigma code.

The age of the Computer was here.

2. Once World War II was over in 1945, the world started rebuilding. Many of the innovations that grew out of the war were now being harnessed to revive economies. The US and the USSR (formerly the Soviet Union) became the two superpowers with very different strategies. While the USSR pushed its communist ideals to build a world order based on government control of resources, the US, western Europe, and Japan used capitalist market economics to privatize companies and innovations. This superpower competition to create allegiance blocs around the world became known as the Cold War. Computers started becoming more popular and more accessible, ushering in the digital world.

   a. As the Cold War heated, the US and USSR entered the space race. Both knew that the space race depended on wireless communication and computing. Computers would calculate rocket trajectories and velocities and relay changes wirelessly. Suddenly remote wireless networks and faster and smaller computers became paramount. Russian cosmonauts won the race by less than a month's margin.

   b. The Russian Sputnik rockets helped Yuri Gagarin become the first man in space in 1961 and Valentina Tereshkova the first woman in space in 1963. The US sent Alan Shepard to be the first astronaut in space in 1961 and Sally Ride the first woman in space in 1978. Doggedly, the US took the chalice with its 1969 Apollo mission carrying Armstrong, Collins, and Aldrin to the Moon.

   c. Although computing and wireless communications were helping explore the edges of space and beyond, the Cold War had a more ominous side. Computer-controller rockets were not only being built to explore space but also carry devastating nuclear weapons. Growing out of Nazi Germany's V2 rocket program, both the US and the USSR stockpiled their nuclear-tipped intercontinental ballistic missiles (ICBMs) and trained them at one another. The US had already used two atomic bombs, Fat Man and Little Boy, in Hiroshima and Nagasaki in 1945, to force Japan to surrender. The world knew the incredible devastation they wrought and nearly every country prepared itself for a nuclear holocaust during the Cold War.

d. In fear of not being able to communicate with its and allied military during a nuclear strike, DARPA, a US military-sponsored an invention of a worldwide digital network. In the 1970s, the US started networking their computers to decentralize and "digitize" information across an "internet" in worries of a Soviet nuclear strike on the US military command. This digital network would be globally widespread like a spiderweb, undersea, and overland. If one part went down from a nuclear strike, the other parts would maintain communication. It was called the DARPANET.

e. But, as history would have it, the USSR collapsed in 1989. The Cold War was over and suddenly DARPANET became a moot military innovation. The US decided to open up the entire DARPANET to the global public. This became the Internet. Instead of 2IR telegraph lines carrying Morse code, the Internet was the digital network that would carry an Instagram picture, Facebook posts, TikTok videos, and Wikipedia pages in milliseconds around the globe.

Did You Know That?

The 1969 Apollo 11 (codenamed Eagle) moon lander had a guidance computer with approximately 32 KB of RAM! Today, we need more than 32 KB RAM to store 2 characters in Microsoft Word!

3. The invention of smaller and faster chips, doubling in processing power every 18 months (called Moore's law), and faster wired and wireless networks led to a slew of commercial computing.

a. Computers started being used for complex engineering, architecture design, and machine operations. As computers got smaller in size, there was, remarkably, a place for computers in the home to replace the typewriter and the pocket calculator.

b. Large mainframes became smaller and smaller. The 1974 Altair became the first popular home computer, followed by famous models such as the 1977 Apple II, 1983 Apple Lisa, and 1984 Apple Macintosh. IBM introduced their PCs that made Microsoft Windows famous.

c. Financial institutions leapt to seize the opportunity by creating ATMs (Automated Teller Machines) that would use computers and secure, wired networks to dispense money 24/7. The ATM bank card became immensely popular, allowing people to simply walk up to an ATM in any part of the world, at the oddest hours, enter their card and PIN, and access their accounts. ATM computers would link to globally spanning networks, verify your identity, reconcile the money you have in your accounts, and dispense cash in the local currency and automatically credit your account. This became one of the earliest examples of digital transformation.

d. At the same time, computers were helping wireless communications grow in reach and range. Home computers, chips, and the space race created a need for remote communications.

e. The coming of smaller and faster computers, cell phones, and wireless technologies, the Internet, along with better information organization in "databases," began the "Digital Revolution."

f. The Internet began the digital revolution that became the next great equalizer. With the entire world able to access data posted in real time from around the world, the Internet suddenly allowed people all over the world a chance to show off their ideas and products, starting the era of E-commerce.

   i. Entrepreneurs like Jeff Bezos' Amazon.com used the Internet to create an online book warehouse that customers could access and order from 24/7 without the need for physical bookshops. Amazon.com's E-commerce business model uprooted and bankrupted centuries-old physical booksellers and bookstores, much like the way Walmart's large warehouses once upended small stores in the 1980s.

ii. Netflix.com equally upended the physical movie-rental stores such as Blockbuster with a massive online E-commerce movie warehouse where customers could rent DVDs (Digital Video Discs) via mail without the need for store visits, being dependent on store inventory, or any late fees.

iii. With data and information (information is data that is more structured to serve a purpose) burgeoning across the world, companies like Google emerged to search, catalog, curate, and categorize information and data to make them more relevant to what we wanted to search for. Suddenly, with our ability to search for information being created and posted in real-time from around the world, the world became our oyster, and the World-Wide-Web (www) became the most popular Internet-based application.

iv. With so much data created and consumed during 3IR, there grew a need to systematically organize data for faster searching and fewer errors. So, 3IR also became the era of Databases, one of the core ingredients of our Digital Revolution!

The 4rth IR (2010–Present): The Age of Digital Convergence and the Metaverse

The computer, superfast 5G wireless networks, and the Internet started the 3IR digital revolution. With the world digitally connected to trillions of data being created and consumed across the globe, the Internet was meant to be the great equalizer, a harbinger of what has come by since. And that paved the way for the **Fourth Industrial Revolution (4IR)**.

The 4th Industrial Revolution is the age of digital convergence. With a proliferating Internet around the world, high-speed wireless networks, cheap computing, 4IR is connecting various devices, databases, and a variety of digital networks over the cloud. The **cloud** is simply a virtual place for an on-demand way to access and store computing and information resources.

The 4IR began with on-demand cloud access to different resources on the cloud. Think movies on the cloud (think Netflix, Hulu, Amazon Prime, Disney+), storage (iCloud, Microsoft OneDrive, Amazon S3), or complex analytics and computing (Google App Engine, Microsoft Azure, Amazon Elastic Compute [EC2]). Individuals and companies no longer required expensive computer updates to store large data or process complex software codes. Instead, we can access storage and run complicated computer code and applications from cloud serves.

4IR started with Applications (such as banking and social network apps) **(SaaS)**, entire Platforms (such as Alibaba in China where you can buy things, pay for services, do banking, invest) **(PaaS)**, and Infrastructure (such as Amazon Web Services [AWS] or Microsoft Azure where you can tackle all your computing needs such as servers, databases, high-powered processing) **(IaaS)** moved to the cloud and using them on-demand.

4IR is also reshaping agriculture, thought to be the first economic organization. 4IR **AgriTech** using a combination of drones, GPS, AI, automation, robotics, and sensors to figure out exact soil conditions and farming strategies. Sensors are constantly measuring soil moisture, sunlight, and pH balances. This information is integrated with weather information to predict farming strategies. GPS technologies guide large combines and harvesters to plant particular seeds in particular parts of the land based on predictive yield using soil and weather data. Drones deliver specific types of pesticides and soil treatments and robots are used to pick and sort fruits and vegetables!

With services, platforms, and infrastructures on-demand and managed remoted on the cloud, all we need is a laptop, a smartphone, or tablet to run the most complex of systems.

In 4IR, technology is poised to run everything, from genome cracks, drug discoveries, drone deliveries, and autonomous-driving vehicles (AVs), to Work-From-Home (WFH), millions of remote smart devices called **IoT (Internet of Things)** for office and home controls (remote door and light sensors, temperature, garage doors), and technologies predicting our health and shopping even before we know it.

4IR will use IoT sensors and **blockchains** to track and trace the movement of things and people by creating a unique digital ID for everything and track the ID's movement over time. Blockchains create a ledger entry for every event, creating a long, immutable, and irreversible block made of transaction chains. Because blockchains are immutable, none can tweak or revise any transaction, ensuring tremendous transparency for people, products, and money.

During the Fourth Industrial Revolution, technology will become a part of our everyday lives, embedded into the smallest of devices, used everywhere, and where technology will gradually interconnect everything (Fig. 1.2).

Did You Know That?

Wally Funk, one of the original female US Mercury 13 astronauts in the 1960s, was denied the opportunity to head to space! 60 years later, Jeff Bezos' invited Wally Funk to become the first passenger and the oldest woman to travel to space flying aboard Blue Origin's New Shepard spacecraft.

4IR Technological Highlights

Automated and Connected Sensors

We could argue that IoT (Internet of Things) kickstarted the 4IR. But what are IoTs? As the name signifies, Internet of Things is a group of common, everyday "things" that are connected to the Internet—not just our computers, tablets, and smartphones, but a panoply of connected everyday "things," making them "smart." Smart lightbulbs, plugs, thermostats, door locks, garage openers, mailboxes, or Fridges, IoTs simply add sensors and Wi-Fi to the most mundane of devices and turn them smart.

Today an IoT sprinkler system can measure the soil moisture, the weather trend and decide on whether, when and for how long to run a sprinkler to water yards, saving homeowners large water bills and increasing environmental sustainability.

It is quite likely that future smart fridges will have specific placeholders for milk, eggs. Anytime the milk weighs less or sensors detect eggs fewer eggs, a smart fridge can place a milk and egg order refill from your preferred grocery store.

Car insurance companies like Noblr and Root are using our smartphone's location tracking and accelerometer IoT sensors to quietly track our driving. When do we drive? Where do we travel? How good are our braking, accelerating, turning? Do we text while driving? These new IoT-based car insurance companies are coming with clever ways to charge insurance and challenging the large insurance companies. They are the next Netflix and Amazon, waiting to take over the world.

Machine Learning and Analytics

Artificial Intelligence (AI) is perhaps one of the most significant 4IR advances. Think of Facebook's AI. Facebook's AI knows a lot about you: Where you walk, what music you play for certain days, and moods when you post messages about feeling elated or depressed. Linked to your IoT data, AI uses machine learning to train itself on when you are leaving work to turn on your house climate control and shut down the climate control when you leave for work.

Simply put, AI does not just automate. It thinks.

AI trains itself just like we do. When we learn something like, "what is a book?" we learn by looking at different types of books and then using

Fig. 1.2 4IR technologies

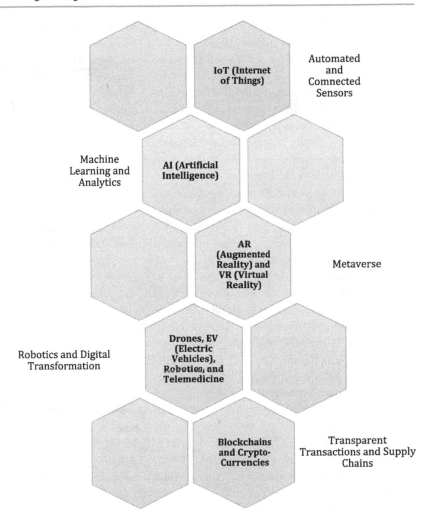

that to create our idea of what a book looks like. Our brains learn from looking, hearing, touching, and smelling various things to "learn" about things in the world. AI does that, exactly. Using neural nets, a sophisticated statistical software, AI systems are fed millions of pictures and sounds as data. AI uses its artificial neural networks (ANNs) to "learn" from the information fed to it. That is how Apple uses facial recognition AI to log you in or Siri's AI to recognize your voice with. This is oftentimes referred to as machine learning and deep learning.

Often, when we visit websites, we are asked to verify ourselves by choosing the correct pictures of cars, trains, animals, etc. Our choices are fed to help AI learn what we choose as cars, trains, animals, etc. When more people choose a picture as a picture of a car, the AI learns that that is the correct choice.

Technically, this is how AI's deep learning works. AI deep preferential learning minimizes $\hat{y}$ based on the heuristic shown below. AI's neural network relies on weights W (W_1 and W_2) assigned to choices b (b_1 and b_2) to predict the outcome $\hat{y}$.

$$\hat{y} = \sigma(W_2\sigma(W_1x + b_1) + b_2)$$

An AI uses an output $\hat{y}$ is fed as a "feedforward" to learn.

AI models and algorithms are a function of their users' inputs. AI algorithms learn based on what is input to decipher user preferences. In the wake of the Hong Kong protests against Chinese mainland control where news media is vastly divided and partisan, AI creates a different preferential learning profile for a user that predominantly clicks on and reads Mainland China news versus a preferential learning profile for a user that predominantly clicks on and reads Hong Kong and western news sites and news. AI uses each candidate's profile to deliver custom content that matches individuals' proclivity as a way to mitigate their news information uncertainty. The AI sends the user interested in Mainland China news information that plaudits Mainland Chinese tolerance toward Hong Kong and China's attempts at maintaining unity under the "One Country-Two Systems" policy. On the other hand, the AI sends the user interested in western news information that plaudit Hong Kong protests against Mainland Chinese oppression and the unnecessary violence being meted out by Mainland China under the pretense of control.

In a 2018 interview Vox (2018) about AI-based preferential learning on search and social media sites, the interview noted that AI on search and Social Media sites are not meant to be paternalistic, ideal neutral platforms, but as a platform that treats its users as customers. "There is safety in saying the consumer is going to make the decision. Yes, there is an algorithm here, but the algorithm is to the consumer. The algorithm is just saying, "What do you want? Okay, we're going to give you more of that."

4IR AI is utilized in our detailed images from X-Rays, GPS, and space telescopes to remotely discover things we had never found—from archaeological sites under the ground, far-flung galaxies, and black holes around the universe, to the faintest heart murmur. Billions of images are fed into AI systems for deep learning. Now, AI is being used to spot everything radiology reports to track the smallest hint of cancer, a faint nebula, or an archaeological find. AI can detect the slightest anomaly and change—something human beings are rarely able to do. In the 4IR age, AI is getting smart enough to write poetry, compose music, and even paint. The latest AI painting sold on Christie's Auction House for nearly $500,000.

Metaverse

What is a metaverse? Well, a metaverse is a multi-dimensional, immersive environment where you experience digital content as you do in real life. These include video, audio, text, 3D, **augmented reality (AR)** (such as taking a picture of a product on your iPhone and placing it in your room), and **virtual reality (VR)** (such as transporting yourself to a different place). In a metaverse, you can virtually walk through a museum, while looking at famous paintings and sculptures, taking pictures, sharing them on social media, take art history, and even having your social media friends join you in a virtual stroll together. Of course, you say, isn't that what the bulky Oculus 3D does? Yes, to a certain degree. But the 4IR metaverse will reduce our 3D immersive experience into a simple pair of glasses by bio-physical integration of high-speed wireless networks, AI, and superfast computer chips.

Robotics and Digital Transformation

4IR is, single-handedly, the dawn of the robotic age. When COVID-19 came to town and social distancing became mandatory, companies needed to run. So, companies heavily invested in robots to fill in for factory assembly lines. Tesla's production robots became very popular during California's lockdown when people weren't allowed to walk into a production facility. Tesla invested heavily in robotics to build its Model 3 because robots don't need to be quarantined you can still operate and these robots 24/7 without overtime or health concerns. A famous Japanese company called **FANUC** manufactures a lot of these sophisticated robots. **FANUC** operates something called a **Lights-Out factory**, where robots run the entire factory with no human presence for more than a year. FANUC robots can even predict and take care of robot maintenance.

China, while catching up with Japan's and the West's innovative prowess, is practicing a slightly different philosophy. China knows that the world is becoming more and more technology and digital transformation dependent which means that a lot more technological hardware is going to be needed to replace the physical hardware that we've used to. China's focus is to dominate the technology supply chain, from controlling **Rare Earth Elements (REE)** (elements from 57 to 71 on the periodic table) supply chain needed for everything from semiconductors to electric car batteries. China now operates hundreds of mines around the world, creating huge logistical networks from Africa to the poles, from China right into the Eastern and Southern European doorsteps, known as China's **Belt and Road initiative, or "The New Silk Road."**

Robotics are also becoming a part of **4IR environmental sustainability**. The idea is to recycle electronics so that we do not have to constantly mine them in dirty open pit mines and create a large energy footprint from transporting them across the world.

Companies like Apple have been at the forefront of sustainability. Because iPhones and iPads are very difficult to disassemble to recycle electronic components, Apple's sustainable operations use **Lisa and Daisy robotic recyclers** to dismantle and disassemble iPhones and iPads to reuse electronics and metals such as gold and cobalt. The robots work swiftly and precisely without any human intervention.

Similarly, Amazon uses thousands of **KIVA robots** in its warehouses. Whenever an order is placed, KIVA robots, that look like Roomba vacuum cleaners with a lifting screw on-top, quietly move to find the right shelves with the ordered items, lift them up, and bring them to the person filling the order. The person does not move. Instead, the KIVA robot does the heavy lifting for them. Because KIVA robots are small and can effortlessly slip between shelves, Amazon can pack many more shelves in their factory. So, using robots, Amazon increases its factory space while reducing the number of people needed in its warehouses.

On the delivery side, COVID-19 is seeing a new set of **Delivery robots and drones**. With COVID-19 lockdowns, companies started using robots to deliver goods.

Remember the proverb "Necessity is the mother of Invention" (based on Plato's "our need will be the real creator"). When Boris Johnson, UK's PM, announced advocated a lockdown,

people still needed food and groceries. But delivery drivers weren't available. In Milton Keynes, a town close to London, a new company called Starship Technologies started during the severe lockdown, using small delivery robots to deliver food and groceries from stores to restaurants and stores. These delivery robots armed with a QR code and an ID would drive up to your doorstep where only your app logic would open the delivery container.

Internationally, a new company called Zipline Drones is using drones to bypass dangerous neighborhoods in war-ravaged countries to deliver medicine and even organ transplants. UPS is a large Zipline Drone investor. With the US FAA (Federal Aviation Authority) opening up the airspace for drone operations, it's just a matter of time before drones become the next generation of delivery logistics transformation.

Nowadays, drones are becoming more and more common in both military and civilian operations. Military unmanned drones called **Unmanned Aerial Vehicles (UAV)** are replacing pilots, delivering supplies (e.g., Zipline drones delivering medicine in Rwanda and Ghana), and well as striking enemy targets (e.g., US Predator, UK's Taranis, China's Rainbow).

Finally, it would be remiss not to mention the growth in **3D printing**. 4IR technologies are using 3D printers to feed bio-organic and synthetic materials into the printer and print everything from repair parts in space stations, prosthetic ears, noses, and skins, and complex architectural models.

Of course, 4IR is experiencing the next generation of space flights, where SpaceX's and Blue Origin's reusable rockets are replacing costlier NASA and Russian Soyuz rockets to deliver satellites and humans to and beyond orbit.

4IR is increasing telemedicine and telesurgeries to increase global access to healthcare. Physicians and scientists can remotely offer medical advice, create vaccines, edit genes, and perform surgeries. Once again, COVID-19 increased virtual consultations, using more AI to figure out common symptoms and problems and resolve them before seeing a physician. At the same time, telesurgery using robotics is becoming a reality, thanks to 5G networks.

Transparent Transactions and Supply Chains

Right after the 2008 global financial crisis, countries needed to recoup their losses and collect internal revenues from taxes. But tax fraud is a common corrupt occurrence in many countries.

Even in higher-income countries such as Italy, cash bribes for tax evasion are frightfully commonplace, with a culture of "only fools pay." This cash-based shadow economy, with under-the-table cash exchanges and people driving Ferraris and Porsches without declaring any income, costs the Italian government €300 billion per year to tax cheats—a sum that could pay off Italy's €2.2 trillion debt in less than eight years. But of course, the *Mafioso (Mafia)* and 'Ndrangheta in southern Italy use cash to extort and grant lucrative contracts.

Around the world, corrupt financial dealings rely on cash, increasing counterfeiting, graft, and corruption.

The first step toward financial transparency is payment digitization. With 4IR, the Italian government started a digital payments platform called PagoPA to digitize all government payments: taxes, car payments, and traffic fines. The PagoPA app carries a QR code to make digital payments, easily traceable. No more cash!

Digital payment transparency is a type of digital transformation where traditional processes and converted into digital processes for cost savings and efficiency!

How Bitcoins and Blockchains Work

Bitcoins (BTC) and blockchains are some of the most talked-about financial transformations focused on transparency. Financial digital transformation (often called FinTech) is likely to be the largest 4IR paradigm shift in the next five to ten years as countries compete to shift from a physical currency to a digital currency.

If there are no paper currencies or coins, every transaction would be digital and transparent.

Nowadays, we invest in and hear about Bitcoins, Litecoins, Dogecoins, and Ethereum. In September 2021, El Salvador, the Central American country, adopted Bitcoin as its currency.

Bitcoin is a digital currency invented by Satoshi Nakamoto that is not controlled by any particular government. Bitcoin uses blockchains to create and manage currency. Bitcoins operate like a real currency where no more than 21 million Bitcoins can be in circulation. By late 2021, the world created (mined) 90% of the allowable 21 million Bitcoins.

Bitcoin mining creates Bitcoins by adding a "verified" 1 MegaByte Block to a long chain, essentially called a blockchain. A blockchain is a verified set of digital blocks, each with its ID, chained together so that any break in the chain can be noticed. A Bitcoin miner has to use powerful GPU or ASIC processors to solve a simple mathematical problem (coded as a 64 digit hexadecimal hash) where the result has to be less than the target hash. The mathematical problem is not difficult but the process of arriving at the hash is extremely resource-intensive. The current odds are 1 out of 5.9 trillion.

The Bitcoin miner that can solve this hash has to include the "Proof-of-Work" as a part of the Bitcoin block ID. Once a Bitcoin miner creates a new, verified block, the miner is paid in Bitcoins. The first miners in 2009 were paid 50 BTC, with payments halving every 4 years. In 2021, a successful Bitcoin miner is paid 6.25 BTC for each new Bitcoin, to be halved in 2024.

The new BTC, a new block on the chain, is registered across a decentralized network of computers or "nodes" around the world. The computers periodically check each BTC's validity.

This is similar to creating an accounting ledger entry, periodically audited, and verified by many different auditors. Every time you mine, transfer, sell, or buy BTC, the transaction is verified as another proof of work across all the nodes. Only when there is consensus about the proof of work from the nodes, the ledger registers that transaction in chronological order. Attempts to counterfeit (change, tweak a transaction) or remove a transaction is impossible as the blockchain would deny them.

Insofar as blockchains are concerned, transactions are trustworthy and verifiable. But, given that Bitcoins can be anonymously traded has made BTC a preferred hacker currency and added tremendous volatility.

So, international governments are jumping onto the blockchain bandwagon to create their digital currencies. These digital currencies use blockchain's verification and ledger but are not decentralized. Instead, these digital currencies are managed by individual governments. China's Digital Yuan is the first national crypto currency. US' Digital Dollar, UK's Digital Sterling, and Europe's Digital Euro are all vying to become 4IR's digital currency.

Blockchain-based digital currencies are particularly useful for the following reasons:
1. Immediate access to money internationally without any fees or transaction costs with no brokers or middlemen.
2. Smartphone apps can replace banks, allowing anybody to be able to bank (there are billions of unbanked people in the world that have to rely on cash transactions and shady cash dealings).
3. Transparency with no counterfeiting or double charging.
4. Income and expenditure transparency with lower tax evasion.

Blockchains in 4IR are equally effective for supply chain transparency. With container ships moving around ports carrying food, cargo, and medicine, open to pilferage and spoilage, companies are using blockchains to track the movement of items throughout the entire supply chain. Blockchains linked to IoT sensors can detect ambient temperatures, location, drops, mishandling (shocks), and immediately register these events to create supply chain transparency. Was the wine exposed to heat or sunlight and for how long? Was a product removed from its packaging? Did the egg carton drop? Did the COVID-19 vaccine delivery maintain a cold supply chain (a very low temperature throughout the entire transportation system to maintain vaccine efficacy)?

Did You Know That?

In June 2021, The El Salvador government declares Bitcoin as a part of El Salvador's legal currency, the first ever country to declare a crypto-currency as a legal tender!

Mini-Case: The Pandemic, Vaccines, and 4IR (4th Industrial Revolution)

The Pandemic Preface

Whether it was a poor bat sold or a poor pangolin sold at China's Wuhan wet market remains a conjecture. All we know is that a wild virus crossed the wildlife-human threshold and attacked the human respiratory system.

Hello, SARS-CoV-2!

By January 2020, an eerie Pneumonia-like respiratory illness engulfed Wuhan, killing people. The Chinese government tabled autopsy results to avoid a panic, chastising anyone that dared discuss them. COVID-19 painted Wuhan red, but nobody knew it.

Yet!

Globalization has always been a pandemic catalyst. Viruses follow trade routes.

Like the 1918 Spanish Flu pandemic that started in World War I battlefields, carried and spread by steamers and newfound railways, COVID-19 followed trade routes across a shrinking globe.

The world took notice.

2020 became the year of the Pandemic. Millions died. Countries went into immediate lockdowns. Businesses closed their operations. Unemployment increased; Markets tumbled, reeling from uncertainty.

Something had to be done!

The Idea

Two ideas emerged.

Pfizer-BioNTech's synthetic messenger RNA (mRNA) fooled the body's RNA by injecting (or doping) one of our four RNA nucleotides with a reprogrammed set, instructing the body on how to defend itself.

Meanwhile, Oxford-Astra Zeneca used a weakened version of the common cold adenovirus (the common cold adenovirus infects us all), to carry the vaccine to deliver antibodies and train our T-cells to block COVID-19 antigens (the virus part harming our body) from entering our cells.

Time to develop ideas into vaccines!

Pharmaceuticals leaped into action. Vaccine development needed global collaborative efforts, from real-time vaccine design, testing, clinical trials, production, and cold supply chains.

4IR to the Rescue

Welcome to the 4th Industrial Revolution (4IR)!

4IR beckons an age of digital and bio-physical convergence. 4IR interweaves sensor and genomics data across millions of smart devices (called IoT [Internet of Things]) over high-speed digital networks. AI (Artificial Intelligence) neural nets perform complex computations. Robotic arms spring to productive dances. Blockchains keep track and tab.

At warp speed, 4IR technologies helped create the COVID-19 vaccine.

China had uploaded the SARS-CoV-2 genetic signature. Within seconds, worldwide researchers started collaborating on vaccines! Globally networked supercomputers fed complex epidemiological models, algorithms, and simulations to replicate viral attacks on the human body. AI, used for cancer response and treatment discoveries, was repurposed to discover immune responses to SARS-CoV-2.

Around the world, scientists uploaded clinical trial data into the cloud. Independent researchers and agencies leaped into action, using complex machine-learning algorithms and analytical engines to verify vaccine safety and efficacy.

Once checked for safety and efficacy, pharmaceuticals green-lighted vaccine production, sharing the vaccines' complex molecular designs for global production.

In a physically distanced world, robotic systems hummed away, unaided, fastidiously producing and packaging vaccines following precise specifications.

Traditionally, vaccine developments take years. But 4IR changed innovation dynamics.

By mid-July, Moderna, Oxford-AstraZeneca, and Pfizer-BioNTech announced vaccine breakthroughs.

Did You Know That?

More than 52% of FaceBook users use FaceBook as their primary news source, regardless of the news source's credibility! During the COVID-19 crisis, Russia use FaceBook to post memes discrediting how UK's Oxford-AstraZeneca vaccine jabs would turn people into monkeys. It was Russia's desperate attempt to promote its own Sputnik-V vaccine!

4IR and Vaccine Delivery

COVID-19 vaccine delivery requires extremely low-temperature storage and transportation, with Pfizer-BioNTech at −70 degrees F and Oxford-AstraZeneca at 36 degrees F. Both require constant refrigeration when transported, known as a cold supply chain.

To prevent vaccine spoilage, cold supply chains entail constant monitoring across transport carriers crisscrossing the globe.

4IR technologies, notably IoT (Internet of Things) sensors and blockchains, are used to monitor vaccine supply chain transparency.

Blockchains are digitally unique information blocks comprising digitally distributed, verifiable, immutable ledger chains.

Using a digital ID, vaccine blockchains monitor and record every vaccine state—ambient temperatures, locations, carriers, time, and even movements, as vaccines travel across locations—from vaccine production to the jab.

Any break in the chain, from tampering, a temperature rise, or a fall, is traceable. Because blockchains are immutable, none can tweak or revise any transaction, ensuring unprecedented transparency for products such as vaccines or services such as financial contracts.

Clever!

4IR beckons a brave new world of interlinked systems, meant to upend non-value-added activities, and create a new generation of innovation where digital will become and remain the new normal.

4IR's Dark Side

But 4IR's bright powers come with their dark parables: Privacy and Misinformation.

Using COVID-19 as a pretext, China capitalized on 4IR to monitor its citizens, investing in AI proximity-tracking apps and IoT thermal and facial scanning sensors, sending data over 5G wireless networks!

Throughout China, thermal scanners constantly registered body temperatures, using high 100+ degree F temperatures as COVID-19 infection evidence. AI facial recognition tracked the individual, matching the person to one's national ID. The information gave Chinese authorities the uncanny ability to monitor where people traveled and who they met. Infected individuals were tracked, forced to self-isolate, and denied travel privileges until treated.

Draconian to the world. Existential to China, desperately containing viral spread within its chockful urban enclaves, and getting its factories purring to global demand for cheaper goods.

4IR can speedily serve misinformation, too, feeding fears and shoving scams at the speed of light. Despite using Oxford-AstraZeneca's vaccine model for its own Sputnik-V, Russia wanted to discredit UK's Oxford-AstraZeneca early efforts. Using a Russia used a slew of anonymous international accounts to post disparaging memes on how AstraZeneca vaccines turned humans into monkeys.

4IR technologies that shared vaccine design information also spread doubt by fear-mongering, leading to echo chambers, conspiracy theories, and, subsequently, vaccine-hesitancy.

China's 4IR practices further exemplify 4IR powers and perils.

1. Suppose you jaywalk on a Chinese street.
2. Street IoTs, linked to traffic signals, sense a pedestrian crossing when the "Walk" sign is off (for computers, something off is read as 0 and on as 1). It is a pedestrian violation!
3. The pedestrian violation triggers IoT cameras linked to the cloud.
4. The IoT cameras zoom in and take a series of pictures or a video of the jaywalker and upload it to the cloud.
5. In seconds, supercomputers in the cloud run their AI facial recognition software on the video, running complex facial and movement (gait) analytics to recognize the pedestrian's identity. With movement and facial geometry, a match is made in seconds.
6. The AI identity match immediately connects to the government database over the cloud. The pedestrian identity is automatically checked across hundreds of millions of national ID card pictures until they match.
7. The Chinese government uses the digital identity match to pull the pedestrian's national ID card.
8. The pedestrian's ID picture and name are digitally plastered on digital billboards strewn across the motorway. It might read "Bad Citizens Jaywalk!" It is Digital Shaming.
9. The pedestrian is blacklisted. An immutable blockchain (like a credit history) is created for the specific ID. Instead of only looking at the person's credit, the blockchain will also look at social behaviors (do you jaywalk? Do you get drunk and fall? Do you double park your car? Do you post negative comments about the Chinese Communist Party on online forums? Did you join an anti-government protest group?).
10. Using blockchain ID information, a person determined by the authorities to be a less-than-stellar Chinese citizen can be penalized and denied certain social and economic privileges, such as joining a specific club or forum, housing, or even a loan.

4IR is Damocles' sword. It offers both power and peril.

Governments, companies, and humanity—
take note!

Exercises

1. Q&A: How do you use each of the 4IR
   technologies in your own life and work?
   What are your concerns with any or each of
   them?
2. Choose 3 technologies from 1 to 3IR that
   you think have been the most influential
   technologies leading to where we are today.
3. Discussions:

   a. Are industrial revolutions, from 1 to
      4IR always prompted by socio-
      economic changes? What are the
      socio-economic punctuations for 4IR?

   b. Discuss/debate on the following:
      Industrial revolutions have bettered
      humanity!
   c. Discuss/debate on the following:
      Industrial revolutions have bettered
      the SDG and the environment!
   d. With 4IR become the linchpin
      towards sustainability and stop
      environmental degradation? How?
   e. COVID-19 has changed the nature of
      work and life. Will 4IR help create a
      better work-life balance? Explain!
   f. Which of the industrial revolutions,
      from 1 to 3IR, most dramatically
      impacted society and globalization?
      Which one has been the most positive
      and which one the most negative?

From Functional to Corporate Thinking

Central to managerial and **executive decision-making** is to learn how to connect the dots that can transform trees into a forest, and a forest into a landscape. The beginning steps lie in thinking beyond the box, beyond your own function. Thus, it is important to first understand globalization and the world. Whether you are a manager or an executive, your job is to figure out cosmos from chaos—discover patterns from messiness; assign structure to the unstructured; match the matchless; make sense of the otherwise obscure.

Our decisions and we occupy a globally diverse and complex world where contexts can no longer be insular; they must span the globe. Today, new markets usher in innovations and profits. Brands are being redefined and frontiers are being merged to create a global society—a technologically interwoven global society interlinked by the flow of humans, capital, products, and services.

One issue all companies face is having managers siloed into **functional thinking**! You might be specialized in your technical function but if you don't understand how your work aligns with the overall company strategy, you create a functional silo that is oblivious to how your work ties into company objectives. Functionaries can often operate like disconnected corporate citizens mainly because they never really understand or care about what's going on with the company. Functionaries are often thought to focus on doing what's good for their department without considering what's good for their company. Yet, as in Shakespeare's Julius Caesar, Brutus, Julius Caesar's best friend says in defense of his assassination of the dictator to save Rome: *"Not that I loved Caesar less, but I loved Rome more."*

In companies, a corporate executive must be willing to sacrifice his or her incumbent functional loyalties to do what is good for the strategic future of the company. That's why you'll find that's why there are so many people who start working especially for technology. They understand technology but only from the technical side rather than on the business end. Unless you turn out to be brilliant at it, you're just going to be seconded to a basement-level operation. The same story follows across other functions, from accounting to HR. You must understand the bigger piece of the business puzzle if you plan on managing rather than simply supervising.

The **conflicting perspective** is that business managers and executives oftentimes think of IT and other functional managers as functional geeks that can't reconcile the importance of tying their work to the overarching business strategy. Business executives often think of IT technicians as people that have no idea what they're doing other than finding errors in the code, fixing logins, or making sure Wi-Fi connections and printers work day-in-and-day-out—fixing and tackling something that nobody else wants to tackle.

© PiaDura LTD 2022
P. Datta, *Global Technology Management 4.0*,
https://doi.org/10.1007/978-3-030-96929-5_2

As a functionary, you are never the puzzle master; you're just a person who cuts a piece of the puzzle and you don't know the overall puzzle picture.

Business managers think of functionaries and IT managers as technocrats that are only interested in new features and technologies and that IT managers have no idea how it makes business sense. On the other hand, IT managers think of business executives and managers as short-sighted that don't understand the importance of technology.

But choosing which technology innovation to invest in or bank upon is often a difficult choice for companies. Just because a recent technology has come to play doesn't automatically mean you need to get that technology unless it serves your business purpose. You can't merely jump around feverishly about any latest technology that's come to town and say "oh! we need to get it." Irrationally exuberant reactions like that will likely make you invest in technology that does not align with your competitive business needs, and it is going to fall short of your expectations and fall short of performance and return on investment (ROI). Yet, if business managers and executives don't see the potential of specific technologies and work closely with IT managers on what technologies to try out (pilot) and implement within their companies, they are likely to get trampled by technologies lurking in their blind-spot or around the corner. So, it is important to make sure that both business managers and IT managers not only communicate across the aisles to understand how latest technologies can change traditional business processes and how a company's strategy can work closely with emerging technologies.

Such conflicting views are commonplace where *good strategies fall by the wayside because of a bad culture* of not communicating or not understanding. Functional or departmental roots can poison even corporate culture. An educational institution hired a senior executive with academic training in Portuguese poetry. Even as an executive meant to think more about the efficiency of the university over a function, the person tried to buoy an otherwise withering Portuguese poetry department at a high opportunity cost of underfunding better performing departments and colleges.

Similarly, a company that grew out of a sales culture had appointed executives that still believed that the way they had traditionally conducted sales as being the only way. Their **functional myopia** (short-sightedness) made them de-value the emerging use of technology to find and manage customers. Then, one day, they were "Amazoned" and went out of business after 35 years. That happened because, even though they were executives, they had failed to ever expand their understanding of what is to come beyond their traditional functional roots.

That is what happened to **Sears**, a global American retailer that began business in 1886. Sears' followed a sales mindset by simply adding more physical locations and services including Sears Rent-A-Car. But Amazon's strategy of online presence and internal cost management pushed the century-old retailer out of business, and Sears filed for Chapter 11 Bankruptcy in September 2018.

Executives and policymakers, although once functional managers, must shed their functional garb to adorn themselves with the toga of the organization. **Functional Managers** excel at their specializations and departments. However, being an **Executive**, the next step up, requires that they think beyond the box, beyond their function to understand the interconnectedness of various functions, markets, and the environment that can affect the company rather than a function, division, or business unit. It, therefore, becomes important for executives to separate themselves from being too close to their original practice.

For example, the department head of Orthopedics is a functional elite. However, for the head of Orthopedics to step in as a hospital executive requires that the Orthopedic surgeon step up to thinking of what benefits the entire hospital rather than Orthopedics. It might even require revisiting the need to even maintain an Orthopedics department if the unit is unprofitable or does not offer strategic value. It might even require shutting down a unit that one may have belonged to because it's no longer beneficial to the company. Similarly, a Director of IT (Information Technology), upon assuming a corporate executive position such as a CTO (Chief Technology Officer) or CIO (Chief Information Officer), might have to rethink the optimal and strategic allocation of IT dollars. The CTO or CIO will have to distance himself or herself from his or her historic relationship to the function and might have to make tough decisions on the financial and strategic viability of a functional unit that might require disinvestments and outsourcing. Carrying the soil of the past might impede optimal decision-making.

The corporate executive needs to be an impresario, not an orchestra piece. You are more than a top-notch clarinet player; you are a conductor controlling multiple musicians and groups (e.g., strings, woodwinds) in a symphony or philharmonic. You need to know when the clarinet begins playing and when it needs to cue the flute. Your job is strategic resource allocation that goes beyond your love for the clarinet; instead, you want the symphony to perform at its fullest.

Exercise

In your own experience or within your own company, can you think of instances of functional thinking at the cost of corporate performance? How would you help fix it? Come us with three solutions.

The Tower of Babel: Culture and Politics in Decision Making

There is a tale told in Genesis in the Bible about humankind coming together to build a Ziggurat, a tall pyramidical structure, called the **Tower of Babel** somewhere in Mesopotamia (modern-day Iraq) to reach to the heavens and defy God. This was the largest architectural and construction project in history. God, realizing that humans were banding together to defy him, presumably, as the story goes, created various languages that made communication impossible. Without the ability to communicate with one another, the Tower of Babel failed to become a reality. Beyond the myth is the very fact that different languages create distinct cultures and soon it separates us tremendously—thus hampering productivity and performance.

Consider Your Landscape

It's important to understand the changing demographics and psychographics when considering the choice of strategy. *Why is it that KFC succeeded in China, but Home Depot failed?* Demographics refers to basic data about people such as age, sex, income, education, and race. Psychographics refers to data about how people feel. Sometimes a good strategy is based on demographics but not good psychographics. **KFC** realized that the Chinese market is interesting. Instead of launching the typical fare of fried chicken in China, KFC cautiously whetted the Chinese appetite by introducing fried chicken with some popular local food such as Congee, egg tarts, and soy milk drinks.

Home Depot, on the hand, focused on demographics to establish large stores in China. China was the perfect market. Housing was booming; people were interested in renovations. But what **Home Depot** did not understand was that China did not yet understand the Home Depot "Build-it-yourself" culture. China, with its recent wealth and cheap labor supply, was a "Build-it-for-me" culture. In China, getting your hands dirty with a home project was looked down upon and the Chinese would abstain from ever carrying a piece of tile, let alone a piece of drywall or lumber. Sadly, Home Depot was too late in understanding Chinese psychographics and, after struggling for six, years, closed the last of its 7th store in 2012.

The heart of technology decisions is understanding and aligning strategy across various facets of operations—between functions, across markets and cultures, across maintaining efficiencies via technology, and yet remaining effective in competition. **Marriott**, the hotel chain, is always trying to simplify its guest experience (also called user experience) by creating check-in kiosks in its hotel lobbies. Marriott is a chain with top-notch properties such as Ritz Carlton, Bvlgari Hotels, JW Marriott, and St. Regis; premium properties such as Marriott, Renaissance, Sheraton, Le Meridien, and Westin; and select hotels such as Courtyard, and Fairfield.

The Marriott chain caters to a lot of seasoned business travelers that prefer a quick check-in convenience without having to go through the hassle of waiting to check-in at the front desk behind a lengthy line of other guests. So, Marriott wanted to use technology to simplify the check-in process and increase its customer experience. So, around the year 2000, Marriott wanted all hotels in its chain to implement check-in kiosks. Travelers that simply wanted to check-in and get to their rooms o rest could simply walk up to one of the Marriott kiosks in the lobby, enter their info like swiping a driver's license or passport scan. Their reservations would pop up with room assignments, allowing guests to upgrade, add services, and print their guest room keys, and head on to catch up on work or a relaxed evening. Marriott liked the concept and wanted to implement it across all hotels in its chain.

Each Marriott Hotel operates like a **profit center** rather than a **cost center**. A profit center manages its budgets, revenues, costs, and expenses. In a profit center, if you can keep your costs and expenses low and increase revenues, you make more profit. After remitting a part of the profits to Marriott corporate, individual hotels can keep the rest of their profits to disburse as they feel fit, whether they be renovations, new service offerings, and/or bonuses. In contrast, a **cost center** operates based on creating and presenting a budget to the corporate headquarters (HQ), like requesting an allowance. The corporate headquarters reviews each request. If one of the hotels did not use its entire allocated budget, instead of being appreciated and rewarded for better cost and revenue management, HQ would reduce the budget for the next period. That's the origin of the term, "use it or lose it." Even if a hotel were to smartly manage its costs so that it

had money left over, instead of being appreciated for its efforts, HW would assume that it does not need the money. Costs centers often are inefficient because it fails to acknowledge positive cost-cutting and revenue-building efforts.

Because each Marriott hotel had a say in what it wanted. While some premium and select hotels opted in to implement the self-sign-in kiosks, the luxury brands, particularly the Ritz Carlton CEO, opted not to implement the kiosks. **Ritz Carlton** had a point and understood that when and where to place technology was a large part of corporate technology strategy. Not that technology and convenience were not important, but that the technology had to be hidden behind personalized service. Ritz Carlton guests expect personalized service and a human touch. You walk into a Ritz Carlton to feel that you are being offered personalized service. You have someone asking you your preferences, the types of flowers you like, the types of chocolates, and the type of cuisine, so that when you return to your room after heading out, you might find your favorite flowers in the vase and a chocolate assortment of your liking on the bed. While each meticulous note of your likes and dislikes are later fed into a database that can be accessed by the next housekeeping shift staff and front desk, technology is used in the background with a human in the foreground. That is what creates and differentiates experiential service. Today, Ritz Carlton offers a smartphone app that analyzes your preferences to create something called "anticipatory customer service" as a part of its **customer-relationship-management** (CRM). CRM is a way by which companies use technology to better understand their customer choices and habits using things such as purchase history, preferences, what customers tend to purchase together (market basket analysis), location, along with basic demographics.

At the end of the day, it's useful to realize that *data is digital, but service is personal.*

Technology remains paramount in importance but knowing where and when to use it and where to show or hide technology are what defines good technology strategy.

Exercise

Based on Marriott and KFC's strategies, how would you advise Home Depot to work around culture to become successful?

The Geopolitical Landscape: Energetic Progression

Let's go around the world in 80 s, viewing it as Santa Claus views it on a dark crisp Christmas evening dropping presents down chimneys and smokestacks. To Santa and space voyagers, this is how the earth looks like at night (courtesy of NASA). Where there are lights, there is energy; where there are energy footprints, there is development. So, let's review the energetic progression (Fig. 2.1).

The Americas

Beginning in **North America** with the tiny specks of lights from Alaskan oil rigs, we head south from the desolate Canadian Yukon territory until we reach the fringes of USborders where Canada's urban centers twinkle the landscape. The western

US Rockies are sprinkled with communities. Seattle and western California glitter. As you head east over the Rockies, you are drenched in a large swathe of lights and action concentrating as we head east of the Mississippi-Missouri rivers. South of the US lies Mexico, a quasi-pariah state debauched by drug and gunrunners and human traffickers. Nearly 32,000 people were murdered in Mexico in 2017, fueled by poverty, drugs, and illegal immigration transits from South and Central America. The few bright energy streaks come from supply chains transporting goods and human cargo. Further south, the lights grow dimmer till we reach the Panama Canal, bracing two oceans, active with sea traffic and cargo movement heading, thanks to NAFTA (North American Free Trade Association), *el norte*.

Enter **South America** and you spot the bright lights on the northwestern rim are from Venezuela and Columbia. Venezuela's Orinoco Basin and Columbia's Cusiana and Capuigna oilfields with their rich oil deposits shine bright with refineries, the Transandino oil pipeline, and transport routes across Columbia into Panama. But the Venezuelan economy is in tatters with a severe lack of energy and economic output. Venezuela, with massive oil reserves, cannot even manage the cost of producing oil to provide

Fig. 2.1 The global world at night (Courtesy NASA)

necessary energy for the country. Once one of the richest South American economies, Venezuelans today are often forced to run to stores to purchase items before prices rise every day from inflation. Venezuela's socialist president, Maduro, talks about women finger-drying their hair instead of using a blow dryer that requires energy. With no economic activity, the Venezuelan currency, called Bolivar, has depreciated so much that the President has asked people to simply add multiple 0s to their existing currency. Ten years ago, in 2008, 1 US Dollar was equal to 2.2 Bolivars. In 2018, 1 US Dollar is equal to 250,000 Bolivars. Heading south, the Andes mountains and the Atacama Desert dim the lights until you reach the eastern parts of Argentina and Brazil.

Brazil, the Latin Jaguar, is the part of the **BRICS** (Brazil, Russia, India, China, and South Africa) (BRICS to be discussed later), emerging economies with once-high rates of growth. Brazil, with oil from the Campos, Santos, and Lula basins, hydroelectricity, manufacturing, and its rich ore, glitters around its eastern shores. Yet, the pomp and circumstance of Brazil's once hallowed president, Lula De Silva, faded as corruption charges against him embroiled the once hallmark South American Economy. His protégé, Dilma Roussef, heralded as the quintessential successor, was consumed by the same doldrums and was out of office. Once the price of oil and commodities (things such as metals, meats) plummeted, the country realized that the heydays were over and rampant corruption surfaced. Add to that the uneasy mix of wealth with miles of poverty-stricken, crime-ridden shantytowns called Favelas. This has created years of entrenched corruption. Corruption in Brazil costs the economy $50 billion a year in 2018 and, with no viable leadership. While Argentinian agriculture and minerals along with Chilean agriculture and wine light up the production and supply routes, Argentina has been reeling from one economic crisis to another. The Argentinian economy imports heavily, and its agricultural exports of maize and soybeans have suffered from drought, increasing consumer prices of goods, thus leading to inflation. Having suffered one of the worst currency crises in 2001

when Argentinian's, fearing massive currency devaluation, made a run-on banks (when everyone wants to withdraw their bank deposits), a weakening Peso (the Argentinian currency) along with high reliance on imports is making imports more expensive, and creating more inflation where the Peso loses even more value.

Europe, Middle East, and Africa (EMEA)

Traveling east across the Atlantic, you encounter **Africa**, the explorer's continent rich with resources, wildlife, corruption, strife, but also a new era of digital innovations.

South Africa, or Zuid Africa, stands as one of the few beacons of economic activity with light streaks from Cape Town with its tourism and wines to Johannesburg with its advanced manufacturing and services.

South Africa's story mirrors the saga of the African continent. Colonized by the Portuguese in the fifteenth century, the British and Dutch East India Companies popularized South Africa as a mid-point for supply chain provisioning during their long voyages to India around The Cape of Good Hope. The Dutch established farming communities and the Dutch farmers (Boers) established homestead colonies that were commonly in conflict with the native Xhosa population. Great Britain formally colonized South Africa to stop it from falling into Napoleon's hands after the French Revolution.

> **Did You Know that?**
> Around 1760's, the French King Louis XV used a flying dinner tables (*table volante*) and chairs to present dinners to guests in Versailles Palace's Petit Trianon! Think of it as the world's first lift (*ascenseur*)!

Discovery of gold and diamonds in the nineteenth century intensified growth of British influence and led to the Anglo-Zulu war against the native Zulu tribe followed by the Boer War against the Dutch settlers. In 1948, South Africa began a draconian era of apartheid based on segregation by skin color. The apartheid era ended in 1994, with open elections that heralded Nelson Mandela, a civil-rights activist imprisoned for 27 years, as the President. But South Africa, since 2011, has been beset by economic maladies, corruption, and widespread economic inequality under the Jacob Zuma presidency.

Moreover, surrounded by impoverished economies, African wildlife is also under threat from rampant poaching of Rhinos and Elephants for their horns and tusks, primarily driven by Asian demand.

Yet Africa is full of silver linings, led especially by 4IR technology innovators!

Take Kenya, for example. For decades, a lack of an accessible banking infrastructure left Kenyans concerned about carrying large sums of cash for various transactions. However, it was commonplace to purchase and transfer "cell phone credits" easily. So, Kenya's cell phone provider, Safaricom, used the "cell phone credit" transfer concept to introduce the world's first mobile phone to mobile phone payment system called M-Pesa. No longer did you need to transfer cash; instead, all you needed was a phone number to collect and send money! Kenya's M-Pesa solved concerns related to carrying physical cash and became an instant success.

Africa's 4IR innovations are creating a new entrepreneurial ecosystem. South Africa and Nigeria are building scalable Healthcare Mobile Payment and Telemedicine Platforms for easier access to healthcare. Uganda is using Robots to guide traffic in busy intersections. Drones are being deployed to monitor wildlife and deter poaching! According to a 2020 World Health Organization (WHO) report, 4IR innovations ruled 60% of African entrepreneurships, with a large boom in 3D printing of parts, robotics, WhatsApp Chatbots, and contact tracing and diagnostic apps and tools in to combat COVID-19 in Ghana, South Africa, Angola, and Rwanda.

Heading north is a vast undeveloped landscape with Namib and Kalahari deserts till you reach the western fringes of Nigeria. The Niger Delta oilfields and the Harcourt port glitter and then darkens again as you head north across the Sahara till you reach the northern perimeters of Africa. Bracing the northern coast of Africa Mediterranean are the erstwhile French and Italian colonies of Morocco, Algeria, Tunisia, Libya, and Egypt. Vainly prodded by then Secretary of State Hillary Clinton to remove their dictator, Gaddafi, the uprising killed Gaddafi on the streets and, created an anarchy and vacuum wherein the US ambassador died in an attack in Benghazi. Whereupon, Libya lies in tatters, trembling with anarchy and terrorism.

This area, once a hotbed of trade and commerce, is now worrisome. Islamic terrorism is rampant north of the African Equator while bad governance is rampant in sub-Saharan Africa. Since the Arab uprising against dictators that began in Tunisia in the early 2000s, the shores of Morocco, Algeria, Tunisia, Libya, and Egypt that once shimmered with active trade routes into the Mediterranean, are suffering from failed attempts at democracy. This is ushering in a political vacuum and, risking falling prey to terrorism from groups such as Daesh or ISIL (Islamic State of Iraq and the Levant)/ISIS (Islamic State of Iraq and Syria), Al Qaeda, Boko Haram in Nigeria, and Al Shabab in Ethiopia and Somalia. Countries like Egypt and Libya, although run by long-standing dictators, were relatively stable. The failed Arab Spring uprising in the early 2000s that wanted to replace dictatorships with democracies has not seen fruitful outcomes. Rather, Egypt is still protesting in Tahrir Square ten years after the Arab Spring; Libya, after the brutal execution of its long-time dictator, Muammar Gaddafi, regressed into chaos and is still at an elevated risk of succumbing to terrorism and a failed state. Somalia suffers from massive corruption and poverty along with Islamic fundamentalism and terrorism. Run by warlords such as the infamous Mohammed Farah Eideed, when the US and the UN presence suffered a loss of life and limb while trying to capture him. Since then, Somalia has gained massive infamy for piracy, its most productive activity, where Somali boats try and hijack cargo in the high seas for ransom, thus making the area, known as the Horn of Africa, one of the most precarious global shipping routes.

East of Africa across Sinai and the Red Sea begins the **Middle East**, in strife for thousands of years and in crises for the past hundred or so years, especially after Transjordan was divided into various countries by the 1916 Sykes-Picot Agreement. The Sykes-Picot Agreement came at amidst World War I where Turkish-held areas of Transjordan were divided into Syria, Lebanon, Palestine, and Armenia along with other areas of control across Great Britain, France, and Russia. A land based on feudal loyalties were forced to be managed by dictators; the Shia and Sunni Muslims hated each other based on centuries of resentment from whether the Shias or Sunnis were truly the inheritors of their prophet. The resentments were accentuated by the birth of Israel in 1948 that was considered an affront to the Arab Muslims by establishing a Jewish state in the area once informally called Palestine. Israel, right after its formation, defended itself from a massive Arab assault from Egypt, Jordan, Syria, and Iraq. In 1967, the same countries attacked Israel. In what became famous as the Six-Day war, the Israeli air force destroyed most of Egypt's air force and ended up controlling the Gaza strip, West Bank, the Sinai Peninsula, and Golan Heights. In 1973, Syria and Egypt attempted an invasion against Israel on the Jewish holiday of Yom Kippur. Although caught off-guard, Israel was able to recover and advance, resulting in a ceasefire.

Did You Know that?

In the 1950s, Israel used computer algorithms to reprogram original color broadcasts to B + W on Israeli TV channel to deter people from importing color TVs in the fear that the Israeli economy would crash!

These wars still carry a bitter taste across the Middle East and Israel's existence has been in constant threat. The hotbed of animosity is even hotter with internal conflicts among the surrounding Arab states. The Kingdom of Saudi Arabia, the largest presence in the area and the largest oil producer, is paradoxically both anti-Israel and pro-west. With an orthodox Muslim population displaying strong underlying support for Wahabis, an ultra-conservative group like the Taliban in Afghanistan, the Saudi monarchy has long felt fragile. Once flush with money from oil exports, the Saudi kings' largesse (free overseas education, subsidized fuel, water, and benefits) to its citizens has long been the Saudi strategy to mitigate a Wahabi takeover. Less than 30% of Saudi citizens own their home and the kingdom provides most benefits. However, with massive oil strikes across the globe in the 2010s, gas finds from hydraulic fracturing (fracking), and alternative energy, Saudi Arabia, along with other oil producing countries in the area, have suffered massive economic distress.

Resource Curse and the Dutch Disease

Why is it that Venezuela, a South American country, with 20% of the world's oil reserves, and contributing to 56% of Venezuela's income (2008 data), suffers from one of the direst shortages of food, medicine, paper, and even electricity? In 2016, Venezuela was forced to reduce the workweek to only Monday and Tuesday from issues of recurrent blackouts.

This phenomenon of a country relying on only one natural resource as its source of revenues makes it complacent. That creates a **resource curse**. A resource curse makes a country not focus on educating its citizens for the future and no skills and intellectual diversity among its workforce. From Venezuela to Kuwait and Saudi Arabia, this resource curse is in play.

A resource curse creates a phenomenon called a **Dutch disease**. A Dutch disease is a putative effect where countries rely too much on exporting one sole product (mostly, a natural resource for which they really did not have to innovate much). The ability to export a large amount of a particular product increases the country's earnings, which in turn appreciates (raises) its currency value. A more expensive currency makes exports more difficult because exports become more expensive. Because of that, a country with one main export suddenly makes all its other industries suffer, then falling into a **resource curse**. Because of oil exports, Venezuelan agriculture suffered. When Norway found oil in the North Sea, it stifled other industries and the economy suffered. Russia's oil has been its resource curse, as are cases with Nigeria, Saudi Arabia, and Iran.

This has forced Saudi Arabia and other similar undiversified economies (that mainly depend on oil or a natural resource as their main revenue source) to rethink its need for economic diversification (rather than simply counting on oil revenues) and restructure its economy with new taxes and cuts in subsidies, making a nervous atmosphere fragile. Saudi Arabia's economy, reeling under dropping oil prices and energy innovations, is scrambling to diversify its economy. One way it's doing so under the new monarch, Price Salman, is by making social reforms at home like giving women more freedom such as being able to drive for the first time in 2018, while crushing all dissent within the country.

Moreover, Saudi Arabia (a Sunni Muslim country and Iran (a Shia Muslim country)) treat each other as nemeses. Since 2015, Yemen, a neighboring country, has become the proxy battleground from Saudi Arabia supporting the Yemeni government and Iran supporting the Houthi Rebels. Iran, once Persia, till it was conquered by the Arabs, has failed to recover its economy. Ruled by despotic dictators such as Reza Shah Pahlavi and then overthrown by a despotic clergy called Khomeini, Iran still suffers from massive economic sanctions and economic crises. After years of war against Iraq's Saddam Hussein, Iran today tries to exert its regional influence on post-Saddam Hussein's Iraq as well as in Syria and Lebanon. Beirut, the capital of Lebanon, bordering Israel, was once regarded as the Paris of the Orient. Since Lebanon's civil war in the 1980s, the country has been reeling from one crisis to another and currently assumed to be a run by Hezbollah, a terrorist group, with Syrian and Iranian support. Syria, under the repressive iron fists of its president, Bashar Al-Assad, is still suffering from a civil war with anti-government rebels as well as with ISIS terrorists.

Since 2011, the Syrian civil war has created mayhem within and beyond its borders. The president, Assad, waged a brutal military offensive against a hodge-podge of Syrian rebels. Although some opposition was legitimate such as The Syrian Arab Republic, the Free Syrian Army, and the Democratic Federation of Northern Syria, ISIS, the terrorist group, was one. With so many shifting loyalties among the rebel opposition, it remains difficult separating legitimate groups from terrorist organizations. Nonetheless, Assad's unrelenting brutality and years of fighting (with Russian and Iranian Hezbollah aid) has resulted in nearly 400,000 dead, among which nearly 110,000 are civilians. Syria's civil war has also displaced 7 million people, creating more than 5 million refugees, propelling a migration crisis. The refugees and displaced population have suddenly crossed borders into Lebanon and Turkey and then to Eastern Europe and crossed the Mediterranean to Italy, Spain, and Greece, trying to make their way into wealthier western European countries, creating a sudden population surge and a perceived threatening of the Western European values and lifestyle. With a slew of recent terrorist attacks, and the growing popularity in Nationalism, the migration crisis is enveloping Western Europe.

Iran, once the center of the Persian Empire has used this turmoil to reestablish its dwindling economy and geopolitical influence. Iran, a part of an Islamic sect called Shia, is daggers drawn against its other neighbors known as the Sunnis.

Western Europe, the birthplace of western philosophy and the renaissance, glitters with development, innovation, and activity. From the UK across the channel into Belgium and into Austria, these are where the top brands of Europe reside with a tremendous need for energy to keep the brands running. Southern Europe, bristling with ports and logistics ferrying legal goods and illegal migrants to the shores of Europe, glitter from Messina to Corfu. Yet not all is quiet on the western front. The **1957 Treaty of Rome** established the notion of a single European Community that later evolved into the European Common Market and the Eurozone. If you look at Greece, Portugal, Spain, Ireland, and Italy in the early 2000s, their governments assumed most of their employment burdens. Armed with low Eurozone interest rates and over-employment, the Greeks were delirious. Countries such as Germany and France, the most productive economies in the Eurozone, want low interest rates to invest in R&D innovations and productivity.

Sadly, when the same interest rates are shared by countries with varying productivities, some remain austere and some profligate. Greece, Portugal, Spain, Ireland, and Italy borrowed cheap (low interest) money and turned prodigal. They could simply borrow for naught yet practice unbridled spending. So, the countries binged on purchasing goods, cars, and inflating the property market without improving their economy, thus increasing their public debt. Edifying their convictions that the common market was the holy grail; the Greek government simply lay down an ultimate for of capitalism…cheap credit and no taxes. In Italy and Greece, not paying taxes was in vogue, a sort of national pastime. It propitiously improved standards of living of the people at the cost of the whole economy. Interest rates from the *troika* were low enough to allow them to indulge themselves on free-flowing credit. And everyone was drinking the Kool-Aid even though the myopia was pervasive. It is similar to building yourself a mansion in a fort with decaying walls. You know that when the walls collapse, your mansion remains to be plundered, yet you intendedly refrain from contributing to patching up the wall or the ramparts. So, the **European Union (EU)** invited more countries, now from Eastern Europe, to buoy up the rest.

Parts of Europe that are very picturesque and highly dependent on tourism suffer from a similar **resource curse**. Many areas of Italy and many Greek island economies that primarily rely on summer tourism often close all operations during the low-winter-season when few tourists visit the island. Tourism based on the beauty of the geography becomes a resource curse, impeding alternative economic development initiatives. Inhabitants in these areas often think of tourism as a quick money-earner, and that disincentivizes some locals from seeking higher education, knowing that they can earn money peddling wares to tourists or working in the tourism-service industry. Over-reliance on tourism, therefore, creates adverse effects by (i) concentrated economic reliance mainly on tourist preference leading to (ii) low economic diversification, and (iii) large environmental footprints from overuse of infrastructure and environmental degradation during high tourist seasons. There are small, picturesque communities that generally do not speak English brandishing signs obviously aimed at tourists reading "Please do not litter."

Venice in northeastern Italy, for example, is a very fragile city with a beautiful maze of waterways and old structures. A massive influx of tourists and cruise ships has caused irreparable damage to the city. With 4 to 5 large cruise ships entering Venice each day during high season, the tides created by the ships cause flooding across the city. In addition, Venice receives nearly 20 million tourists every year, often 120,000 tourists a day, concentrated in certain parts of the city and over-using its water and sanitation infrastructure. With more tides causing flooding and overuse of water and sanitation facilities, the sewers overflow, forcing refuse and sewage into the streets, creating a serious health and environmental hazard. Yet, Venice, so dependent on tourism, is caught in the resource trap, where it must precariously balance its disastrous environmental consequences and its economy. The story is the same for the Greek islands such as Paros, Mykonos, and Santorini. Even Mount Everest, the highest mountain peak in the world, is being closed to tourists from over-commercialization. With 4,000 people paying to climb Mount Everest, Nepal, home of some of the most picturesque mountains in the world, is pulling the plug on tourism because of the negative ecological footprints from littering and even 11 climbing deaths in 2019 (Fig. 2.2).

Did You Know that?

It was Napoleon's invasion of southern Europe created the first Kingdom of Italy (with only northern Italian states) and chased Portugal's King Pedro who exiled himself and founded the Empire of Brazil!

Fig. 2.2 Venice during high tides (Courtesy Flickr)

Heading into **Eastern and Central Europe**, economies dim from large manufacturing closures due to cheaper Asian labor. Subsequently, several Eastern and Central European countries have succumbed to populist leaders choosing to ally themselves with either Russia or the EU.

East of Europe and North of China lies **Russia**, the White Bear, spread across Europe and Asia. Russia, glows on its western fringes of St. Petersburg and Moscow, and then grows dismal as you head east into the Ural Mountains. Russia, head of the erstwhile Soviet Union, has been a part of several important historical events over centuries, its brutal winters thwarting Napoleon's *Grand Armee* and Hitler's Blitzkrieg. The twentieth century saw Russia's most momentous changes. Once a land of Tsars, the 1917 Russian revolution replaced monarchism with a Bolshevist form of Communism led by Lenin and then Stalin.

Russia, once invaded by the Mongols and Tatars such as Genghis Khan, Kublai Khan, and Timur Lang, has been the juxtaposition of the east and west, creating a transcontinental country. During the sixteenth century, Ivan the Terrible (Ivan IV) annexed kingdoms to unify Russia and become the first Tsar. During the eighteenth century, Russia became more westernized and industrialized under Peter the Great's age of reform and Catherine the Great's age of enlightenment. Tsar Alexander I thwarted Napoleon's march to Moscow. Still, Russia remained largely feudal and oppressive and Russia's economic misery from costs of fighting against the Austro-Hungarian army in World War I culminated in the 1917 revolution.

The Revolution executed the last of the Tsars, Nicholas II, and, under Lenin, created the first socialist country in world, the USSR (Union of Soviet Socialist Republic) or the Soviet Union. Stalin succeeded Lenin and began the great purge, where hundreds of thousands of dissenters disappeared and were executed. USSR became a part of the allies during World War II and pushed back Nazi Germany's siege of Stalingrad and later participated in the fall of Berlin. After the war, the Potsdam Conference let USSR annex parts of Germany and eastern European states. Then began the Cold War with the USSR against Western Europe and the US, often verging on nuclear conflict. In 1991, after the fall of the Berlin wall separating East and West Germany, USSR collapsed, lost its annexed territories, and became Russia again. The Russian economy reeled from sudden upheaval with internal wars with Chechnya, a Muslim-majority territory and a 1998 financial crisis.

With an unexpected resignation of the affable President Yeltsin in 1999, a new strongman, Putin became the new Russian president. Under Putin, Russia has been trying to reassert itself as the returning superpower. Since then, Russia, under Putin, has reverted to more petulant geopolitics, despite international condemnation. In 2014, Russia ran a unilateral referendum in Ukraine, an independent country, and annexed Crimea from Ukraine. In 2015, Russia militarily intervened in Syria in support of Syrian President Assad, an ongoing war.

Did You Know that?

Although Western Europe did not condone Russia's annexation of Crimea in 2016, Europe's dependence on Russian Nord Stream 2 energy pipeline forced Europe to turn a blind eye! Such is our energy dependence in the 4IR world!

Even with large oil reserves, the Russian economy has been in rapid decline and social purges have become common. Only 7% of Russians belong to the middle class and Russia,

today, is more embroiled in reasserting its international prowess rather than developing its
internal economy and human rights.

A land of incredible talent, from scientists to
artists, despite communist reforms called *Glasnost
(openness)* and *Perestroika (restructuring)*, the
Soviet Union collapsed in 1991. Facing economic
crises, Russia relied on its vast Siberian oilfields to
supply energy to Western Europe using the Nord
Stream pipeline. But Western Europe's energy
reliance on Russia's Nord Stream gas and oil
pipelines has allow Russia to evade sanctions.

In today's 4IR world, Russia is restarting the
Cold War with multiple state-sponsored hacking
and ransomware groups such as *Fancy Bear*,
intent of disrupting western infrastructures and
commercial interests.

As you cross into Asia, the Caspian Sea and
Black Sea areas shimmer with their Tengiz oilfields and oil pipelines. Then it goes dark heading into Afghanistan and Pakistan till you reach
India with small clusters of development across a
swathe of more than a billion people littered with
corruption and illiteracy. Despite an educated
workforce and entrepreneurial talent, India suffers from overpopulation and poverty along with
a beleaguered physical infrastructure. However,
India's rich technology talent has allowed India
to become a popular software-development and
call-center-support offshoring destination.

East of India, the port cities of Thailand and
Malaysia, guide you to the services hub of Hong
Kong into the manufacturing Mecca in mainland
China with its east coast sparkling like a necklace
reading millions of containers ready to be shipped around the world. East of China are Taiwan
with its manufacturing base and Japan with its
innovation, still steeped in samurai tradition—
polite, precise, and sometimes brutal.

Japan is a country simultaneously steeped in
modernity and tradition. Japan has remained
isolationist for over 600 years, ruled by feudal
lords called Shoguns. Commodore Perry, an
American naval officer, forced the opening of the
Japan to the outside world. Then came the Meiji
restoration when Japan was rapidly westernized
and industrialized. Japan rapidly armed itself and
defeated China and Russia, annexing Korea and

Taiwan from China and parts of the Sakhalin
island from Russia. Although Japan stayed with
the allies against Germany during the World
War I, Japan's expansionist policies made it
invade China in 1931 and joined the axis powers
(Germany and Italy) during World War II. The
surprise Japanese attack on Pearl Harbor in the
US got the US involved in World War II and
Japan surrendered after the US dropped two
atomic bombs on Hiroshima and Nagasaki in
1945. With a formidable military but forced to
renounce any right to declare war or use military
might, Japan is one of the West's strongest allies
and Japan's economy grew to become the second
largest economy in the world until 2009, primarily driven by technological innovations,
manufacturing, and industrial automation. Yet,
Japan is equally traditional where work is performed in all intensity while life outside of work
is meant to be slowed down and enjoyed.

Asia

As we head south into **Asia**, we find India. India,
the Saffron Elephant—the seventh largest country and the world's largest democracy with the
second largest population in the world—is a
country of oddities. Centuries of invasion and
conquests, from the Greeks under Alexander, the
Arab invasion, and then British colonization
have left India divided between fatalism and
superstition for a large swathe of its population
while the other, albeit smaller part of the population attempts to be scientific and enlightened.
India's educational institutions are well regarded,
yet its literacy rate is merely 75%; its economy is
the 6th largest in the world, yet its GDP per
capita is 140th in the world; it is one of the largest IT services exporters in the world, yet its
infrastructure and health conditions remain one
of the poorest. Corruption is rampant with pronounced social and economic inequalities, with
poverty dwelling side by side with billions. India
suffers from a dreadful general infrastructure,
from roads to transportation and sewer systems.
While India has tried to emerge out of its own
ruins of overpopulation and extreme practices of

caste and religion with intellectual thinkers, India has yet to deliver. India is trying to rethink its urbanization and developmental strategy, figuring out a way to balance its technology services exports on the one hand and tackling aspects of large-scale illiteracy and primitive living with high levels of social intolerance, pollution, and population explosion.

North of India lies **China**, the middle kingdom of the Red Dragon. China, buoyed by massive cash inflows from global exports, wants to establish itself as a dominant super-fulcrum, if not a superpower. So, China is following a three-pronged strategy. First, China forces all companies that wish to establish a presence in the large and lucrative Chinese market to assume a local partner and share its technology and expertise. The aim is to build up Chinese technical know-whow without much regard for **IP (Intellectual Property)** rights. IP rights are meant to protect novel ideas and innovations through patents, copyrights, and trademarks. Countries with little or no regard for IP will infringe (steal) ideas and make it their own. For example, if you created a new type of medicinal drug compound after years of and many millions in **R&D (Research and Development)** (investments in research, innovation, and new products and services) but the minute your drug hits the market, someone reverse engineers and steals the chemical composition to produce their own, you have lost a sizable proportion of your revenues to recoup your R&D costs. This is a form of IP infringement. It is estimated that IP infringements and relaxed enforcement of IP laws in China cost US companies nearly $50 billion per year.

Did You Know that?

China's one-child policy created a significant gender imbalance, with more males than females. With fewer women available for marriage, it is not uncommon to find Chinese parks with boys' parents handing out flyers to girls' families, urging them to consider marrying their sons!

Second, China, after multiple unsuccessful attempts to build lucrative global brands, has opted to acquire reputed global brands. In recent years, Chinese companies have acquired famous brands including GE Appliances (US), AMC Cinemas (US), Motorola Mobility (US), Volvo (Sweden), London Cab (UK), Gieves and Hawkes Clothiers (London), Cerruti Clothiers (Italy), Waldorf Astoria Hotels (US), AC Milan Football (Soccer) Team (Italy), Sandro Clothiers (French), Pirelli Tires (Italy), Hose of Fraser Department Stores (UK), and Hamleys Toy Stores (UK), to name a few.

However, China's growth has come at a cost. First, thousands of Chinese factories operating to feed global demand have prompted overurbanization along with serious environmental costs. Most Chinese citizens have never seen blue skies. Beijing's air quality is often so polluted with microparticles that public health agencies regularly warn residents to avoid leaving their homes to protect their health. Second, with a weak and unreliable investment market, Chinese investors have overinvested in properties, creating a large real estate bubble. Chinese properties have become frightfully expensive. In 2021, Evergrande, one of China's largest property developers, reported bad multi-billion dollar real estate investments, furthering concerns about China's property market (Fig. 2.3).

Third, China is heavily investing in building and owning infrastructure around the world, especially supply chain infrastructure that it can use to transport its own goods across the world. China has acquired commercial shipping ports in Sri Lanka (below India on the Indian Ocean), Djibouti (on the Horn of Africa by the Red Sea, the eastern shores bracing Africa and Middle East), and Brazil (TCP, the 2nd largest port as a South Atlantic Gateway). China controls European ports in key locations in Greece (Piraeus, near Athens, linking the Aegean and Adriatic Seas), Spain (Valencia as a link to the Mediterranean Sea), and Belgium (Zeebrugge, with access to the North Sea and the North Atlantic) supply chain routes. Beyond controlling shipping, China's new **Silk Road or Belt and Road**

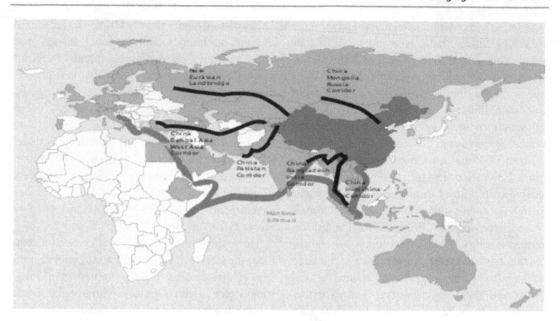

Fig. 2.3 China's belt and road initiative map (Courtesy Wikipedia)

Initiative is meant to create high-speed transportation routes as land bridges across Asia and Europe with links to Russia, Turkey, Germany, and India. Combined with the shipping ports, the Belt and Road Initiative will give China an open passage to supply its goods across the world without heavy reliance of shipping delays and costs. China is also heavily investing in Africa. China's Africa Fund is investing nearly $60 billion in Africa, converting Africa into China's second continent. China is building long road and rail networks in Nigeria to the west, Congo in the center, Algeria in the north, and Kenya, Ethiopia, and Tanzania to the East. China is developing cities in Egypt to the north and in South Africa in the south. China loans African nations funds with incredibly low interest, unsupervised loans as long as the countries grant China control of their supply chain infrastructure. From oil in Angola to copper in Zambia, China is red hot in pursuing Africa as a part of its expansionist supply chain neo-colonization.

Internally, China is focusing on leapfrogging its previous technological shortcomings with rapid technological advances, often at the behest of the government and at the cost of privacy. In 2019 and 2020, faced with the Trump administration trade war, China devised a long-term strategy for technological supremacy as a way to reduce reliance on US technological exports.

It started with the Trump administration's hard-handed trade war tactic with the first salvo against Huawei's 5G network, claiming that such installations could compromise security. While it is true that China sponsors a lot of corporate espionage (stealing of intellectual property), reprimanding China is a global dilemma. China took bold steps to build its own homegrown global technology companies. Alibaba was already China's Amazon; Weibo was China's Google search; WeChat was China's FaceBook. But China did not muster the technology dominance in emerging technology. China needed a spark to kindle its ambition. And COVID-19 provided that spark.

The coming of COVID-19 AI, Social Credit, Space, and FinTech suddenly forced the world into a new-found health isolation. Travel cease. China capitalized on the crisis to rethink its strategic position in the world. Not as the world's factory but the World's technological champion. **"Made in China 2025"** meant to extricate China from jest being a manufacturing destination to becoming the world's next Silicon Valley in areas of *robotics and advanced manufacturing, electric cars, FinTech, artificial intelligence (AI), chip manufacturing, and space exploration.*

As a **Communist-part-controlled market economy** (the state controls the government with private companies that can develop, innovate, and sell products and services for profit), China used its COVID-19 isolation to start building its technology-capabilities.

With the origin of COVID-19, China began building and implementing technologies to contact-trace and keep tabs on its citizens. China started by deploying cameras everywhere, loaded with facial recognition technology to capture people's faces at various angles and use the information to train its Artificial Intelligence (AI) software for facial recognition. Combines with location services, China could now trace and locate its citizens wherever they went. The contact tracing app added to this track and trace originally meant to control COVID-19 contagion. But, beyond the contagion, the crisis gave China the ammunition to constantly and continuously geolocate and even geofence it's citizens, regardless of privacy.

For example, if you were jaywalking in China, an artificial intelligence software in a CCTV wood automatically capture your image, match it to your driver's license or state-ID picture on the government database and suddenly ding you, and what the Chinese call **Social Credit** for being a good or bad citizen. If you jaywalk too much or voice too much dissent against the government, it will negatively impact your social credit. Suddenly getting a loan, getting your application approved, and getting into University or even finding a job might prove difficult.

If your luck would have it, your picture of being a bad citizen could even appear on a billboard as a form of social chastising! While this might sound draconian in the West, this type of AI recognition is helping China fool-proof its AI authentication techniques with a training database full off rich identifiers.

Did You Know that?

China's Chang'e 5 lunar module was the first ever to land on the far side (the dark side) of the Moon!

China is also trying to lead the world electric car making and battery technologies. Companies, such as NIO which promotes battery swaps rather than battery charging for electric cause, are revolutionizing China's battery technology expertise. Tesla already has a batter-making Gigafactory in China, mainly because China controls a large supply of the world's precious metals that's may comp the components of sophisticated electronics and battery tech.

In the area of fintech (financial technology), China has long been on the forefront of innovation. It is quite common to finds people paying for goods and services via Alipay or via WeChat instead of paying via credit cards or cash. In late 2020, the Chinese government also began a trial pilot form its own digital currency cold the digital Yean as a part of its digital currency electronic payments (DC/EP) system. It is a very innovative venture, trying to remove hard currency in circulation that is difficult to trace, and increasing improving access (for people in rural areas with no banks) while simplifying transactions.

On the space frontier, China became the first country to land Chang'e 5 (named after China's Moon Goddess) on the far side of the Moon to retrieve rock samples and return to Earth. Tianwen-1, China's deep space explorer, launched in July 2020 and is expected to reach Mars in March 2021.

In the next decades, China will steadily rise, closely watched by international communities as China develops its technological might but facing social issues such as its repression of Muslim minorities in the west of China and its crackdown on Hong Kong democracy.

In the quick trip, the glittering dots embody development and progress. In the 4IR world, progress requires information; the flow of information requires electrical energy; the glitters at night trace the concentration of energy. But where does this progress originate? *Innovation or Production*?

Exercise

Choose any three countries and compare their business cultures. Are there certain cultures that are better for global businesses? Why? Explain.

How can technology help solve the resource curse of over-tourism where economies that mainly rely on tourism in the short-term also degrade their own education, living, and infrastructures in the long-term? Offer 2–3 solutions.

Adam Smith, Productive Efficiencies, and the New World

To begin mulling on matters of production and innovation, it is useful to consider the notions of **efficiency versus effectiveness**. Efficiency is a hallmark productivity metric. Deep-seated in notions of productivity, *efficiency is simply the ratio of output divided by input.*

Efficiency is tactical (short-term) fix focusing on producing the "cheapest" or "quickest" result. Effectiveness, on the other hand, is more strategic (longer-term) focusing on producing the "best" result.

Whether we call it productivity or efficiency, we simply mean the ratio of output to input. In short, *all efficiency calculations are nothing but outputs/inputs*. So, if someone were to ask the productivity of a machine, we would calculate the throughput of the machine, i.e., the amount of material or number of parts the machine can create in a particular time. If we were to calculate the energy efficiency of the same machine for sustainability, we would calculate the ratio of the amount of material or number of parts the machine can create to the amount of energy needed to create them. If we are calculating sales productivity of a salesperson, it would be the ratio of sales by the salesperson per period to the cost of the salesperson per period.

Efficiency is necessary but not sufficient for success. *Being effective is more important than being efficient.* For example, an "efficient" physician in a hospital can cursorily review multiple patients throughout the day and increase the number of patients flowing through the system. That is efficient but may not be effective. Patients might get a quick diagnosis but may find the results to be dissatisfactory. An effective physician is more focused on providing quality healthcare to relatively fewer patients but ensuring loyalty and satisfaction with the care, increasing patient satisfaction and revenues over time.

When the Scottish economic philosopher Adam Smith published "**The Wealth of Nations**" the central theme was increasing productive efficiencies where less input would be required to produce the same output. The key to increasing productive efficiency was labor specialization by dividing large tasks into small (or modular) pieces and using labor trained and specialized only for that task to perform it over and over and over again.

Let's consider **labor specialization** in producing a single pencil. One labor group cuts wood blocks the size of a pencil. The next uses a circular saw to create semicircular "pencil slats" in the shape of a pencil. The next waxes and stains the pencil slat. Next, a groove is cut inside the pencil to drop the graphite core. The next places and glues the graphite and clay writing-core into the groove and sandwiches the other slat to create the circular look. The next labor group passed them through a shaper to shape and machine the pencil. Another group lacquers the pencil. Next, the pencil is checked for quality control. Finally, a group packages the pencil for shipping.

© PiaDura LTD 2022
P. Datta, *Global Technology Management 4.0*,
https://doi.org/10.1007/978-3-030-96929-5_3

The same labor specialization philosophy is used for manufacturing a microprocessor (chip) or admitting a patient to surgery.

1. Microprocessor manufacturing begins with the design team drafts a new chip for a specific technology need.
2. Upper-level designers review the draft to check for functional operation.
3. Next, IC (integrated chip) designers will simulate and check functional specifications.
4. Once the system specifications are refined, RTL (Register Transfer Level) designers will convert the specifications into hardware level components and circuit design connecting the components.
5. Next, a hardware verification group checks if the RTL design functionally operates as required.
6. Next, the RTL design is transformed into a physical design using various specialized teams such as logic integration, floor-planning (assignment of functions to physical sections of the IC), routing wires and connections.
7. Finally, a group conducts extensive error checks and then releases the physical to manufacturing.

Hospital surgeries follows a similar division of labor.

1. In a hospital surgery, the admissions group checks in the patient.
2. Next, theatre orderlies escort the patient to the operating theatre suite.
3. Clinical teams confirm patient identity for the operating procedure, explain the process to the patient and obtain written consent for the patient.
4. Next, an anesthetic team reviews the choice and administration of the anesthetic.
5. Next, the surgical team and the surgeon discuss the surgical procedure and then perform the surgery.
6. Then, the post-operative team assigns the patient to a post-surgery unit for recuperation and post-operative care.
7. Finally, the billing team takes care of the finances and discharges the patient.

Regardless of whether we are manufacturing a pencil, a microprocessor, or a patient operation, each group specialized in an individual task based on "division of labor" to increase the speed of performing a task repeatedly without disruption. Specialization would also make labor expert in each task and they can come up with more ingenious ways of doing their task better to increase productive efficiency. Specialization and repetition also reduce the learning curve. **Learning curve** is the rate of effort a person must put in to learn and perform a task. Labor performing an extremely specialized task turns the task into a habit that requires no extra effort because of repetition and practice. Remember the first time you used software, rode a bike, or learnt to swim. The initial effort of learning goes down dramatically as you practice using it more and more.

Specialized labor can conduct their task better and faster to create a product or service that will be demanded by others who will be willing to pay to receive the labor, the good, or the service. That gives you **job mobility,** that is, your ability to stay in demand and change jobs. But job mobility creates **labor wage inflation**.

Labor specialized in a task can be more productive and companies are willing to pay more of productive labor to speed up operations and productivity. In fact, companies often compete for labor in demand and start a bidding war on the labor. This creates **labor wage inflation** by increasing upward pressure on labor wages. **Inflation** is a crucial piece in decision-making. **Inflation** is the rate of change in prices we pay over a period. If the price of a gallon of organic milk is $8.00 in 2017 and $8.40 in 2018, we can say that organic milk price inflation was 5% between 2017 and 2018. Labor wage inflation, similarly, is the rate of change in labor prices over a period. Inflation, therefore, is a good yardstick for companies and countries to budget in price changes in the future.

Suppose an energy analyst in the alternative energy market specializes in predicting solar energy price trends. This analyst might be in tremendous demand and a think-tank offers the analyst 10% more salary to come work for them; another firm ups the competition for the analyst by offering the analyst 10% more salary than the think-tank. This is an example of wage inflation where the salary of the analyst rises (inflates) dramatically and suddenly the market salaries jump for good solar energy analysts.

This is a constant struggle in emerging economies that rely on **outsourcing** (the process of having a third-party create a product or service that you need) such as China and India. In China, skilled production workers such as iPhone assemblers are well-trained and in so much demand that other assembly companies are eager on luring them from their present job with a higher pay. Similarly, in India, trained tech workers, programming for popular software or areas such as smartphone applications, automation software of AI (artificial intelligence) are in high demand, constantly changing companies for higher salaries. Assume a trained (skilled) production or tech worker in China or India earns $20,000 (around 120,000 Renminbi (RMB) or yuan in China; 1.4 million equivalent Indian Rupees in 2017) per year. This worker is in high demand and is sought out by other companies that need trained workers to reduce costs or training and hasten production. The company lures the worker with a $25,000 salary. That's a 25% increase in pay. The worker jumps ship and goes to work for the new company. In a couple of years, the worker gains more expertise and jumps ship again to another company willing to pay 25% more than the workers present wage (pay) at $31,250. If the worker moved from a wage of $20,000 to $31,250 in a period of, say, 7 years, the **labor wage inflation** is 62.5% in 7 years. That means that companies must be willing to budget in an extra 62.5% of their specialized labor costs for popular specialized labor. Now, that's an expensive proposition. The only way companies and countries can temper and manage such high labor wage inflation is by increasing supply of specialized training via apprenticeship facilities and universities that will create a constant and consistent labor supply. That is why good, robust economies have a great higher education system that collaborates closely with companies to train students and apprentices for the near future.

Did you know that?

Because China's stock market is thought to be notoriously corrupt, most Chinese invest in properties as their only other alternative. This has created a huge property price inflation.

Exercise

Can you think of instances where labor specialization might be an advantage and instances where labor specialization might be a disadvantage?

The Invisible Hand

Adam Smith's idea of labor specialization is based on **free-market or laissez-faire economies** such as the UK, USA, Germany, France, Israel, among others. In a free-market, specialized labor has mobility where they can seek any employer that provides them the best salary or wages. In short, specialized labor, by being incredibly good at their work, can work in their own self-interest to increase their success, and thereby that of the community, society, and country.

Assume you are an entrepreneur that has come up with a fantastic product. You begin manufacturing in your basement. You build a quality product, and the market demand increases. Soon, your basement can no longer support the demand. You look for an affordable space to grow and you buy a small spot of land in a countryside village to build your manufacturing. You keep up with and outrival your competitors and demand grows even further. The gravel roads can no longer support the large trucks you need to maintain your logistical and transportation needs. So, you work with the municipality to share the costs of building paved roads. Your company grows and suddenly there is a need for employee housing. Builders come in to construct houses and existing real estate demand increases. As your employees grow, other vendors come to build malls, groceries, and shops to serve the employee market. Suddenly, invisibly, your self-centered focus on growing your business creates a city out of a village and creates an economic climate with greater employment and activities.

This is Adam Smith's **invisible hand**, a metaphor by which laissez-faire free-market economy ends up distributing wealth across other economic entities without requiring the government to force welfare. This later became a business philosophy, called paternalism. Paternalism, like *noblesse oblige* (obligation of the nobility), drew on the belief that company owners ought to advance society as well as their own self-interests as "capitalists with a conscience." Lever brothers-built Port Sunlight by Cheshire, UK; Cadbury brothers-built Bourneville near Birmingham, UK; Hershey built Hershey, PA, USA; and tech companies-built Silicon Valley in Palo Alto, CA.

4IR companies exemplify the working of Adam Smith's invisible hand. Highly specialized innovators, from Apple's Steve Wozniak and Steve Jobs or Microsoft's Bill Gates have built prosperous cities from their innovations, namely Palo Alto (Silicon Valley) in California and Issaquah in Washington, respectively.

Are We Capitalists or Socialists?

We, in the US, are a market economy. We are neither capitalists nor socialists but a combination. If we have Social-Security and Medicare, we are already quasi-socialists where the government has a safety net for the population.

Capitalism is driven by private control of production and distribution of services based on market demand and competition. Communism, the other end of the spectrum, is the total government (state) control of all means of production and distribution. The motive of pure capitalism is the production of goods and services for profit with no requirement toward any social development. **Socialism** is a softer version of communism where private companies can control few or some production but control the distribution of products and services. For example, under Nazi (National socialist party) Germany, private companies such

as the one of famous Oskar Schindler, notable for saving more than a thousand Jewish lives from the holocaust by hiring them at his unprofitable factory produced for the Nazi party. The Nazi party would then decide how to distribute the products and services based on their assessment of population and state needs. Other forms of socialist economies allow employees to spend their income as they wish, offering them more market options than a communist economy.

Many countries have purely capitalist economies but no social freedoms. Russia and Singapore do not offer social freedoms; India has no social net—if you don't work and earn a livable wage, you die. However, countries such as the US, the UK, France, Germany, and Switzerland sprinkle bits of socialism in a capitalist free-market economy. The 1215 Magna Carta (particularly the right to justice and fair trial to all) in the UK and its influence of the US Bill of rights and along with the Amendments to the US constitution are examples of social freedoms. So are the concepts of social security, free education, national healthcare, Medicare. Most progressive economics provide a safety net to ensure none of its citizens falls too hard while creating the opportunity to create productive efficiencies and effectiveness to play the "invisible hand" of enterprise. Yet, if lower costs lie beyond borders, companies will move to lowest areas of costs and highest areas of sales. That's the basis for **globalization**, a phenomenon where the world is interconnected by product, service, and capital flows by virtue of the Internet, technology, and supply chains.

Did you know that?

Almost all developed and industrialized countries are a mix of socialism and capitalism! Socialism such as medical and unemployment benefits and capitalism via the free and private market system! Countries like Afghanistan and Rwanda are the most capitalistic because they offer no government welfare or benefits. If you can't work, you starve!

Exercise

Think of a purely capitalist economy? Can you think of any? Why is a market economy more useful than a capitalist economy?

The PIIGS: Portugal, Ireland, Italy, Greece, Spain

Not All PIIGS Are Napoleon

PIIGS stands for Portugal, Italy, Ireland, Greece, and Spain. PIIGS is a set of weaker economies/countries within the Eurozone, along with countries of stronger economies such as Germany, France, Belgium, and the Netherlands. The PIIGS were a point of grave concern because of the precarious roles they played in the 2009 **European Sovereign Debt Crisis**, marked by dropping GDP, high unemployment, and high (risky) bond yields, that nearly brought the Eurozone to the brink of failure.

In George Orwell's dystopian novel, Animal Farm, Napoleon was the pig that staged and led the alluded socialist uprising. *But not all PIIGS are Napoleon.*

Of the seventeen countries that then made the Eurozone, the PIIGS, comprised 30% of the Eurozone countries, but only contributed to 6% of the Eurozone GDP. The PIIGS story is a remarkably interesting case of strategizing when a group of countries are integrated but each country has unique needs and challenges. How do you cope with various members with diverse levels of strengths, weaknesses, attitudes, and productivity?

The **Eurozone** (a group of countries sharing the same common currency, the Euro) is run by a single central bank called the **ECB** (European Central Bank) and a signatory to the Maastricht Treaty which limits the amount of debt each EU country can assume. But the Eurozone is such a diverse bloc of countries with dramatically diverse levels of innovation, productivity, and labor quality, that managing such a diverse group became the toughest of all juggling acts for the ECB. The dawning of the 2008 financial crisis started showing deep fractures across various countries in the Eurozone. With a common currency comes common interest rates and the more innovative countries want interest to be low. Innovation is risky and not all R&D (research and design) is transformed into profitable products and services. So, countries with innovative companies such as Germany, France, Belgium, and the Netherlands like to hedge their risks with low interest rate borrowings. Low interest rates signal cheap money. Cheap money means different things for the prudent versus the prodigal. Prudent countries and companies use cheap money to try innovating new products, new services, new markets. The prodigal, with less sophisticated labor and industry, and few, if any, innovations, and productivity, on the other hand, has no idea what to do with cheap money. Such was the circumstance that highlighted the PIIGS.

Each of these countries that make up the PIIGS, were primarily focused on traditional industries such as tourism, general construction, and some agriculture. Yet, with so much cheap money floating around prior to the 2008 financial crisis, the governments, companies, and the public of these countries decided to use the low interest rates to borrow vast amounts of Euros from the ECB and squandered their borrowings on things they couldn't afford such as: real estate, cars, and luxuries. Real estate developers in places such as Malaga, Spain, used cheap credit from the ECB to build thousands of apartments on the sunny coast of which 30% was vacant, thus reducing the developers' ability to repay their loans (also called default), which in turn increased the banks' default rate. Banks in default can create chokeholds on the economy because a bank's inability to loan money affects everyone; from the general contractor paying labor before they get reimbursed for his or her project, to large employers that need to borrow capital for new products, services, and/or facilities. This creates a domino effect where defaults from borrowers will strain a bank's ability to recoup its loans, which then can reduce the bank's ability to loan additional to more dissevering borrowers, and thus stagnating the economy.

Did you know that?

The Big Tech Five—Google, Apple, Microsoft, Amazon, and Facebook—now make up a record 23% of the S&P 500 index's total value! In Europe, countries with high technology innovations such as Germany and France are deemed the least-riskiest countries!

The general confidence in the PIIGS was waning during the 2008 financial crisis. If you ever wonder how confidence in a country, or even a company is measured, the answer lies in its credit rating, specifically its **Bond Yield**. A lower credit rating sends a signal to the market that that country or company is a risky investment. Yet, countries need to borrow money and selling bonds is one of the more popular strategies for countries. A country with a low credit rating will have to promise higher yields (rate of return) to borrowers (countries, companies, or individuals). Therefore, the riskiness of a company or country, is easily traceable by looking at their bond yields. Even during the 2008 financial crisis, market optimism in the US for an overall US recovery was high enough that US treasuries were in high demand. With a low credit risk, the US Federal Reserve was able to reduce its interest rates to increase borrowing and consumption without worrying about a lack of demand for its bonds across the globe. In short, US treasuries (Bonds) offered low yields yet had no global dearth buyers. Across the Atlantic, the PIIGS were experiencing a completely different ball game.

Add to that situation, overly liberal government programs such as early retirement with full pensions, draconian labor laws that protected underperformers, and reliance on foreign investments to bolster employment and their economies, further dampened competitiveness among the PIIGS.

Portugal

Portugal, a part of the Eurozone, was still a traditional economy, focused on construction, manufacturing, and tourism. Becoming a part of the Eurozone suddenly made Portugal uncompetitive where Portuguese workers would be paid Eurozone wages while lacking competitive industries or worker productivity. With a low ability to compete in the global marketplace, Portugal increased public spending by hiring more workers in the government rather than in the private sector, thus leading to more bureaucracy and a bloated government sector that was hiring and paying for 4 workers even when one worker would suffice. During the European Sovereign Debt Crisis, Portugal had to freeze government worker salaries to control public spending and practice financial austerity (financial cost-control). At one point, with high unemployment, the Portuguese Prime Minister asked the Portuguese youth to look for work overseas and asked teachers to relocate to Portuguese-speaking countries such as Angola in Africa or Brazil in South America because Portugal could no longer support them.

Ireland

Ireland tried to use low taxes to attract international companies and **FDI (Foreign Direct Investments)**. Indeed, many companies came and set up shop in Ireland, not because the Irish market or that Irish labor supply was attractive but because these companies could escape high taxes in their home countries. When the global crisis came with the housing bubble, these companies left. While they were in business in Ireland, these companies borrowed money at incredibly low interest rates and splurged, creating a real estate bubble (inflated property prices from excessive bidding and buying of property). Ireland's property prices were 192% inflated between 1996 and 2007. This meant that properties were being sold at three times their original prices and people were borrowing money from banks to buy real estate at 3 times their value. Banks, overextended from borrowing and loaning money to satisfy an inflated appetite, realized that they were overextended. Once the 2008 economic crisis hit home, these overextended banks and inflated property prices fell out of confidence as the same companies left in a hurry, creating an economic vacuum. Moreover, as a part of the 16-country Eurozone, Irish banks had borrowed and lent money across other European banks, creating a **domino or contagion effect** where massive drops in property prices in Ireland and the Irish banks' inability to collect on its overextended loans would have a negative ripple effect across the 16 countries. Ireland relied heavily on US firms such as Dell Computers, for employment so much so that when Dell decided to save on labor and move its Irish operations to Poland in 2009, nearly 10,000 Irish jobs were lost, creating economic meltdown for local Irish economies. On the other hand, countries such as Germany that had been practicing strict fiscal discipline were using the cheap money from low interest rates to increase innovations, efficiencies, and labor productivities, by investing the money into cutting edge R&D, automation, and labor policies.

Now is a good time to talk about the idea of **tax inversions**. Multinational companies, i.e., companies that operate and have divisions across multiple countries in the world, are a large part of technology producers, user, and consumers. Once upon a time, multinational companies used to be based in their country of origin, sell around the world, pay local taxes, and taxes on overall earnings in their countries where they were headquartered. With the coming of technology that connected financial networks all around the world, it created a global economy where a company could be based anywhere and everywhere and choose most lucrative trade and tax zones to call that place its home base. Multinational companies' source from different places, assemble the toy in another location, sell in tens of other countries, and pay taxes somewhere else. With technology allowing companies to send specifications for components online, create virtual designs, and remote work and production across the world, multinationals try to save costs by relocating their "legal" domicile. A legal domicile is the formal place and country you declare as the designated formal HQ location for the multination while maintaining various other operational and functional sites as subsidiaries where most of the work is done. The reason for claiming a different "legal" HQ location is for **Tax Inversion.** Tax inversion is a practice where multinational companies choose low tax areas as

tax havens to create their legal HQ. If a multinational were legally based in the US in 2016, it had to pay 39% taxes on company profits. However, if the multinational is legally based in Ireland, it must pay 12.5% taxes on profits, a 26.5% savings. The Trump presidency in 2017 lowered corporate taxes from 39% to 25.7% to reduce losses from multinational tax dollars moving to other countries.

Did you know that?
The 2021 G20 summit of the top-20 economically developed countries tentatively agreed on a minimum 15% tax on technology companies to reduce tax inversions and pay their tax burdens! That would bring in hundreds of billions in taxes lost to Tax inversions.

Italy
In Italy, labor laws make firing underperforming employees impossible. For example, Article 18 of the Italian "workers' statute" law that governs employee rights states that employers in Italy cannot simply fire or sack underperforming employees. All sacked employees can request Italian courts to decide on the justification of sackings. Interestingly, most judgments require reinstatement of sacked employees. Although Article 18 was originally created to protect employees from unscrupulous behavior such as rampant sexual harassment and terrible work conditions, the abuse of Article 18 had turned Italy uncompetitive and regressive. Companies could not downsize or automate to cut costs. Productivity was low given the inability to sack underperformers in a competitive economy. With very few full-time employees simply signing in at work without being productive and never leaving a company, Italian youth unemployment was staggering at 40%. As a result, employers opted against hiring full-time employees to circumvent Article 18 and instead hired "*precarios*" or short-term employees with low pay and a slim probability of gaining a permanent position. These, taken together, made Italy an unpromising venue for international companies.

Greece

Arcane laws and bad government policies added to the woes of cheap money, inflated real estate prices, and prodigal splurging. Labor unions further dragged their economies with primitive pressures and undue demands. In Greece, a hairdresser could work till the age of 50 and retire with a full pension. The average age of retirement was 61, the lowest in Europe. With so much pension obligations, Greece owed nearly 9 times more than its GDP earnings. Moreover, Greeks practiced tax-evasion as a "national sport" and corruption was rampant. In 2010, nearly $35 billion of Greek taxes were uncollected. *Fakelaki* or *small envelopes* were a popular part of daily lives, used to stuff money to bribe everyone, from government employers to secure employment to doctors for false health claims.

Greece, along with Portugal, both suffering from economic hardships in recent years, have devised alternative ways to attract international investments. While selling property to tourists on sunny Greek isles was one commonplace, in recent years, Greece and Portugal created the **"Golden Visa Programme"** to attract **foreign direct investment (FDI)**. The Golden Visa Programme is primarily aimed at countries that require visas to enter the EU. The Golden Visa Programme grants a Greek or Portuguese passport (essentially, an EU passport) to anyone willing to invest €250,000 in Greece or Portugal.

For foreign nationals, especially from countries such as China, India, Brazil, Russia, and others require visas to travel to and conduct business in the EU, the Golden Visa Programme offers a way to circumvent existing checks and balances to enter the EU, allowing unfettered access to the larger EU countries such as France and Germany by simply investing €250,000 in Greece, whether an apartment to rent out via **Airbnb** (a crowdsourced apartment and home rental website) or a business gateway to sell goods and services to the rest of Europe. In the process, Greece and Portugal and offering unfettered access for any company or individual to Europe.

Did you know that?

Cash-strapped Greece and Portugal's Golden Visa Programme became a hit for Chinese individuals trying to get their feet into the European Common Market!

Food for Thought: Is the Golden Visa Programme a good idea for Greece and Portugal? Offer two reasons why it might be a good idea and two reasons for why it might not be a good idea.

Spain

Spain, flush with taxes from a booming property market bubble because of low Eurozone interest rates, used the banks to overextend their loans and hide their losses from regulators. The property bubble reached a fever pitch and, in a country of around 17 million people, there were more that 24 million houses with a lot of them empty. Average house prices were skyrocketing while average incomes were low. In order to sell houses, banks were offering 40-year and 50-year mortgages. The overabundance of housing supply compared to housing demand lowered house prices (whenever supply is more than demand, prices drop because buyers have many more options/choices). Places like Valdeluz in Spain became ghost towns with more than 20,000 houses with only 700 or so residents. With an over-reliance of tourism, Spanish unemployment grew deeper as the financial crisis led to a drop in tourists visiting Spain. Unemployment for youth under the age of 25 was nearly 50%. With a **recession** (defined as 3 consecutive decreases in GDP), high unemployment, and unsustainable property debt from the real estate bubble forced Spain to seek an EU bailout in 2012.

Together, to avert a major calamity, the **ECB (European Central Bank)** had to spend $750 billion Euros to bail out the PIIGS due to the PIIGS' mismanagement of capital, organizational, and human resources.

We see the same story repeat every day in companies and perhaps even in your own teams. In project teams, some members are diligent and prudent while other members may be prodigal or wasteful. Yet, the success or failure of the project, much like the success or failure of the Eurozone, will depend upon all the members. As students, you may have experienced similar tribulations of some members carrying the weight of a good grade while others show laxity. And then you must bail them out to save your own grade. Therefore, managing diverse countries, companies, divisions, teams, or people, require the right orchestration of resources, capabilities, and motivation. Miss one and the music will fall off tune.

There was a lot of global uncertainty about the PIIGS economic outlook and countries were reluctant to buy bonds from them (to invest in these countries) even when PIIGS' bond yields were 5% or higher compared to 1% or less for the United States. Right when the PIIGS felt the world was shunning them, China came to their rescue. The 2008 economic crisis had reduced people's earnings and created an opportunity for the BRICS to become the production centers for the world with their cheap labor and cheaper real estates. China seized the opportunity. The world needed cheaper goods to maintain its levels of consumption, and China was willing to provide.

The agreement was such. China would purchase PIIGS' bonds even when the rest of the world was reluctant; in return for taking that risk, China would entertain contractual privileges from the PIIGS where China would not only be lobbied for at the United Nations but also be given special consideration in large-scale infrastructure projects that were to come once the PIIGS economies had stabilized. For example, if Portugal were to privatize its energy sector, Portugal might offer special consideration to Chinese firms interested in investing in Portugal's energy sector. Such deals are not only coming to fruition but also gaining spotlight as China completes its **Belt and Road Initiative** in 2018 by creating massive land and sea transportation routes from China through Greece and Italy into the rest of Europe.

Exercise

How are the PIIGS economically performing, currently? Explain two ways how their economies have improved and two ways that their economies have not.

The Economics of Globalization

Productive Forces

All economic forces rely on productivity, the ratio of economic outputs to economic inputs, also called the **factors or means of production**. There are **four economic inputs and related outputs**: Land, Labor, Capital, and enterprise. **Land outputs rent** (after all, even real estate purchases are long term-rents with a discount); **labor outputs wages**; **capital outputs interest** (as a return on capital); **enterprise outputs profits**. Between a capitalist and communist economy, the difference lies in who controls the four economic inputs and outputs. A free-market economy based on a capitalist model allows private individuals and companies to own the means of production while a socialist or communist economy limits private ownership of a few means of production (socialist) or all means of production (communist).

A core issue in controlling the factors of production is deciding who does a better job at managing productivity—the state or the government. China's property-driven economy is an interesting case in point. Mind you, buying a property in China does not mean owning an eternal deed on the property. Instead, the multi-billion-dollar Chinese real estate is based on a 70-year lease of the property from the government. Seventy years from the date you purchase the property, the property is returned to the government unless you purchase it again at the end of the seven decades, assuming government regulations still favor private ownership of land.

A government control of labor often leads to overemployment and loss of efficiencies.

Countries like China, India, South Africa, Italy, Greece, and Brazil are notorious for overemploying labor in the government sector. Where you might have needed one worker in the private sector, you hire three in the government sector. That offers a quick but inflated fix to unemployment numbers, but productivity suffers. Productivity suffers because the same output requires three times higher input costs from overemployment. Add the costs of employee benefits and costs skyrocket while efficiencies bite the dust. More employees add to more bureaucracy and shaking off the garb of bureaucracy later becomes a nightmare, as we will find when we discuss various countries later.

Now comes the control of capital. Here, regardless of the economic philosophy, the government controls capital to an extent by controlling interest rates. Interest rates often become the backbone of an economy by implicitly influencing three **economic propensities**: **Propensity to Consume, Propensity to Save,** and **Propensity to Invest**. Commonly represented as percentages, these three propensities add up the 100% of income, be it an individual, a company, or the government.

Propensity to consume is the percentage of our income we are inclined to spend on consuming various goods and services, including housing. Housing is a prudent piece to add to consumption calculations. After all, we need shelter till we perish, and the value of a house is purely nominal until actually sold. Conservatively, it is best treated as an expense. Propensity to save is the percentage of our income we save in fixed interest generating accounts. Propensity to invest, then, is the percentage allocated to the rest of our income that we invest in a portfolio of corporate and financial assets such as stocks, bonds, ETFs (Exchange Traded Funds), Mutual Funds.

But how can the government attempt to influence these propensities by controlling the interest rate? Assume that interest rates are close to zero. A near-zero interest rate makes borrowing money incredibly cheap because interest payments on debt are very low. Individuals, companies, and countries find low interest rates an attractive proposition to borrow more money to consume

(buy a house, car, appliances) and invest (in operations and innovations by purchasing company stocks). Low interest rates, on the other hand, reduce the need to save money. That's because of **inflation, a mechanism** where the prices of goods or services increase over time (measured by periodic **CPI (consumer price index)**). After all, because of inflation, keeping money in a bank account offering an interest rate less than that of the rate of inflation simply means that money is losing its value over time. For example, if our checking accounts offer 0.5% interest while there is 2% inflation in the economy every year, keeping the money in the checking account is tantamount to losing 1.5% every year. Suddenly, saving does not sound promising. So, the propensity to save drops. Instead, it becomes more tempting to consume and invest the income. So, propensities to consume and invest increase.

This very idea is the basis for all economies. Controlled in the US by the US Treasury Secretary and in the UK by the Chancellor of the Exchequer and various ministries of finance worldwide, the government tries to fine-tune interest rates to drive economic momentum. The sweet-spot is approximately a 2-percent inflation in major industrialized economies in the US, UK, and Western Europe. **Inflation-targeting** tries to stabilize market prices and manage unemployment by controlling interest rates. If money becomes too cheap while high employment, there is a chance that there is too much money flowing in an economy. With such cheap money supply, there is a chance of overspeculation in investment that can create price bubbles waiting to burst at the slightest hint of worry. A targeted inflation also prompts people to consume more as long as the savings interest rates are lower that the inflation rate.

But can a government eternally drive consumption? Well, it can't. This is the realm where the private enterprise as a factor of production in a competitive (free-market) economy becomes central to the puzzle.

Enterprise is the fourth and final factor of production. Enterprise outputs profit. The question is, who controls the economy, the private sector, or the public sector (government)? The private sector distributes its profits across shareholders while the public sector is a not-for-profit entity distributing its profits across earmarked budgets following an oft-inefficient clause of "use it or lose it."

The government is not very enterprising. In communist countries, including the erstwhile Soviet Union, production is allocated to individuals while it is the role of the state to be enterprising. That is one reason why state-owned heavy industries building weapons and heavy machinery are such bestsellers in communist countries while the consumer sector languishes under a lack of options in goods and undue rationing, leading to long bread lines. As the joke goes, *communist countries have a fabulous infrastructure of good education, manageable healthcare, and available housing; the only things missing are breakfast, lunch, and dinner.*

The question is, why should we innovate if ingenuity does not offer us the payback on the risks we assume? Instead, we find it more prudent to stay within the allotted quota and refraining from innovative enterprising given that all profits belonged to the state rather than to the innovative producer. That was the issue with socialist and communist economies. A farmer was asked to grow, say, 200 lbs. of cabbage each season. The farmer would try to grow exactly that amount or close to that amount, not more. The farmer knew that ingenuity would backfire. If the farmer used innovative farming to grow 10% more, i.e., 220 lbs. of cabbage, the farmer's innovativeness, rather than receiving an incentive for productivity, would be assigned a quota to produce 10% more every season. There was no incentive for risk-taking and innovation. It was much more beneficial for the individual to barely maintain the assigned quota rather than be enterprising.

Did you know that?

Cash-strapped Greece and Portugal's Golden Visa Programme became a hit for Chinese individuals trying to get their feet into the European Common Market!

Win on Currency; Lose on Trade!

If you were to choose, would you opt for a weaker dollar or pound or a stronger dollar or pound? Take a minute. Think. A strong currency always seems the way to go—a sense of pride! But, as the reality of trade and economics would have it, a stronger currency weakens your position. But why? Well, a stronger dollar makes your currency dearer, i.e., more expensive, and other currencies in other countries you trade with, relatively cheaper. Think of this instance. The US trades a lot with China and the current **exchange rate** (the rate of currency conversion) of 1 US Dollar is 1 USD = 6 RMB (China). This means that 1 US Dollar can purchase 6 RMB worth of Chinese products or services. Assume a few month later, the US Dollar gets stronger at 1 USD = 7 RMB and now can buy more Chinese RMB. Is that good? Well, it's good only if you are **importing** (purchasing products and services overseas to bring back to your country) a lot of Chinese products and services. **Exporting** (selling goods and services from your country to another country) becomes more difficult because other countries will now have to pay more for your goods and services.

Suddenly buying things from China become cheaper because your 1 USD can but 7 RMB worth of Chinese goods. That's nearly 17% (16.66% precisely) more products and services that you can buy. However, for the Chinese, your products and services become more expensive to purchase. A Chinese customer or company will have to pay 17% more to buy your products and services. Instead of being able to spend 6 RMB to buy 1 USD of products, China will have to shell out 7 RMB to buy 1 USD of products. When that's the case, the US customers and companies would rather import from China and have their currency flow out to Chinese manufacturers instead of Chinese customers and companies willing to buy more US products and add to the US coffers. That's why some countries such as China and Japan try to manipulate their exchange rates to keep their currency value lower. That makes their products more attractive to import or cheaper to offshore. When the price of 1 Euro (currency used by the Eurozone) falls, people from the US and UK love to travel to or invest in Europe because it becomes more affordable. On the other hand, people from the Eurozone will find it more expensive to travel to or invest in the US or UK. Once again, a cheaper currency attracts purchases by others and investments, leading to more exports. A more expensive currency attracts purchases from others and less investments, leading to more imports. This impacts a country's **balance of payments**, i.e., the difference between how much it earns from exporting and how much it spends on importing. A weaker currency often has a positive balance of payments because it sells more and buys less, and a stronger currency will often have a negative balance of payments because it buys more and sells less. You may win on your currency, but you might lose on trade.

Profit on the Product; Loss on Production

The Smile Curve

Win on the product. Lose on production. That is the basic gist of the **Smile Curve**. The Smile Curve looks at value addition from a product in its Y axis and the design to sales lifecycle on the X axis. As it is with a broad smile across a face, the highest value-added **Returns on Investment** (**ROI**) lie at the beginning and the end, notably the innovation phase and the sales phase. ROI is the return on your money or the economic benefit in money you receive for every dollar invested in a project or an initiative. ROI and the Smile Curve are particularly useful for both companies and countries in figuring out when to develop a product and when to outsource it.

Given that the highest value addition is in the innovation and sales phases of a product, companies would be smart enough to manage those phases in-house. When time comes for branding, design, manufacturing, distribution, or marketing, is a strategic move to outsource, even offshore these phases (Fig. 3.1).

> ## Did you know that?
> Called the Radium Girls, women in the 1920s dipped tiny paint brushes in Radium and licked them to sharpen brush edges to paint watch dials that glowed at night (called "lip, dip, paint")! They were paid 1.5 pennies per dial and painted 250 dials per day.

If you look closely, manufacturing offers the lowest ROI even though it is the central and the largest piece of building a product. That is because while manufacturing is important, the ones who manufacture are simply smaller pieces of the puzzle that follow instructions and routines rather than define the product. For example, Apple's "Designed in California. Assembled in

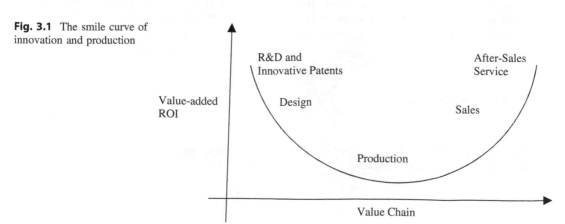

Fig. 3.1 The smile curve of innovation and production

China." Markings on every one of its products, tells you a strategic but somber story. Apple's designers and engineers spend years creating a product and then ship out the specifications to companies such as Foxconn and Pegatron in China that fastidiously follow these specifications to assemble Apple products using cheap Chinese labor. Apple controls its innovation Intellectual Property (IP) and Sales and Servicing, the two value-added ends of the Smile Curve, while offshoring manufacturing to its Chinese/Taiwanese partners. This strategy allows Apple to recoup 60% of the profits from device sales while companies that manufacture for Apple recoup about 1% of the profits.

In a chat with some Chinese regulators and executives, the executives mentioned how haute couture brands run 80% of their fabrication in China but use a legal loophole (such as double stitching) as a workaround for the final product label to read as a western originator (e.g., Made in France). And the margins are extreme Pareto cases where the brand assumes over 90% of the profits. For a country running a fiscal surplus from being the "factory for the west" with its major cities overcast with the hazy shade of industrial progress, the regulators and executives painfully inquired "where is China's Prada?"

Controlling production does not automatically mean controlling the product. The brand controls the production and then manufacturer, production. Every Apple product reads "Designed by Apple in California. Assembled in China." It is the production volume that pays the wages and salaries of employees in factories such as Foxconn. They don't have the privilege to enjoy the Apple retail premium. Rather, Apple stores in China were simply mobbed when Apple's iPhone 4S officially debuted. If you think Apple is an aberrant Giffen good (i.e., a product or service whose demand is not price-sensitive), consider the growth of stores such as Tesco, Carrefour, and Walmart. These stores essentially source and sell medium-quality goods often originating from China, sometimes fabricated even a few miles away. Instead of buying shirts at one of the many vendors littered across the pavement, Chinese customers pack Walmart shopping for clothing at a premium even with explicit knowledge that they were sourced from spots a few miles away.

And there's more to it. Production depends on production technology and that too is a brand. From Ford's assembly line to Devol and Engleberger's robotic arm that GM deployed in 1962, even the technology of production is controlled by Western and Japanese oligopolies. As clients and vendors demand eternal cost control, the assembly line infrastructure must undergo large reinvestments periodically. Yet, assembly line technologies are imported although the assembled products are exported.

So, what does that leave the vendor controlling production? Only labor—especially a large supply of cheap labor. There is a looming peril in that equation: if a country's only mettle is its low-wage labor force, where the production technology and the product are beyond its control, what lies ahead when neighboring economies converge in like a pack of hyenas to steal the carcass?

The same story repeats itself over and over again with across many companies throughout the world from Microsoft outsourcing software design to Indian companies to banks outsourcing Call Center Support to companies in India and Mexico. China competes with its inexpensive factory labor and India with its inexpensive technology labor force. Yet, ask yourself, what exactly do countries like China and India control? Companies are constantly seeking cheaper pastures. Tomorrow, if Vietnam or Mongolia were to offer better tax shelters and cheaper labor, companies would move their production and servicing infrastructures to the new kids on the block. That is the cost of controlling production but not the product or service innovation.

And there's more to it. Production depends on production technology and that too is a brand. From Ford's assembly line to Devol and Engleberger's robotic arm that GM deployed in 1962, even the technology of production is controlled by Western and Japanese oligopolies. As clients and vendors demand eternal cost control, the assembly line infrastructure must undergo large reinvestments periodically. Yet, assembly line technologies are imported although the assembled products are exported. There is much more money to be made with selling manufacturing technology that finished products that use Western and Japanese manufacturing technologies and carry these brand monikers. So, the vendor is merely left with control of labor—especially a large supply of cheap labor. There is a looming peril in that equation: if a country's only mettle is its low-wage labor force, where the production technology and the product are beyond its control, what lies ahead when neighboring economies converge in like a pack of hyenas to steal the carcass.

Countries like China and India know how much their economies are at risk. Newer, emerging economies in Southeast Asia, Eastern Europe, Central Asia, and Africa have started offering cheaper labor and tax breaks. Recently, Vietnam has been competing against China as an offshoring venue. To reduce threats from these newer economies, China tries **hedging** (an insurance against risk) to reduce these threats. Hedging is a way to reduce risk such as buying insurance to protect our health or our car.

In our 4IR **Knowledge Economy** where knowledge and enterprise create innovations and brands that garner the most profit, the highest ROI (Return on Investment) is commanded by innovation rather than production. Overtime, Knowledge Economies migrate from production factories to innovations centers. The next time you look around and find factories disappearing while company-profits burgeoning, you'll know that it's the Smile Curve in action.

The Evolution of Business Innovations and the S-Shaped Curve

A knowledge economy is a wellspring of innovations. Innovations end up introducing new products and services in an economy. But, these new products and services, just like everything else, have a life cycle. The S-Shaped (sigmoid shaped) curve tells the story of how an industry begins and matures. When a new type of company or product enters the market, the company, e.g., smart watches, there are no competitors. The

market has little idea about the product itself. So, there are a few early adopters. This the Entry Phase. At that point, the innovation has a small market but, within the small market, the product has a large market share. As the product gains popularity, other companies get interested in getting a part of the market share and profits and start building their versions of smart watches. This is the Growth Phase. The market grows as more people start buying and wearing smart watches. With soaring popularity (demand), more companies start getting into the smart watch business. This is the Maturity Phase. But as the market gets crowded with competition, profits fall (Fig. 3.2).

At one point, the market gets saturated with too many competitors and outstrips demand. The point of saturation is called **carrying capacity**. Then, because the market can carry no more competitors, profits fall. With the market chock-a-block with competitors, profits fall so much that some companies are not able ends meet and close shop. This is the Decline Phase. The market stabilizes itself, left with a few competitors that match customer demand. When profits decline, smart companies and economies must figure out a way to diversify and innovate to maintain their profits. Failure to do so will spell demise.

IBM was one of the first to enter the PC market during the early 1980s and the IBM ×86 architecture became synonymous to personal computers. IBM ThinkPad's remarkable growth

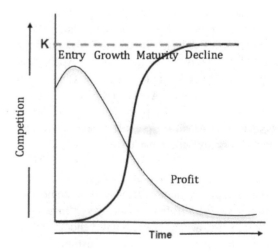

Fig. 3.2 S-Shaped Curve of Competition and Profit

attracted a slew of competitors such as Sony, Toshiba, ASUS, HP, and Dell, each with its unique business model. As the PC industry matured, rivalry increased and marginal profits slimmed! It was time for IBM ThinkPad to exit. China's interest in acquiring international brands gave IBM ThinkPad the opportunity to exit the market before a potential decline. So, IBM sold its ThinkPad and tablet divisions to Lenovo in 2005 as a profitable exit.

To Innovate or to Manufacture

We all try to brand ourselves. On the teeter-totter of efficiency vs. effectiveness, countries and companies must choose between leading on effective innovations or efficient manufacturing. **Effective innovation** changes the world with novel ways of doing things using products and services. **Efficient manufacturing (and servicing)** tries creating more output using less input. After all, efficiency and productivity stem from increasing the ratio of output to input. Reduce input costs and increase output value. We try differentiating in ways that become hallmarks— identities recognizable to the world. Yet, of the millions companies in the globe, less than 1% are recognizable brands. That's because innovation brings recognition and most of all, innovation commands profit.

Around mid-2000, I was in China dining with a wonderful group of Chinese media officials around Beijing. The officials were bemoaning the pollution from China serving as the **"factory of the west."** When I asked why China chose the path of manufacturing rather than of innovation like Japan, the officials went silent with furrowed brows.

China is no fan of Japan. In China, deep animosities fester like a gastro-intestinal ulcer from looking back at Japanese brutality on mainland China. Japan considers herself to be the British Isles in the Pacific having beaten the Russians during the Russo-Japanese war. When its occupation of Manchuria in Mainland China was castigated by the League of Nations (the old version of the United Nations), Japan walked out of the League of Nations in 1933 and invaded China in 1937, butchering over 200,000 Chinese civilians in the city of Nanjing alone in less than six weeks.

Once the initial sense of offense of my remark dissipated, a very astute official remarked how top fashion brands often fabricate more than 80% of their products in China using Italian fabric, ship them back to Italy for buttoning and double stitching, and then, using loopholes in the international labeling protocols, often label them as "Made in Italy," sending them back to China to be sold at a premium over prices in Europe. Although China ends up contributing upward of 80%, China merely garners 5–7% of the price charged in the Chinese market. The Italian fashion houses (brands) *effectively innovate* to build market demand for their styles and then send their designs to China for *efficient manufacturing (fabrication)* to reduce costs. The lesson—the brand that embodies an innovation takes home the lion's share of profit and spoils; the business of labor and fabrication gets a pittance. Even Apple's products read "Designed by Apple in California; Assembled in China." The entire product is assembled in China, and then sold back into the Chinese market, with Chinese consumers a 20% premium over US prices.

Brands that build upon innovations create and push innovations in design and function and the market is willing to pay them a premium for innovative risk-taking; but brands that build on efficient manufacturing are constantly pressured by the market and innovators to lower their prices. *In the age of globalization, a knowledge economy covets innovators and offshores production.* Companies pay more for an architect than for a construction worker; more for a physician than for a nurse; more for a designer than for a fabricator.

Did you know that?
Madam Curie discovered Radium and Polonium and won the Nobel Prize twice, one for Physics and one for Chemistry in 1903 and 1911. Sadly, she passed away from radiation poisoning!

To Build, to Buy, or to Acquire

The Smile Curve helps companies strategize on one of the more important aspects of operations: build or buy. A company can decide to build a product in-house from scratch or to outsource/offshore the building/manufacturing of a product through other third-party suppliers, vendors, or assemblers.

Let's revisit the Apple iPhone as an example. Apple buys its processor chips from Samsung (South Korea) and Texas Instrument (United States); its display screens from Corning (United States), Japan Display (Japan), and LG (South Korea); storage chip from Toshiba (Japan); its touch ID from TSMC (Taiwan); its NFC chip from NXP (the Netherlands); gyroscope for motion sensing from ST Microelectronics (France); iPhone assembly by Foxconn (Taiwan) and Pegatron (Taiwan) in China and Brazil. That is just a small sample of what goes inside the belly of the beast. The only pieces that Apple builds itself is the IOS software and the R&D design and innovation. In fact, Apple buys more than 90% of the components that make up the iPhone (components that make up a product are often called BOM [bill of materials]). Apple's strategy to build less than 10% and buy more than 90% for its iPhone product line allows Apple to control and leverage the Smile Curve for highest profitability. A 32 GB Apple iPhone 7, sold by Apple as a finished product for $549 has $219 of components (39% Direct Materials (DM)) and Apple pays $5 for assembly (1% of the Apple iPhone price) (Fig. 3.3).

But what happens when a company needs a certain product or service so much that it can't afford to have a third-party control it? That's when companies acquire other companies, that is, they change their strategy from buying from the company to buying out the company.

eBay, perhaps the world's most famous online auction site, had created a perfect marketplace for buyers and sellers to gather around and transact. However, eBay faced a serious hurdle: even if the price was right, how would payments be transferred? A company called PayPal came to the rescue. PayPal had come up with a simple innovative solution for financial transactions without sacrificing financial confidentiality. PayPal allowed buyers to keep their financial private information from sellers by using email addresses to mask (hide) user financial information. Now, users would not be weary of divulging their financial information. PayPal, therefore, became the backbone for eBay payments. PayPal was an independent company. That posed an interesting problem for eBay; what would eBay do if PayPal were to leverage its prowess and either work with eBay's competitors or even try to strong-arm eBay by asking for higher commission and fees.

eBay, faced with this problem, could (1) build a platform like PayPal from scratch, or (2) buy PayPal as a platform. Of the two choices, eBay chose the latter. Realizing that it would take eBay years to build a platform like PayPal from scratch, it was a better strategy to acquire PayPal. Acquisition is often a good strategy for companies planning on extending their product line by buying out competitors, vendors/suppliers. In eBay's case, this acquisition was a vendor acquisition because PayPal offered financial services for eBay's auction platform. The acquisition of vendors or suppliers is often called Vertical Integration (Amazon accruing Whole Foods to create a physical presence) and the acquisition of competitors is called Horizontal Integration (Porsche acquiring Volkswagen, Kraft Foods acquiring Cadbury). If a company needs to expand its product line or depends a lot on specific partners, a buy (rather than a make) strategy can end up being a "Buy it Out" strategy (acquisition). From a buy strategy (outsourcing / offshoring) to a buy-it-out strategy (acquisition).

The general principle is as follows: if something is mission critical or core to your company's survival, build it (for example innovations, R&D); if something is not core to your survival (for example manufacturing where companies can change vendors), buy it. However, if what you are buying becomes mission critical to your business survival, rather than building it, acquire it.

Fig. 3.3 Apple iPhone X Complex Linkages (Courtesy Bernstein Research)

PARTS AND PROFITS
Key suppliers for the iPhone X

🇹 Taiwan 🇺 U.S. 🇸 South Korea 🇨 China 🇯 Japan 🇦 Austria 🇭 Hong Kong 🇸 Switzerland

DUAL CAMERA
Lens
Largan Precision 🇹
Most valuable stock per share in Taiwan; net income, revenue surged over 700% in decade through 2016
Genius Electronic Optical 🇹
Shares have jumped over 160% in 2017
CMOS image sensors
Sony 🇯
Shares have risen over 50% in 2017

Revenue up over **700%**

TRUEDEPTH 3-D-SENSING CAMERA
Receiver
Largan Precision 🇹
Genius 🇹
Kantatsu 🇯
Sensor
STMicroelectronics 🇸
Infrared filter
Viavi 🇺
Sensor assembly
Tong Hsing 🇹

PROJECTOR
Vertical-cavity surface-emitting laser (VCSEL)
Lumentum 🇺
Finisar 🇺
II-VI 🇺
Wafer-level lens
Himax 🇹
Ams 🇦
Defractive optical element (DOE)
TSMC 🇹
Xintec 🇹
Optical parts assembly
Ams 🇦
Laser manufacturer
Win Semi 🇹
Laser tester
Chroma 🇹
3-D camera module assembly
LG Innotek 🇸
Sharp (Japan-based unit of Taiwan's Foxconn)
Ceramic substrate
Kyocera 🇯

CASING
Glass back, cover glass
Biel Crystal 🇭
World's largest cover-glass maker; also key supplier for Samsung; planning Hong Kong IPO

Lens
Technology 🇨
Biel's rival; also key supplier of screen glass for Samsung, Oppo, others; stock has risen over 130% since Shenzhen IPO in 2015

Stock up over **130%**

Stainless steel frames, casing assembly
Foxconn Technology 🇹
Foxconn unit; main business is metal casing, mechanical parts; also key assembler for Nintendo

DISPLAY
OLED panels
Samsung Electronics 🇸
3-D force touch module
TPK Holding 🇹
Also supplier for iPad touch module, MacBook touch bar
General Interface Solution 🇹
Foxconn subsidiary

ASSEMBLY
Foxconn 🇹
Longtime major iPhone assembler; Taiwan's biggest company by revenue; sales climbed 155%, net income doubled from 2007-2016

Sales up over **150%**

Sources: Companies, Bernstein Research

Complex Linkages

Modern age is the age of brands. The invisible hand of the brand offers the most socio-economic handfuls. But the relationship between the innovator whose brand and logo define a product or service and the producers and assemblers that build the product and service is a **complex linkage**.

To begin to fathom how truly "bonkers" the new world is, next time you pick up your laptop, phone, or tablet, ask yourself this question: If you were to break down all components of each of these devices into individual parts (called **BOM (Bill of Materials)**), what percentage of these components are made by the brand whose logo appears on the device? The brand logo might be that of Apple, Google, or Samsung, but the concept remains the same.

Consider Apple iPhone's components. The list of components as a BoM (Bill of Materials) includes flash storage by Samsung and Toshiba, Camera lens from Taiwan, Battery and Displays from Japan, Qualcomm transceiver and Texas Instruments touchscreen controller from the US, Metal casings from Taiwan. Foxconn and Pegatron, Taiwanese companies with sophisticated assembly lines in China, assembles the final product and packages the iPhone, readying it to become the next worldwide phenomenon. In the BoM, Apple only offers the iOS software. Yet, it is Apple that controls the logo, the brand, and the profits that encompass the iPhone.

This is the world of complex linkages, a world of **interdependencies**, where components from various vendors (suppliers) are hidden under the logo of a brand. If your iPhone's Wi-Fi appears dodgy, you don't blame Broadcom, the Wi-Fi component provider; instead, you remark how rubbish your phone's Wi-Fi reception appears to be. Customers and consumers (consumers are the ones that use a product, or a service and customers are the ones that purchases a product or service and may or may not use it) that buy the brand, are often, if not always, unaware of the components and the component manufacturers that make the brand. While brands reap the profit by enveloping (hiding other components under its skin), choosing these complex linkages in today's global world must be underpinned by strategic choice of vendor and quality, not just costs. The choice of the correct suppliers (vendors), logistics and transportation companies (e.g., FedEx, UPS), payment processors (e.g., Visa, Mastercard, American Express), retailers (e.g., Best Buy, Nordstrom), and customers and consumers, altogether define a company's **ecosystem**. Choosing the right ecosystem based on your brand is a key to success and maintaining a competitive advantage.

Chasing the Sun

Chasing the sun is a phenomenon where we tend to create offshoring venues in countries like China and India that are nearly 12 hours away (about 12 time zones). Chasing the sun is a type of operational strategy that multinational companies follow when they operate in multiple markets at the same time.

This 12-h choice is interesting because, by the time the designers in the US head home around 7 pm after submitting a design specification for manufacturing or building in China or India, the workday is just beginning in those countries. By the time they finish their fabrication and leave for home around 7 or 8 pm, the workday in the US is starting and the fabrication results are ready for inspection at the US HQ. With a strategic choice of time difference, a company is now "chasing the sun" by having its operations run 24 hours a day (12 hours in one time zone followed by 12 hours in another).

There was once a time when countries colonized other countries; for example, the famous phrase that the sun never sets on the Union Jack represented how Great Britain and her colonies spread across the world. When the sun set in Great Britain, dawn arrived in areas such as India. Chasing the sun has replaced the metaphor of a flag with the metaphor of a brand. It is the new dawn of economic colonization. The term "The sun never sets on the British Empire" with the Union Jack is being replaced by "The sun never sets on the brand," regardless of what flag the brand belongs. But, as brands expand their global production and presence, they must ensure that they are modular enough to be nimble and agile to meet various market preferences and demands.

Today, in Post-Colonial times, a new generation of economic colonialism has come to task. A company that has operations in China and India (mind you, these countries are typically twelve hours ahead of the US), that company is chasing the sun with 24-hour operations. When dusk falls on its US operations and employees leave, they leave with design specs ready for production or development in China or in India. When the employees in the US leave the work at 7 or 8 pm every evening, the employees in the Chinese and/or Indian divisions begin their workday. As they arrive at work, specifications are waiting for them from their US counterparts. These employees work throughout the day to build prototypes and develop programs that they can conveniently hand over their US counterparts by the end of the Chinese or Indian workday, respectively.

So now, when the Indian or Chinese workers return home, the US workers begin a new day of work, ready to receive prototypes and programs handed over by the Chinese and Indian divisions. This creates a twenty-four-hour factory without the US company having to incur US labor costs for twenty-four hours. Therefore, the strategy of chasing the sun offers tremendous cost benefits for multinational companies while running their operations around the clock.

Of course, technology plays a hand in simplifying such strategies. Whether it is online file sharing via corporate Share Point, Dropbox, or Google Drive, specifications can be easily transmitted without errors from traditional modes of communication such as telephones or faxes. And the world gets smaller and more efficient.

Modularity and Postponement

As markets have grown global, so has consumer demand. But global consumers do not display the same demand. Different cultures have different tastes and brands must adjust their products and services to match the taste and culture of various global consumers. BMW creates a 4-cylinder engine variant to cater to the Chinese market where roads are crowded, petrol is expensive, and comfort is valued more than drivability. Rolls Royce, Mercedes, and Jaguar offer cars with longer wheelbases in China because the Chinese affluent enjoy chauffeured rides and more space in the back than in the front. Driver comfort is secondary if the owner is chauffeured.

KFC's (Kentucky Fried Chicken) rapid expansion in China is a result of KFC's ability to build a menu that matched the tastes of the Chinese consumer without increasing its own costs of managing too many ingredients and inventory. KFC did so by adding Chinese items to the menu. Instead of simply serving fried chicken with chips, KFC served fried chicken with congee, a traditional Chinese porridge to whet the appetite and interests of the Chinese. More ingredients in the inventory means more complexity and cost. So, the key is to increase variety in the end product without increasing the number of items in the inventory. The answer: modularity and postponement.

Modularity is basically a business philosophy, borrowed from biology and engineering, where a product or process is divided into small, manageable pieces that can be joined together to create various finished products and services. Even specialized labor is modular. Each laborer does a specific task that can be used in various ways to create or assemble a complete product. McDonald's uses less than 20 pieces in its inventory to mix and match to create over 30 different menu items. Modularity is similar to Lego blocks. Each Lego block is modular. Lego blocks can be combined to build various designs, from fire engines to lorries to rockets.

Modularity adds tremendous cost savings as well as strategic benefits for companies. Dell computers used this idea of modularity in the 1990s to become a global leader. Instead of building finished computers with specific hardware configurations that may or may not sell in the market, **Dell** used the idea of modularity to create a strategy of build-your-own computers for its customers. Dell maintained an inventory of modular components such as memory, hard drives, optical drives, and processors. Each component had about 3–5 different options, e.g., memory and hard drive sizes. Customers were empowered to combine these components based on their choice to design their own computers. Once the customer had made a choice and paid for it, Dell assembled the order based on the specifications and shipped it to the customer. While other competitors were pre-assembling computers based on wildly fluctuating demand forecasts, Dell was using modularity to reduce costs of carrying inventory that might not sell while strategically positioning itself as being driven by "real" rather than "estimated" customer demand. Car companies are seriously into modularity. Car manufacturers are building modular assemblies and sub-assemblies that they can combine to build the right car based on market demand. If a customer or market wants a different trim, wheels, leather color, or engine size, modularity allows companies to simply mix and match these components as per customer or market orders rather than wild guesses on what might sell.

Did you know that?

Rather than selling preconfigured computers that people did not care for, Dell computers was the first company that empowered customers to build their own PCs from a select set of options! It was one of the earliest examples of postponement in the computer industry!

Using modularity as a stepping-stone, post-ponement is strategy where companies finish products and services for sale closer to the market and based on what customers demand rather than building a finished product early on and trying to sell it through distributors and wholesalers. Dell's build-your-own computer or Ford's customize-your-own-Mustang are examples of **postponement** strategy. The idea is to "postpone" the building of a finished product till someone actually orders it. Once an order is placed, the right modules are assembled to build the product to sell to the customer.

Postponement works off a pull rather than a push strategy. Traditionally, companies followed a "**push-strategy**" for their goods and services. Push strategy is based on building finished products in large batches and hoping that the market likes the products they have built. Pull strategy is based on building products only when customers demand them. Customers "pull" production by demanding products. Producers "push" products by manufacturing and supplying them.

Capital Markets and FinTech in a Global World

If we were to take a take a step back, two threads interconnect and weave globalization: the flow of data and information via technology and the flow of money and investments via capital markets. So, if anyone were to ask you, during the direst economic conditions, old chap, who and what should we save on Noah's Ark? The answer: Technology and Capital Markets (banking).

However ill we speak of banking, it is a love–hate relationship. We need banks but we are always apprehensive of their control over the money flow. And we cannot come to a compromise. Knowing that you need someone you otherwise doubt is no fun.

There exists a strange propinquity between apprehensive perceptions and our actions. There is no greater fear than fear itself. We act optimistic but the slightest errancy triggers our deep-seated pessimism. We chastise quicker than we praise; we sell-off faster that we buy-in; we like

hope, but we love fear. Perhaps, deep in us, we are all like the Russian novelists who marvel in a gray, dystopian world and, like vampires, hate an optimistic sunshine.

Decades ago, **Kahnemann and Tversky** talked about something called the loss-aversion theory. Elementally, it points to our actions that are driven irrationally by sentiment, particularly negative sentiments where we feel a greater negative emotion for a loss than the positive emotion for a gain, even if they are the same in value. For example, if you were to be walking down an east-end alley and chanced upon a 100 quid bill. You pick it up and pocket it, muttering "finders' keepers," brandishing a tiny chuckle. As you walk on with the undeserved 100 quid in your pocket, you hit a pub, get a drink, and in the process, mistakenly lose the 100 quid. Therein lies the irrationality of pure market economics.

Assume, for a bit, that banks are no longer there, no interest rate regulations are stipulated by the Federal Reserve and capital structuring, i.e., the D/E or debt/equity ratio, is zero, which means there is no debt leveraging, just pure-play market value generation. In this pure-play market-based equity, a company that might need some funds for equipment or payroll or R&D will either have to disburse internal funds or generate capital from the market. Given there are no banks that can offer a loan with a fixed cost interest payment, the company will have to brave the volatility of the market for capital. Of course, there are some brave hearts, e.g., Apple and Google that have evaluated their unleveraged mettle.

So, how would companies raise money? One way could be the issuance of stock for capital but that simply dilutes the stock without ascertaining exactly whether the stock issuance would generate requisite capital based on current market perceptions. But, caprices of the equity market have, indeed, weighed on firms so much that reliance on shareholders has become a nuisance. Just like large donors in democracies, large institutional investors and fund managers hold a rather large sway over the dynamics. Their support (investment) or pullout (disinvestment) can create large ripples toward or away from the core. After all, companies need investors that are like barnacles rather than butterflies. Capricious investors can be calamitous. In fact, Alibaba, in February, requested the Hang Seng to delist its shares of alibaba.com because, as The Economist points out, to untether itself and be "free from the pressure of market expectations, earnings visibility and share price fluctuations." And that is a malady that besets every publicly traded firm. Look at Google's 1st quarter earnings report where the company had a solid CAGR (Compounded Average Growth Rate) but missed market expectations by a few cents and its stock plummeted by nearly 10% at the news. At that point, companies can find solace in being debt leveraged instead of the volatile sentiments that underpin our sentient beings. And if the denouement of existence is caprice, *damn democracy, welcome leverage*!

Banks offer money supply that creates leverage. Leverage allows us to borrow money to buy a house, a car, or the latest appliance with a promise to pay it back with interest. A world without banking to issue debt is a world left at the mercy of market caprices with mind-numbing uncertainty. That is why saving the banks becomes an agenda under dire straits, much like Churchill's plea to save St. Paul's Cathedral during the Luftwaffe blitz on London. From spirituality to money flow, some institutions are interwoven into the fabric of life and living, making them, rather than "too big to fail," to "too useful to fail."

Banking is dead, long live banking! 4IR has reintroduced banking with a series of innovative **FinTech**s. FinTechs are 4IR technology-driven financial products, services, and business models that offer distinct financial value-propositions meant to bridge and substitute traditional financial offerings!

In Africa, companies like Fawry, Interswitch, Jumia, and Flutterwave are simplifying cross border payments via Facebook and Uber platforms as well as building digital wallets during COVID-19.

China's Ant group's Alipay settles ecommerce transactions and even offers banking services for the unbanked population. Malaysia's Razer Pay is building cashless wallets. India's PolicyBazaar is creating a one-stop shop for financial services comparison and shopping.

Mexico's Bitso is creating Bitcoin accounts for unbanked people while Kueski and Confio offer micro-credit on the fly. Brazil's Bit.one is using blockchains to monitor and verify cross-border payments and NuBank is offering totally online banking with clever credit scoring.

In Europe, the Netherlands' Ayden, and Italy's Nexi are streamlining payments while Sweden's Klarna is building integrated payment solutions and UK's Greensill is simplifying supply chain finance.

In North America, companies such as Betterment and Wealthfront are using robo-advisors for investment decisions. Better is offering one-stop online mortgage services. Companies such as Robinhood are offering zero-fee stock and crypto-trading platforms. Meanwhile, companies such as Square and Stripe are challenging payment gateways.

Insurtech is another 4IR FinTech innovation that is reshaping the insurance industry. Insurance is based on gauging risk to charge a premium. A riskier person or company would pay a higher premium than a less-risky person.

However, insurance companies have traditionally relied on large aggregate data: age, income, gender, race, ethnicity, profession, address, and sometimes a credit score, to define risk. These aggregations are often too nebulous. For example, you and I, among many other similar individuals, might belong in the same large aggregate category! But are we the same? Do we carry the same risk? Even credit scores cannot pin the exact amount of risk! So, how do we differentiate riskiness? This is where Insurtech comes in.

For decades, I used large insurance agencies to offer me auto and home insurance based on large aggregates and averages. Then I heard of auto insurance companies like Noblr and Root. All they asked me to do was download a smartphone app and allow the app access to my smartphone tracking. While I drove around with my smartphone, the app quietly used mt smartphone's built-in accelerometer, gyroscope, and GPS-module to track mt specific driving

3 Business Concepts in Globalization

behavior. The accelerometer data provided information on how quickly I accelerated and braked. The gyroscope data informed whether I took sharp or cautious turns. The GPS and device showed when I traveled, the distance I covered, and the routes I took, as well as whether I drove distracted, texting or looking at my phone. Together, the Insurtech app created a composite for me and just for me. The Insurtech company used these data points in their proprietary risk-assessment algorithm that came up with a specific personalized risk premium. The risk premium was less than half of the best rates I had ever received. If my driving suffers, my rate goes up. If I drive better, my rate goes down.

Did you know that?

Because Insurtech uses our real behaviors to assess our risk premium, Insurtech implicitly promotes better self-management, with driver and homeowners knowing that better driving or homecare carries lower insurance rewards.

Today, 4IR technological convergence is reshaping insurance, with startups using smart home device information to move away from historical aggregates to more personalized, dynamic, realtime quotes based on how we behave and live. For example, if my smoke alarm goes off more frequently than that of my neighbors', my insurance rates might go up, even if my neighbors and I might have the same exact demographics!

Mad Markets, Madder Multitudes

In a world of surfeit consumption options, most of us belong to a group called "prodigals anonymous." We are wasteful yet unrepentant. We like spending too much, eating too much, and entertaining ourselves too much. Responsibility has been overrun by laxity. Revisit the financial crisis once more and the answers are obvious. As Shakespeare writes in his play, Julius Caesar, "*the fault, dear Brutus, is not in our stars but in us.*" But that's me, a fiscal

conservative, talking. But mutter that to the general populace and be prepared for some furrowed brows.

The world is replete with indebtedness, more financially than theologically. We consume more than we pray. And why not? After all, God is granted, financial prosperity is not. This the basis of the new MAD (Mutually Assured Destruction).

We all love debt, whether social or economic. Debt allows us immediate fulfillment and post-hoc repayment. Sometimes it is an imperative for survival; other times it is for a quick high.

Credit as a Survival Imperative

Credit flow for survival has played itself out over millennia. During the age mercantilism, wars were funded by vassals who were promised loot and royal warrants in return. During the Napoleonic wars, privateers sailed the oceans to capture enemy vessels with the promise of loot. Credit is a promise of money. Simply put, acquiring money as credit has been an imperative since the dawn of civilization. Take credit away and state and corporate machinery can grind to a halt.

The 2nd world war was an unexpected war in some regards. Chamberlain had succumbed and allowed **Hitler** to assume Czechoslovakia on the premise that it would pacify Hitler and Nazi Germany of their feeling of slight for the unjust reparations imposed by the Treaty of Versailles at the end of the First World War. Germans had seen their economy stumble after the First World War; unemployment was rampant; production was abysmal because economic sanctions imposed had reduced credit flow to a trickle. That was the juncture where the Nazi party gained momentum. With a feeling that Germany were unjustly condemned by its adversaries after the war and forced into economic servitude with no creditworthiness, Hitler's intention was to seize what was made unavailable. Thus, the beginnings of *Lebensraum* to acquire resources and the horrific mass deportation and incarceration of Jews were meant to reduce German unemployment and exert misbegotten internal control and legitimacy. The fall of the Hapsburg dynasty had left Germany no vassals that could lend to its coffers. Invasion, incorrectly, appeared as the only legitimate option. Thus, the annexations of Czechoslovakia, Austria followed by the invasion of Poland in 1939 and the Soviet misadventures. The rest is history.

The UK faced a similar existential crisis based on credit supply after the war. With continental Europe in German chokehold, the UK was the last bastion across the channel. Nazi Germany decided to siege and level the UK into submission through aerial bombardments via the Luftwaffe and sever its supply chains via its Atlantic U-Boats. On a wing, a prayer and tremendous fortitude, the UK held on. Their invention of the Radar (radio detection and ranging) for early air-raid detection, the Marlin Spitfire crushing of the Luftwaffe Messersmidts and Junkers, and the dogged courage by Montgomery's forces against Feldmarshal Rommel's (the desert fox) Panzer tank divisions in North Africa were the first signs of Nazi defeat. By the time the US actively entered the war after Pearl Harbor and the Russians after the Siege of Stalingrad, the UK was exhausted. Physically and economically in ruins after the war, the UK sent **John Maynard Keynes** to the US to request more than a Billion Dollars in credit to rebuild the country. That was Keynes' economic perspective which is often called a Keynesian injection—an adrenaline shot into the veins to jumpstart the heart. Credit is the Adrenaline and the Economy is the heart. Had the UK not received the credit from the Americans, she would have succumbed to decrepitude or communism that was rapidly knocking on doors in the continent.

A similar scene is being reenacted for the past three years in Greece and Spain who feel illegitimately burdened the Euro, the EU labor directives for open immigration across EU member countries and the lack of productivity. It desperately needs credit but is parched for the same. The ECB (European Central Bank) has denied Greece any further credit unless Greece pays back the cheap billions (at incredibly low interest rates) it had borrowed and drunk itself silly on the cheap liquor of credit. For high productive areas like Germany and France, low interest rates were welcome because it allowed

the countries to invest in projects with returns more than the interest rates. A rate of return higher than the interest rate is a positive addition to the economy. While some used the low interest rates wisely for productive returns, others splurged on non-productive consumption purchasing goods, Range Rovers, and houses with swimming pools they couldn't afford. Greeks further abandoned their scruples by reneging on taxes, building camouflage nets over swimming pools to evade property taxes. Suddenly, credit became a premise for laxity rather than leverage. Cheap money without productive ends can often lead to laziness and misspent economics.

The European sovereign debt crisis further compounded the political malaise. Since 2008, globalization and cheap credit had turned Italy, along with Iceland, Portugal, Greece, Spain, Ireland, profligate. The 1992 Maastricht Treaty required Eurozone members to control their annual government deficit (the difference between government earnings and spending per year) to gross domestic product (GDP) ratio to remain under 3%. The Treaty also required member states to control gross government debt (the accumulation of previous government deficits) to GDP ratio to remain under 60%. Both rules required reining in government spending and increasing revenues from productivity and taxes.

Despite Maastricht Treaty guidelines, some member states failed to heed the troubling signs. Italy, Greece, and Ireland were carrying government debts more than 120% of their GDP. Italy had a €2.2 trillion debt. With cheap money and cheaper goods from globalization, the government and people were spending beyond their means. Governments were getting larger and inefficient, funding over-generous pensions, while foregoing investing in technology and resources that would keep them competitive in an age of globalization. Productivity was low and tax evasions, rampant. People were purchasing houses and cars on cheap credit with high default risks. Firing inefficient workers were constitutionally impossible. Governments borrowed, bloated, and squandered more to veil low productivity and government inefficiencies. Several banks had funded bad debts, and, under threats of insolvency, these banks requested bailouts from already cash-strapped, indebted governments.

Such profligacy and government mismanagement of debt led to a massive loss of trust and confidence in European businesses and economies, making borrowing (from selling bonds) more difficult. S&P, a financial-ratings agency, downgraded Greece's Bond Rating to junk status followed by an S&P downgrade for Italy. A downgrade signals uncertainty in an economy and investors want higher interest (or yields) to cover their risks of buying bonds (similar to how a person with a low credit score has to pay higher interest rates on credit cards). Prior to the debt crisis, EU countries offered an average of 4% bond yields. By 2011, the debt crisis had spiked 10-yr bond yields to 7.31% for Italy, 8.17% for Ireland, 11.57% for Portugal, and a dramatic 27.63% for Greece. With one of the largest bond markets in the world, high bond yields would spell a world of trouble.

Iceland and Greece were the worst managed and became the epicenter of the European sovereign debt crisis. The debt crisis began in 2008 with the collapse of Iceland's banks, spreading like wildfire to Portugal, Italy, Ireland, Greece, and Spain in 2009. In 2010, in order to keep their governments running, the ECB (European Central Bank) agreed to a €110 billion package for Greece followed by €85 billion for Ireland and €78 billion for Portugal in 2011.

As the old adage goes, with carrots come sticks. The ECB, fearing further bailouts and debt crises, instituted strict conditions. Although Italy did not need a bailout, Italian banks were carrying much of the loans and were stretched thin. Italy needed to force financial austerity, drastic pension, and labor law reforms that increased labor mobility, youth employment, and economic productivity and competitiveness. Following and ECB ultimatum and a promise to buy poor-performing bonds to fend off another debt crisis, Italy was forced to accept austerity and fiscal reforms in 2011. But, after years of indulgence and profligacy, such reforms came at a high social and political cost.

Today, Greece, while hating Germany for demanding payments back to the ECB, is striking worrisome chords on two sides of the spectrum. One the one hand, parties like the Golden Dawn are chanting Nazi slogans, meting revenge on immigrant labor, and reading Goebbels (conveniently forgetting the iron yoke of the Nazis during World War II). On the other hand, Anarchists and Communists parties are decrying capitalism and seeking freedom in neo-communism. The Neo-Fascists and Neo-Communists have one common thread unless further credit flows from being in the Eurozone, a revolution is nigh.

The Economics of Leadership Succession: How Money Supply Made Hitler

Money supply, simply put, is the way by which an economy maintains the flow of money to individuals and businesses. Money supply includes various measures such as maintaining short-term assets that can be liquidated for cash, bank liquidity and reserves to avoid bank runs (where a bank can become insolvent if all customers withdraw their deposits at the same time). If money supply is choked, the inability of individuals and companies getting money (through withdrawals or loans) can create economic havoc. Companies would not be able to fulfill payrolls, borrow to build and innovate, thus dragging the economy to a crawl. Increasing money supply commonly reduces interest rates and increases the ability of an economy to borrow money to consume and invest toward productivity and innovation.

It was this very lack of money supply that introduced Adolph Hitler, one of twentieth century's abominable characters, to the German and the world stage.

The treaty of Versailles and the ending of the First World War on the 11th hour of the 11th day of the 11th month in 1918 suddenly created a storm of events. The most substantial was the dismantling of the Austro-Hungarian Empire into states such as Austria, Hungary, Czechoslovakia, Latvia. Among others, once assumed to be a part of the overall German unity, these small states suddenly created myriad German minorities who longer could travel across borders to unite with their dissipated families separated by the drawing of political lines on a map. Moreover, small enclaves of Germans across political boundaries reduced their mobility and threated the German nation and its national pride.

Then came an economic debacle that allowed Germany to sow the seeds of **Nazism** and war. The economic debacle was the 1929 Wall Street Crash that sent a ripple effect across the world. Germany's pride was long hurt from feeling forced to sign the treaty of Versailles. Germany had never lost the First World War militarily; its loss was driven by severe economic shortages at home from the ongoing war outside its immediate borders. The **1929 Wall Street Crash** became a perfect stepping-stone for Hitler and the Nazi (National Socialist Party).

The October 29th Black Tuesday Wall Street Crash could not have come at a more opportune time for Hitler and Nazi Germany. The Roaring Twenties prior to the 1929 Wall Street Crash was driven by low-interest money supply. With so much money available as such low interest rate, people and companies started amassing more and more debt and channeled the borrowed money toward riskier speculative investments. After all, if interest rates are that low, even making a small amount from risky speculation could easily offset interest payments.

So, companies also used the "cheap" money to over-produce and over-market their goods and services. However, consumer demand did not stay in line with supply. With too much wheat production and supply, too much steel produced and too many cars built, suddenly companies had too much inventory that they could not sell. What happens when you can't sell something at a set price? You lower it. When none purchases that either, you lower it further. Your competitors follow suit to get rid of their inventory, bringing prices down even further. However, with too much in supply, there is not enough motivation for consumers to purchase. On the other hand, lowering prices means lower revenues for companies. Lower revenues with large costs force companies to take measures to reduce their costs. The lowest hanging fruits are employees.

For ages, firing employees has been a quick solution to reduce costs without addressing core problems of production design and consumer demand. As employees get the sack, their ability to generate an income to demand goods and services decreases dramatically, further increasing the gulf between supply and demand. Investors get worried about companies' ability to meet their costs and that triggers a bearish selloff. That's what happed in 1929. In the two days leading to **Black Tuesday**, the market dropped precipitously and $30 billion of investments simply disappeared. Hundreds of companies filed for bankruptcy and laid-off more and more workers, adding to the vicious cycle of lost productivity and inventor confidence. To an extent, the loss of consumer confidence in the investment market and overall negative sentiment became psychological foundations for the **Great Depression** to follow from 1929 to 1939.

The 1929 Wall Street Crash sent an ominous shock wave across the world, particularly with the US experiencing an economic depression in the aftermath. To revamp its economy, the US government was forced to call back its foreign loans from various countries, including Germany. *Bruning* was the German Chancellor of the *Weimer Republic* at the time. Being forced to repay US loans, Germany had to take severe measures internally by cutting off public expenditures and pay to government workers. Germans saw unemployment rise dramatically and there was resentment among the public antsy for a regime change. But who would be the right successor?

With growing economic malaise and disparity, Communism was becoming a popular choice under the Marxian slogan *"workers of the world unite."* About a decade earlier, the Russian revolution (read John Reed's "Ten Days that Shook the World" for more information) had lay waste to Tsarist Russian and formalized the **Bolshevik** creation of a communist state. The romanticism of communism rallying against a "class whip" that controlled capital and production was palpable all across Europe. Gentrification was dead; the proletarian revolution against the bourgeois was beginning. The promise of Communism as the great socio-economic equalizer was spreading its tentacles across Europe. However, communism was greatly feared by the general aristocracy as well as the bourgeois knowing that they would cease to exist, perhaps even in life and limb, as with the Russian revolution.

The other option was a more right-wing dictatorial command-and-control economy. The Nazi (*Nationalsozialismus*) party, started during the Weimer republic, thought to be the lesser of the two evils. Incumbent aristocrats and producers of goods and services supported the Nazi party as a hedge against communism.

> ### Did you know that?
> Faced with economic sanctions after World War I, Germans suffered from Zero-Stroke. Zero-Stroke was a mental condition from hyperinflation where the German Mark kept losing value. In 1922, a loaf of bread cost around 160 Marks. By the end of 1923, the same loaf cost 200,000,000,000 Marks!

The Nazi party had a strong anti-communist *Freikorps* presence. The party championed land reforms and nationalization of certain industries such as energy and touted the importance of nationalism over parliamentary democracy. **Adolf Hitler**, a firebrand, was the party champion—sharp in tongue and ruthless in action. His radical rhetoric incriminating Jews as the bane of German society along with his fierce nationalism made him a popular choice under times of severe austerity. With political arm-twisting, Hitler forced President Von Hindenburg to appoint him Chancellor in 1933 as he dissolved the Reichstag as the law-making body and the Nazi party as the single authoritarian presence in Germany. Hitler sealed his dictatorship in 1934 with the **Night of the Long Knives**, getting rid of Nazi left-wing members such as Strasser, the paramilitary Brownshirts (called SA (*Sturmabteilung*) along with their leader, Rohm, and conservative anti-Nazi figureheads such as former Chancellors Schleicher and Kahr.

Nearly three-quarters of a century later, the 2008 financial collapse signaled the incredible power of money supply.

The Allure of Credit and US Financial Crisis

So, why is **credit** so alluring? Credit's Latin origin means "belief" or "trust." A trust that one can borrow money to consume (borrow for utilization such as food, clothing, leisure) or to invest (borrow to purchase financial products (on margin) such as equity, derivatives). A creditor (lender) such as a bank lends money to a debtor (borrower) as a loan protected by a contract (also called an IOU (I owe You)) that trusts that the money will be paid back in full along with an additional interest. The interest is meant to cover the risks of trusting the debtor, and the cost of money losing its value over time and the opportunity costs of investing the same money in something else instead of lending it.

An important concept called **default risk** underlies the idea of credit interest. The higher the default risk, the more the interest rate.

Default risk is the risk of lending money to the debtor. What if the debtor defaults on the loan or fails to pay back the amount on time? Creditors try to hedge (or cover) the risk by loaning the money at a higher interest rate to individuals and organizations that appear to have a higher default risk. That's why credit scores from agencies such as a FICO (Fair Isaac Corporation) in the US and the ICO (Information Commissioner's Office) in the UK working with various credit data collection companies such as Experian, Equinox, and Transunion have become commonplace in gauging credit default risk. While changing higher interests to debtors with higher credit risks is one way to offset the probability of loss, Credit Default Swaps (CDS) offer an additional hedge. A CDS is a credit insurance that is traded in the open market. Much like a health insurance or an automobile insurance where a premium is paid to protect against issues arising from health or accidents, a CDS requires a premium from the creditor that protects the creditor from defaults by the debtor. The CDS seller is the insurance provider that changes the premium to protect the creditor if a debtor defaults on the loan. Suddenly, hoping for a default appears promising.

Default risk was at the heart of the 2008 US financial crisis.

The problem is that banks thrive on debt and deposits. For banks to issue credit, they have to hold deposit. Yet, depositors can flock and request withdrawal at any time and the bank would not be able to cater to their requests. And that would be a default. Banks work on the probability of maintaining liquidity (capital buffer) while considering the chances of a run-in (mass customer withdrawals). That is why, during the onset of Russia's 2022 Ukrainian invasion, Russian banks limited the amount of *Rubles* Russians could withdraw to prevent a run-in and maintain capital buffer to shore up the Ruble in the face of international sanctions. Banks therefore have to hold capital to sustain themselves against bad loans, investments, or sudden surge in withdrawals. A bandwagon withdrawal effect has happened many times, recently in Argentina in the 90s and currently in Greece where depositors have stormed in to withdraw their deposits to be rudely reminded of withdrawal rationing.

Now here is the rub, the large banks around the world that have grown organically, over time, or mainly via mergers and acquisitions, have suddenly built capital clusters that are so deep that it makes them too large to fail. These banks include Belgium's Dexia, BNP Paribus, BPCE, Credit Agricole and Societe Generale in France, Commerzbank and Deutsche Bank in Germany, UniCredit and Intessa Sanpaolo in Italy, China's Industrial & Commercial Bank of China (ICBC), Japan's Mizuho Financial, ING and RaboBank in the Netherlands, BBVA and Banco Santander in Spain, Sweden's Nordea Bank, Credit Suisse and UBS in Switzerland, Barclays, HSBC and Royal Bank of Scotland in the UK and Bank of America, BNY Mellon, Citigroup, Goldman Sachs, JP Morgan Chase, State Street and Wells Fargo in the US. These banks control most of the money flow across the global economy. Post-Graham Leach Bliley Act when banking and investments were merged, these banks, as global financial firms, created lumped and bundled products to create lucrative but often poisonous porridges.

With some many banks eagerly competing to lend money, gone are the days of consumer buying based on what one can afford. Lender's free structures are revised based on defaults by customers. High fees are a way to spread the contagion of default by distributing the costs to the rest. Still, while banks have become chary about lending, consumers keep the tills working with borrowed plastic. With this kind of princess posturing, consumer attitudes have changed, shifting from "aspiring to be just above their pay bracket to aiming a long way above their pay bracket" notes Steve Rees in The Economist. A little cut above income spurs welcome debt; living too large simply creates a calamitous recipe for default, spiraling down household economics. With property mortgages carrying the most debt to income ratio, prodigality in stores is simply a harbinger of household headaches.

Recently hunting for another house for a change of scenery where I encountered an interesting pattern, I spotted some quaint brick houses selling in the mid 300 k. The interiors were quite a show with hardwood floors, granite countertops, sunk stone basins, tiles, and large plasma sets everywhere. The statistics from the realtor painted a dismal portrait. The current owners had bought the property for 360 k. Within the next year, they refinanced the property and cashed over 70 k on which they lived large, bought designer clothes, redid what did not need to be done, and splurged on the latest electronics on another store credit card. As asset prices boomed, they had refinanced again for another 50 k which they spent frivolously and prodigally. When the housing bubble came to a screeching halt, falling prices and burgeoning unemployment ushered in a rude awakening and the house, with an existing mortgage of more than 400 k, was debuting in the market for 340 k plus 8% realtor fee and closing costs. The owners had lost it all.

It was a travesty led on by greed. Rather than using the house to live and love, they were using it as a cash wellspring. Even when money was tight, budgeting and rationing took the backstage —after all, if the house does not feel our prodigality, what will? Their friends in San Francisco were flipping houses and making a quick buck, why couldn't they? After all, the American dream was not owning your house but flipping it for a neat profit. Give me inflated real estate equity or give me death. In a special report on Debt in The Economist, Charles Stanley, a stockbroking firm, sarcastically drove home the underpinning psyche of the western consumer, "please fund our lifestyles but don't hold us to any commitments." Now there is some truth to that.

After the Black Monday Wall Street crash in 1929, the Glass Steagall Act introduced the Federal Deposit Insurance Company (FDIC) and the separation of investment and commercial banks in 1933, only to be repealed by the Graham Leach Bliley Act under Bill Clinton, a democrat with an unflinching agenda to provide homeownership as the extended American dream beyond Life, Liberty, and the Pursuit of Happiness. The British and American models rest on similar laurels with the British motto of "Dieu et Mon Droit" or "God and My Right." Yet, during the Clinton administration, the pursuit of happiness took on a new dimension that implied a syllogism: happiness comes with homeownership; most homeowners are happy; therefore, to pursue happiness, you have to be a homeowner. Adding to the nota bene, Freddie Mac and Fannie May were given the charge to rule the roost on egalitarian homeownership. Come ye, come all, and the band played on. It was the beginning of what would turn into the calamitous 2008 financial crisis.

The Clinton-era push toward economic prosperity promoted that but all Americans should be homeowners. Full steam ahead, they said, and suddenly, like no child left behind, no consumer wishing to buy a house would be deprived, regardless of their financial wherewithal. No 20% minimum down payments, no credit checks, no logic. If the homebuyer had low-income relative to the property they wanted to purchase,

banks swept such high default risk concerns under the carpet. Banks would systematically ask customers to claim higher incomes and increase house valuations. A customer earning $50,000 per year would report exaggerated earnings of $150,000. Houses valued at $200,000 would be falsely appraised to $350,000 to build a false sense of affordance and equity.

And the subprime drumroll began. Yet, everyone, capital rich or capital starved, wanted to become quick millionaires. Suddenly, a new investment opportunity was introduced on the shoulders of Fannie Mae and Freddie Mac—the government would shoulder the responsibility of debt and default. That was the start of a housing bubble.

The Graham Leach Bliley Act allowed banks to ramp up their creative financing with ARMs and hedging risky assets with creative hedging in the form of innovative swaps and bundling of risky assets. **ARMs (Adjustable-Rate Mortgages)** offered incredibly low interest rates (less than the market-base prime rate—also known as **subprime**) to homeowners and then, after a few years, dramatically increased the rate. Suddenly, a homeowner could pay $1000 mortgage per month to live in a $500,000 house, forgetting the fact that a few years later the mortgage would jump 3 to 4 times.

The banks knew the risks. So, banks came up with a combination of macabre financial innovations to deal with a market replete with toxic property asset bubble with high default risks. They were **MBS, CDO, and CDS**.

The combination of banking and investment houses via the GLB Act during Clinton's administration gave the government a lot of room to play using MBS, CDO, and CDS.

Consider this scenario: Suppose you have a slight allergy toward peanuts and particularly do not care for shellfish. If presented separately, you are not likely to pay for either. So, what I do is add a few things you like: veal, ginger, vodka sauce, scallops, a hint of curry. I dice them up and bake them with a nice hint of rosemary and a pretty, flaky flour. In mixing them, I use a larger proportion of shellfish and peanuts to get rid of my "risky" inventory that I will have a tough time selling separately. I, then, mask the shellfish paste with curry and ground peanuts with vodka sauce. Then, I bake them in layers. Once the concoction is done and delivered, I slice the layers vertically to further hide the taste within the complexity. The entree has spread the risk in a complex concoction that you are somewhat uncertain of, yet the price is enticing enough to take a bite…after all, you can't taste the shellfish or peanuts to make a sound decision—and you go for it.

This is an example of an **MBS (Mortgage-Backed Security)**. An MBS takes a pool of mortgages with various levels of default risks and packages them into small pieces cut in various ways to make them look attractive and mask their weaknesses. So, banks started selling MBS to thousands of banks around the world. **CDO (Collateralized Debt Obligations)** offered one more complication. Instead of simply buying MBS, you would buy specific payments made by homeowners that comprised the MBS. For example, one group of CDO investors might receive the first five years of interest payments from all homeowner properties in an MBS. Another investor group might receive first five years of principal payments from all homeowner properties in an MBS. A third investor group might receive principal payments from the same MBS from years 11–15. So, no single bank was owning a mortgage. The mortgage was being divvied up into many small chunks packaged with other mortgages and sold across the world.

Banks heavily bought MBS and CDOs because they looked attractive and the virus had spread throughout the world economy. But they had an uneasy feel about the hidden risks. So, companies like AIG and Lehman started selling something called **CDS (Credit Default Swap)** as an insurance against default of MBS and CDOs. Banks would purchase CDS as an insurance for their MBS and CDO investments. AIG complacently lucratively sold CDS but never envisioned the mortgage bubble bursting or reserving for impending MBS and CDO failures.

In the mid-2000s, globalization opened world markets to cheaper production, better communication and information sharing via the Internet, and more efficient supply chains that crisscrossed

the globe. Suddenly, companies realized the potential for cost savings and started moving their production to China and India. Between 2000 and 2014, the US lost more than 5 million manufacturing jobs. As US and Europe started importing cheaper goods from around the world and using technology to increase productivity with fewer workers, US and European companies also started cutting payroll and moving their operations overseas for cost savings. With a run-up in property prices and loss of jobs, people started selling their overvalued properties in a super-saturated market. With too many houses to choose from and homeowners looking for cash in an economic downturn, property prices started crashing. May 13, 2008 was the beginning. Bear Stearns, the 7th largest securities firm in the world, realized that it was carrying more than $28 billion in highly risky "level 3" assets and CDOs. In a matter of days, Bear Stearns' value dropped by 93% and was merged by JP Morgan Chase. Bear Stearns disappeared. AIG took a dramatic hit and had to be bailed out by the government for $180 billion.

The rest is etched as a calamitous history from which the world is still digging out to the surface.

The Greek tale of Icarus offers a cautionary aid. Remarked by Aristotle in his Nicomachean Ethics, Icarus was born with wings. In his hastiness to fly, Daedalus, his father cautioned him. If he flew too low and close to the water, he would wet his wings and drown. If he flew too high, the sun would burn his feathers and he would plummet to earth. Central to this tale is the age-old advice of seeking the Golden Mean, moderation over extremes—pointed by wise men from Aristotle to Confucius.

Aftermath and the Paradox of Choice

The aftermath of the financial crisis led to more regulation. With raging financial turmoil around the globe and the revision of the Basel Committee of Bank Supervision guidelines, banks are therefore being asked to carry more buffer capital. These banks, working off Dodd-Frank, are called **g-SIFI** (global systemically important financial institutions) and they are the ones that require a greater buffer. But here is the catch and the moral hazard.

First, a greater capital buffer requirement reduces the percentage that can be loaned or invested. Therefore, the more you buffer, the less you can lend, increasing the cost of lending (because you are losing interest or investment income from the buffer). Second, increased cost of lending has to be, one way or another, factored in, sending a message that credit could have factor costs. If consumers feel that the cost of lending is rising, it could dampen their initiative to borrow. Finally, to defray higher costs of lending, banks have to hedge via investments or complex financial products. Suddenly, the very risk-taking that the law was meant to curtail goes topsy-turvy. And there lies the logic of cross-funding and proprietary trading—something that the Volcker rule will attempt to stem.

On the far side of the SIFI spectrum lie small, community banks, often the link to small business loans based on relational presence. The Troubled Asset Relief Program (TARP) lent money to these community banks to shield them from volatility. Then, in 2011, the federal government disbursed $4 billion to boost small business growth via the community bank lifelines. Unsurprisingly, as the Wall Street Journal reports, these community banks used about 45% of the 4 billion to pay back the interest-based TARP loans. Only 55% of the money aimed at spurring small business. The result, with less money available for lending, community banks ended up rejecting more small business applications and issuing less credit. Such is the paradox of choice.

Given the bi-modality of banks, one that are behemoths and the others that are cash-strapped saplings, there is a scent of blood in the water. Basel Accord or not, the coming of 2019 for greater buffer capital or not, mergers and acquisitions will create larger banks, bigger investments firms, and more complex financial derivative instruments and swaps to defray and shift risks from one part of the operation to another. It has to happen. The more you are regulated, your costs go up and your usable capital goes down. Yet, your shareholders request better earnings. So, you take more risks (and buy more complex insurance as a hedge). Suddenly over-regulation that was set to reduce your risk exposure forces you to expose yourself to a new set of complex financial instruments you don't know very well. When your friendly government becomes a fiendish regulator that makes you walk the perimeter of uncertainty is when **black swans** (high impact but low probability events) appear. Then markets go topsy-turvy.

Did you know that?

In 2021, a large group of investment neophytes on a Reddit thread called "Wall Street Bets" used the motto "YOLO" (you only live once) to have thousands of its members buy small chunks of shares of languishing companies like GameStop and AMC. This crowd movement sent GameStop and AMC's stocks soaring, creating a "short squeeze" against large Wall Street hedge funds betting against these companies. The power of the crowd led to billions in hedge fund losses.

Managing Costs, Managing Mortality

Marginal, Fixed, and Variable Costs

Traditionally, companies were built on the basis of production volume. Focus was on reducing **marginal costs** (costs of producing one more product or service) by distributing fixed costs across more and more units. With **fixed costs** or overheads, the more units you produce in a single batch, the lower the cost per unit (total fixed costs divided by total units produced). This is called **Economies of Scale** where marginal costs fall as more and more units are produced. However, creating bulk orders of finished goods builds up a finished goods inventory that cannot be used anywhere else. If they don't sell, it's sunk cost (cost that cannot be recouped). Modularity and postponement offer a hybrid approach. Modular components are built as a "push" batch order using economies of scale. These components are assembled based on "pull" demand using **economies of scope**, where choosing the right set of modular components can save money by allowing a company to build multiple products using various combinations of components. The concept of economies of scope is similar to be able to prepare various tasty recipes by combining a small set of cooking ingredients.

Why is it that there are restaurants and bars booming at the beginning of every economic recovery and also being one of the firsts to close shop? An Ohio State University study found that 60% of restaurants change ownership within the first year and 80% of restaurants close within five years. Although there is a myriad of reasons for restaurant and bar failures such as mismanagement, over-reliance on employees, location, customer preferences, and competition, one of the most important reasons is not understanding fixed costs, variable costs, and BEP (breakeven point)—the number of products of services you need to sell in order to recoup your costs.

Break-Even Point (BEP): The Key to Cost Control

Fixed and variable costs are important for calculating **BEP (Break-Even Point)**. Costs should not be confused with price. Price is what customers pay and costs are the amount you incur to produce a product or a service. Fixed costs are costs that you have to pay regardless of whether you sell any product or service. For a restaurant, fixed costs include monthly rent if leasing (or mortgage payment and property tax if owning) the property, basic utilities such as water, heat, sewer, and electricity, employee wages (even if there are no customers), and maintaining basic food and drink inventory. Variable costs are costs that depend upon the number of products or services sold. For example, a $999 Apple iPhone might cost Apple $499 to build; a craft beer pint sold for $8 might cost $1.50 to purchase (based on a $9 price for a six-pack); a burger sold for $12 might cost $4 to prepare (cost of food items and cost of electricity and oil for the grill and

fryer). In short, fixed costs are costs you have to bear regardless of whether you sell anything or not. Variable costs are costs you have to bear only when you sell a product or a service.

Let's use this to look at a restaurant or bar's cost structure using fixed and variable costs. Suppose the restaurant or bar rent is $2500 per month, its utility bills are $500, and it employs 3 fixed staff (2 servers and 1 cook) for 12 hours a day, 7 days a week for $10 per hour. Assume that there are 30 days per month. Therefore, the total fixed costs per month are $10,200 ($2500 + $500 + $10 per employee × 12 hours a day × 3 employees × 30 days of operations) = $10,800. Suppose the average variable cost of your food and drink items are 30% of the sale price and the average customer orders $30 of food and/or drinks. So, the variable cost is $9 per customer.

For the restaurant or bar to remain in business, the restaurant or bar needs to make sure that it is at least covering its fixed and variable costs. The question is, how many customers must the restaurant or bar have per month to make ends meet? The answer lies in BEP. Let's try it out:

Average Sales per customer × # of Customers = Fixed Costs + Variable Costs per Customer × # of customers

Average Sales per Customer × # of Customers – Variable Costs per Customer × # of Customers = Fixed Costs

Then,

# of Customers × (Average Sales per Customer – Variable Costs per Customer) = Fixed Costs

Therefore,

# of Customers (i.e., the BEP) = Fixed Costs/ (Average Sales per Customer − Variable Costs per Customer)

In business, Average Sales − Variable Costs is also called contribution margin. So,

# of Customers (i.e., the BEP) = Fixed Costs/Contribution Margin.

Using this calculation for the restaurant or bar, the # of Customers (i.e., the BEP) = $13,800/$(30 − 9) or $13,800/$21 = 657.17 which, rounded up, is 658 customers per month. This means that the restaurant or bar should pay attention to attracting at least 21.9, i.e., 22, customers per day to break even. In terms of food and drink sales, that means 22 customers × $30 average sales per customer = $660 of sales per day. The BEP is an incredibly important concept that you should use to understand how much you should sell to cover costs. Anything more, you are making a profit. Anything less, you're running at a loss and bleeding money.

The problem is compounded when restaurant and bar owners start borrowing more money to pay their fixed costs. In addition to the fixed costs, they now have to meet their fixed costs from debt obligation, i.e., interest and principal payments that may be additional to what they may have borrowed from banks in the first place to start their restaurant or bar.

BEP is integral to business decisions. Whether it is Disney+ figuring out how to price their streaming subscription or Apple deciding how many iPhones or Macs it needs to sell before making a profit, every company, from 1 to 4IR, needs to understand and use BEP for making core decisions.

Did you know that?

Modern Air Forces are rapidly transforming their fleet by using less pilots and more drones. BEP analysis is regularly used to figure out the growing need for Drones over pilots to reduce fixed costs and effective attack fleet sizes based on enemy offenses and defenses!

This importance of BEP is not just limited to companies. It is also prevalent in countries' governments where their debt is far greater than their revenues (gross domestic products (GDP)). In 2017, the US commonwealth of Puerto Rico had $74 billion in debt and $49 billion from unfunded pension obligations. Puerto Rico was not making enough taxes and revenues to break even and was forced to accept debt restructuring (a way to rethink how to manage and pay off debt and attract more revenues—much like restaurants and bars that often get new management). Having fixed costs from debt is not an issue. Not making enough revenues to bred-even is the main worry. The US' debt is $19 trillion, about 98% of its GDP but there is a promise that US companies are productive enough to break-even. If you show more promise, you can manage more debt. For example, a student studying to be an Orthopedic surgeon can borrow $200,000 with ease but a student studying to be an apprentice mechanic may be hard pressed to find a lender willing to lend $50,000. That is because the probability of recouping the $200,000 loan from a physician's income is higher than the probability of recouping $50,000 from a mechanic's income.

However, for countries that have lower earnings or productivity (like restaurants or bars with bad menus, drinks, and customer service), there is little chance to recoup its costs from debts unless they completely restructure their economies to lower their costs and focus more on innovations that will drive revenues in the future. The PIIGS' 2017 debt to GDP is as follows: Portugal (216%), Ireland (684%), Italy (124%), Greece (228%), and Spain (167%)). Ireland's debt is 7.84, i.e., nearly 8 times that of its GDP revenues, which means that its fixed costs just from having to pay interest on its debt takes up a large chunk of its GDP revenues and paying off the principal will take some serious restructuring. In comparison, the BRICS, with high GDP revenues earned from outsourcing, offshoring, and increasing incomes within their countries, have some of the lowest fixed costs from debt. In 2017, Brazil's debt was at 30% of its GDP; Russia at 40%; India at 20%; China at 14%; and South Africa's debt at 48% of its GDP. Breaking even is less of an issue for BRICS and a concern for the PIIGS.

Transition Exercise

How will Technology shape Globalization?

Purpose

The purpose of this exercise is to help you apply your understanding the intersection and confluence of globalization and technology. The assignment will help you examine bottlenecks and roadblocks related to implementing emerging technologies across the world while paying close attention to issues and concerns that differentiate efficient versus effective strategies.

Globalization was driven by cheap labor and technology, but technology, particularly AI and robotic automation, is creating a new world order where the same cheap human labor in China and India may be left for naught. Assume you, as a think-tank analyst, have been asked to assess the impact of technology on globalization.

Come up with two opportunities where technology can make globalization blossom and two threats where technology can make globalization wither. Explain your choices.

This part introduces a set of useful strategic and analytical metrics and models to build up an analytical repertoire. The part begins with an overview of some emerging technologies that can be used to contextualize analytical thinking! Students learn a useful set of strategic models to guide their abstract and long-term thinking based on organizational objectives and purposes. After that, students are introduced to useful and popular statistical and econometric analytics using Microsoft Excel to apply and analyze numerical facts for decision-making. In the search for the best decisions, a combination of strategic and statistical analytics provides students the right tools and techniques to offer applicable solutions and insights.

Learning Outcomes

By the end of this part, students will be able to:

- Understand how strategy and analytics intersect in technology innovations, especially Artificial Intelligence (AI).
- Evaluate strategic models and tools for company and industry analysis.
- Critically assess the importance of Metrics to measure decision-making performance and outcomes.
- Examine statistical and econometric models to for Data Mining for prediction and

Prescription (optimization) analytics to guide strategic decisions.

- Understand and utilize an important set of Data Mining tools for statistical and econometric analysis and reference.

There are two major shifts shaping the world. One is globalization. The second is 4IR technology innovations.Globalization and technology innovations are changing the way companies and customers purchase, sell, manufacture, service, and even communicate. An Apple iPhone includes parts from 8 different countries and is sold in 130 countries. GM is closing manufacturing operations in the US and focusing on manufacturing electric cars in China. Barcelona, in Spain, is becoming the 3D manufacturing capital of the world. Drones are being readied to deliver packages. Uber and Lyft are upending taxi services around the world. Amazon is using big data and analytics to predict what we will purchase one year in advance!

Oil prices are dropping as oil supply is increasing and countries and companies are shifting to alternative, sustainable energy options. Tesla's electric cars and batteries are reducing pollution. Artificial Intelligence (AI) is taking care of basic accounting, basic health diagnostics, and even basic recruitment screening. Companies like Alipay in China are using cellphones as wallets and changing the way customers pay for everyday purchases. Globalization and technology threads bind our new, connected world. And this is just the beginning!

Strategic and analytical tools are core to managerial and executive decision-making. This module will briefly introduce useful strategic and analytical metrics and models to build the executive repertoire. Strategic models guide thinking based on organizational objectives and purpose. Analytics is all about using facts for decision-making. In the search for the best decisions, analytics applies the right tools and techniques to offer solutions and insights.

How 4IR Technology Innovations Change Competition

Netflix and Blockbuster

Technology is nothing but a device or service that improves an existing process by making a traditional process faster, more cost-effective, better, more accessible, and/or easier to operate and use. The advent of the wheel made moving things easier and faster. Gutenberg's Press made printing books cheaper and accessible. The **industrial revolution** made mechanization its *tour de force*. The coming of electricity made heating and lighting cheaper and more accessible and prevalent. Telephones and telegraphs increased accessibility by connecting people across the world and allowing them to communicate easily. The steam locomotive simplified travel by cost-effectively carrying more people over longer distances. The airplane made long-distance travel even easier. The coming of computers made information processing cheaper and easier, allowing companies a faster way to gather and store data. The Internet made global communication even easier, allowing multiple, simultaneously active channels. Robotics automated laborious tasks into cost-effective processes run by preset programs. AI, the current holy grain of technological innovations, is reshaping tour comprehension, thinking, understanding, and decision-making.

From changing human experience to costing, technological innovations have upped the ante, often dissolving hundreds of years of tradition with novel thinking and processing.

Take the case of **Blockbuster** and **Netflix**. Once upon a time, there was a company called Blockbuster, so popular and prevalent that you could spot its stores anywhere, just as common as an Asian takeout. Founded in 1985 Blockbuster became the largest video game and movie rental chain in the world with over 9,000 video stores, serving about three million customers each day in the US and 24 other countries. Nearly 20% of Blockbuster's revenues came from late fees alone. Blockbuster prided itself on being everywhere. If you needed a video, Blockbuster was your stop. While Blockbuster was basking in its omnipresent glory, a small start-up called Netflix was using technology to change customer experience and manage costs.

But, in 1999, a small start-up call Netflix was about the up-end the landscape. Netflix's business model started the first online DVD rental where customers could subscribe to DVD rental services online and have their DVDs delivered by mail. This subscription model took off. Customers could order what they wanted, have it quickly delivered with free return packaging and shipping and not worry about late fees. Netflix leveraged the Internet to increase convenience as a product differentiator. Netflix also reduced costs by only shipping disks in protected sleeves. As the Internet became more prevalent and **bandwidth** (the volume and speed of data that can be transferred) got cheaper, Netflix innovated

© PiaDura LTD 2022
P. Datta, *Global Technology Management 4.0*,
https://doi.org/10.1007/978-3-030-96929-5_4

with **on-demand** streaming. On-Demand streaming is a business model that allows customers to watch a movie or show or listen to a specific music whenever they want rather than when it is played. A radio station or TV channel typically used a **push-strategy** where shows, movies, and music are broadcast or supplied to customers via the radio or TV channel to watch or listen. HBO broadcasting a show like Game of Thrones every Sunday at 9 pm Eastern Time is an example of a traditional push-strategy where viewers (customers) would have to wait for the program. On-Demand is a **pull-strategy** where customers, instead of waiting for certain music to be played or show to be broadcasted, can login to their channel of choice and watch Game of Thrones any time they please. An On-Demand pull-strategy empowers customers to control their choices of what to watch and when.

Netflix's on-demand pull strategy grew on the heels of digitization and online streaming. A typical Blockbuster store carried thousands of DVDs in its inventory. The minute a customer rented a movie, the movie would be off stock. If a store carried 5 copies of a particular DVD, say, Rogue One, and 5 customers rented a copy each, the store would have no more copies left even if there were a line of customers waiting to rent the DVD. Only when one DVD is returned can it be rented again. A short stock is a lost sale. Netflix realized the disadvantage of physical media and the advantages of using digitization to simultaneously differentiate its service while reducing costs dramatically. Suddenly, Netflix could use digital content and stream movies and TV series over the Internet to hundreds of millions of global customers without worrying about logistics, packaging, or manufacturing. Netflix simply changed the competitive landscape. For Blockbuster, having multiple physical stores was no longer an advantage because Netflix movies and TV shows could be streamed on any device 14/7. By 2018, Netflix had nearly 100 million subscribers around the globe and its **market valuation**, calculated as the price of each share times the number of shares in the market, topped a $100 billion, making it more valuable than industry media giants such as Comcast or Disney. Moreover, Netflix started producing its

own TV shows such as House of Cards and Orange is the New Black that made Netflix not only a service provider but also a media and content producer competing with big Hollywood studios and distributors. Blockbuster ended up filing for bankruptcy by 2010 and was forced to auction its assets. By 2013, Blockbuster announced their plans to close the remaining US stores.

Consider the technological landscape in the past decade. **Telecommunication** oligarchs, behemoths in their own right for years, are suddenly challenged by fledglings of the near past! Once cable companies laid their hardwired lines to households, they discovered, somewhat serendipitously, the wonders of the technological flux. First, the age of the Internet had dawned. Second, they discovered multiplexing. And voila! The cable providers allowed customers to discover the magic of broadband access. A DSL line was just a turboprop, not a jet. Damn the torpedoes, full speed ahead—and cable companies, once regarded as puny entertainment providers, suddenly started controlling digital content—leaving behind the telecommunication behemoths leasing backbones and seeking greener pastures beyond western borders. Companies like Vodafone, Airtel, and France Telecom have donned colorful multinational feathers on a hat scarred by domestic hyper-competition.

Did You Know that?

The Telephone landline that took billions to build, from across deserts and over mountains, is perhaps one pf the shortest-lived technology investments, totally routed by the advent of Mobile Telephones! How many of us have a landline telephone in this age?

But the era of landlines was waning. Emerging countries were **leapfrogging** the developmental hurdle. Leapfrogging is a strategy that allows companies and countries to skip one or more technological innovations and adopt the latest technology. For example, countries in Africa, Asia, Eastern Europe, and Central and South America had little or no telecommunications such as telephone landlines. That was because laying landlines required a lot of infrastructure resources and many countries did not have the ability to spend money or the technical knowledge to install millions of feet of telephone cables and hundreds of thousands telephone poles and towers. That meant most of the population in these countries had no mean of communication using telephones or telegraphs. However, the coming of mobile (cellular) phones suddenly offered these countries a chance to jump or "leapfrog" from little or no telecommunications to hooking up to the cellular ether. A mobile or cellular phone is wireless. It does not need millions of miles of wired landlines. Satellites in orbit can handle traffic with little marginal cost but ample marginal revenues. The age of wireless telephony was in. And in was a new breed of nascent firms. Internet and wireless were converging rapidly, and the momentum is still palpable. Telecommunication deregulations opened up the market and fledgling firms challenged the status quo competing on flexibility against calcified rigidity. Telecom behemoths were fighting two flanking attacks. On the Internet front, companies like Vonage and Skype were challenging the incumbent with voice-over-IP (using the Internet for telephone calls). On the wireless front, companies like NTT DoCoMo and Qualcomm flanked the oligarchs while Wi-Fi access points started ruling the local roost. Then, of course, are game changers—a sharp punctuation confounding the attacks. Take Apple and the iPhone and how the iPhone wrested the power dynamics from the telecom networks with a revolutionary device and rewriting the competition. In another vein, take **Google Voice**. One single virtual number of your choice- connected to multiple phones, custom greetings for various numbers, voicemail transcribed as delivered as digital documents. A search engine from two Stanford geeks reconfigured the landscape—creating wastelands out of the telecom oligarchs' long-term plans.

Film vs. Digital Cameras

Kodak is another case in point. Founded in 1892 as Eastman Kodak, Kodak established an entrenched position in professional film products with a catchy slogan, "You press the button, we do the rest." Kodak in a contemplating a long-term strategy to preempt competition by raising barriers to entry instituted a distinct brand of quality control. Kodak started revising its value chain on the philosophy of end-to-end quality control. Kodak was reputed for its film and the halides and nitrates used in film required one particular metal- silver. The long-term strategic approach was to insulate itself from sudden fluctuations in the commodity market for silver and to maintain quality as a hallmark of its reputed film division, the largest of its revenue source. Second, control over silver would further raise barriers to entry and reduce competition from Fujifilm, Ilford, and others. Kodak vertically integrated its operations, buying silver mines and processing companies to maintain end-to-end long-term quality control. The strategy seemed sound till the advent of digital cameras. The age of films was waning. The famous Ektachrome line was discontinued. Images were digitized and stored online or offline. Price per gigabyte of hard drive was falling rapidly. Film prints were falling in disfavor. The strategy to preempt competition became Kodak's albatross. Kodak was suddenly carrying around deadweight of fixed operational costs that was limiting Kodak's ability to flexibly counter threats from Sony, Nikon, and Canon. Suddenly, Kodak, a symbol of quality control, was now outsourcing its digital camera production to Flextronics International, shedding quality control just to keep its head above water. Although Kodak, in 1975, had invented the digital camera, Kodak worried that digitization would cannibalize its own film business. **Cannibalization** is a situation where one company's product can steal profits out of another product made by the same company. Kodak was so large that it took Kodak decades to change its strategy even though it was threatened by digital cameras and digital images. By 2012, Kodak was forced to file for bankruptcy protection. Kodak, the company largely popular for bringing photography mainstream, had succumbed to its own weight, tradition, and the rapid onslaught of technology.

Technologies and Differentiation

In a world where competition is saturating markets, ensuring sales can be a difficult proposition unless your products and services are truly differentiated. Companies that stay ahead of the curve differentiate themselves by following a combination of strategies. Differentiation is a strategy by which companies can offer a sense of value to their customers that sets them apart from the competition. Companies generally differentiate themselves by offering:

1. **Product and Service Differentiation** that no Other Industry Rivals Can Offer or Match.
2. Internal cost-control for **Cost Differentiation** that allows a company to increase its margin (the ratio of a company's profit to its sales) without sacrificing its competitive edge.

Leveraging Technology for Product and Cost Differentiation

In the 1970s, banks heralded the use of technology for product differentiation. Banks had largely been traditional companies focusing on personal, tangible, services carried out by tellers, managers, and a variety of staff across the board. Suddenly, banks realized that customers needed cash 24/7, 365, and banks couldn't afford to be open every hour of the day. To differentiate themselves, certain banks leveraged technology to give them an edge over the competition. In 1967 Barclays Bank in England introduced a cash-dispensing machine that used a card to read a customer's information across digital networks and dispense cash to customers regardless of the time of day or location. But it was Lloyd's Bank of England that made the ATM mainstream.

Did You Know that?

Lloyd's Bank differentiated its services with its 24/7 ATM cash-machine that only Lloyd's customers could use to get cash while customers at other banks had to queue up during office hours to fill out forms and get cash.

The **ATM (Automated Teller Machine)** created a competitive edge for Lloyd's Bank in England. Shepherd-Barron, the inventor of the ATM, said, "It struck me there must be a way I could get my own money, anywhere in the world or the UK. I hit upon the idea of a chocolate bar dispenser but replacing chocolate with cash." Lloyd's Bank could differentiate its services by creating a 24/7 ATM cash-machine that Lloyd's customers could use to get cash from a Lloyd's Bank ATM anytime, regardless of the hour of the day. No other bank offered the service, and this service differentiation gave Lloyd's bank an edge up against other banks.

Product or service differentiation often changes the way people and industries have traditionally operated things. Technology and globalization, especially global politics, and policies, have immensely affected the past, the present, and the future. In 1978, the US deregulated civil aviation, i.e., passenger airline industry. Previously, the US government played a major role in regulating airline tickets prices, schedules, and routes. **Deregulation** meant that airlines could now compete in the open market without government intervention and let the market decide on which airlines are to be profitable and which are to disappear. This meant that airlines could set their own competitive fares, schedules, and routes.

However, getting the right route and fare was not an easy task. Suppose you wanted to fly from Denver, US to London, England, the old method for booking a flight would have been as follows: You would call a travel agent about for ticketing the travel agent would place you on hold and call multiple airlines across multiple routes. If the flight from Denver to London meant two stopovers; Denver to Chicago, Chicago to New York, New York to London, then the agent would call multiple airlines operating on each of those routes. Each airline would offer schedules and fares for each route. The travel agent would then show you the various route options and their accompanying fares. If you wanted a schedule slightly different than what was offered, the process would re-start. American Airlines' information systems division, called AMRIS, wanted to seize the deregulation opportunity to create a product/service differentiation that would change the future of airline reservations.

Using technology, AMRIS created a computer system called SABRE that could simultaneously search multiple routes, schedules, and fares, in less than one hundredth of the time it took for a travel agent to call and confirm. AMRIS offered free computer terminals installed with SABRE to travel agents explaining to them how using SABRE would improve the traditionally painful process of flight reservation for clients. **Time increases complexity** because it increases the chances/probabilities of things going wrong. The longer the process, the greater complexity. The greater the complexity, the greater the cost. This product/service differentiation offered travel agents and American Airlines a win–win proposition. Travel agents could now use the SABRE terminal to book flights with ease, and, with American Airlines the only flight network offered via SABRE, would guarantee American Airlines more profit and a leg-up over its competition.

While Barclays and Lloyd's Banks were **first movers**, i.e., companies that are the first to use or introduce an innovation to the market, with ATMs and American Airlines with SABRE, there are companies that practice product and service differentiation as a **second mover**. A first mover has multiple advantages as it is the first one to bring an innovation to the market:

Brand Recognition: Companies that introduce products to a market oftentimes become the most recognized brands associated with the innovation. Xerox photocopiers, Bell telephones, Sony Walkman, Tesla electric supercar, Coca Cola soft drinks, Microsoft Windows—the list goes on.

Switching Costs: First movers, if able to capture a lot of market share, can increase switching costs. Switching costs are the costs that one has to bear to change from one company to another. For example, if you have a store, hotel and airline card that offers you points every time you shop, you start accumulating points that you can use later. Suddenly, you are locked-in to the brand because you cannot you're your points if you choose to move to another store, hotel, or airline. A Windows computer user is so used to the way a windows computer works that switching to a Mac increases learning costs—the cost to learn a new technology or interface. First movers try to lock-in by making

you rely on their innovation so much that you will feel that moving to another competitor will be costs, both in time, money, and effort. Now you see why companies like Google offer services such as Gmail for free. Users get used to using Gmail so much so that they don't care about changing their email service provider.

However, while first movers try to capitalize on brand recognition and increased switching costs, there are second movers.

A **second mover** is a company that waits and watches how markets react to the initial innovations by first movers, and then, learning from first movers' mistakes and initial market reactions, introduce a better version of the same innovation. **Apple** products are particularly famous for capturing large market shares using second mover advantage to differentiate its products and services. In the late 1990s, first-mover companies such as Creative and Diamond introduced the idea of a portable mp3 player where you could store songs on a portable hard drive with a digital screen. The idea was an innovative solution that would allow people to carry a large number of songs in an mp3 format instead of hundreds of CDs. Apple waited out the market reaction to the first movers and observed customers complain about the clunky interface and the difficulty in searching and finding songs. As a second-mover, Apple observed these market reactions as it introduced the iPod to the market in 2001. The iPod was an instant success with great navigation, fantastic interface, and user-experience.

User experience is the level of enjoyment and engagement users get from using a technology. With a minimalist crisp screen and the scroll and click wheel for navigation, Apple used a second-mover advantage with the iPod for product differentiation that redefined the market. Apple has kept on pursuing second-mover advantages. In early 2000, multiple first-mover companies such as Palm Pilot, Blackberry, and Sony Clie had been innovating on touch-screen phones. While these phones were popular, they suffered from issues with touch-screen sensitivity, expensive data plans, and incredibly low battery life. Apple, using its second mover advantage, introduced the iPhone that partnered with cellular companies to offer cheaper plans with an iPhone purchase, simple colorful navigation, and a relatively long battery life. Once again, Apple led the competition and every cellphone since has tried to copy Apple's design from the first iPhone in 2007 to iPhone X in 2017.

Google is another case in point of a 2nd mover. Prior to Google, Yahoo was the most popular **search engine** in the 1990s, surpassing other incumbents such as Alta Vista, Excite, and AOL. Yahoo. Although the other companies were first-movers, Google's search algorithm, i.e., the logic behind the operation, was brilliant. Previously, web search was based on matching keywords to web pages. Google, founded by two Stanford PhD students, came up with an approach that scientists used when ranking papers.

A good paper is a paper that is cited by other papers and those papers used by other papers and so on. This was called the web-of-science. So, Google came up with a system called Page-Rank where the search ranking for a particular word or phrase was based on whether the website that carried the word or phrase was also popular among other websites that were themselves popular among other websites. Google, with its more scientific approach, suddenly upended the competition as a second mover. But there was more.

A good search engine was immensely helpful but there were no definite ways of **monetizing** the search engine development. After all, search engines were free. Suddenly, this company called Overture comes along with a remarkably interesting proposal of "cost-per-click" where every time a user would click on a relevant link that would take the user to a product or service website, the product or service website would have to pay a referral fee. A **referral fee** is a fee that you charge for referring someone to a business or opportunity, much like a finder's fee. Now search engines could become profitable as long as they offered relevant results.

Did You Know that?

During the initial uncertainty around COVID-19, Google search found an increasing search trend for the term "corn-teen." Google's AI was able to figure out that people were misspelling "quarantine" as a part of their search!

If a user was searching for the best deals on trainers, a better search engine could provide the most relevant trainer sales websites. If the user clicked on the website, the website vendor would pay a referral fee to the search engine for connecting the user to the site. Instead of companies paying hundreds of thousands of dollars to marketing research companies to **generate leads** or run about doing cold-calls, the search engine could change the name of the game by creating leads based on user searches 24/7. Google seized the opportunity and partnered with Overture and reaped the benefits—so much so that Google became eponymous with the word search. Yahoo once had adverts that asked, "Do you Yahoo!?" but that has been replaced by Google where we commonly say—"just "Google" it." Even though Yahoo ended up buying Overture later on, Google had surpassed Yahoo. The rest is history.

Artificial Intelligence (AI)

Today's world is run by and replete with technology. Anywhere you turn or look, there is some technology we are using (smartphones), interacting with (checkout systems), watching us (cameras and GPS location services on our phones), helping us (robotics), and guessing what we might want or do next (predictive systems). One of the most important emerging technologies is that of **Artificial Intelligence (AI)**.

So, what is AI? **AI** is a type of software technology that acts like a thinking-and-learning machine. AI uses data collected from various different sources and use sophisticated analytics to learn and predict what can happen. Data is plentiful. From voice software to our social networks, from online browsing to supermarket checkouts, we are helping companies collect massive amounts of data that companies can use to stitch a profile for us. **Machine learning** is a part of AI that uses previous data to continuously improve.

Did You Know That?

In the 1800s, during 1IR. Europe was fascinated by the Mechanical Turk, a Chess Playing robotic machine that beat more than 80 competitors. It was later discovered that the Mechanical Turk was not a machine; Rather, it was a person playing chess while hiding in the box!

An AI GPS system will not only use its built-in features to figure our routes based on shortest route, fastest route, routes with or without tolls, etc. but also learns from your driving when you deviate from the route and find a better route yourself. Internally, the software AI will calculate changes in route and the time it took to get to the destination along with other data such as the number of stop-and-go (more stop-and-go reduces mpg), number of turns to "learn" which might be a better route. If the new route seems to be quicker and more efficient, the AI will learn to use it as a better route option. **Deep learning** is a further enhancement on machine learning because it a software that learns on its own. Deep learning tries to mimic human learning.

Think of how a child learns what a car is over time. The parents show the child a car for the first time and every time the child sees another car, the parents remind the child that it's a car. Over time, the child learns to connect various features from all the times the child has seen a car to learn what features define a car, regardless of a sedan, SUV, coupe, convertible, and others. In Deep Learning, an AI system is fed millions of images representing a car and the AI is programmed to create its own ability to gauge what defines a car. Once that is done, the AI is fed many more millions of images to differentiate between types of cars such as a convertible versus a sedan and so on. From an analytics bend, deep learning uses Neural Networks as a popular technique to figure out what something is by connecting dots

© PiaDura LTD 2022
P. Datta, *Global Technology Management 4.0*,
https://doi.org/10.1007/978-3-030-96929-5_5

across millions of images, just like a human brain.

AI design is getting so good that AI is supposed to be the next killer-app that will disrupt and redesign the future of competition and work. Here are some examples.

Around 2010, a father, living with his teenage daughter in Minnesota, received mail addressed to his daughter from Target, the supermarket. Curious, he opened his daughter's mail to shockingly find coupons related to pregnancy and post-natal products. Furious, the father spoke with Target, asking them how egregious it is for Target to promote teenage pregnancy. Little did the father know that Target used AI analytics from the daughter's shopping behavior to find shopping patterns. Target's AI analytics traced a pattern that girls and women purchasing large amounts of unscented lotion tend to do so around the beginning of their second trimester, especially when closely purchased with supplements like calcium, magnesium, and zinc, lots of scent-free soap and extra-big bags of cotton balls— getting close to their delivery date. This is why stores offer customer cards so that can link your card to your shopping cart, every time you make a purchase. This is called **market-basket analysis**.

New **voice recognition** devices such as Apple's Siri, Amazon's Alexa, Microsoft Cortana, and Google Home are using AI to predict and decipher what you are saying and using the information to return you a result you want. For example, if you say, "play me some of Black Sabbath's best songs," the voice recognition AI will decipher that you want (i) music played from (ii) a group called Black Sabbath and (iii) songs that are the most popular (best). Then, the voice recognition AI will update your profile by adding that you like Black Sabbath. Based on that information, the AI will recommend that you try similar music such as Iron Maiden or Deep Purple. Moreover, if a new album of single similar to the Black Sabbath's music is released, the AI will recommend that you try it out as a sample or for purchase.

IBM's AI software called Watson is overhauling voice recognition and AI. **IBM Watson** was the first AI to win on Jeopardy, an American quiz show where Watson had to figure out what was being asked by a human being and then provide an answer. Watson was trained using all Wikipedia data and millions of pieces of latest information from newspapers, magazines, and books. Watson using machine learning algorithms, learned how to figure out the meaning of a question, find patterns in the massive amount of data fed to it, and come up with a response that matched the question and the data. Watson is also being used in healthcare to reduce patient waiting times. Watson AI uses millions of health case data files to become the first line of healthcare. Watson AI can scan, read, and understand millions of health documents and diagnostics in seconds, read them and understand coverage for a specific patient. Watson can listen to a patient's problems to do a preliminary assessment of illnesses and potential drug reactions. Watson AI can perform basic diagnosis based on patient charts and lab tests, specify which specialist to visit, and what medical fees to expect.

Similar AI software is helping societies in dire need of healthcare. Nigeria, an African country has a 1:4000 doctor-to-patient ratio. Aajoh, an AI-based Nigerian technology firm, uses AI for remote medical diagnostics over a smartphone app. According to a 2018 Stanford Social Innovation Review article by Lexi Novitske titled *The AI Invasion is Coming to Africa (and It's a Good Thing)*, "patients input their symptoms in the app using a range of communication options, and receive an instant diagnosis and, if prescribed, information about where to purchase medication."

A 2016 CBS interview[1] on AI put it as follows. *"The ultimate goal for some scientists is A. I. that's closer to human intelligence and even more versatile. That's called artificial general intelligence and if ever achieved it may be able to perform any task a human can. Google bought a company named Deepmind which is at the AI forefront. Google's Deepmind learned how to*

---

[1]CBS News, Artificial intelligence positioned to be a game-changer, 60 Minutes, October 9th, 2016.

play world's most difficult board game: Go. The real progress is less in what they did than how they did it. The technology taught itself and learned through experience without any human instruction."

In HR, AI is being used for selection and employee management. AI in employee screening can remove biases and just focus on competencies. For example, AI found a pattern that job postings using the word "developing" rather than "managing" attracted higher quality females than males. This information allowed the company to level its gender balancing by rewording their job postings. AI is being used to create Chatbots that can offer more thorough policies, training, and employment related questions to current employees as they begin work (onboarding) or over their time with the company.

AI can even gauge from employee communications, interactions, and evaluations chances of low motivation, job satisfaction, and even turnover and attrition. AI, especially, can read between the lines to figure our sentiments by a combination of the pictures we post, the emoticons we send, the food we eat and post on Facebook, the news we read. For example, if you post a picture of a cupcake at 5 pm on Facebook after a quick series of sad and stress emoticons and phrases such as "another day," and a Google search on vacation spots, AI can learn from your posts that you are likely stressed and unhappy at your job and might be looking for a break. AI can use this information to offer you books on motivation, jobs that match your profile and resume, and travel or vacation opportunities from 3rd parties. Together AI can create composites that can figure out who we are, perhaps, often better than we can ourselves.

For example, **Walmart** uses AI from real-time data collected via SAP software across point-of-sales across its 11,000 stores to figure out what is likely to run out and what is not selling on the fly. If Walmart's AI realizes that one of its stores is selling a certain type of bicycle very quickly, the AI will predict how many more bicycles might sell in the next few weeks and when to ship out more bicycles to the store without any human intervention.

Similarly, Walmart or Target might use AI to collect data on weather trends and demographics to forecast when there might be a blizzard or a thunderstorm so that the sores would be prepared with shovels and umbrellas even before customers know what to expect. By the time the blizzard hits and customers scurry to the store needing a shovel, Walmart or Target will not only have shovels but the right number of shovels (based on the proportion of the population in the area that might need new shovels).

AI and Shopping: Amazon's AI looks at your profile and purchasing behavior to figure out what you might want to purchase or what you might need in the future, sometimes even before you know it.

Every order or business is adopting AI to make better predictions, enhancing market relationships, increasing competitive edge, and lower costs. According to The Economist, one of the most prescient magazines in the world, according to IHL, a research firm, the 2015 cost to companies of overstocking was around $470bn and of understocking $630bn worldwide. Amazon's AI today is so sophisticated that it can predict what will sell 1 month down the line. That allows Amazon to stock its warehouse based on what it might ship now versus what it might need to ship later.

AI and Package Deliveries: AI is also being used to come up with better and safer delivery routes. For large companies such as UPS and FedEx, savings of 1 mile per route can save them nearly $50 million dollars every year. In production, AI is offering major cost savings. Large manufacturers and production firms are training AI and using AI to use computer vision to spot errors in products, even if it is a smallest of a hairline crack or a small change in a precision mold angle. AI even predicts when a particular piece of component, machinery, or equipment might fail.

AI and Winemaking: AI is even making headway into complicated activities such as grape picking for **vineyards**. *Botrytis cinerea*, or gray mold, is called noble rot. The mold infects grapes and increases sweetness and longevity in wines such as Sauternes. However, the same mold can devastatingly negative effects when producing dry red wine, costing vineyards hundreds of millions. Human pickers during harvest season have difficulty figuring out if a bunch of grapes include some moldy grapes. Nowadays, vineyards are using AI and photography on a robot to pick the right grapes that would make a better-quality wine batch without fear of contamination and large losses.

AI and Banking: Banks have long used AI in the form of mobile banking and AI-based customer service that takes care of transfers, bill payments, credit checks, loan applications, and account services. AI is meant to remove clutter and increase convenience while reducing the need for human interventions and the costs associated with managing physical infrastructure, expensive real estate costs and of course, large employee expenses. Investment finance is steadily increasing its use of AI, especially creating autonomous AI Robo-Advisors that can use algorithms to understand clients' risk tolerance and financial objectives to create custom investment-portfolios for them.

Investments firms such as Renaissance Capital runs an AI-based hedge fund called a Quant Hedge Fund that uses AI to create investment prediction models and trains the AI to readjust predictions and portfolio balancing based on new market data, everything from political changes to weather changes that can affect financial markets. In fact, driven by AI and technology, **FinTech** (Financial Technology) is a rapidly growing area in Finance that is changing the investment landscape.

AI and Driving: Then, of course, is the predominance of AI in the coming age of **autonomous vehicles**. An autonomous vehicle is an automobile that has the ability of driving and maneuvering itself without any human intervention. Germany's Deutsche Post DHL Group (DPDHL), the largest package and mail delivery organization is working on using smaller-sized driverless electric trucks to deliver mail and packages. These driverless trucks are light trucks that can easily maneuver through narrower European streets. The driverless (autonomous) systems are developed in collaboration with ZF

ProAI that uses AI to run through millions of data pieces to accurately assess its environment for variables such as traffic conditions, parking spot identification and parking, and pedestrian behavior.

How AI and Sensors Run Autonomous Driving

In contrast to human drivers prone to individual driving styles and reaction (including road rage), autonomous cars accurately follow traffic rules with better driving quality (gear shift and acceleration that reduces ecological footprint, exact spacing between cars (called platooning synchronized braking), and quick reaction time (less than half of human reaction time), all calculated by sophisticated AI. Sensors, cameras, **LIDAR** (Laser Radar), and radar feed data into the AI system that accurately learns from the environment and trains itself to better handle roads and routes without falling prey to driver fatigue, human error, and lost time along with huge cost savings in the last mile of fulfillment from the final warehouse to the delivery destination, typically the most expensive and time consuming in supply chains and logistics (Fig. 5.1).

The way an autonomous vehicle works is as follows. An autonomous vehicle is fitted with a variety of sensors whose main jobs are to scan the position, the environment and send the information to an AI computer that then sends signals to various parts of the car to perform certain functions such as braking, acceleration and deceleration, turning, swerving, reversing, and parking. The GPS system constantly checks the position of the vehicle based on multiple satellites and combines them with altimeters (to measure altitude), tachymeters (to measure speed), and gyroscopes (to measure angles such as turns, climbs, etc.) to know exactly where the car is and where its heading every millisecond. The GPS figures out the exact location, changes in speed limits, type of area, direction, speed, and so on. The LIDAR module scans the nearby environment by bouncing multiple light pulses like SONAR (Sonic Radar) used in ships and

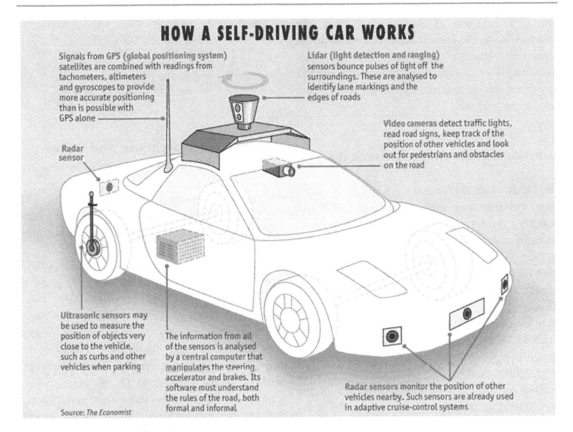

HOW A SELF-DRIVING CAR WORKS

Signals from GPS (global positioning system) satellites are combined with readings from tachometers, altimeters and gyroscopes to provide more accurate positioning than is possible with GPS alone

Lidar (light detection and ranging) sensors bounce pulses of light off the surroundings. These are analysed to identify lane markings and the edges of roads

Video cameras detect traffic lights, read road signs, keep track of the position of other vehicles and look out for pedestrians and obstacles on the road

Radar sensor

Ultrasonic sensors may be used to measure the position of objects very close to the vehicle, such as curbs and other vehicles when parking

The information from all of the sensors is analysed by a central computer that manipulates the steering, accelerator and brakes. Its software must understand the rules of the road, both formal and informal

Radar sensors monitor the position of other vehicles nearby. Such sensors are already used in adaptive cruise-control systems

Source: *The Economist*

Fig. 5.1 Self-driving car (Courtesy Robot Report)

submarines to scan the immediate environment around the car. These include people walking or standing, other cars nearby, road conditions like potholes, pavements, and curbs, buildings, and other objects.

Did You Know That?

LIDAR (Light Detection and Ranging), a popular technology in Autonomous Vehicles, uses hundreds of light pulses per second to map our surroundings, generating 1.5 million data points every second!.

High-resolution video cameras armed with image recognition AI software further define the environment by figuring out various things such as obstacles, lane markings, traffic signals, road signs, pedestrians, and other vehicles. Radar sensors all around the car check for things happening nearby such as getting too close to an obstacle or other cars or people. Ultrasonic sensors try to determine how close you are to various objects on the road. Together, this massive data is fed into an AI-based central computer that analyzes everything and sends various signals to operate the car. At a roundabout, the GPS will geo-locate and specify that a circular turn is coming with a specific speed limit, the LIDAR will check for pedestrians crossing and incoming vehicles; the video camera will identify signs and markings such as lane closures and yield signs along with verifying cars, pedestrians and other fixed and mobile objects as well as sounds such as police and ambulance sirens and construction drills; and the radar and ultrasonic radar sensors will check if you are close to other objects and how close they are to the autonomous vehicle.

Altogether, the autonomous vehicle acts like the autonomous nervous system in the human body. Different senses from our eyes, ears, nose, and skin function as sensors that relay the information to the central nervous system in the brain (the vehicle's AI system). The brain that analyzes all the information and sends signals via peripheral nerves to various parts of the body that makes the body react.

Autonomous Driving and Trucking

The heart of an AI system is its ability to automate routine and complex tasks. With AI changing the future of work, the shape of competition, and the nature of emerging products and services, the question is, what is at stake and want isn't? AI in autonomous driving is poised to impact the trucking industry in the next 5–10 years.

In October 2016, Budweiser used **Otto**, an AI-based self-driving autonomous trucking company owned by **Uber**, to deliver a beer shipment from Ft. Collins to Denver, Colorado, a 125-mile journey on I-25 on a driverless truck. Volvo has been operating an autonomous truck in the Kristineberg mine in Sweden. Fabu Technology, a trucking company in China, plans to run driverless autonomous trucks for intercity and within-city freight transportation by 2020. Uber, Tesla, Baxter, and Google are among the many autonomous trucking companies that are entering the AI-based driverless delivery vehicle sector. These trucks are expected to run 24/7, there is a high probability of wide-ranging unemployment in the trucking industry that employs the most unskilled workers in the country. With truck drivers often amounting to nearly 70% of logistics costs, AI and autonomous trucking will perhaps end up sacking more than 4 million trucking jobs. In 2017, *The Guardian*,[2] a venerable newspaper from the UK, mentioned,

> "The only human beings left in the modern supply chain are truck drivers. If you go to a modern warehouse now, say Amazon or Walmart, the trucks are unloaded by machines, the trucks are loaded by machines, they are put into the

warehouse by machines. Then there is a guy, probably making $10 an hour, with a load of screens watching these machines. Then what you have is a truckers' lounge with 20 or 30 guys standing around getting paid.
> And that drives the supply chain people nuts."

Autonomous Warehouse and Delivery Robots and Drones

On the warehousing end, Amazon, UPS, and FedEx are massively investing in AI and robotics. In 2012, Amazon acquired **Kiva**, a robotics firm that upends traditional warehouse management. Instead of workers in warehouses and distribution centers walking around picking things from aisles to fulfill customer orders, Kiva robots slide under each shelf stack, lift, and bring the right shelf over to the worker. This means that warehouses and distribution centers don't have to worry about having spaces between shelves for the workers to move. Instead, they can more than double warehouse capacity by staking shelves tightly side by side as the robots slide under the shelves and carry them to the right order fulfillment worker. According to a recent Deutsche Bank report, Kiva robots have cut warehousing operating costs by about 20% for each fulfillment center.

Today, FedEx and UPS are using robots to move large goods that could reduce insurance costs from using human workers (e.g., workmen compensation from back-pain). These large robots, called "luggers" at FedEx can move large and bulky items. UPS is also trying out **drone** deliveries using the top of its vans as a mini-helipad to fly the drone from the closest base to customer's house or business. UPS is invested in drone deliveries that use AI to spot the right house and drop zone. UPS mentions that using drones to cut just one mile per day from each of its drivers' delivery routes, it would save more than $50 million per year in fuel. Amazon has created a logistics branch called Amazon Prime Air where it plans to drop off shipments using multiple drones to customers in 30 minutes or less.

---

[2]End of the Road? Will Automation Put an End to the American Trucker? By Dominic Rushe, *The Guardian*, 10th October 2017.

Did You Know That?
According to UPS, using drones to cut just one mile per day from each of its drivers' delivery routes would save more than $50 million per year in fuel costs alone!

While the US designed and developed a drone delivery strategy, it is China that is actually implementing it. **JD.com**, a massive Chinese E-commerce retailer and the Chinese version of Amazon.com, has begun a massive drone delivery network to deliver packages to more than 500 million rural Chinese. The Chinese government is speeding up the development of unmanned drones for delivery. When a Chinese customer orders a product via his/her cellphone from JD.com, JD aggregates items ordered for a particular village and packs them into a single package.

The package is latched to a drone that flies with it and drop ships it at a central location—a landing zone in the village. JD works with a 3rd party company that then gets the items and delivers the items to individuals on motorbikes. While western democracies are focusing more on drone regulation for safety, China, with its single line of authoritarian government, is promoting drone delivery technologies to strategically corner the global market. With massive **subsidies** (government assistance such as tax breaks, easy credit, and simplified regulations) and less regulatory hurdles, China dominates the world in inexpensive solar panel production and wants to recreate their success in the area of commercial drone deliveries.

Autonomous Robotic Factories

AI-based autonomous work using complex **robotics** is pervading manufacturing and services around the globe. Philips Norelco, the electric razor and grooming arm of the electronic giant, Philips, uses 128 robots in its Netherlands factory with only 7 human beings for quality assurance.

Complicated assembly lines are rapidly being automated using AI and **robotics**. FANUC, a Japanese precision robotics and engineering firm, has been, for over 10 years, running something called a **lights-out factory**.

A **lights-out factory** is a manufacturing setup where manufacturing goes on with little or without any human presence. Robots run the show here, controlling every part of the manufacturing process. They run 24/7 and do not tire. Robots check the quality of work and even know, using predictive AI, when to remove one robot for maintenance and replace it with another robot. At FANUC, Robots built 50 robots every 24 hours and can run unsupervised for more than 30 days. According to a Wikipedia article on FANUC, "Not only is it lights-out," says Fanuc vice president Gary Zywiol, "we turn off the air conditioning and heat too." With Apple and Tesla pumping more than $1 Billion into FANUC, AI and robotics are scaling up even further.

Japan has long been at the forefront of robotics and wants to begin a "robot-revolution." Robots are creeping into many parts of Japanese firms and culture. Mitsubishi Financial, one of Japan's largest banks, has introduced Nao, a 4 ft, 15 lb. robot, as a bank teller that can converse in 19 different languages and help open bank accounts, set up exchanges and money transfers. In Nagasaki, Japan has opened a hotel called **Henn Na** (Strange Hotel) that is completely staffed by robots. A dinosaur robot greets you at the front desk, a robot bell staff carries your luggage to your room and robots manage your housekeeping needs. The Henn na Hotel uses facial recognition for room access and its climate control adjusts automatically based on guests' body temperatures. In 2013, Japan sent the first robot astronaut to the International Space Station where it stayed for 18 months before returning to earth.

Change is in the air and coming to every profession. As long as the profession involves routine work that requires repetition. From HR to manufacturing, AI and automation are supposed to reduce 45% of human jobs in 60% of professions, according to a 2016 McKinsey Report.

In particular, work that requires physical movement and labor is likely to be automated. Jobs such as mining, heavy lifting, delivery, driving, dishwashing, fast food cooking, assembling, and packaging, retail customer servicing, accounting, and bookkeeping, data collection and data processing, among many others.

The key to survival is to make sure that your role is one of complex decision-making rather than routine work. For jobs that are at the mercy of being automated, it is important that we help transition our employees into skills for tomorrow.

Did You Know That?

Since 2001, FANUC, the 4IR Japanese Robotics company operates a "lights-out factory." At FANUC, robots build 50 robots every 24-hours shift, totally unsupervised for up to 30 days!

Exercise: Leading in an Automated World

Purpose

Emerging technologies can change global operations by reducing costs and increasing efficiencies. The purpose of this exercise is to help you apply your understanding of global operations, strategy, and security and how to assume leadership in a period of rapid change and uncertainty.

Assignment: Assume you work for a global logistics company with more than 2000 truck drivers across the world on its payroll. A corporate executive has asked you help the company prepare for its future:

a. Explain why the coming of autonomous vehicles, especially autonomous trucks, will create a "disruption." Come up with *two points* why that disruption is good for the logistics firm (one has to be a financial/cost reason) and *two points* why that disruption can be bad for the logistics firm (once again, one has to be a financial/cost reason).

b. The executive wants you to create a mechanism to transition the drivers so that there is no large strike or setback (remember that truckers are a part of the teamster union). Explain to the executive why social friction can be a problem. Come up with *three suggestions* on how you would tackle the "undercurrent of denial" and "social friction."

c. Technology innovation is a social disruption. Emerging technology operations can disrupt the status quo. How will such disruptions ripple across society and how do you analyze and manage such disruptions? Think about economic, cultural, and social disruptions. Do these disruptions need separate technological infrastructures? Can autonomous vehicles increase sustainability? Why or why not? Explain.

How 4IR Technologies Are Changing Global Business and Society

Technology & Conservation

Sharks are no strangers to the fisherman's hook. It is estimated that tens of millions of various shark species end up as bycatch in commercial fishing nets and open sea fishing every year. New technology from the company Shark Defense out of New Jersey, US, has created a SMARThook that will remedy this issue and thus radically reducing the number of innocent sharks caught by fisherman. The SMARThook, once activated in seawater, sends an electronic vibration, which should deter a significant percentage of sharks from the hook. So far, tests have up to 94% decrease of shark bycatch. A simple idea that updates a tool used by humans for hundreds of years. The SMARThook is available for both the average fisherman as well as commercial fishing boats. A small piece of tech that is saving a big part of the ocean.

Poaching is a serious and growing concern for many animals around the world, but how can technology help? The World Wildlife Foundation, WWF, is using technology to help prevent poaching in the Kenya wildlife parks. WWF is utilizing infrared cameras atop stationary poles lining the border of the park as well as a mobile infrared camera placed on a truck driven by the park rangers. However, this is a two-step approach. Once the infrared cameras, provided by the company FLIR, detect heat emitted by an object that crosses their viewpoint, the paired software, developed by the WWF's conservation engineer, Eric Becker, determines whether the heat signal is human or animal. The FLIR thermal cameras pick-up heat emitted by people and animals as they cross their viewpoint. The thermal cameras come from the company FLIR and pick-up heat emitted by people and animals as they cross their viewpoint. The accompanying software determines whether that heat came from a human or animals. If the software identifies the heat signature as human, an alert is sent to the head warden, who can then deploy a quick response ranger unit to confront the intruder(s). If a human is identified, the computer sends an alert to the head warden, who then deploys a quick response ranger unit to intercept the intruder.

Technology & Healthcare

The pharmaceutical industry has long been plagued with extended and expensive periods to evaluate and discover new drugs. But Based in California, Atomwise, a leader in Artificial Intelligence (AI) for drug design and discovery, is using the prediction of AI algorithms and supercomputers to try and help with these issues. For example, with the use of AI algorithms the company discovered two drugs which could significantly reduce Ebola infectivity and other dangerous endemics worldwide. In addition, the company continues to use AI to further research drug and design and partners with pharmaceutical companies such as Pfizer.

Many people who live outside big cities have difficulty receiving the healthcare that they need. In an attempt to remedy the problem, the Chinese government approved the implementation of "Internet Hospitals" in Guangdong province, China. Approval was granted in 2014, and by 2015 the Internet hospitals were working with

over 500 patients a day and prescribing over 120 prescriptions a day. Since the approval, there are nearly 100 Internet hospitals, which provide accessible outpatient care to many who could not readily travel to a regular medical facility. Patients visit a local medical facility where they have access to an online platform that allows the patient to have an online video chat with the doctor. The patient answers medical questions and can upload pictures of medical concerns. While the patient and doctor have an online meeting, the patient is hooked up to machines onsite that send the patient's vitals to the doctors in real time. Through this platform, the doctor is able to make a diagnosis as well as prescribe necessary medication for the patient, the script prints out for the patient while the patient is at the facility. Now, many more people are receiving the effective healthcare, thanks to the utilization of simple web-based technology.

Technology & Society

Companies exist not only for profit but also to positively shape society. Faced with massive amounts of gasoline pollution from cars and trucks, Tesla, an American company, introduced the first electric supercar and accelerated the alternative energy vehicle industry. Today, Tesla is not only the most popular global electric car manufacturer, but also a company that provides battery and solar powered energy solutions that can light up your home and your city. Another company is using technology to combat the workers' health and safety. BHP, a global Australian mining company, uses heavy earth movers. In order to increase driver safety, BHP has designed Smart Helmets for its copper mines in Chile. The Smart Helmets actively monitor driver (operator) brain waves to trace driver fatigue to reduce chances of accidents and worker injury.

In developing countries, water is not just a source of life but also an exceedingly rare commodity for many people. In order to try and combat this, eWATERpay solution developed a "water ATM." Throughout villages by the Lilongwe Water Board and Nairobi Water

Company's Agtap, eWATERpay solution vending points are being evaluated. Many people in rural Africa lack access to clean and safe water, but with these eWATERpay solution vending machines is working on scalable technology to increase access to clean and safe drinking water. To obtain water from one of the vending machines, customers use a pre-paid Near Field Communication (NFC) card to purchase the water. This has reduced the distance they have to travel to get water and reduced the risks of contamination. This pre-pay system allows consumers to monitor their own water habits, in terms of both consumption and finance. The long-term goal is to scale up access to water with more people opening vending locations throughout the country, greatly increasing access to clean water. In addition, the eWATERpay solution could even be implemented into households so that people would always have access to clean water and there would be less risk for the company with the pay-as-you-go system. The combination of a simple idea and monitoring technology has the potential to bring clean drinking water to millions of people throughout the world.

Technology & Marketing

How does Amazon always know what to recommend to you before you even know what you want? Amazon does not guess, and the recommendation is not a coincidence, its Amazon's recommendation system. The retailer uses an algorithm based on remarkably simple components such as what have you bought previously, what you have sitting in your Amazon shopping cart, and products you have liked and rated. In addition to the data you provide Amazon based on your habits and clicks, Amazon combines all of your information and shopping habits with what other customers have recently viewed, purchased, rated, and/or have sitting in their shopping carts as well. With this "item-to-item collaborative filtering," Amazon can create a highly customized browsing and shopping experience for returning customers. Someone who frequently buys books from Amazon will go onto the Amazon homepage to find new recommended books based on their previous searches and purchases, while someone who is a new mother will go onto the Amazon homepage to find infant and baby supplies recommended. The beauty of this simple algorithm is that the consumers feed the algorithm data and the algorithm can grow to make a variety of recommendations for the consumer based on the changing interests and lifestyles of the customer. A lot of Amazon's recent growth has to do with the way that Amazon has integrated and utilized their recommendation system for the customers; every step of the purchasing process has listed recommendations for the customer to add to their shopping cart.

Alibaba is a successful company for many reasons, one of which is its ability to incorporate technology into its marketing strategy for the company. Through its use of technology and data, Alibaba maps consumers' intent, which is where the majority of its direct sales and revenues comes from. In order to do this, Alibaba uses micro-moments, which allows the company to instantly map consumer intent. Once Alibaba looks at the real-time engagement and sales from the consumers, Alibaba then shares this information with the retailers. This use of data and technology helps Alibaba by helping the retailers make necessary adjustments based on the consumer information data. With a focus on marketing for the retailers to deliver better inventory and products and prices to the consumers, Alibaba thus becomes a more effective and successful company, thanks to its technology focused marketing strategy.

Technology & Finance

Many FinTech creations are evolving to help people with their finances and investing. And Acorns is no exception. Created as an investing app aims to make "investing a small decision." By using an app-based investing platform, Acorns allows the investor to invest a little at a time, or even "round up" invest by linking a bank card to the app. It's a simple idea, without a brick-and-mortar location, and without utilizing brokers for the investors. Instead, the app, in a few quick and simple steps, sets up the account for the investor using modern portfolio theory and an algorithm to help the investor have a diversified and healthy portfolio based on the investors selected level of risk and investment contributions. The app is an easy, safe, and accessible way for many people to invest, especially those who may not have previously invested traditionally. Through its use of technology, Acorns makes investing a simpler proposition for new or experienced investors.

Alibaba, the Amazon.com of China and one of the top 10 most-valued companies in the world, realized that bank loans from Chinese banks are often in the hundreds of thousands of dollars. However, most small businesses require small loans, often between $50 and $1,200, in order to keep their operations running. Dealing with banks was time consuming and often not worth the bank's time and costs. Alibaba realized the opportunity and started Ant Financial, a microloan business. Since 2012, Ant Financial has loaned more than $15 billion to more than 3 million small and medium businesses. Collecting data from its borrowers, Ant Financial can monitor every transaction, every communication, every bill payment, and every customer service complaint or praise automatically to derive a credit score for its customers (there are no formal credit scoring systems in China). Borrowers with low credit scores are deemed risky and charged higher interest rates while borrowers with better credit scores are offered lower interest rates. All this is done with using technology and no human involvement!

Technology & HR

Traditionally, HR has been a human-driven function, today data, powered by technology, drives HR decision-making for companies like Google. It is no surprise that the technology company, Google, has a technology-driven approach to Human Resources. By using people analytics to examine people operations of the company, Google can optimize its HR practices to analyze everyday concerns to analyze what makes workers happy or unhappy. Google's approach is to mix qualitative and quantitative methods to examine an array of problems such as how long employees enjoy waiting in the line for lunch and why management at Google is effective or ineffective. Google uses a variety of methods to collect the data, one of which is surveys to gather the real-time data on the mood of the Google employees. By having such a technology-driven HR approach, Google can ensure that the workers at Google are effective and happy, which can benefit Google in the short and long run.

Armed with education and knowledge, students are always the best source of labor for companies. But finding the right set of students often requires dealing with University bureaucracies. Side, a French company, has created a student network that companies can tap into for small but useful company tasks. This not only allows companies to access the student market and get things done on-demand but also vet the best students for future employment based on their work performance. HeyJobs, a German company, is using CV and resume data to create a better profile of the right-candidate. Once recruited, companies like Peakon in Denmark and Jubiwee in France are using real-time data analytics to offer real-time feedback to employees in order to correct performance errors early on and ensure employee success.

Technology & Supply Chains

Can a company know what you might want before you actually order it? Amazon is using sophisticated sales and supply chain analytics to figure out what areas tend to demand what products are what times. Amazon plans to use the information to ship and item to the area; the final customer destination will be filled en route when the customer actually orders the product. For example, Amazon might forecast that a certain part of Texas might want more orders of scarves during an upcoming, unusual pattern of cold weather. But Amazon may not know which customers would order the scarves. Using anticipatory shipping, Amazon would ship the scarves to the region, and once specific customers order the scarves, the customer's name would be added to the scarf that's already *en route* for delivery!

Even with wide-scale poverty, more than $6 billion of food is wasted in India every year because of bad logistics. While India is one of the world's largest banana producer, it holds less than 1% of the global banana market. Keeping food fresh requires something called a Cold Supply Chain where a certain temperature is consistently maintained across the entirety of production, transportation, and delivery. New technology such as blockchains can allow temperature monitoring of every food item as food moves from the farm to the final customer. Blockchains use IDs for each food package where temperature sensors monitor and control possibilities of spoilage. Today, Walmart uses blockchains to monitor the origin and handling of pork across China into the US and Provenance, a UK company, uses blockchains to trace and monitor the Tuna supply chain in Southeast Asia.

Technology and Operations

Uber is the company that is everywhere, yet nowhere. Uber's operations have made it a part of our daily lives. Instead of saying, "why don't you catch a taxi?", we now say "why don't you Uber it?". Yet, no car carries large markers that spell out, "Uber." Uber's operational platform cleverly hides an Uber car, which could be any car on the road. Instead, Uber's operation is transparent. Both passengers and drivers are well aware of each other's exact location, although to the passerby, they are just cars and people. Combining such operational efficiencies quietly tucked away under cool technology, Uber's operations have single handedly upended more than a century-long taxi service and transportation monopoly. By leveraging data collection and even heat-mapping, Uber can deliver accurate information to both driver and passenger, to bring a better business experience for both. The end result is an "invisible" company that continues to shake up the entire industry from taxis to food delivery.

Mining oil and other natural elements doesn't seem like a high-tech job, but one mining company has changed that perception. BHP is an Australian-based mining company that extracts and processes not only oil, but also gas and minerals world wild. The Chief Technology Officer of BHP, Diane Jurgens, said that she had to find for the company to accommodate rapid international demand and growth as global population increased and the stand at of living rose for many countries. One way of solving these issues for the company was to implement more technology into its operations. One example is autonomous trucks that have the capacity to move 250 tons of material.

Another example is automated dills at many of the iron ore mines, which have increased productivity and cut down on maintenance costs. In addition, there has been a human advantage too, the drill operators no longer to be in the hot weather manning a dangerous piece of equipment, becoming fatigued or overworked. Now, the workers can monitor the autonomous drills from a safe and comfortable facility. Another example is BHP's use of lasers to load train cars, which helps the process be more cost effective and efficient. By incorporating more technology into the company's operations, BHP has been able to grow international, keep up with global demand, cut costs overall for the company, and keep the workers safer and more effective.

Did You Know That?

Microbial fuel cell (MFC) (branded as "Pee Power") technology converts urine into electricity. Microbial fuel cells use microbes that feed on urine to generate electrons, which can be collected as electricity, while the by-product can be used as a crop fertilizer!

Questions

Come up with two ways that a company can use SMARThook for other applications.

What is another interesting technological innovation that can be used to prevent poaching?

Think of a social issue or issues important to you or your community. How would you use technology to work towards a solution for the issue or issues?

What other technology would help solve the freshwater crisis around the world?

Can you come up with better ways to increase transparency for the food and drug supply chain?

Is AI the answer for the future of pharmaceutical industry? What might be some disadvantages to using AI in healthcare?

What other technology would improve the ability of internet hospitals to be more accessible to not only the people of China, but to people around the world?

What Is Strategic Analytics?

Analytics is all about using facts for decision-making. In the search for the best decisions, analytics applies the right tools and techniques to offer solutions and insights. For analytics to work, companies must realize the following:

Analytics must work toward creating competitive advantage for a company.
Analytics is more than crunching numbers. It's what corporations can learn from the past to prepare them for the future.
Analytics is a corporate activity, not a functional routine. Analytics requires corporate championship.

Analytics needs both strategic models as well as data models. Data models without strategic thinking make Analytics a short-term functional tactic; Strategic thinking without data models makes Analytics anecdotal and amorphous. Together, Analytics can use numbers to guide executive decision-making that aim into the future.

Analytics ROI (Return on Investment): Actionable Insights

It is important to realize that analytics is not statistics. Statistics, mainly statistical techniques, is just a part of analytics that is used to numerically validate answers to problems. *Statistics offers facts. Analytics offers insights.* Here are the differences between the popular numerical techniques used in business.

Analytics begins with **Data Mining**. Data mining is the stepping-stone toETL (Extract, Transform, Load). ETL includes Extracting data from databases, transforming data by cleaning and structuring data into a common format, and Loading the "clean" extracted and transformed data into data warehouses and data marts for further mining and BI. Data mining forms the basis for KDD (Knowledge Discovery in Databases) by extracting and structuring the data for econometric and statistical analyses. Data mining has become even more popular with **Big Data** representing massive amounts of data collected online through social media, at checkout counters, in healthcare and sciences for statistical investigation.

Statistics focuses on techniques and **Econometrics** uses statistics to solve economic problems. **Business Intelligence (BI)** moves a step further by finding and visualizing interesting patterns in existing data. Using data mining techniques, BI discovers patterns and often focuses on finding information from historical data useful for maintaining existing operations. **Strategic Analytics (CA)** *learns from the past but models for the future.* Competitive analytics builds upon BI. CA leverages knowledge gleaned from the past and focuses on the future through a combination of strategic and

© PiaDura LTD 2022
P. Datta, *Global Technology Management 4.0*,
https://doi.org/10.1007/978-3-030-96929-5_6

statistical/econometric models. The objective of competitive analytics is to offer insights using good KPI (Key Performance Indicator) metrics, appropriate strategic, operational, and statistical models.

As in Data Mining, Competitive analytics should follow Deming's (the father of Analytics-driven quality control) **PDCA (Plan-Do-Check-Act)** cycle:

Plan: Choose the appropriate model and metrics
Do: Choose the appropriate tools and techniques for analysis
Check: Benchmark. Compare actual with expected. Evaluate for feedback
Act: Decide on an appropriate course of action based on analytical insights

Cases and Articles

The 3Ms of Competitive Analytics

Competitive Analytics relies on 3Ms to solve various problems: Metrics, Models, and Mining.

Metrics are measures that offer "quantifiable" objective and specific assessments for a variable's behavior or performance. Finding and using the "correct" metric is extremely important. In order to find the correct metric, it is important to know what you are measuring? If you're unsure of what you're measuring (i.e., the measurement question), you're likely to choose the wrong metric and arrive at a number that does not offer the right information for decision-making.

Did You Know That?

In Douglas Adams' philosophical and satirical farce, A Hitchhiker's Guide to the Galaxy, human beings ask a supercomputer, Deep Thought, the ultimate question:

"What is the Answer to Life, the Universe and Everything?"

Deep Thought, after seven and a half million years of computation, arrives at an answer.

On the day of reckoning, billions of people crowd to hear the answer to the ultimate question. Deep Thought asks whether people are ready to hear the answer. To the anticipating crowd, Deep Thought says, "The answer to the ultimate question of life, the universe and everything is 42." The crowd thinks the answer is meaningless. In response, Deep Thought points out that the response appears meaningless because the "Ultimate Question" metric was meaningless, not the answer.

Moral of the tale: If you want to find a meaningful answer, choose the right metric for right question. Flawed Questions create Flawed answers or "garbage in, garbage out."

Models are abstract graphical or numerical representations of inter-relationships between organizational resources and relevant organizational outcomes. These models are a combination of soft and hard tools and techniques that logically depict and solve organizational problems. Models can denote economic, operational, and strategic solutions combining ESSO (environment (market), strategic, structure, and operations).

There are many different types of models. Decision models follow a decision logic and can use various strategic, operational processes, economic and statistical aspects to evaluate scenarios and problems and formulate solutions.

For example, SWOT (Strengths, Weaknesses, Opportunities, and Threats) is a strategic model to analyze a company's competitive position. Pareto Analysis analyzes how certain small operational changes can create large differences (based on the Pareto rule that 20% of issues create 80% of problems). Critical Path Model (CPM) Analysis is a process model to analyze interdependencies among processes and activities to prioritize activities. Similarly, Decision Trees model various If–Then processes based on various scenarios.

Mining is a process by which data is extracted, organized, and analyzed from large databases and market observations to reveal important insights. The success of data mining relies on choosing the right metrics and models as prerequisites to data mining. Data mining becomes useful when companies are proactive than reactive. With the rapid growth of computing and big data, a lot of data mining is becoming programmed as algorithms and integrated with machine learning.

However, mining requires you to understand and choose the right metrics and models for usable analytical ROI.

Good data mining can drive better recognition of hidden patterns, relationships, and predictive ability for competitive advantage. Logic, not technicality, is the central premise for successful data mining. Data mining can use sophisticated techniques. Some include Bayesian Belief Networks relating dependencies between random variables to find probabilities of an outcome based on conditional dependence on other factors; Influence diagrams to create decision models under uncertainty; Naive Bayes Classifiers for artificial intelligence in recognizing speech, text, and medical diagnostics; Artificial Neural Networks (ANNs) for pattern recognition with unknown and uncertain inputs and connections used in biometrics, among others. Although such techniques are beyond the scope of this book, an overview of analytical tools and techniques introduced in this text offers the stepping-stones for conducting preliminary but useful competitive analytics.

Metrics for Competitive Analytics

You can't check or improve anything unless you can measure it. Competitive Analytics must rely on the right metrics. A good choice of metrics that competitors ignore can provide key competitive advantages. *Such metrics can serve as key performance indicators (KPIs).* Therefore, choosing the correct metric has to be deliberate.

For example, China uses "# of real estate constructions" rather than "3 of houses sold" or "# of houses occupied" as a measure of real estate growth. This has created tremendous mismeasurement with ghost cities in Kangbashi, Dantu, Ordos, among many others. Similarly, a company that measures preferences of customers (buyers of a product or service, e.g., parents buying toys) vs. consumers (the actual users of the product or services, e.g., children playing with toys) can trigger mismeasurement.

Therefore, some important parameters for choosing metrics are as follows:

- Metrics should be reliable (be consistent over multiple tests) and valid (meaningful).
- Metrics should offer the best impact and improvement.
- Metrics should reflect the mission, vision, and values of the company.
- Metrics should be driven by measurable evidence.
- Metrics should be simple to collect and analyze.
- Metrics should have more than one dimension.
- Metrics should try to offer complete information. It is important to not use absolute values but consider ratios as metrics. For example, converting a fraction into a percentage creates a common floor or 0 and a ceiling of 100, therefore standardizing the data.
- Metrics should be assessed for changes over time.
- Metrics should be audible for accuracy and transparency.

Here is a sample of popular performance metrics in various functions and industries. If you look carefully, you will find that many of the popular metrics offer incomplete information (Table 6.1).

Exercise and Food for thought: Do these metrics provide a complete picture or do they provide incomplete information? Think of how you could make them better.

Table 6.1 Popular metrics across industries

Function	Popular metrics
Healthcare	Structural (ratio of physicians to admitted patients); Process (% of patients completing preventative or follow-up treatments); Outcome (Survival rate for cardiac arrests); Experience (Negative to positive feedback ratio); Lab turnaround time; Average ER waiting time; Average length of stay
Operations	Productivity (output/input); Yield (% of quality finished products from WIP (work in progress) without scrap or rework; % of Customer Returns; Throughput (# of completed products per time period); MTBF (Mean time between failure); Capacity utilization (capacity used/available capacity); Continuous improvement spending
Accounting	Return on Assets (Revenues/(Fixed Assets + Working Capital); Current Ratio (Current Assets/Current Liabilities); Inventory Turnover (Costs of Good Sold/Average Inventory); Net Profit; Gross Profit (Revenues − Costs of Goods Sold)
Finance	Earnings per Share (EPS) (Net Income/# of outstanding shares); Price-to-Earnings (P/E) (Market price per share/EPS); Dividend Yield (Dividend per share/Price per share); Interest Coverage Ratio (Earnings before interest and taxes/Interest expense); Debt to Equity (D/E) (Total liabilities/Total shareholder equity)
Human resources	Average Absence Rate (total number of absent days/total number of employees); # of vacancies filled; % of staff turnover per period; Change in demographic diversity between periods; % of staff operating above productivity level; Average workforce qualification
Marketing	Marketing ROI (Total Sales Revenues from Marketing/Total Marketing Expenditures); Customer Relationship Management (CRM) (% of retained customers); Market Growth Rate; Market Penetration Rate; Online marketing traffic; Sale-uplift (increase in sales/increase in marketing expenditure)
Technology and IT	% System Downtime; # of incident work orders; Average response time; Average resolution time; Program quality (# of errors per period/Total # of lines of code); % of backlog per request; Change Quality Index (Total Defects/Total Components Changed)
Project management	Schedule Variance; Cost Variance; Quality Variance; Cost Performance (cost overrun if < 1) (Earned Value (EV) (estimated budget consumed to date)/Actual Cost (AC)); Schedule performance (time overrun if < 1) (EV/PV(Predicted time value)); % over budget; Schedule Performance (completed on-time/total completed)

Who and What to Measure (Frame and Unit of Analysis)?

Searching for metrics can be daunting, and if not practiced cautiously, can create problems from mismeasurements and offer no **Analytic Return on Investment (ROI)**. The key is figuring out the subject (who and what) to observe and measure, also called the *Unit of Analysis*. Should you measure at the corporate level, functional level, the project/process level, the activity level, the task level, the group level, or at the individual level? The diagram above shows a structural breakdown in organizations from which you can choose your unit of analysis.

The *Corporate Unit* is made up of multiple industries (SIC (Standard Industry Classification) or NAICS (North American Industry Classification System) codes, span multiple geographical

markets (e.g., China, UK, USA) and have various divisions and Brands (e.g., HP has multiple divisions such as printers and computers; Mercedes has divisions such as vans, sedans; Toyota has brands such as Total and Lexus). *Each corporate unit is made up of multiple functions* such as Technology, Marketing, Finance. *Each Function runs multiple project processes and workflows* (sequence/steps toward delivering a product or service for the function). *Each Project Process/Workflow is made up of multiple activities. Each Activity can be broken down into multiple tasks. Each Task has one or more Task Group. Finally, each Task Group has individuals associated.* Your choice of Unit of Analysis should correspond to choosing appropriate KPIs as metrics. For example, it would be mismeasurement *if you chose the group as the Unit of*

Analysis but used Return on Equity (ROE) (a corporate KPI metric) for analyzing the group performance. Instead, Trust or Conflict Management may be a better group KPI metric.

Understanding Interdependencies Across Processes

Table 6.2 offers a matrix for you to show process interdependencies that can be useful when planning your metrics and KPIs (Key Performance Indicators). The reason is that, if you understand the interdependencies, you might have a better understanding of how your choice of metrics and units of analysis can influence other KPI metrics as you move higher or lower from the organization to the people or from the people to the organization level. *If the metrics are out of sync because you have not paid attention to the interdependencies, you might encounter unwanted resistance to change management or your analytics outcomes.*

Useful Analytics Terms

Market Basket Analysis is based on Correlation and Association Rules where analytics for a shopping basket or shopping cart can reveal what and how a customer purchases together to make future coupon and purchase predictions. Market Basket Analysis (MBA) is especially useful in CRM (Customer Relationship Management) Analytics, used to attract new customers and retain current customers.

Churn Analysis is a predictive modeling analysis that analyzes the probability and reasons for customer attrition, i.e., discontinuing and not repeating purchases. Customer churn is a measure of customer retention given that the cost of retaining an existing customer is considerably lower than attracting a new customer. Churn rate is calculated as the percentage of repeat customers per period. Churn analysis can explain specific customer traits, segments, and reasons for churn of future prevention and reduction in churn.

Payback Period is the *time* it takes to recoup an investment. *Payback Period = $ Invested/Periodic Cash Flows from Investment.* Payback Period is a quick analytical measure where a longer payback period is less acceptable.

Breakeven Analysis & Contribution Margin: Breakeven Analysis calculates the breakeven point as the number of items or services that need to be sold to balance the costs of producing the item or selling the service. Every operation has associated fixed costs and variable costs. **Fixed Costs** are the overheads (e.g., machines, facilities, employees) and Variable Costs are specific costs (e.g., labor, material, electricity for the item) for each item produced or service offered. *Breakeven Point or Quantity = Total Fixed Costs for the item or service / (Average Revenue per item or service − Average Variable Cost to produce each unit or to offer each service).* Because **Contribution Margin = Revenue − Variable Cost**, *Breakeven Point or Quantity = Total Fixed Costs for the item or service / Contribution Margin for item or service.*

Return on Investment (ROI) is the value (benefits − costs) of an investment based on the ratio of investment value and investment cost. ROI = (Total Investment Benefits − Total Investment Costs)/Total Investment Costs. A −ve ROI means a loss on an investment; A 0 ROI means an investment has been recouped. A +ve ROI is important for investment consideration.

Table 6.2 Interdependent process mapping

Process	Corresponding activities	Corresponding tasks	Resources in use (human, technology ...)
Innovation deployment	Design criteria	Component design	R&D scientists
		R&D signoff	IE engineer
	Feasibility analysis	Market analysis	Business unit executive
		Integration	VP of operations

An ROI of 1 (100%) means 2 times the return-on-investment dollars.

Net Present Value (NPV), Future Value (FV), and Time Value of Money are some of the most important analytical metrics. While Payback period simply looks at the time it takes to recoup an investment based on periodic cash flows, what is often missed is the value of money that changes over time. A cash flow of $1,000 today is not the same as a cash flow of $1,000 five years later. The value of money is reduced over time and $1,000 five years later is likely to be less valuable (because of inflation and the opportunity cost of investing money somewhere else for a return) than $1,000 today. NPV shows the value of an investment by incorporating future cash flows over multiple periods with a specific discount rate (rate at which money loses value − if no specific corporate discount rate is available, inflation rate or the yield on a treasury can serve as a proxy). NPV = Sum of all Future Cash Flows per Period $(C_t)/(1 + \text{Discount Rate } (r))^t$ − Present Investment (C_0) where it is a specific period. So, t = 5 for a cash flow 5 years later.

Schedule Performance Index (SPI) is a useful analytical metric for project budgeting. SPI measures project efficiency in terms of how much it is on schedule. SPI is calculated as a ratio of *Earned Value (i.e., % of work completed × total budgeted cost)/Planned Value (i.e., % of work completed based on time planned × total budgeted cost)*. So, if a project has a $60,000 budget to be completed in 10 months, after 3 months, 33% of the work should have been completed per schedule but 40% work has been completed with an actual cost of $40,000, the earned value is 40% × 60,000 = $24,000; the planned value is 33% × $60,000 = 20,000. *The Project SPI is Earned Value/Planned Value = 24,000/20,000 = 1.2 or 20% ahead of schedule.*

Gross Margin and Net Margin are analytical measures of corporate financial and accounting performance. **Gross Margin** is calculated as (Revenues − Costs of Goods or Services Sold)/Revenues. Gross margin measures how well a company manages its operations, production, and material costs. **Net Margin** is calculated as Net Income after Taxes/Revenues. Net margin measures how well a company manages its bottom-line profits with an eye on costs as well as expenses (e.g., salaries, administrative, marketing).

EVA (Economic Value Added) and MVA (Market Value Added) are useful financial and economic profit measures based on the return-on-investment capital and the cost of capital (often called WACC (weighted average cost of capital)) for the **Expected Value** (probability of occurrence or proportion in use × $ value). **EVA** *is calculated as Net Operating Profit after Taxes − (WACC × Invested Capital)*. **MVA** is calculated as the difference between the Market Value of the Firm − Capital Invested in the Firm.

Throughput, Cycle Time, and Takt Time are measures of operations and production efficiency. **Throughput** is a measure of production efficiency calculated as the number of units produced per period. **Cycle time** is the average time it takes to produce one good or service. **Takt time** is calculated as the available production time (subtracting breaks and idle time) for production per period/required units of production per period.

Probability Distribution shows the shape of a random variable based on its probability of occurrence. Some popular probability distributions include:

i. Normal (symmetric bell curve where most values are in the middle with a mean of 0 and standard deviation of 1 with examples such as customer and patient preferences, a person's height, and weight).

ii. Lognormal (asymmetric positively skewed distribution with few values below 0 such as pricing, stocks).

iii. Uniform (distribution with a minimum and maximum will all values having the same probability of occurrence such as revenues from an innovation).

iv. Triangular (distribution with a minimum and maximum being the two ends and the most likely being the vertex with examples such as the time to finish a project, time to receive a delivery).

Optimization is an extremely useful analytical technique for finding the optimal allocations required to achieve an objective (typically minimization or maximization of an objective) given various constraints. For example, a company may want to minimize the number of errors of defects by changing the number of quality control quality personnel at various points in the production and service delivery keeping in mind that there are budget and resources constraints. Optimization will create a best possible solution without sacrificing constraint issues.

Monte Carlo Simulation is a type of **Scenario Analysis** technique that uses random samples to create multiple solutions for what-if scenarios where there is uncertainty about possible choices. Monte Carlo simulation uses multiple random values chosen from a probability distribution (e.g., Normal, Uniform) with thousands of calculation iterations to show multiple outcomes for multiple scenarios ranging from least likely to most likely.

Neural Nets or Artificial Neural Networks (ANN) is an analytical technique modeled after the nervous system and neurons. A typical ANN has three or more neural layers: one or more input layers, one output layer, and one or more hidden layers that learn from the observed data but assigning different inputs different weights to offer optimal outputs. Neural nets are often used to find hidden patterns that explain outcomes and provide solutions including biometrics and cancer detection.

Strategy Models in Analytics

SWOT Analysis (Strengths, Weaknesses, Opportunities, Threats)

SWOT stands for Strengths, Weaknesses, Opportunities, and Threats. Strengths and Weaknesses are internal characteristics of a company. Opportunities and Threats are external to the company, often underpinned by the environments including regulation, competition, and the market.

It is important to ensure that we use SWOT for Product-line based industry analysis rather than using SWOT for the corporation. *Note that the old adage of using SWOT for corporate analysis within an industry no longer holds.* Today, innovation is driving companies to diversify rapidly and being listed across multiple industry classifications and categories. For companies that are marked across multiple industry-NAICS codes, (for example, Apple, Sony, Siemens), a corporate SWOT will create a misspecification. For example, Apple's iPhone belongs to a different industry (mobile phones) category compared to its Mac OS (Operating System) (software industry) or its iTunes (Media). *Rapid acquisitions and diversification have led to tremendous industry overlap where the days for single-industry classifications for companies are speedily waning. It's more prudent to analyze strategy based on product lines (also called line-of-business – analogous to product category) than on a single industry.*

Porter's Five Forces Analysis

Porter's Five Forces is a popular and useful strategy analysis technique. Porter's 5 Forces is particularly useful in periodically auditing a company's market position *based on individual product lines*. Assessing and analyzing changes in the market can have tremendous impacts upon the product-line and industry standing of a company. A change in the market can be a boon or bane for a company's product-line SWOT. Here are some examples:

Threat of New Entrants and Barriers to Entry: An attractive product line is an invitation for competition. If large profits are to me made in a high-growth product-line segment, more competitors will flock in to get a piece of the pie. Established companies in specific product categories (e.g., cable companies, print media) want to increase barriers to entry of new companies in that product line to reduce threats of entry. Newer firms (e.g., wireless fiber broadband such as Google, blogs, and social media), often because of a specific technological innovation, instead want lower barriers to entry to increase threats to incumbent firms. To increase barriers to entry and threaten newer entrants, companies will often try to acquire competitors. Governments will often use anti-monopoly regulation such as antitrust laws.

Threat of Substitutes: Product lines that are *sensitive to pricing or consumer preferences* have high threats of substitutes. Companies try to reduce buyers *switching* from their products to another substitute by differentiating their products and services to "*lock-in*" buyers. For example, in April 2015, Apple TV media player partnered with HBO to offer a monthly subscription-based cable service for its users to differentiate Apple TV from other media players such as Google Chromecast, Roku, Amazon Fire TV. Similarly, **Amazon** combined its Amazon Prime media with free 2-day Amazon Prime shipping along with specific amazon.com shows to differentiate itself from Netflix. *Note: More entrants from fewer barriers to entry can increase threats of substitutes.*

Buyer Power: Buyers (or clients) can exert low or high power over producers and vendors. For example, because Walmart does large volumes purchases, it can exert a lot of price pressure on manufacturers and suppliers. Buyer power can increase price competition, quality, and differentiation. Producers/manufacturers and vendors can try to reduce buyer power by increasing buyer dependency (e.g., Facebook) and raising costs of choosing substitutes (such as amazon. com with its Prime 2-day shipping and free returns). *Note: More new entrants and more substitutes can increase buyer power.*

Supplier Power: Suppliers, vendors, producers, and manufacturers can have low or high power over buyers and clients. For example, Russia's control of petroleum allows it to exert tremendous supplier power over Eastern and parts of Western Europe. Similarly, in 2014, OPEC (Oil Producing and Exporting Countries) increased its oil production and supply to out-compete shale-gas producers in the US as well as curtail Russian revenues from their over dependence on petroleum sales. Suppliers try to increase their power

through lock-ins and monopolizing their products and service. Buyers try to curtail supplier power by threatening suppliers with substitutes such as alternative energy choices to reduce petroleum dependency.

Competitive Rivalry: Competitive rivalry refers to levels of competitive intensity for a product line or service. Companies use strategies such as innovation, marketing, and pricing to reduce competitive rivalry while lower barriers and supplier power and higher buyer power and number of substitutes can increase competitive rivalry.

Gap Analysis

Gap Analysis is a simple but effective periodic analytical tool to assess strategic performance and financial returns from various strategic and project initiatives and assessments. In gap analysis, the gap refers to the difference between actual and expected performance across one or more metrics for specific assessments. If actual performance is equal to or greater than expected performance, there is no gap. A gap exists when actual performance falls short of expected performance. *Note: Once a gap is found, it might be analytically useful to trace the reasons for the gap using Root-Cause Analysis.*

Root-Cause Analysis

The Root-Cause (Ishikawa) analysis technique, also called a Fishbone diagram, is possibly one of the most important operational analytics tools started as a part of *Kaizen* (continuous improvement). Root-Cause Analysis is an excellent strategic analysis tool for an in-depth depiction and assessment of any outcome or effect. It starts with deciding on what outcome we need to assess. Next, decide on the major causes. These categories can be as general or specific as we want. For example, suppose a company finds that the actual number of product returns (outcome) is more expected. This increase in product returns is a gap. There may be several causes for the gap, e.g., people (involved in the production, distribution, and fulfillment), processes (methods and steps involved), policies (procedures involved), and technology (equipment and systems). Now, drill deeper. Treat every cause as an effect and find the causes. For example, if people involved in managing and handling the product or even using the product may be a cause, what caused people problems—lack of training, lack of motivation, unclear user manuals? *Note: You can drill down as many levels you want as long as you have good measures for each cause. You will find that as you drill deeper, you will find common causes. These common causes are the root causes that impact your outcome.*

McKinsey 7s

McKinsey 7s is a strategy analysis tool for organizational performance and effectiveness. The 7s are divided into two categories of hard and soft elements. Strategy, Structure, and Systems are hard elements. Shared values, skills, style, and staff are soft elements.

Hard Elements:

Strategy (mission, market environment, competition, customers)
Structure (hierarchy, functions, coordination, communication, centralization/decentralization)
Systems (Technical, HR, Financial systems, controls, and audit processes)

Soft Elements:

Shared Values (culture, beliefs, perspectives, mission)
Style (leadership, supervision, board composition, project teams)
Staff (level of specialization, contract vs. full-time, position and promotions)
Skills (mission-critical skills, skills gap, rewards, and remuneration)

Note: The 7s analysis can be used to create the initial list of causes in a Root-Cause analysis.

Market Segmentation Analysis

Markets are getting more and more fragmented every day. **Market fragmentation** happens when newer market segments (categories) are created because of small differences in tastes (preferences), geography, demographics, and behaviors. More fragmentation creates more segments. More segments require more differentiation. Products such as salt, once thought of as a commodity that required no differentiation, is getting fragmented into iodized/non-iodized salt, kosher salt, Himalayan salt, cooking salt, table salt, mineral salt, herbal salt, spiced salts, etc. Companies will differentiate what to offer based on the market segment.

Today, companies face hyper-segmentation with thousands of **customer segments** based on preferences, demographics, and behaviors. Geographically, there are segments based on geographical areas and sub-segments based on specific regions and cities. In the US, New England is different from Boston and New York City; New York City is different from Manhattan. New England is different from the Midwest which is different from Chicago. The Midwest is different from the Pacific Northwest which is different from the West. The West is different from the South and the South is different from the Southeast. Austin, Texas, a university town in the southwest is quite different with its art and hipster bars and innovation enclaves from the rest of Texas with a more western, blue collar lifestyle. Italy has multiple segments, from the science and innovation-driven areas by Milan to the laid-back Piedmont and Ligurian areas to the more artistic areas of Rome to the more provincial areas of Puglia and Napoli. In the UK, the Midlands is quite different from Essex or Sussex or Cornwall, notwithstanding the different segmentations originating from Wales, Scotland, England, or Northern Ireland. In China, Shanghai in the east is vastly different from Beijing in the north and Xian in Shaanxi province to the West. Shaanxi is different from the shipping areas of Dalian in the northeast and packed commercial areas of Guangdong province in the Southeast.

Demographic segmentations can be based on rural/urban, income, gender, etc. There are Libertarians (social liberals but fiscally conservatives), Yuppy (Young, Urban, Progressive, Prosperous, Young), DINKS (Double Income No Kids), GLAM (Grayed, Leisured, and Moneyed), Empty Nesters, etc.

Behavioral Segments are based on psychological and behavioral preferences in the market. They include Tech-Savvy vs. Luddites (non-tech), early vs late adopters, price-conscious, quality-conscious, time-poor (lacking enough time outside work), social influencers, among others.

Integrating Strategic Analytics

Combine Porter's Five Forces and PEST modeling to analytically link how Porters 5 forces and PEST can impact a company's SWOT. Porter's 5 Forces and PEST, both strategic analysis of the product line, industry, and market, can significantly affect a company's strengths, weaknesses, opportunities, and threats. Various industry, competitive and market shifts can trigger opportunities and threats and how opportunities and threats can turn strengths to weaknesses and weaknesses to strengths. In order to reduce weaknesses, add to their strengths, exploit opportunities, and mitigate threats, companies must perform periodic audits analyzing the performance of each aspect of SWOT (e.g., strength from increasing operational cash flow, weakness from too many product returns, opportunities from dropping interest rates, threats from increasing supply chain costs). The periodic audit can be done using Gap Analysis. Once a gap has been identified, the McKinsey 7s can provide a stepping-stone for assessing the causes for the gaps (e.g., Systems, Staff…). Finally, we can use Root-Cause Analysis to lay the groundwork for a numerical model linking outcomes and causes (Figs. 6.1 and 6.2).

Strategic Human Resources Analytics

Strategic human resources or human capital is another important part of assessing organizational performance. Every *resource has dimensions*: each resource (i) has a purpose, (ii) is measured using performance metrics (iii) is a part of a process, and (iv) follows organizational policies.

Companies like Ritz Carlton and T-Rowe Price make managers combine customer service "key success factor" metrics to strategically and analytically explain and appraise resource allocation choices, operational dependencies, and technology-human combinations for optimal performance analysis and analytical prediction of future performance (Fig. 6.3).

Allocating Humans as Strategic Resources is an imperative. Effective employees are a scarce resource. This is a fundamental business puzzle. We have unlimited wants, but we have to deal with limited resources. Because of limited, scarce resources, we always have to economize on our business decisions. And guess what, the Human element is the scarcest resource in the organization. Why? Mainly because a machine or a system can be produced and duplicated to exactly the same specifications at will. However, you cannot duplicate a human element. Developing the human element to replace another takes considerable cost, effort without any sureties of success.

Every economic decision must be done to allocate resources efficiently. To meet unlimited wants, businesses need unlimited resources. Alas! That's impossible. Every resource is a cost and you simply can't use unlimited resources. Therefore, businesses have to tighten their belts, bite the bullet, and decide on which resource to invest in as well as which resource to use at various times and for various purposes. This is the law of resource scarcity.

As we mentioned, because resources are scarce, we have to use them diligently and not with wanton abandon. This is called **resource allocation**. Therefore, businesses have to consider the need for resource allocation. A right resource at the wrong time can prove ineffective, costing you money but not delivering the value. Consider the legend, Babe Ruth. He was an excellent resource as a hitter and a pitcher, but slightly better as a hitter than a pitcher. Because Babe Ruth is a scarce resource, he had to be

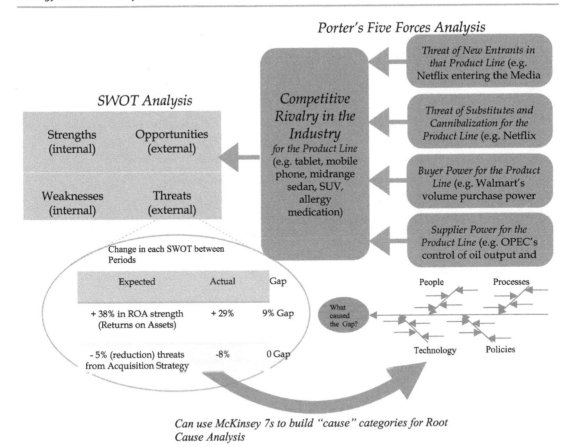

Fig. 6.1 Tying together strategic models for decision-making

allocated to best serve the team. If he was to be misallocated and asked to pitch more than bat, he would wear out prior to his batting and the team would lose. "He was better than most other pitchers, but he was much better than most other hitters, especially when it came to hitting home runs. That's why he played in the outfield and batted in the line-up every day, instead of pitching every 4 or 5 games." This is an example of resource allocation.

Another aspect of allocating scarce resources is not just who to allocate but when and how to allocate. "When making up the line-up, a good manager will lead off with the player who has the highest on-base percentage and is fast enough to steal bases. The third batter is usually the team's best all-around hitter. The fourth hitter is a slugger. He may not have a high batting average, but he often hits the ball over the fence for a

home run. Home runs are more efficient when the1st, 2nd, and/or 3rd hitters are already on base. The weakest hitter bats near the end of the line-up. That way they don't bat as often as the others." (http://www.sonic.net/~schuelke/Baseball_USvsCuba.htm).

Therefore, to manage human resources, we have thought of managing human capital as a resource that has cost and benefits and learn to make the most out of measuring and managing it with diligently. But what is the best way to allocate HR assets? The answer is simple when following these steps (Fig. 6.4).

Begin by defining a work process. Keep the work process short. Begin by drawing out the steps in a process.

In viewing Human Resources as Human Capital Assets, you might ask: All right, if human elements are the scarcest of resources,

Fig. 6.2 Steps in analytical decision-making

why companies have downside and fire/sack their human capital? While we will discuss issues of downsizing later, it's useful to understand differences between resources and assets.

Human capital is a scarce resource that can maintain its usefulness only when it's an asset.

According to the IFRS (International Financial Reporting Standards), an **asset** is a resource controlled by the enterprise as a result of past events and from which future economic benefits are expected to flow to the enterprise. For human capital to transform itself from a resource to an asset, human capital has to consistently provide economic returns and benefits to the company. But we know that already. Companies are constantly gauging employees from recruitment to retirement. They create performance reviews and appraisals to ensure that the human resource is an asset providing a consistent and measurable return every period.

If hiring human capital is an investment, there has to be a **return-on-investment (ROI)** to designate the human capital as an asset. But how do you gauge returns from human capital?

Just like an asset we invest in, ROI for human capital is the present value of all future value offered by the specific human capital asset. So, what's value? **Value** is nothing but the difference between benefits derived from an asset minus its costs. So, if a company is paying you $10,000 per month (the cost of employing you as a human capital asset), the company needs to ensure that your benefit to the company is greater than $10,000 per month.

A problem with Human Capital Assets is that, unlike other capital assets, human capital does not depreciate but appreciates over time. Here is an example. A machine (including a robot) is used to complete routine tasks with tremendous efficiency. From a cost perspective, these assets can be depreciated to the end of a useful period. This means that the value of a machine or a building as an asset decreases over time. However, it is not so with Human Capital Assets.

Fig. 6.3 A 360-degree view
of the human element in
companies

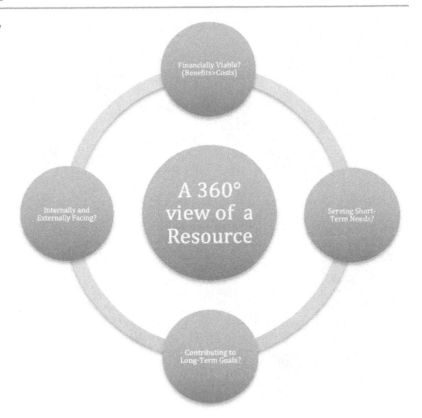

Human capital assets can be trained, and they can learn better than any other company asset. But this training takes place at the company expense. Suppose a company spends tens of thousands training you in a highly valuable area. For the company to receive positive value from this training cost they've gone through, the company might need you to collaborate with them for the next three years. However, once you've received this training, you might find another company, a competitor, willing to pay you more than what you're getting (note that they will be saving on the training costs because you're already trained). Suddenly, your present company might find itself in a fix. To retain you would mean paying you more, notwithstanding the training costs they've already undertaken. Thus, because human capital can learn, evolve, and adapt, they can turn themselves into assets with better and better prospects and income over time.

On the other hand, human capital that remains as a resource and fails to transform itself into an asset is always at the mercy of time or the environment. Consider Detroit, the heart of the American Auto Industry. Once, just having a high school degree provided a factory job and training in this thriving city. There was no motivation for a resource to become an asset. Unions promised that jobs would always stay there. Suddenly, a high-school graduate would join and remain as a stamper or a machinist for his/her whole life. There was no motivation to learn more to adapt and evolve. This created a skills gap as competition changed and profits got squeezed. Sadly, when the economy went south in 2008 and companies scrambled to save every penny, routine skills could not be replaced with robotics or simply outsourced to another country with lower labor costs. *Failure of a resource to translate itself into an asset that can learn to adapt and change with the times will be perceived by a company as not adding positive value over time, making the human capital resource replaceable.*

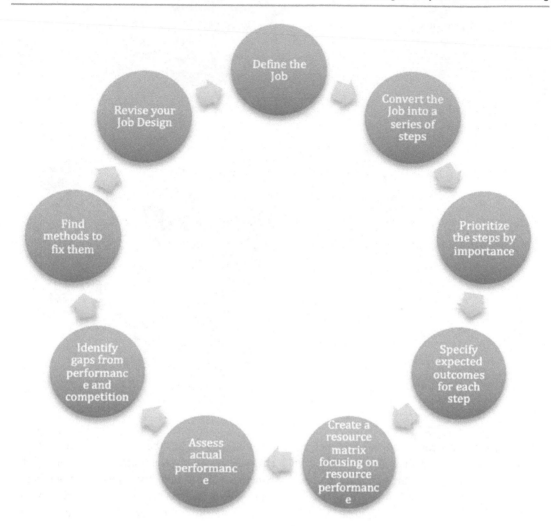

Fig. 6.4 A guide to resource allocation in companies

Strategic Positioning

Faced with a variety of internal strengths and weaknesses and external opportunities and threats, constantly negotiating with suppliers, catching up with competitors, enticing buyers, keeping an eye out for new entrants, and differentiating services and products, countries and companies focus on a positioning strategy. Positioning is how a company or country wants its customers and other countries around the world to perceive it and what it offers.

In a global world, countries are as competitive as brands. The reason why presidents, premiers and heads-of-state are constantly traveling is to strategically position their countries to create a positive perception. A positive perception can warm other countries and companies to come and invest in the country, buy products from the country, and create strategic partnerships for mutual benefits. Just think about how you perceive a country (of course, with considerable variance based on your own education and experiences; this is a sample snapshot from asking multiple people across 11 different countries): US positions itself as powerful and innovative; Saudi Arabia, lavish oil wealth and religious; Iran, belligerent and repressive; India, poor and traditional; UK, sophisticated and advanced; Japan, polite and technological; France, cultural and romantic; Italy, artistic and provincial; China, industrious and communal, etc.

Companies operate on remarkably similar principles. Apple positions itself as stylish and innovative; Toyota, affordable and reliable; LG, smart and fun; Siemens, well-engineered and industrial; Bose, sophisticated and cool; BMW, quick and edgy; Rolls Royce, imperious and conservative; Alfa-Romeo, fast and fashionable; Google, smart and free; Amazon, huge and fast; etc. In order to maintain competitive advantage, companies consider various types of positioning: **Market positioning** is the perception a company wants its consumers to have about its product and the overall brand. For example, in late 1990s, Dell, an emerging computer manufacturer, positioned itself in the market as the brand that allowed customers to customize their computers by choosing a mix of high-performance computer components that **Dell** would assemble and ship to the customer. Dell's market position is dealt with empowering the customer the ability to customize and build their own computers with personalized customer service at a time when larger rival companies sold pre-configured computers in a box.

Dell's market positioning was based on **product differentiation**. Once other competitors like Acer capitalized on Dell's niche differentiation and also entered the market with customizable computers, they eroded Dell's market position and threatened Dell's competitive advantage. Competitive advantage is one or more ways by which companies try to protect and sustain their market position from eroding to rival companies. Dell, rather than innovating more on product and service differentiation, decided to build more affordable, cheaper computers, sacrificing quality and service. This led to **Brand Dilution**, where a brand's high market position is threatened because customers no longer feel that the brand offers the same level of product and service quality. Dell's market position was diluted and felt in disfavor.

For example, if Burberry or Prada were to start selling at Target or Carrefour or cheapen the quality of their materials and design, they might be diluting their brand. Apple products are often a sign of elegance and high differentiation. It took Apple several years before deciding to sell Apple products at Walmart, whose market positioning is based on **price differentiation** with inexpensive, affordable products with "rollback prices" in a warehouse setting.

Often brands will create new product lines to maintain product differentiation and avoid brand dilution. Burberry's market positioning differentiated its own product lines with the high-end Burberry Prorsum (Latin for "forward"), the classic Burberry London, and the casual Burberry Brit. Toyota, known for its reliable but affordable cars, created Lexus as a new product line for a luxury car market positioning strategy. Honda created Acura, Nissan Infiniti, and Chrysler Cadillac.

Product Positioning is a strategy where companies use product and service features rather than customer perceptions to differentiate themselves. Companies often practice product positioning based on their core competencies. A **core competency** relates to what a company does best. Amazon.com's Amazon Prime positions itself with a free same-day and 2-day delivery. Google's product positioning is based on search and integrating search into other products such as Google Maps, Google Home, etc.

Dell's product positioning is based on the choosing the right set of customizable computer components for best performance, speedy assembly, and delivery. Toyota's product positioning is its world-famous Toyota Production System (TPS) that uses a number of best practices to build some of the most reliable cars with very few defects.

Think of Apple's vs. Microsoft's product positioning strategy. Apple Mac's product positioning is built on user experience and control of hardware, software, and suppliers that form its ecosystem. Apple Mac OS (operating system) requires stringent quality control. Only Apple builds Macs. No other company is allowed to use computer hardware to run Mac OS. Apple scrupulously checks and verifies every 3rd party software that runs on a Mac for compatibility. Apple Macs were rarely found in the international arena, especially in developing countries lacking finances to purchase Apple Mac computers for $1,000 or higher.

Microsoft PC's product positioning was based on creating features that could be installed by any supplier across any international ecosystem. Microsoft's Windows OS could be installed on any PC that anyone wanted to build across the world. Microsoft did not require checking for compatibility, quality of the hardware, or anything else. Microsoft PCs are often sold for a tenth of the price of an Apple Mac. This made Microsoft PC's running Windows the most popular computing device in the world. On the other hand, Microsoft's product positioning that allowed Windows OS to run with incompatible hardware and software with little quality control resulting in Microsoft Windows OS tarnished by the disparaging term "blue screen of death."

However, Apple devised a clever strategy to combat Microsoft PC's popularity using a combination of market positioning and product positioning. For a long time, Apple used Motorola Power PC chips to run its computers. However, Windows PCs used an IBM $\times$ 86 architecture, supported by Intel Chips. Realizing that even Mac OS users needed to run software that ran only on Windows OS, Apple terminated its relationship with Motorola. Instead of using Motorola Power PC chips that it had since its inception, Apple redesigned its computer architecture and switched to Intel chips for its Mac computers. Today, Mac computers can dual boot (run two different OS) both Mac OS as well as Windows OS.

Channel Positioning is a strategy where companies choose the right market channel (i.e., the way and place by which a product or service is sold or fulfilled). Every product or service has a channel. A channel can be the medium, such as physical or digital, as well as the place, such as the specific store. Higher end perfumes such as Aqua di Parma often chooses Barney's New York as their channel position.

Even expensive fashion companies like Versace and Balmain occasionally use H&M (a Swedish fast fashion company known for affordable clothing with fast-changing styles— hence, fast fashion) as a channel to increase their visibility to a younger client base. There are online financial, banks, and investments firms, also called **FinTech** (Financial Technology) such as Capital One (banking) and Betterment (investment) in the US, M-Pesa in Kenya (money transfer), and Alipay (payment transaction) in China. On the other hand, companies like Chase Bank and Morgan Stanley in the US, Bank of Kenya, and Industrial and Construction Bank of China (ICBC) primarily use physical channel positioning. These companies only offer online channels.

Acquisitions

Some are more interesting. Amazon.com's channel positioning is essentially digital. If you want to purchase something from Amazon, you can't go to a store and pick it up. You have to order it online and have it delivered. Amazon, however, revised its channel positioning strategy when it purchased Whole Foods, an upper end grocery in the US. Amazon's Whole Foods acquisition was an example of changing Amazon's channel footprint from purely digital to a mix of physical and digital channels. Amazon now has Amazon Lockers in Whole Foods stores where Amazon.com customers can get their orders delivered for pickup while shopping for groceries at Whole Foods. Groceries are perishable, making online deliveries difficult. So, shoppers that visit Whole Foods to shop for groceries can now pick up their Amazon purchases. On the other hand, shoppers that have ordered Amazon.com purchases can visit Whole Foods to pick up their products and while there, they can get some grocery shopping done at the store. This is **Hybrid Channel Positioning**, where a company's channel position is a mix of online and offline channel choices.

In recent years, **omni-channeling** is emerging a new channel positioning strategy. Omni-channeling is a channel positioning strategy where companies try to combine inventory across physical stores and online warehouses to make sure that a customer finds what he or she is looking for. You step into a store and search for a shoe style and size. You might like the style, but the store might not carry your size. Instead of losing a sale, omni-channeling will have the salesperson immediately find another store or the company warehouse that carries the right combination of size and style.

Omni-channeling allows every store to view inventory across all other stores. Suppose the store finds the right combination in another store's inventory. The customer's store will place the order. The employee in the store carrying the inventory will receive the order via the store's computer system and will immediately ship the order from the store. Omni-channels merge inventory across physical and digital channels so that an online order can be fulfilled by an offline store or warehouse and an order at a store can be transferred digitally for fulfillment by another store or warehouse. Every store is a sales point as well a warehouse for fulfilling orders.

Strategic Audit

An **audit** is a way by which companies monitor and review their various activities and functions. A financial audit is the monitoring and reviewing of a company's financial statements. An operational audit is the monitoring and reviewing of a company's operations. A strategic audit is the monitoring and reviewing of a company's strategy.

Companies evolve with time. Markets, competition, customers all keep changing. A company needs to evolve in line with changing times so as to not fall behind. This means that companies need to revisit and revise their strategies to stay ahead of the competition and evolving market needs.

Strategic audits have multiple facets. They are:

Customer Audit: Companies want their customers to be barnacles—loyal, stable, and unswayable. Sadly, customers are butterflies, constantly changing preferences and loyalties to search for the best value for their money. The customer base is always changing, and companies know that it costs 6 times more to acquire a new customer than it is to try and retain an existing customer. Amazon.com therefore relies on analyzing its massive amounts of customer purchasing data to predict how its customer preferences are changing. Amazon.com can use predictive analytics to predict customer purchases more than a year in advance, constantly revising its analytical models to accommodate for changes in purchasing behaviors. Companies such as Sears in the US, once market giants, failed to audit their customers' purchasing changes. Sears kept focusing on large physical stores when its customers were purchasing more and more online, thus falling prey to its customers' changing preferences. Sears filed for bankruptcy protection in 2018. A slew of newspapers went out of business or were bought for dimes on the dollar because they had failed to audit their customer evolution from reading cumbersome physical newspapers once or twice a day to digital news snippets in real time. The growth of digital media spelled demise for a lot of newspaper companies.

Competitor Audit: Competitor audit refers to periodically monitoring and reviewing competitors. In a technology-driven age of international business and globalization, competitors can emerge out of anywhere. Taxi services have long been either a monopoly (where one company controls the market such as the Yellow Cab or the London Cab) or an Oligopoly (where a handful of companies control the market). Taxi services created high barriers to entry, requiring expensive taxi licenses and permits (sometimes called medallions) to deter other competitors. While these taxi services focused on other large fleet owners as their primary competitors, they missed on technology-driven companies like Uber and Lyft that used a platform model to create newfound competition.

Rather than owning a fleet of cars and drowning in the fixed costs of ownership, maintenance, and upkeep, Uber and Lyft built a crowdsourcing platform for rides. **Crowdsourcing** is a way by which companies use the general public to offer resources and in turn, get paid for their services. Uber and Lyft, instead of owning taxis, have created a technology platform where interested car owners can sign up and offer rides to passengers for a fee. Uber and Lyft provide a transparent platform where rides can be availed quickly, and fares are affordable. Uber and Lyft blindsided established taxi services and have upended taxi services not only in multiple cities but also in multiple countries.

Context and Market Audit: Market audit refers to monitoring the changing market and revising existing strategy to respond accordingly. President Barack Obama was able to sense that the changing voter market in 2008 was much more attuned to social media as the platform for engaging and rallying voters. President Donald Trump sensed the changing economic agitation and maladies of the white middle class and he used Twitter to empower his voter base. Both were successful in their efforts in securing the US presidency. Japan and Germany are experiencing a rapidly aging population with decreased birth rates and new companies such as Senior Living communities and Charity Trusts (for bequeathing estates) have opened to capitalize on these market shifts.

GM's Dilemma: A Strategic Audit

General Motors (GM), one of the largest car manufacturers in the world, announced the closure of multiple plants in the US and laid off 14,000 workers in January 2019. Perhaps, GM's case of massive layoffs reflects a strategic market audit. The world of automobiles is dreadfully competitive. There are too many car companies in the market offering too many car models around the world. Yet, markets are evolving, and a confluence of events may have shaped GM's strategic choice. GM's official excuse was weak sedan and electric car sales in the US. Of course, cheaper oil prices in the market will always drive consumer demand for larger vehicles such as SUVs and Pickup trucks. And oil at around $60 a barrel is cheap. But GM's audit of the international market may have played a more important role.

China quite fancies GM. Of course, China's first love has been Volkswagen, mainly because

Volkswagen was the very first foreign auto company China invited after its 1980's market liberalization under Deng Xiao Peng. Since then, China has become a global automotive manufacturing base. However, GM cars have become one of the more popular brands among Chinese customers. In fact, GM's Chinese market is much more profitable than its US market and GM extensively uses its China R&D center to design a variety of GM models.

As Chinese income grew, so did its appetite for cars. But prosperity comes at a cost. With Chinese factories spewing smoke to satiate worldwide appetite for cheaper goods, pollution is severe. It has been more than a decade or so that the major Chinese cities have seen blue skies. The air is heavy with smog from pollution particulates and Beijing, China's Capital city, will occasionally suffer from such terrible air quality that it will ask its residents to stay indoors to avoid breathing in the smog. Adding more cars on to the road would simply amplify pollution.

So, China came up with a strategy. In 2016, China announced that China would like to invest in electric cars and become a global leader in the electric car market. In that vision, GM would be one of the main beneficiaries. China asked GM to build its next generation of Electric Cars. Just the way China has cornered the global solar panel market, China wants to be the world's "Electric Car Central."

But being the world's electric car central is not an easy feat. Electric cars need massive battery (energy storage) innovations and large-scale precision electronics and engineering. China knew that it had to build these ancillary capabilities as a pre-requisite. So, China strategically approached its ambitions using a multi-pronged approach.

First, China decided to build a presence in Africa, a continent known for its natural resources, especially rare-earth elements such as lanthanides and actinides (the bits you see at the bottom of your periodic table in Chemistry). These rare earth elements that are sought after for their conduction properties. China has rapidly built a presence in Africa, purchasing mining rights, offering obligation free loans to tin-pot dictatorships, maintaining a blind eye toward human rights abuses, while building road and rail infrastructures to streamline its supply chain. It's not uncommon to find and correlate metaled roads and highways in Africa to Chinese investments.

Second, China recently invited Tesla, the world's foremost electric car and energy storage company, to build its next generation Gigafactory, Tesla's battery and energy storage division. We might safely suppose that China is likely to offer Tesla Gigafactory special benefits. One important benefit is China's control and supply of the rare earth metals required for precision electronics to Tesla at subsidized rates. Second, China might offer Tesla large tax subsidies to sweeten the deal. And that could set China's market ambitions to become the world's "Electric Car Central" in motion.

Let's return to GM. GM is wildly in the throes of competition. GM's US customers expect special deals such as employee pricing even when margins are incredibly low. GM's US electric car initiative called GM Cruze received disappointing interest in the US because of low gasoline prices and demand for larger vehicles. But GM realizes that, in China, the tribulations of competition may not be that high.

The Chinese government's patronage is likely to give GM the sales boost with mandated government-wide electric car adoption. In addition, the Chinese government may sweeten the deal by offering GM preferential pricing on electronic component supplies for its electric cars as well as a way to access Tesla's Gigafactory batteries. Tesla has positioned itself to become not only the world's electric super car manufacturer but also the predominant supplier of energy storage for cars, homes, and businesses. That means that Tesla would be the most likely battery supplier for GM electric cars being built in China under Chinese government patronage. GM's market audit might have simply reinstated the new operational norm: **Build Local, Sell Local.** China offers a captive market as well as the value network of electronic components and battery technology required to manufacture electric cars.

Total Costs of Ownership (TCO) in International Markets

If you were to purchase real estate property at a purchase price of $500,000 and you used it for 5 years, how much is your **total cost of ownership (TCO)**? TCO is one of the most important business analysis philosophies that looks at the true cost of ownership rather than the initial purchase cost. *Every investment or cost decision a company makes must be based on the total cost, not the base or initial cost.*

The $500,000 property purchase price will add on closing costs (assume 2% of property price) of $10,000, another 2% (assumedly) property taxes amounting to $5,000 per year, insurance of $1,000 per year, and maintenance and upkeep costs of $3,000 per year. After 5 years, the investor sells the property for $550,000 with a 5% sales commission cost. Owning the property rather than renting saves $30,000 in rent per year. So, how much is the property owner's TCO?

One quick guess is by simply calculating the total costs and sales. That includes:

Costs: $500,000 purchase + $10,000 closing + $5,000 property taxes × 5 years ($30,000) + $1,000 insurance × 5 years ($5,000) + $3,000 upkeep × 5 years ($15,000) + $550,000 × 0.05 (5% commission). Total costs amount to $500,000 + $87,500 = $587,500. Total revenues amount to $550,000 after 5 years + $30,000 5 years ($150,000) = $700,000. The basic calculation would subtract $587,500 from $700,000 showing a TCO of $112,500.

While this calculation is generally acceptable, there is an inherent problem. The value of money drops over time. This is **inflation** or the change in the **Consumer Price Index (CPI)**. The way inflation is calculated is by first creating a basket of essential food items people need for basic living. The basket typically contains one dairy item such as cheese or milk, one staple such as rice or wheat, one vegetable item, one meat item, etc. Countries will measure the price of this item combination each period and measure the change in prices. The change in CPI is called inflation. Of course, countries want a little bit of inflation. Why? Some inflation is good because the fear of rising prices will prompt customers to purchase now rather than purchase later. Think of it. If you felt that house prices are likely to remain the same or fall, would you purchase a house now or wait? When you delay purchases, consumption and investments fall and the economy starts to sputter. So, some inflation (typically around 2%) is good. Anything more starts creating hardships because affording things get more and more difficult (Fig. 7.1).

Let's try out inflation as a concept to understand its importance. Assume inflation is at 4% per year and your income/salary growth is at 2% per year. Inflation is overtaking your income rise by 2% every year which means that your living costs are going up by 2% every year. That also means your **standard of living** is falling by 2%

© PiaDura LTD 2022
P. Datta, *Global Technology Management 4.0*,
https://doi.org/10.1007/978-3-030-96929-5_7

Fig. 7.1 The value of money over time

every year, year after year. Look at the chart to see the impact of inflation surpassing income rises on your standard of living. At that rate, it will merely take 25 years for your standard of living to drop by half. That means you will be able to afford less than half of what you can afford today. Even though a 2% drop may appear to take 50 years for standard of living to diminish by half, **compounding** accelerates diminishing standards-of-living by 25 years. *So, what's your country's average rise in income and inflation? Where do you stand in terms of the Total Costs of Inflation and its influence on your own Standard-of-Living?*

So how does compounding work? Here is a basic, but very important compounding formula. FV is the future value of the asset, PV is the present value, n is the number of periods (e.g., years), and i is the rate at which the value increases over time.

$$FV = PV \cdot (1+i)^n$$

Based on the compounding formula, suppose someone has a 2% salary increase per year on an annual salary of $100,000 and a 4% increase in inflation. Using the compounding formula, the person's salary will amount to $104,040 after 2 years ($100,000 \times (1 + 2\%)^2$) and $164,060.60 after 25 years ($100,000 \times (1 + 2\%)^{25}$). On the other hand, a 4% inflation compounding on $100,000 will amount to $108,160 (($100,000 \times (1 + 4\%)^2$) and $266,583.63 after 25 years ($100,000 \times (1 + 4\%)^{25}$).

Resource or Asset Performance: Return of Investments (ROI) for HR Assets

So, let's use compounding to measure the TCO and value of human capital assets. **Human**

Capital TCO is important because it can help you gauge how much productive value you'd expect from the employee and manage out of pocket costs related to the employee.

How do we calculate value? To recap, value is nothing but the difference between the benefit from the asset and the cost of the asset (Table 7.1).

Here is an example. You have just hired a line manager to deal with international operations. Here are the valuations by year.

Now, let's look at the numbers. Surprisingly, *after 10 years of working, the human capital resource truly becomes an asset.* Why? That's because the total value (adding all the Human Capital Asset Value numbers in the last column) is $1,251 after 10 years. That means that the employee broke even after the 9th year. So, if this employee decided to leave the company before their 10th year, the company actually would have to sustain a loss on that human capital before the resource could turn into an asset. To make the most off the employee (assuming there are no further training costs, and that performance continues to grow at the same rate, the employee will truly start returning a

good value for the investment), the employee has to stick with the company more than 10 years.

Now you might ask yourself, so what? For the company, this information is extremely beneficial. The company will try to retain the employee more than 10 years and will try to increase employee motivation after 10 years so that their Human Capital choices fetch a good ROI, something that is imperative for keeping the company's costs under check. So, next time you think of Human Capital in a company, make sure that you consider important factors such as Value, Costs, Benefits, Resources, Assets, and ROI.

Human Capital and Performance TCO in Global Business

Let's suppose a company has branches around the world—in France, in the US, and in China. Company policy requires that all its **expats** (employees originally recruited in one country that relocate to work for a branch in another country) must get paid the same regardless of the country of operation.

Working hours in France are 35 hours a week, 40 hours a week in the US, and 45 hours in

Table 7.1 Valorising human capital TCO (total costs of ownership) by cost and performance (in dollars)

Year	Selection cost	Salary costs	Benefits costs	Total direct costs (increasing by 3% per year)	Training costs	Indirect costs (vacation, sick leave, office real estate, etc.)	Performance benefits	Human capital asset value
1	3,000.0	70,000.0	20,000.0	90,000.0	4,000.0	1,500.0	75,000.0	−23,500.0
2	0.0	72,100.0	20,600.0	92,700.0	2,000.0	1,500.0	89,000.0	−7,200.0
3	0.0	74,263.0	21,218.0	95,481.0	0.0	1,500.0	99,000.0	2,019.0
4	0.0	76,490.9	21,854.5	98,345.4	0.0	1,500.0	107,000.0	7,154.6
5	0.0	78,785.6	22,510.2	101,295.8	0.0	1,500.0	111,000.0	8,204.2
6	0.0	81,149.2	23,185.5	104,334.7	7,000.0	1,500.0	114,000.0	1,165.3
7	0.0	83,583.7	23,881.0	107,464.7	2,000.0	1,800.0	114,000.0	2,735.3
8	0.0	86,091.2	24,597.5	110,688.6	0.0	1,800.0	116,000.0	3,511.4
9	0.0	88,673.9	25,335.4	114,009.3	0.0	1,800.0	119,200.0	3,390.7
10	0.0	91,334.1	26,095.5	117,429.6	0.0	1,800.0	123,000.0	3,770.4
Total	3,000	802,472	229,278	1,031,749	15,000	16,200	1,067,200	1,251

France. France has 22 national holidays, 11 in the US, and 12 in China. France requires a 1:1.6 benefits contribution, US 1:1.4, and China 1:1.2. In every 10-hours workday, in France, employees get a 2-hour lunch break and 4 15-minute breaks during the day. In the US it is a 1-hour lunch and 3 15-minute breaks. In China, it is a working lunch where food is delivered to employees, and there are 3 15-minute breaks.

Assume the employee is in software development and each employee is paid $80,000 as yearly salary. Each employee is expected to write 400 lines of software code every day. As an executive, you have been asked to decide on which of the three countries offers the best human capital ROI (i.e., the lowest TCO).

Based on the daily work schedule, we could surmise that a 10-hours day will produce 300 lines of usable software code. We often measure performance by cycle time, i.e., the number of lines of code you'd expect the software developer to produce per time unit. In that case, **Cycle Time** should be 300 lines of code/ (60 minutes × 10 hours) per day. That is 300/600 or 0.5 lines of code per minute. The software team lead should be happy if a software developer had a **Throughput** (time required to do a unit of work, in this case, one line of code) of 1/0.5 = 2 lines of usable code per minute.

Sadly, we'd be underestimating. If the software lead were to benchmark 1 line of usable code writing per minute as being productive, the software lead would be overbudget because more hours would be needed to achieve the same performance. The reason is that cycle time based on formal working hours in never the same as our performance based on true working hours.

A German term called **Taktzeit** offers the solution. Taktzeit is a type of metered time, like a metronome for work. What Taktzeit does is that it removes all unproductive hours from cycle time calculations. Calculating productive work hours would require subtracting unproductive hours. So, in France, for every 10 hours of scheduled work, each software developer loses 120 minutes from lunch and 60 minutes (4 × 15 minutes) from breaks. That leaves 420 minutes of productive work. That does not

even include the lost productivity from lost time in between lunches and breaks. So, using Taktzeit, the cycle time in France would be 300 lines of usable code/420 minutes of productive time, or 0.714 lines per minutes compared to the assumed 0.5 lines per minutes. That is 43% more lines of code that a software developer will have to write in order to maintain the 300 usable lines of software code performance per day.

If the software developer wrote 0.5 lines of usable code per minute and worked for 420 productive hours, there would only be 210 lines of code compared to the expected 300 lines. So, let's try it across the three countries:

- **France**: Lost Productive Time: 120 minutes from lunch and 60 minutes (4 × 15 minutes) from breaks = Total 180 minutes of 600 scheduled work minutes per day = 420 productive minutes.
  - Taktzeit Cycle Time (code lines) = 300/420 = 0.714 lines of software code per minute. This is equal to a Throughput (in minutes) of 1/0.714 = 1.4 minutes available to write one line of code.
- **US:** Lost Productive Time: 60 minutes from lunch and 45 minutes (3 × 15 minutes) from breaks = Total 105 minutes of 600 scheduled work minutes per day = 495 productive minutes.
  - Taktzeit Cycle Time = 300/495 = 0.61 lines of software code per minute. This is equal to a Throughput of 1/0.61 = 1.64 minutes available to write a line of code.
- **China**: Lost Productive Time: 0 minutes from lunch and 45 minutes (3 × 15 minutes) from breaks = Total 45 minutes of 600 scheduled work minutes per day = 555 productive minutes.
  - Taktzeit Cycle Time = 300/555 = 0.54 lines of software code per minute. This is equal to a Throughput of 1/0.54 = 1.85 minutes available to write a line of code.

For an international manager and decision-maker, software developers in France will have to be prompted to performed better to meet code performance per day. However, if the company were to run a company-wide training to increase code-writing performance to 0.714 lines of code per minute, software developers in the French division would match the required 300 lines of code per day but it would also raise US and Chinese productivities. In the US, productivity would rise to 0.714×495 work minutes = 353.43 lines of code per day, 53 lines more than the required 300 lines. That's nearly 28% more productivity and savings. In China, productivity would rise to 0.714×555 work minutes = 396.27 lines of code per day, 96 lines more than the required 300 lines. That is 32% increase in productivity and savings.

If the company operated for 20 days a month, there would be $20 \times 12 = 240$ workdays a year. 300 lines of usable code each day would amount to 300×240 days = 72,000 lines of code per year. The French division might need all 240 days to meet requirements. However, the US division would need 72,000/353.27 = 204 days to meet requirements, with 240 − 204 = 36 days of labor savings. The China division would need 72,000/396.27 = 182 days to meet requirements, with 240 − 182 = 58 days of labor savings.

Now if we were to add holidays, vacation days, and required sick leaves based on each country's labor laws and regulations, you start gauging how productivity can differ by regions.

This shows how, in international business decisions-making, work schedule, and country choices can have large ramifications in TCO and ROI.

PESTLE: Feasibility Modeling and Planning

Feasibility Modeling and Planning is a technique used by companies and agencies to assess their own capabilities in deciding on an initiative, whether it be the choice of a merger and acquisition, creating a new product, or entering a new market.

Feasibility modeling takes the general acronym of **PESTLE**: **Political**, **Economic**, **Social**, **Technological**, **Legal**, and **Environmental** feasibilities.

Political Feasibility

Political factors are related to impact of the government or a political party on business decisions. In the US, President Trump taking office buoyed the stock market because of President Trump's promises of lowering taxes and infrastructure spending. President Trump's election also led to a *quid pro quo* tariff rise against Chinese imports and business practices. The Chinese stock market suffered wide losses when President Trump, rightly in my opinion, decided to raise Chinese import tariffs to level the open market playing field. In particular, ZTE, a Chinese telecom company, found to be doing business with Iran and North Korea, was banned from selling its devices in the US. The move would have bankrupted ZTE and led to a loss of 75,000 Chinese jobs. Granted, the ban was lifted after high-level talks but political feasibilities shape business. In December 2018, France's President Macron imposed a diesel tax to reduce carbon emissions. Unfortunately, the diesel tax also impacted lorry and truck drivers and people driving from rural areas to make a living. This led to massive protests called *"Gilet Jaunes,"* based on the yellow vests required to be worn by lorry drivers. The demonstrations and protests on the Champs Elysees, a main thoroughfare in Paris leasing to the Arc de Triomphe, were not only large but turned violent, forcing President Macron to put the taxes on hold. The UK Brexit political referendum resulted in Britain leaving the European Union. However, the aftermath of the Brexit vote created chaos. The incumbent PM, Brown, resigned, and the new PM, May, is trying to discuss points of separation with Brussels (the EU HQ) and soften Brexit's blow on businesses.

The Case of Zimbabwe

A large part of political feasibility is based optimal resource allocation and decision-making.

Political decisions from tax policy, labor law, environmental law, trade restrictions, tariffs, and political stability, impact economic, and business resources, and decision-making. A **resource** is an asset, human, technology, knowledge, land, or anything else that gives you a positive Return on Investment (ROI). Companies and countries need to both *manage and allocate* (know which resource to use for what purpose) their resources.

When Robert Mugabe won the 1980 British-supervised election in **Zimbabwe**, Southern Rhodesia was assumed to breathe in a fresh air of ZANU-PF rule. 12,000 miles away, the conservative leader Maggie Thatcher treated Mugabe's ascendancy as a hallmark of expedient and tolerant transfer of all that was the best of the British. Chamberlain's "winds of change" were in motion in Africa and Mugabe carried the fluttering pennant. England herself was in her descendance. It was a calamitous affair in her home-front—England was facing the worst economic crisis since 1935—inflation was 20% and climbing—unemployment was regressively rampant and a chill penury was in the air. Mugabe's ascendancy as a progressive African president was a triumph for Thatcher. While the French President, Jacques Chirac, snubbed Thatcher as a housewife whose economics were for naught, Thatcher embraced Mugabe as a landmark British-institution suffrage who would champion Zimbabwe into a beacon for sub-Saharan African politics. It was a sound decision in the middle of an otherwise losing dawn of a decade.

But "as flies are to wanton boys, are we to the Gods- they kill us for their sport" (Shakespeare's King Lear). Thatcher's gleeful support of Mugabe would only lead to a confiscation of lands from domiciled white farmers in the next two decades. Mugabe, the elixir of British expectations, had suddenly gone rogue. He assumed executive powers, liquidated opposing voices, and misused Zimbabwe's 1992 Fast Track Land Reform Act to nationalize the farmland and coercively remove existing white landowners without compensation or legal recourse. Yet, the white landowners knew the technology and best practices. They were Zimbabwe's greatest resource. But, Zimbabwe, in a feverishly hasty attempt to return the land to indigenous dwellers, forgot to learn how to transfer the technology and knowledge of mechanized agriculture from the white to the indigenous black population slowly over time, ensuring that the people could be trained to be resources and be allocated to doing the right type of job. But Zimbabwe did not, and calamity ensued.

The land was badly parceled and redistributed to government members and their families who had no training or interest in agricultural operations. In a short period, the "breadbasket" of southern Africa plummeted into starvation and famine. Zimbabwe, the 6th largest producer and exporter of tobacco, a cash crop, fell to its lowest levels in 50 years. Investors perceived operational risk and withdrew their capital, original landowners migrated, and the government forced banks to lend to the new, untrained landowners with high default risk. Risks of operations affected Zimbabwe's internal production acutely. Maize production, Zimbabwe's largest export produce that had helped build its agrarian supply chain, was approximately halved in a few years.

Astoundingly painful, Zimbabwe, once a major exporter of maize, became a net importer. According to Wikipedia, Inflation rose from an annual rate of 32% in 1998, to an official estimated high of 11 million % in August 2008 according to the country's Central Statistical Office. Suddenly, what once cost 1 Zimbabwean Dollar now cost 11 million Zimbabwean Dollars. This is called **hyperinflation**, and Zimbabwe's central bank had to introduce a new 100 billion Zimbabwean Dollar note to keep the economy running. In fact, in 2009, the Zimbabwean government advised Zimbabwean people to stop using the Zimbabwean Dollar and instead try using a more stable foreign currency such as the US Dollar, the South African Rand, or British Pounds. Zimbabwe won its populism but lost its currency!

Did You Know That?

During Zimbabwe's economic and financial mismanagement leading to hyperinflations, an item that once cost 1 Zimbabwean Dollar ended up costing 11 million Zimbabwean Dollars! Even printing the Zimbabwean Dollar became so expensive that Zimbabwe switched to the US Dollar in 2015.

Economic Feasibility

Economic feasibility relates to the economic impacts of decisions. Economic decisions include interest rates, exchange rates, inflation rate, tax shelters, subsidies—aspects that affect businesses operations. To examine various bits of economic feasibility, let's examine a simplified financial income statement:

Revenue (Sales)	$1,000,000
Costs of Goods Sold (COGS) or Cost of Sales	$400,000
Gross Profit	**$600,000**
Gross Margin	600,000/1,000,000 = 60%
Expenses	$400,000
EBITDA (Earnings before Interests, Taxes, Depreciation, Amortization)	**$200,000**
Earnings Margin	*200,000/1,000,000 = 20%*
Interest paid on Debt	$5,000
Depreciation of plant, equipment, technology…	$25,000
Taxes (e.g., 20% on EBITDA)	$40,000
Net Earnings or Net Profit	**$130,000**
Net Margin	*130,000/1,00,000 = 13%*

Economic feasibility analysis looks at whether strategic, global decisions makes economic sense.

The choice of a particular international location would impact most aspects of the income statement. A country with a growing population and income will increase sales revenues. US, French, Japanese, and German car companies such as Ford and GM from the US, Citroen, and Renault from France, BMW and Volkswagen from Germany and Toyota, Honda, and Nissan from Japan generate most of their sales revenues from overseas markets rather than their own markets. Having access to local supply of cheap labor and materials for inventory and production will lower their COGS and increase gross margins.

Access to cheaper services such as marketing, logistics, repairs, etc., will reduce expenses and increase EBITDA. **Earnings before interest, tax, depreciation, and amortization (EBITDA)** is a measure of a company's operating performance. Essentially, it's a way to evaluate a company's performance without having to factor in financing decisions, accounting decisions, or tax environments.

Countries and locations also offer specific modes of depreciation as per their accounting laws that can impact net profit. Particularly, international locations play an important role in interest expenses and tax obligations. The Federal Reserve in countries can use interest rates to attract businesses and promote consumption. If the cost of raising capital is lower (also called **Cost of Capital**), the company's debt and interest expenses are lowered. For example, right after the 2008 US financial crisis, the US Federal Reserve lowered its interest rates to 0.25%, therefore, promoting more business borrowing for R&D and new product development meant to offer more innovations that would pique purchases with dirt-cheap financing.

Countries and international locations can also offer other economic advantages such as tax shelters and subsidies for specific types of industries and sectors to attract internal investments as well as FDI (Foreign Direct Investments). Countries will often create **ETZs (Economic Trade Zones)** or **FTZs (Foreign Trade Zones)** as tax-subsidized areas where international companies can operate without worrying about local regulations and taxes, as long as they utilize local labor. Countries such as Ireland, Bahamas, and Bermuda always advertise themselves as great destinations for business incorporation because of their tax shelters. Switzerland has long been a haven for financial prudence, leading a lot of businesses and wealthy individuals to move their money to Swiss banks.

Social Feasibility

Social feasibility relates the ability of a business to leverage social aspects of a country or an international location. International businesses pay particular attention to how their business decisions will be perceived socially. Businesses will often choose locations that will not only help them but also enrich the local community. In South Korea, Samsung, and LG fund large research centers at universities so as to not only attract talent but also train the best talent for future supply. Amazon.com US HQ2 (2nd Headquarter in addition to its original Seattle HQ1) attracted multiple bids from cities with special operational privileges to liven not just the economy but also the community, attracting a more educated workforce with higher incomes that might add to the educational system (local schools), culture, and quality of life. Hospitals will constantly monitor trends in aging and diseases to consider which location is the most feasible to open a new

Fig. 7.2 A Marriott Hotel Sign. In Saudi Arabia, women are often not allowed in hotels without a male "guardian" (Courtesy Wikipedia)

hospital or clinic specializing in issues related the local region (Fig. 7.2).

Cleveland Clinic, a famous US hospital specialized in cardiac surgery and care, opened a division in Saudi Arabia. Cleveland Clinic in Saudi Arabia realized that Saudi Arabia's population was aging, and the growing inclinations for fast food would lead to potential cardio vascular issues. Cleveland Clinic could thus ensure that it could leverage it specialized cardiac care in Saudi Arabia. Similarly, international businesses such as McDonald's and Pizza Hut avoid serving beef and pork products in India and pork products in Middle Eastern Arab countries.

Other pieces of social culture often verge on the unethical and immoral. When social and cultural beliefs end up harming a part of a population or other living creatures, there is a need for education and reform.

In many countries around the world, corruption and cronyism are a part of everyday life. In India, Russia, and many other developing countries, domestic and publicly tolerated violence against women is often overlooked by courts referring to the fact that men are violent toward women because of love and protection. Similar unethical issues abound with other groups in society, from an intolerance toward homosexuals and transgenders in countries such as Russia and Iran where public beatings and forced sex-change operations as a "fix" are commonplace. In parts of Central Africa, even albinos (a skin condition because of a lack of pigments) are prey to killings. In some more macabre and ghastly instances, witch doctors often concoct recipes using albino body parts for consumption (based on ignorant, arcane beliefs that consuming albino body parts can increase power).

Similar social issues abound with the indiscriminate killing and poaching of wildlife. A year ago, during a photo safari in South Africa's beautiful Kruger National Park, we drove past a congregation of vultures in the distance. The park ranger bemoaned how beautiful creatures such as elephants and rhinos are being poached into extinction based on ignorant and misplaced Asian social notions that rhino horns are aphrodisiacs (substance to increase virility). **Poaching** is the illegal killing of wildlife and is driven by social demand for collecting trophies or misplaced assumptions of medicinal values.

As progressive human beings and decision-makers, we need to change so that such regressive and ignorant notions and attitudes that pose a harm to the global society, the environment and humanity. But how should we approach such issues without offending social beliefs and cultures?

The Need for Code Switching

Building social feasibility requires **code-switching behavior**. An acquaintance once visited a fishing community in the Far East. The lagoon the fishing community bordered was tremendously overfished, and they were running out of fishes to catch and sell in the open market. Acquaintance offered a long and logical talk on why the fishing community should temper their fishing from the lagoon that had fed their predecessors for centuries so that they could save the for fishing for their future generations. Upon finishing, one of the fishermen asked my acquaintance her profession and she said that she was in environmental conservation law. The fisherman then said, "What do you know of poverty and hardships? I want my children to be lawyers like you, not a wretched fisherman like their father. I toil day and night and still live hand to mouth. If catching every fish here will help my children become lawyers instead of becoming a fisherman like their father, I will happily overfish the lagoon."

This is not an atypical scenario where trying to push our own sense of social values can be met with resistance. We are and we shall be presented with similar scenarios. The poaching aftermath was not just an indiscriminate killing; it was done by poachers crossing the border from Zimbabwe to South Africa. These poachers are often extremely poor and getting paid $5,000 for killing an endangered and helpless rhino or elephant is like winning a lottery. In a country so desperately in need of an economy, the value placed on animals may seem to the poachers a notion of the privileged few.

This is where code switching is important. Code switching allows communicating our social values as a low-level narrative that resonates with the subject without alienating the subject. It is one of the most important pieces of communication that needs a combination of logic and empathy in order to deliver and have buy-in for our message.

Easier said than done!

Technological Feasibility

Technological feasibility relates to a company's capability to acquire, build, and manage the requisite technological capabilities in order to meet market needs around the globe. When an international company decides on a venture, it has to consider whether its technological capabilities can match its choice of market. Building technological capabilities is not just a matter of having access to and using high-end technologies. Building technological capabilities also requires having access to a series of complementary resources such as the proper labor supply and capital access. I once visited an agency based in northeastern Africa with rooms full of brand-new computers networked to the Internet.

Yet, most had no access Internet connection. That was because the agency did not know of a single person that could repair broken Ethernet cables. There was no educational training related to technology in that area and the latest devices were simply withering in the absence of a trained labor force. That is why technological feasibility requires the right access to trained labor as well as access to good technology. Good technology without a good labor force cannot last. Technological feasibilities also require access to a robust capital market. Technology requires capital investments and a lack of capital markets (such as easy access to credit, loans at affordable interest rates) can disable an international venture.

Technological feasibility assessment requires companies to analyze their current technologies and operations and redesign it to meet various market needs. Tesla's Model 3, an electric car, was high in demand, and Tesla had to find a way to ramp up production to meet all customer orders. Tesla achieved the technological feasibility by redesigning its entire production line. Tesla's Model 3 production line uses only 43 steps compared to the 130 steps or more required by other car manufacturers. Fewer steps mean fewer chances of errors.

Technological feasibility also involves a company's capabilities with product disassembly for recycling and reuse. Older generation Apple iPhones still carry multitude of reusable components. Yet, iPhones are time consuming to assemble and disassemble. So, Apple created Daisy, a disassembly robot that can meticulously disassemble very iPhone component, right up to the iPhone's BOM (Bill of Materials or the list of components required to build the product) so that all components can be properly reclaimed and reused.

Legal Feasibility

Legal feasibility relates to assessing whether the legal infrastructure (e.g., efficient courts, due process of law, corruption factors) of an international market holds promise. Google and Facebook have been trying to access the Chinese market, but the Chinese governments' demands for censoring information have been a feasibility concern. In 2018, Google was in the works to operate in the Chinese market, but Google's own employees protested and made it infeasible for Google to wrap up the international business deal. Apple was able to get Apple Maps accepted by the Chinese government as long as the government could collect data from it. Other legal feasibility issues are equally important in business decisions. With more than 70% of EU members using Google for search, the EU is questing whether Google might be operating as a monopoly. Similarly, a lot of western firms are wary of China because of the China's weak IP (intellectual property) record. Chinese law requires any western company planning on setting up international business in the Chinese market must jointly partner with a Chinese firm

and transfer technology and product knowhow to the Chinese company. Chinese companies are rarely privately held entities as the government carries a stake in them. With widespread patent infringement fears, companies may often feel a bit wary about the legal feasibility of conducting business in China, especially if the company's patents and technologies are the company's only competitive advantage.

Environmental Feasibility

Environmental feasibility relates to business decisions that impact the ecology and environment such as impacts on climate change, deforestation, water contamination, as well as socio-environmental issues such as living wages and fair trade (where poor indigenous populations or farmers are not being unscrupulously abused for multinationals' benefits). Companies choose international markets and locations based on the impact of their operational on the environment.

For example, a company that requires large lorries and trucks entering the city of London during peak hours may find their location choice infeasible because of the high "congestion charges" they have to bear. Other companies lower their environmental footprints to not only create more environmentally friendly practices but also raise their environmental goodwill among the more caring customers of today.

IKEA's practices environmental stewardship via resource management in sourcing. I-WAY is IKEA's sourcing code-of-conduct for solid wood and board product suppliers—which requires documenting the origin of the hardwood and passing supply chain audits. IKEA tries to ensure that forest managers to have a certified afforestation and conservation values and that all of its wood come from forests verified as responsibly managed. The Reformation, a clothing company, practices resource management in its forward logistics by having its materials delivered locally and by using local fabricators. UPS recycles cell-phone electronics as a reverse supply chain process to reuse electronics and reduce the toxicity of electronic components. According to the EPA, for every million cell phones recycled, 35,274 pounds of copper, 772 pounds of silver, 75 pounds of gold, and 33 pounds of palladium can be recovered. The reusable, recycled, and reclaimed metals are worth over $4 million.

Learning from History

Around 500 BC, Persia (currently, the region of and around Iran), under Kings Darius I and his successor, Xerxes, tried to invade Greece multiple times. Even though the Greeks were outnumbered by the size of Persian forces and ships, the Greek city states (Greece was then a loose amalgam or mix of many city states such as Athens, Sparta, Platea, Thebes) heroically resisted and won, mainly because of **strategic resource allocation**. The Persian forces were larger and their ships far bigger than that of the Greeks. So, how do smaller forces strategically allocate resources to win large victories? Here are some lessons from some famous battles:

Battle of Salamis

Greece was a land of feudal city states, with multiple kings and lacking central, unified, **governance**, i.e., a common set of laws and politics for unified administration. Persia knew that they could capitalize on the feudal enmity among Greek city states and use that as an opportunity to invade Greece. In 480 BC, the Persian march under Xerxes panned on large contingents and bear advances into Greece.

Xerxes was calcified by his prior although pyrrhic (a costly win with a lot of lives lost by the winner) victory, with an overwhelming show of force in the Battle of Thermopylae. The Persians would take the southern route into Attica and Peloponnesus. Preparing themselves against the massive push by the Persian juggernaut, the outnumbered Greek city states laid a naval blockade at the Straits of Artemisium to force the Persians into the narrow gully at Thermopylae. The Greeks established small battlements with

quick retreats to fall back and reorganize (including the evacuation of Athens). Thermopylae was defended by Leonidas with a small contingent of 300 Spartan and Thespian hoplites. The contingent held Thermopylae for three days against massive Persian offensive until betrayed by a flanking mountain path. Thermopylae fell, and the Greeks suffered massive losses at Artemisium. Calcified by his decision to use the massive juggernaut, Xerxes pushed forward, rested at Athens (while burning the city), and moved against the Athenian triremes (Greek 3-oar ships) toward the island of Salamis for a decisive battle.

In 480 BC, led by King Leonidas of Sparta. Xerxes had thousands of archers lined up against the Spartans and Thespians at Thermopylae—enough to cover the sun. "Good. Then we will fight in the shade" said the Spartan Dianekes'—a retort immortalized by Herodotus. Yet, the Spartans fell after three days of heroic battle against the size of the Persian force. With another victory at Artemisium, Xerxes decided to move his huge fleet of 800–1200 ships against a considerably smaller naval force of 360–370 Greek triremes in Salamis. Knowing that the Greek triremes were smaller in size, Themistocles realized that a battle in close conditions would work to their advantage.

The Persian pursuit of a quick victory drew them to an unnecessary narrow channel in the straits where the Greeks used close-quarter skirmishes to confound the first line of Persian ships. Unwieldy, when the first line of Persian ships attempted to retreat in the narrow straits, they ended up ramming their rear guard. With little maneuverability and too many ships committed to a narrow passage, the Greeks inflicted tremendous casualties on the Persian ships. The Persians lost over 300 ships compared to 30–40 Greek losses. Xerxes' strategic calcification spelt the end of the 2nd Persian invasion that suffered the same fate as Darius after the Battle of Marathon a decade ago.

The story is about **resource choice and allocation**, i.e., choosing the right resource for the right role or job is equally important. In an uncertain landscape in flux or change, *resource* *mobility and resource agility hold the edge.* **Resource mobility** is the ability to use a resource in many different ways. **Resource agility** is the speed at which a resource can be deployed or implemented.

Think of resource allocation as casting in a movie set. You have to choose and allocate the right actor, the right set, the right costume, the correct lighting, the proper director, the right location, among others. War, unlike a movie set, is where resource allocation is an imperative, and, unlike a movie set, the costs are too real and too hard to bear.

Assignments and Exercises: How Technology Firms Are Reshaping Strategy

Purpose

Now that you understand how global politics and technologies intersect, this assignment will help you apply your understanding for reviewing strategies for Tech Titans. With companies such as Apple and Amazon entering healthcare, Google in autonomous cars, Tesla in energy utilities, and Elon Musk's SpaceX changing space exploration, this assignment will help you integrate your learning as you use your knowledge to start assessing and modeling company strategies using the strategy toolkit you have learned in this module.

Assignment 1: Assume you are a technology strategy consultant for the US Commerce Department that is worried about companies using Facebook's popularity to disseminate fake news. Facebook, like Google and Amazon, is commonly used by over 70% of the market, can become a hub to spread a lot of news, fake or otherwise. The US Commerce department believe that this is tantamount to antitrust, i.e., the ability of a single company to work like a monopoly and reduce competition. And free competition is the very idea that underscores a free market.

You have been asked to assess the industry position of Facebook Social Media using Porter's Five Forces and based on your assessment, offer 3 ways, by which globalization can reduce Facebook's single-handed influence on social media and using it to shape public opinion.

Assignment 2: Elon Musk's SpaceX is not the dominant space transporter, followed by Jeff Bezos' Blue Origins.

Conduct a comparative SWOT analysis between these two companies.

Assignment 3: You have joined a large bank as a business analyst. Under COVID-19, the bank's costs of managing its many physical branches, paying for employees and its real estate without any customers is disconcerting. In this digital world, the bank is worried about a growing threat—FinTechs.

1. Research the term "FinTech" on the Internet. What is FinTech and why are FinTechs threats to physical banks. Explain well.
2. Find 1 FinTech company in each of the following countries: France, China, and Kenya. Briefly explain, in your own words, why you chose each FinTech company (i.e., how is each FinTech adding value to each of these countries?).
3. Based on your research, your bank executives have asked you to conduct a PEST (Political, Economic, Social, and Technological) Feasibility analysis on why these FinTechs are becoming such threats. You can choose ANY ONE of the 3 FinTechs.

Assignment 4: As a business analyst, a large car fleet operator (e.g., Enterprise, Hertz, SixT) is considering replacing its current fleet of 2020 Fiat Pandas with Tesla Model 3s. The CEO has personally asked you to understand the TCO (Total Costs of Ownership).

1. Explain to the CEO the importance of using CEO when thinking about replacing the fleet.
2. Conduct a 3-year TCO between the 2020 Fiat Panda and a 2020 Tesla Model 3. Each fleet car is driven approximately 50,000 miles every year. Tabulate your responses based on (i) purchase costs, (ii) fuel costs, and (iii) sustainability (CO_2 emissions).

3. Based on your 3-year TCO analysis, which car would you recommend and why. Write a brief 300 word memo to explain your recommendations.

Assignment 5: Autonomous cars are becoming the trend of the future. Yet, autonomous cars are not purely a technological issue. There are multiple social, cultural, political, and legal aspects that companies and countries need to address.

You have been asked to serve as atop consultant for a company such as Tesla embarking on entering multiple global markets, particularly India and Italy. Your advice will guide leadership and strategy.

Based on your reading and understanding of the strategy slides, you plan on doing customer and context audits to assess feasibilities.

a. Begin by researching the Internet to reveal and explain 3 differences from a customer audit and 3 differences from a context audit between India and Italy.

b. Now that you know have strategically audited between the countries, use the audit to recommend 3 solutions each to Tesla's leadership for entering India and Italy. Pay close attention to the socio-cultural as well as technological cues.

Did you know that?

Data Analytics without a strategy has no relevance! Strategic Analytics without data has no credibility!

Data Analytics Begins with Data Collection (ETL)

Data analytics and data mining begin with data collection. Data mining is the process of **extracting** (E) data from databases, **transforming** (T) data following a predefined structure, and **loading** (L) data for performing various analytics. Data mining is commonly associated with big data because it is the basis for systematic analytics for describing and predicting based on data. Here are some useful steps in using Data Mining for Competitive Analytics:

1. **Sample and Collect the Data**: From point-of-sale systems to an online shopping cart, data is everywhere. Companies need to actively seek data that is valuable for decision-making. The data should be (i) relevant, (ii) timely, (iii) accurate, (iv) credible, and (v) useful. In collecting the data, focus on *secondary "explicit" data* sources such as market, point-of-sale, and Internet clickstream data as well as on *primary (1st hand) "tacit" data* from surveys, questionnaires, tests, interviews, and best practices.

Practice good sampling techniques so that *your sample represents the population* (it is time and cost prohibitive to collect data from an entire population). Ensuring that your sample represents your population is therefore especially important for arriving at good analytic conclusions. Here are some popular sampling methods:

a. *Simple random sampling* (probabilistic) is when you randomly draw your sample from the entire population and the chance of drawing each unit in the sample is the same. The random selection is often computer-generated, and it is useful if all members of the population are homogeneous (same). An example would be a sample of 100 Fortune 1000 companies.

b. *Stratified random sampling* (probabilistic) is when you divide the population into relevant segments after which random sampling is done within each segment. An example would be segmenting Fortune 1000 firms by industry category and then choosing a random sample of 10 companies from each of the industry categories.

c. *Convenience sampling* (non-probabilistic) is when you choose a sample because of the sample's convenience and availability. An example would be choosing Fortune 1000 companies that are close to your city or area that are willing to share their data.

d. *Purposive sampling* (non-probabilistic) is when you choose a sample with a specific objective in mind. An example would be

© PiaDura LTD 2022
P. Datta, *Global Technology Management 4.0*,
https://doi.org/10.1007/978-3-030-96929-5_8

choosing a sample of Fortune 1000 companies that are practicing CSR (corporate social responsibility) or a sample of shoppers in a mall based on whether they are carrying a shopping bag from a store.

2. **Structure and Recode**: Data mining uses data warehouses where data is structured, recoded based on organizational rules, and stored for availability, quick access, retrieval, and analysis. For example, Walmart has more than 5 petabytes of data, eBay over 9 petabytes and growing. According to a 2013 gigaom.com article, "A manufacturing customer generates 20 terabytes of data per hour while testing products, although that volume is ultimately reduced to about 1 terabyte after the valuable data is filtered out" based on relevance, timeliness, accuracy, credibility, and usefulness—only then is it information.

3. **Create a culture of systematic metrics, models and mining for knowledge discovery in databases (KDD)**: Analytics is not a functional activity. It is a part of corporate competitive strategy. Creating a culture is important and requires executive championship. Therefore, it is important to define appropriate metrics for measurements at the proper units of analysis, creating useful data models for descriptive and predictive relationships. Ask proper questions and practice out-of-the-box thinking. If your question is problematic, analytics will fail to reveal appropriate insights.

4. **Infer and Interpret analytical findings**: Once results from analytics are on hand, it is useful to draw proper inferences and interpret the findings in light of corporate strategy.

5. **Deploy and Integrate**: Converting analytics into action is the reason for practicing competitive analytics and data mining. With new insights, establish a mode of action to incorporate, deploy, and integrate them into the corporate strategy. Strategy should evolve in light of analytic insights.

6. **Learn and create best practices**: Good competitive analytical practices with appropriate data mining can deliver insights often

unknown to companies. Practice to both unlearn and relearn based on the analytical insights. Assimilate useful insights with strategy to create best practices for competitive advantage.

7. **Audit your Analytical progress**: Practice periodic audits of your analytics to create good benchmarks and rethink the choice of metrics, mining, and models in line with the changing environment.

Useful Data Analytics Concepts

Causation or Correlation?

Both causation and correlations are based on two variables moving together because of a positive relation (if one variable increases, the other increases) or a negative relationship (if one variable increases, the other decreases). However, the question is whether one variable caused the other (causation) or because of a common relationship (correlation) or coincidence. So, *all causations are correlations but not all correlations are causations. Choosing causation without proper logic can create confirmation bias where we define a relationship based on our bias instead of logic.* The key to assessing causation is time. The cause must occur prior to the outcome. For example, movement of a company stock (also known as a Beta) has a correlation with the movement in the returns of the overall market. However, it does not always mean that the stock will cause changes in the market. Because strife in the Middle East is related to increase in crude oil prices, the relationship is causation. Strife in the Middle East has to occur as one of the reasons before an increase in the price of crude oil. *Note: Tests for Correlation mainly include Tests for Linear Relationship between two variables using (Pearson Product Moment Correlation r) or Rank Correlation to compare ranking s between variables (Spearman's Rank Correlation Coefficient, Kendall Tau Rank Correlation Coefficient, Goodman, and Kruskal's Gamma). Tests for causation are based on predictive and* *experimental techniques and **Multivariate analysis** is used if there is more than one outcome.*

Stochastic or Deterministic Analytics?

Deterministic models assume a strong understanding of the causes, effects, and relationships that define a phenomenon. In a deterministic model, specific numbers are included as input and results are output as numbers following the deterministic formula. In short, based on the input values, you can consistently derive the output. Stochastic models, on the other hand, try to incorporate uncertainty into the model by introducing a constant term in the model. Because this "extra" constant term can follow a distribution, the model output varies even if the inputs remain the same.

Fixed or Random Effects?

Fixed effects are used for variables that include all of their levels possible. For example, gender can have 3 levels: male, female, and transgender; an experimental design can only have a treatment and a control group; an industry variable specifying a list of industry codes. However, if a variable uses a sample of all possible levels (e.g., physicians in a healthcare group), the variable can be treated as a Fixed effect as long as it is not generalized and limited to "physicians in that specific healthcare group" in scope.

Random effects are used for variables where only a few levels are chosen out of all possible levels. For example, level of satisfaction using a 5-point Likert scale is unlikely to capture all possible levels of satisfaction. Therefore, for fixed effects, analytics mainly tries to provide insights into the differences between the levels/groups. For random effects, analytics mainly tries to offer insights into how an increase or decrease in the random effect variable explains the outcome. Often, fixed effect variables are used as control variables. In analytics, if there is an interaction term combining a fixed and a random effects variable, the result is a random effects factor.

Induction or Deduction?

Induction (from specific to general) is often inferential where empirical (observations) are used as the basis for analytics in order to reach a conclusion to create a theory or model. Deduction, on the other hand, uses theoretical logic to create a model and then uses observations to confirm or disconfirm the assumptions. In induction, data from observations (1st hand) and/or archives (secondary data) are used to create hypotheses. In deduction, logical hypotheses are generally presented before collecting data for analysis (*Hypothetico-Deductive*). For example, Darwin's seminal evolutionary analysis or the study of genomics is inductive where data drives the research. In comparison, Einstein's theories of relativity are generally deductive.

Validity and Reliability

Reliability is simply the assertion that results will remain *consistent* even when the data is collected and evaluated multiple times across multiple periods. Reliability can ensure that the analytical model is valid and can offer consistent results over time (longitudinally). Some common reliability tests include:

Test-retest reliability: Consistent results over time. *Test: Pearson Product Moment Correlation.*
Inter-rater reliability: Participants consistently rate the tests. *Test: Correlation.*
Internal consistency: Different tests consistently measure same results (e.g., IQ). *Test: Cronbach's Alpha.*

Validity asserts that your metrics/measures and variables in a test or model *accurately* measure what you expect them to measure. Some common validity types include:

1. **Content validity**: Metrics and items appear to accurately reflect the variables. *Test: Basic Logic*.
2. **Construct validity**: Metrics and items accurately measure the **unobservable variables or constructs** (*i.e., variables that cannot be directly measured and need more than one metric to measure them, e.g., patient satisfaction*). One important check is for convergent and discriminant validity. Convergent validity checks whether metrics for one variable shows strong relationship. Discriminant validity checks whether metrics for different variables show significant differences and that metrics for one variable does not relate to another variable. *Test: Factor Analysis*.

Type I or Type II Error

Type I errors occur when analytics end up *incorrectly showing evidence of a relationship when, in fact, there is none*. Type II errors occur when analytics end up *incorrectly showing evidence of no relationship when, in fact, there is a relationship*. Type I errors are called false positives (incorrectly rejecting the null) and Type II false negatives (incorrectly not rejecting the null). For example, it is a Type I error if analytics from a mammogram incorrectly shows the presence of cancer when there is no cancer. It is a Type II error is analytics from the mammogram incorrectly shows the absence of cancer when there is cancer. *Test for Type I: α (alpha) (significance) level, e.g., α = 0.05. test for Type II: Power Test or Analysis (with 15 times the number of items and metrics in the model)*.

One-Tail or Two-Tailed?

A one-tail analysis is more appropriate if there is a specifc direction associated with the cause and effect, e.g., higher education increases income.

For example, if a drug treatment (cause) can reduce incidence of a disease (outcome), the reduction signifies a drop in the direction of the relationship and a one-tail test is more appropriate. Note: Most statistical tests report two-tailed p-values, you can calculate one-tailed p-values from two-tailed p-values, divide the two-tailed p-value by 2.

What Do We Do with Outliers and Missing Values?

In general, outliers are important and good analytical practice should try to understand and interpret the outliers. However, if the outliers do not seem to offer much interpretation and add to noise, there are some techniques managing outliers. *Trimming or Truncating* data removes the outliers as extreme values. However, trimming or truncating data reduces the sample size (observations). *Winsorizing* data does not reduce the observations in the sample. Winsorizing is based on replacing extreme values in data (outliers) with a specific percentile value from each end. For example, a 90% winsorization would require replacing all values over the 95th percentile with the value of the 95th percentile; all values lower than the 5th percentile would be replaced by the 5th percentile value.

Missing values in data can happen because of a bias or pattern (e.g., asking questions that respondents do not have or do not wish to furnish) or purely at random called MCAR (Missing Completely at Random) or MAR (Missing at Random). The safest way to manage missing values is *listwise deletion* where all observations (cases) with missing values are removed from the data sample. But that reduces sample size. Other ways include (i) *mean imputation* where a missing value is substituted with the mean of that specific variable and (ii) *regression imputation* where the missing value variable is predicted from observations and used as a substitute (Table 8.1).

Table 8.1 Choosing appropriate data mining, statistical, and econometric analytics models

If outcome variable is	...& the predictor/s is/are	...then recommended statistical analysis...
Discrete (nominal)	Nominal	*Nonparametric* (no assumptions about distribution of population from which samples are drawn) *Chi-Sq Goodness of Fit Test* (χ^2) *or Fisher's Exact Test* to compare Frequencies of Occurrence between observed and expected frequencies (not for percentages, proportions, means, ratios) *Null: Observed and Actual Frequencies are the same*
	Ordinal	*Nonparametric Chi-Sq Goodness of Fit Test* (χ^2) *or Mann–Whitney* (2 independent samples) *Mann-Whitney Null: Medians of the two samples are equal*
	Continuous normal	*(Binary) Logistic* (dependent variable is dichotomous; independent variables are either continuous or categorical variables) or *Multinominal Logistic Regression* (dependent variable is dichotomous)
	Continuous non-normal	*(Binary) Logistic* (dependent variable is dichotomous; independent variables are either continuous or categorical variables) or *Multinominal Logistic Regression* (dependent variable is dichotomous)
Discrete (ordinal)	Nominal	*Nonparametric Chi-Sq Goodness of Fit Test* (χ^2) *or Kuskal Wallis* (nonparametric analysis of variance of more than 2 samples). *Extends Mann-Whitney test* to more than 2 independent samples. *Null: Medians of all groups are equal*
	Ordinal	*Nonparametric Kuskal Wallis or Spearman Rank* (relationship between two ranked or one ranked and one continuous variable—one outcome and one predictor). Spearman rank correlation is a *nonparametric version of Pearson Moment Correlation* and can be used as an alternative to linear regression and correlation. *Null: Spearman correlation coefficient, ρ (i.e., rho), is 0 where the ranks of one variable do not covary with the other variable*
	Continuous normal	*Poisson or Negative Binomial Regression* for count data (count data is assumed as discrete because of a 0 lower-bound)
	Continuous non-normal	*Poisson or Negative Binomial Regression* for count data (count data is assumed as discrete because of a 0 lower-bound)
Continuous (normal)	Nominal	*ANOVA used to analyze differences between group means* and variances *when you have more than 2 groups.* Use *t-test* if you have two samples only and want to test if means of two samples are equal. Use *Student's t-test* if variances are assumed equal. It is called Student's because a Guinness brewery chemist published this test in Biometrika under the nom de plume of Student. *Null: Means of two populations are equal. F-test, Levene's test or Bartlett's test* can be used to check for equality of variance
	Ordinal	*Spearman Rank Correlation* and/or *Linear Regression.* Linear Regression *Null: Slope (β) of relationship between predictor and outcome variables is equal to 0 (β = 0)*
	Continuous normal	*Pearson Moment Correlation* and/or *Linear Regression.* Linear Regression *Null: Slope (β) of relationship between predictor and outcome variables is equal to 0 (β = 0)*
	Continuous non-normal	*Pearson Moment Correlation or Spearman Rank Correlation* and/or *Linear Regression,* Linear Regression *Null: Slope (β) of relationship between predictor and outcome variables is equal to 0 (β = 0)*

(continued)

Table 8.1 (continued)

If outcome variable is	...& the predictor/s is/are	...then recommended statistical analysis...
Continuous (non-normal)	Nominal	*Nonparametric Mann-Whitney test or the Wilcoxon rank sum test* compares two unpaired groups Null: Distributions of both groups are identical. *Use Kruskal Wallis One Way ANOVA or Friedman Rank Test for K Independent Samples*
	Ordinal	*Nonparametric Kuskal Wallis or Spearman Rank* (relationship between two ranked or one ranked and one continuous variable—one outcome and one predictor). Spearman rank correlation is a *nonparametric version of Pearson Moment Correlation* and can be used as an alternative to linear regression and correlation. *Null: Spearman correlation coefficient, ρ (i.e., rho), is 0 where the ranks of one variable do not covary with the other variable*
	Continuous normal	*Linear Regression. Linear Regression Null: Slope (β) of relationship between predictor and outcome variables is equal to 0 ($\beta = 0$)*
	Continuous non-normal	*Pearson Moment Correlation* and/or Linear Regression. Linear Regression *Null: Slope (β) of relationship between predictor and outcome variables is equal to 0 ($\beta = 0$)*

Other Mining Techniques for Analytics

Factor Analysis

Factor Analysis is an *analytical method used to reduce large sets of variables into more manageable, yet "unobservable" or "latent" set of constructs*. Common correlations across the variables are used to reduce variances between the variables and "load" one or more interrelated variables (or items) into one or more "latent" sets. Factor analysis includes EFA (exploratory factor analysis) and PCA (Principal Components Analysis). CFA (confirmatory factor analysis) is a factor analysis that is not exploratory and used to validate that certain variables will in fact "load" onto certain "latent" set of constructs. Factor analysis is used for convergent and discriminant validities for validity testing.

When variables load to latent factors, the values are called factor loadings representing the correlation (similar to Pearson's Correlation Coefficient r). A rule-of-thumb for loadings is >0.7 correlation coefficient or Eigenvalue ≥ 1 for each variable loading to a factor. *Note: To check how much the loaded variables explain variance in the factor, we can calculate it* as: *Sum the squared factor loadings for each factor/number of variables.*

Applications: *Is there a common set of unknown cross-functional performance variables for a company? Do various metrics for patient satisfaction reveal some unknown common performance? What could be some diagnostic tests that can be run together or where are preventative regimens that can be practiced in tandem?*

Cluster Analysis

Cluster analysis is used to group variables into multiple categories. Like factor analysis, cluster analysis is used to reduce large groups of data into meaningful clusters based on similarity. However, unlike factor analysis that groups multiple variables (columns) into factors, cluster analysis reduces multiple observations (rows) into clusters. Cluster analysis typically does not require any "statistical significance" calculation or rule-of-thumb because cluster analysis algorithms, by default, deliver the most optimal set of clusters. Two popular clustering techniques are (i) hierarchical clustering where the clustering algorithm reveals the clusters but is slow and resource intensive. The other is (ii) *k*-means clustering where the number of clusters *k* has to be specified but is relatively more time- and cost-efficient.

Applications: *Can a customer's shopping purchases over time reveal what the customer tends to buy together? Are there microbe classifications based on their behavior of antibiotic resistance? What type of products should a store shelve together?*

Text Analytics

Text analytics is used to search text to explore patterns in order to retrieve information and match them with and build the lexicon (vocabulary) based on natural language processing (NLP). Text analytics mines large bodies of text using sophisticated conditional analytics such as Named Entity Recognition where the meaning and use of a name is defined by the context (e.g., English referring to a people vs. a language), and Sentiment Analysis used to explore emotions, moods, and opinions from reading texts. Text analytics relies upon semantics to understand the nuances and meanings of words and phrases.

Applications: *Can a transcribed conversation reveal a patient's nervous condition? Can a salesperson's interaction with a customer reveal the customer's sentiment about a product purchase? Can an email about a printer problem suggest an interest in buying a new printer (e.g., as in Google's AdSense)?*

Recommendation Analytics

Recommender analytics use content, classification, and collaborative analytics to (i) explore and find characteristics from content to create a profile based on some classification (e.g., style/genre of movies watched or actor/actress watched); (ii) explore other users' similar ratings of other items; (iii) clustering the similar items along based on common user ratings; and (iv) use the similar items and similar ratings to recommend otherwise unknown items across users for purchase or consumption.

Applications: *What products and services can a company cross-sell and up-sell? How can a hospital come up with a recommended set of services based on common services availed by patients with similar characteristics (demographic and health)? How does Netflix or Amazon recommend different movies and products based on behavior of similar consumers?*

Social Network Analysis (SNA)

Social Network Analysis is an analytical technique to reveal the structure of a network where various nodes (companies, divisions, employees, resources, people, etc.) are directly or indirectly connected to one another. SNA can analyze and show various characteristics of a network such as:

Connections based on *similarity* of node characteristics (homophily), *strength* of the node links based on sharing more than one common connection (multiplexity), and connections based on geographic proximity (propinquity). Applications: *How is information shared between companies (nodes) in the Silicon Valley? What individuals or employees share common professional and social connections? What companies share investments as well as R&D? What types of similar and dissimilar individuals and companies are used in successful R&D collaboration?*

Distributions based on a *weak network position* (bridge) as the *only link* between two nodes or network groups (clusters) and the *importance* of the network position (centrality). Applications: *Who is the right group/person that can influence both patients and administrators? Line workers and management? Which users should companies target their marketing on Facebook that can influence other Facebook users?*

Segments based on groups (cliques) that share common characteristics and purpose and minimum number and level of nodes that would make up the group (cohesion). Applications: *How can companies connect their employees across functions and divisions to build creativity? What researchers and practitioners should be involved to create a university-industry hub or regional business consortium?*

Predictive Analytics

Predictive models are centerpieces of finding the relationships between cause and effects that can be used for decision-making via *Hypothesis Testing (confirming causal relationships)* and estimating future changes via *Prediction*. It is used in every aspect of business that requires analysis and estimation of causes, relationships, and forecasting.

Regression analysis is one of the most important predictive modeling techniques in Analytics. Regression analysis is one of the cornerstones of competitive analytics because you can understand relationships between causes and outcomes better with the (i) logical choice of model variables and the (ii) right choice of metrics. Regression analysis will draw a line that defines the slope depicting the relationship between variables.

Regression analysis (i) links causes to outcomes, (ii) shows various levels of usefulness of causes on the outcome, (iii) reveals levels of impacts of each of the causes on the outcome, and (iv) generates a model that can be uses to predict future outcomes based on different values of the causes (factors). *Note: In regression terminology, an Outcome or Dependent Variable is also called effect, criterion variable, endogenous variable, prognostic variable, or regress and. A cause or independent variable is also called exogenous variable, predictor variable, regressor, explanatory variable, treatment variable or predictor variable.*

Linear regression is the simplest form of prediction equation. It is the most popular and one of the most important statistical analysis techniques. It is called linear because a rate of change between a cause and effect is fixed, i.e., it is assumed that a unit change in the cause will always reflect a fixed amount of change in the effect or outcome.

Regression models predict the expected value of the outcome based on prior observations, fitting a straight line through the data in a way that the sum of the squares between the data and the fitted line is the least.

Simple Regression is used when there is one explanatory variable; Multiple (multivariate) regression when there are more than one predictor variable (β for each variable assumes other variables are held constant).

Steps in Running a Regression Model for Predictive Modeling

1. Begin by writing out and crafting the analytical model in sequence:
   a. *What is the result (outcome) you want to improve?* For example, what factors impact credit score, customer loyalty, brand equity, pricing, positioning, the spread of a contagion, technology adoption, infant mortality, price of oil 6 months later, inventory and product returns, and customer satisfaction?
   b. *What are different causes that can impact your result and outcome?*

2. **Setup and Organize the data**: *The first step is to choose the right sample that is representative of the population and collect data based on well-defined metrics.* Organize the data in columns. Each column should separately represent each of the outcome and predictor variables. In this example of housing data, for each house observed, data is collected for Price, Area (area of the living space), Beds (no. of bedrooms), Baths (no. of bathrooms), Garage (no. of car spaces in garage), Lot Sq. Ft Apx (approximate square feet for the whole lot), Year Built (year the house was constructed), and DOM (no. of Days the House was on Market). The summary specification and explanation of each of the variables are called **Metadata**. In fact, this type of mated is called *Descriptive Metadata* while structural specification and information of the variables (when it was collected, format of the data, who

Table 8.2 Structured house sales metadata

	House #	Price	Area	Beds	Baths	Garage	Lot Sq Ft Apx	Year Built	DOM (days on market)
2									
3	1	$1,350,000	1301	4	2	3	20,000	2004	14
4	2	$1,350,000	1301	4	2	3	20,000	2004	14
5	3	$574,999	1302	5	3	2	5,319	2003	7
6	4	$349,000	1601	4	2	2	3,750	1993	0
7	5	$379,000	1701	3	2	2	6,300	1961	1
8	6	$279,000	1703	1	1	0	3,500	1939	4
9	7	$379,888	1703	3	2	1	6,000	1942	1
10	8	$558,000	1703	4	2	1	4,800	1951	5
11	9	$580,000	1703	4	3	1	6,000	1951	0
12	10	$275,000	1704	3	1	1	4,050	1948	1
13	11	$349,000	1704	4	2	0	7,500	1943	2
14	12	$625,000	1707	4	2	1	5,200	1904	15
15	13	$499,000	1800	1	1	0	5,500	1940	2
16	14	$499,000	1800	1	1	0	5,500	1940	2
17	15	$529,000	1800	3	2	2	4,850	1955	13

collected the data) are called *Structural Metadata* (Table 8.2).

3. **Run a Scatterplot** to check for the graphical relationships between two or more sets of data. It is useful practice to run the scatterplots between various predictor variables (as *x*) and the outcome variable (as *y*). The scatterplot will help you check the shape of the relationships, whether they are linear (increasing, decreasing or flat (unrelated) or curvilinear). Knowing the shape of the relationship will allow you to choose the right type of transformation and regression model.[1] Examine the trend and the scatter.

4. **Setup the Regression Model**: *Choose Y and Xs. Leave the confidence level at 95%.* The level of confidence is 1-level of significance. So, a 95% confidence level means a 5% level of significance. This is your benchmark criterion for assessing whether results from your regression model have statistical significance. The linear regression model format is as follows:

$$\text{Output} = \text{Constant} + \text{Coefficient of Impact} * \text{Predictor} + \text{Error}$$

expressed as $y = a + \beta_i x_i + \varepsilon$ where

- β_i is the coefficient of impact (called slope) for each predictor variable *i*.
- Here, "*a*" is the intercept or the constant in the model. This constant refers to the facts that *y* will still hold a value even if the impact or slope of the predictors is 0. For example, if we were looking at various predictors (*x*'s) of cost control (*y*), suppose we model that cost control (*y*) depends upon governance style (x_1), contract procedures (x_2) and productive efficiencies (x_3), we can set up a regression model formatted as follows:

$$\begin{aligned}\text{Cost Control}\,(y) = {} & \alpha + \beta_1 * \text{governance style} \\ & + \beta_2 * \text{contract procedures}\,(x2) \\ & + \beta_3 * \text{productive efficiencies}\,(x3) \\ & + \varepsilon\end{aligned}$$

The question is, are there other predictors that could also explain cost control is organizations? The answer, in this case, is an obvious yes. The intercept *a* captures what is unexplained by the model coverage.

- ε is the random error term or the remainder from the regression equation not being able to "exactly" predict the outcome. If the prediction were exact, the error would be 0. The error gives you the residuals.

---

[1]It is best to run a regression without transformations. Once we have run regression analysis on the raw data. Construct a scatterplot with residuals vs. predicted values. If the scatterplot looks random, don't transform; transform only when the scatterplot has a pattern.

1. **Useful Checks for Prediction/Regression:** Gauss Markov Assumptions for Ordinary least squares (OLS) Regression[2]:
   a. **Linearity** (straight line function)
      i. Test: Symmetric data distribution in observed vs. predicted and residual vs. predicted plots. Check for normality of the dependent variable; independent variable normality is moot.
      Normality ($\sim N$ (mean of 0, std.dev.(σ) of 1).
      i. Test: Kolmogorov–Smirnov and Shapiro-Wilks (should be > level of significance, e.g., 0.05)
      Variable Independence
      i. Test: Durbin-Watson (should be > level of significance, e.g., 0.05) (Durbin-Watson d should be between the two critical values of $1.5 < d < 2.5$)

2. **Residual Errors should be Homoscedastic** (variables should have the same variance)
   a. Test: Koenker–Basset or Breusch–Pagan test (should be > level of significance, e.g., 0.05)

3. **Covariates are Exogenous** (outside the system): Endogeneity (multicollinearity where two or more predictor variables in a multiple regression model are highly correlated)
   a. Test: Multicollinearity Test: Variance Inflation Factor (VIF) (where redundant predictor variables can relate "double counting" and inflate the results without explaining the model better): If VIF$j \geq 4$ then there is a problem with multicollinearity.

4. **Check for Specification** (reduces problems from Misspecification) for Regression model with appropriate metrics for Effects

[2]For Logistic and non-normal regression, assumptions of (i) Response/dependent variable does not have to be normally distributed, (ii) independent variables do not need to be homoscedastic, (iii) Errors do not need to be normally distributed, and (iv) Independent variables can be of any type (e.g., interval, ratio, ordinal, categorical…).

(Response/Dependent/Outcome/Criterion) variables and Causes (Regressor/Independent/ Explanatory/Treatment/Predictor) Variables.

5. **Check for Influence** (too large or small y and/or x values) and Leverage (too large or small x value) by assessing Outliers. Large outliers (>1) should be removed from the model and run again.
   a. Test: Cook's D (Distance) measures the influence of each observation for outliers. A general rule-of-thumb is to remove outliers if $D_i > 1$. More conservative cut-offs use $D_i > 4/(n - k - 1)$ or $D_i > 4/n$ (n = sample size; k = # of variables).

Check the Model: When you look at the results, ensure that you are asking the following questions:

1. Is the overall linear model valid? Check the following for overall model Goodness of Fit:
   a. Adjusted R^2 (coefficient of determination) The R^2 value (varies between 0 and 100%) = (Proportion of Explained Variance explained by Predictors) $\div$ (Total Variation). It's prudent to use Adjusted R^2 over R^2. It is better because it uses degrees of freedom and penalizes the model for adding too many predictors).
   b. p-value (Prob > F or Prob > t) corresponding to the overall model F-Statistic. You want the p-value to be lower than α (level of significance). Most will have a default $\alpha = 0.05$. The overall model p-value < 0.05 is acceptable for rejecting the Regression Model Null: All non-constant coefficients in the regression equation are zero.

2. What does the Intercept say? The intercept is the point at which the regression line cuts the y-axis. Generally, the intercept tells you that the outcome may still occur regardless of our choice of predictors (that there are other predictors not included in the model that also explain the outcome). This means that if the β estimates of the predictors were 0, y would still have a value. Had you included every possible predictor (which none can); the intercept

would be 0. The intercept should always be included, regardless of whether it is statistically significant (p-value < level of significance) or whether it makes common sense.

3. Do the predictors offer a good explanation of the variation in the outcome? Check the following for assessing the validity and usefulness of each predictor you modeled as impacting the outcome:

   a. Significance (are coefficient estimates statistically significant and practically significant)? For predictors to be useful, the beta coefficient for each predictor should be significant, e.g., for each predictor, the p-value < 0.05.

   b. Magnitude (impact) and Trend of Impact (regression estimates): Once predictor significance is acceptable, ensure proper interpretation of β: By how much will each cause x impact the effect y? The β coefficient for each predictor shows the magnitude of the impact of the predictor on the outcome. A $\beta = 0$ means that y does not change based on the predictor; a $-$ve β means a diminishing trend; a $+$ve β means an increasing trend. Each β

impact controls for other variables in the model (Tables 8.3 and 8.4).

Predict and Forecast based on *Regression Model trend, Magnitude, and Significance*: Your *initial regression model* with all the predictors is particularly useful *for hypothesis testing* (proving whether and which of your "hypothesized" causes are significant).

However, in order to predict and forecast, you need to *only include predictors that are statistically significant*. Here are the basic steps:

1. Once you have run the regression, check for goodness of fit (Adjusted R^2) and β significance for each predictor.

2. Note the predictors that are statistically significant (p-value < level of significance [e.g., 0.05]).

3. Re-create the regression model including only the statistically significant predictors. Drop the predictors that were statistically insignificant in your initial regression.

4. Run the Regression with the y and the statistically significant predictors (x_1, x_2,...). You will find that the β coefficients have changed for the new model.

Table 8.3 Regression choices for predictive analytics

Regression model	Response variable	Coefficient (β) interpretation	Examples
OLS (Ordinary Least Squares)	Continuous, normally distributed	β increase in outcome for unit increase in predictor	Productivity; intention to purchase; use of a product/service; contract costs
Poisson Outcome Y is $Log_e(Y)$	Count of occurrences	e^β *(exponential of β)* increase in outcome for unit increase in predictor	No. of successes; no. of people waiting in line; no. of products returned; no. of months of recession; no. of complaints
Logistic/logit (binary) or probit Outcome Y is $Log(p/1 - p)$	Yes/no	e^β *(exponential of β)* increase in outcome for unit increase in predictor	Accept/reject; win/lose; success/failure; buy/not buy
Multinominal logistic or logit	More than 2 nominal responses (unordered nominal categories)	e^β *(exponential of β)* increase in outcome for unit increase in predictor	Choice of a specific market out of many markets; choice of a brand; choice of a major; choice of a physician
Ordinal logistic or logit	Categorical (ordered nominal categories)	e^β *(exponential of β)* increase in outcome for unit increase in predictor	Income level; size of soda; education level; tax bracket; satisfaction level; performance level

Table 8.4 Interpreting regression choices for predictive analytics

Regression model (Transformed)	Impact of x on y
$\log(y) = \beta_0 + \beta_1 x + \varepsilon$ *Outcome only*	If x changes by 1 unit (whatever the unit is), the outcome y will change by $\exp(\beta_1)$ expressed as a % Suppose β_1 is 0.09, a unit change in x increases y by $\exp(\beta_1) = 1.094$ or 9.4% (1.094 as a %)
$y = \beta_0 + \beta_1 \log(x) + \varepsilon$ *Predictor only*	If x changes by 1% (the unit is %), the outcome y will change by $\beta_1 \times \ln(1.01)$. (1% is 1.01) Suppose β_1 is 3; the impact of a 10% (1.1) change in x on y is "$\beta_1 \times \log(1.1)$" = 0.124 or 12.4% change in y
$\log(y) = \beta_0 + \beta_1 \log(x) + \varepsilon$ *Predictor & Outcome*	If x changes by 1% (the unit is %), the outcome y will change by 1.01^{β_1} (1% is 1.01) Suppose β_1 is 0.7; the impact of a 10% (1.1) change in x on y is $1.1^{0.7}$ or 6.9% (1.069 as a %)

5. Specify the Prediction Model with the new β coefficients as $y = a + \beta_i x_i + \varepsilon$
6. In order to predict, you can replace each or any of the predictor's x values with your specified value.
7. The new y-value predicts the impact of the change from different values of x.

Basic Regression Illustration

Suppose in order to predict house prices, we need to understand what house features impact house prices (Fig. 8.1). We begin by:

1. Hypothesize the relationship as: y (house price) $= a$ (intercept) $+ \beta_1 x_1$ (House Area) $+ \beta_2 x_2$ (# of Bedrooms) $+ \beta_3 x_3$ (# of Bathrooms) $+ \beta_4 x_4$ (# of Cars Garage) $+ \beta_5 x_5$ (Lot Sq Ft) $+ \beta_6 x_6$ (Yr. Built) $+ \varepsilon$
2. Run the Regression with x and y variables.
3. Check Goodness of Fit: The model shows an Adjusted R^2 of 52.74% (0.52735). This means that the hypothesized predictors explain about 52.74% of the variance in house prices. Not all predictors are significant.
4. Check β significance for each predictor: The regression analytics shows that not all hypothesized predictors are statistically

Regression Statistics

R	0.75848	
R Square	0.5753	
Adjusted R Square	0.52735	
S	253,833.26796	
Total number of observations	70	

ANOVA

	d.f.	SS	MS	F	p-level
Regression	7.	5.41126E+12	7.73037E+11	11.99784	0.
Residual	62.	3.99474E+12	6.44313E+10		
Total	69.	9.406E+12			

	Coefficients	Standard Error	LCL	UCL	t Stat	p-level	H0 (5%) rejected?
Intercept	-2,292,635.01203	2,497,584.65864	-7,285,235.60603	2,699,965.58197	-0.91794	0.36221	No
House Area	200.62237	74.65751	51.38415	349.8606	2.68724	0.00924	Yes
# Bedrooms	142,218.9703	38,837.73437	64,583.44552	219,854.49608	3.66188	0.00052	Yes
# Bathrooms	-38,048.38938	49,654.30243	137,305.92563	61,209.14687	-0.76627	0.44643	No
# of Cars Garage	113,808.68704	48,658.07787	16,542.57612	211,074.79957	2.33895	0.02258	Yes
Lot Sq Ft Apx	7.27065	3.49903	0.27619	14.26511	2.07791	0.04187	Yes
Yr. Built	1,024.75333	1,294.12455	-1,562.16478	3,611.67145	0.79185	0.43147	No
DOM (days on market)	5,422.21466	3,302.91096	-1,180.21027	12,024.6396	1.64165	0.10573	No
T (5%)	1.99897						
LCL - Lower value of a reliable interval (LCL)							
UCL - Upper value of a reliable interval (UCL)							

Fig. 8.1 Basic regression statistics for predictive modeling

significant at $p < 0.05$. Significant predictors are House Area, # of Bedrooms, # of Car Garage, and Lot Sq Ft Approx. Insignificant predictors are # of Bathrooms and the Year Built.

5. To predict, re-create the regression model including only the significant predictors. The new prediction model is shown as: y (house price) $= a$ (intercept) $+ \beta_1 x_1$ (House Area) $+ \beta_2 x_2$ (# of Bedrooms) $+ \beta_3 x_3$ (# of Cars Garage) $+ \beta_4 x_4$ (Lot Sq Ft) $+ \varepsilon$

6. Rerun the new regression model with x and y variables. Note that the new Adjusted R^2 is 51.74% (a small drop from 52.74% even though two predictors have been removed) is all predictor variables are statistically significant. The prediction model is y (house price) $= -299,959$ (intercept) $+ 188*x_1$ (House Area) $+ 128,714*x_2$ (# of Bedrooms) $+ 135,198*x_3$ (# of Cars Garage) $+ 7*x_4$ (Lot Sq Ft)

7. Use the new model for prediction. Based on the results from the sample of 70 houses, every extra sq. ft. added to the House Area raises the price by nearly $188; adding another bedroom increases the price by $129,000; adding one more car garage by $135,000, and one lot sq. ft. by $7.

   a. Suppose we wish to predict the estimated price of a house in that area that is approximately 4000 sqft., 5 bedrooms, 3 car garages on a lot of 20,000 sqft. All we do is input these values into the variables as y (house price) $= -299,959$ (intercept) $+ 188*4000$ (House Area) $+ 128,714*5$ (# of Bedrooms) $+ 135,198*3$ (# of Cars Garage) $+ 7*20,000$ (Lot Sq. Ft). Based on this information, we can predict that a house price of approximately $998,279 at which it is likely to sell.

   b. We can use this information for competitive analytics which allows us to make pricing decisions as well as home improvement decisions. For this specific area, it might be prudent for the homeowner to add a garage space for one more car because the impact of # of Car Garage is the highest and thus provides the biggest investment on every invested dollar.

   c. Of course, it is especially important to use some strategic sense in this decision-making. It is relatively easier and cheaper to add a garage space than to add a bedroom. So, when deciding on whether to add a garage space, it would be useful to assess the costs of building a garage. We know that the price of a house increases by approximately $135,000 from adding a garage space. Suppose it costs $5000 to add a garage space, we could calculate return on investment (ROI) for an additional garage space as approximately $135,000/$5,000 $\sim$ an ROI of 27 or 27 times return on investment. This appears to be a welcome decision that could help you competitively improve and price your house based on your market (Fig. 8.2).

Other Regression Analytics Concepts

Dummy Variables: If you have a predictor with more than two nominal or categorical variables, you can use dummy variables to create a proxy to check for specific effects. Suppose we hypothesized that House Prices are also a function of (depend upon) a specific area of the city (5 nominal values of East, West, North, South, Central). In this case, *you can create 4 dummy variables (n – 1, i.e., 5 – 1 = 4 dummy variables). Each column would represent the specific area of the city* such as East, West... If a house were in the Eastern part, the dummy variable of East would take a value of 1, else it would be 0. If a house were in the West, the dummy variable of West would take a value of 1, else it would be 0. *We do not have to create a dummy variable for Central* (i.e., the last of the areas) because it automatically assumes a value of 0 because others can be a 1. *Note that, for dummy variables, the variable values cannot overlap, e.g., in this case, there cannot be a north-west or south-central area of the city.*

Regression Statistics							
R	0.73849						
R Square	0.54537						
Adjusted R Square	0.51739						
S	256,492.48012						
Total number of observations	70						

ANOVA							
	d.f.	SS	MS	F	p-level		
Regression	4.	5.12975E+12	1.28244E+12	19.49339	0.		
Residual	65.	4.27625E+12	6.57884E+10				
Total	69.	9.406E+12					

	Coefficients	Standard Error	LCL	UCL	t Stat	p-level	H0 (5%) rejected?
Intercept	-299,959.34299	196,358.19501	-692,113.73786	92,195.05189	-1.52761	0.13146	No
House Area	187.99913	73.32668	41.55564	334.44263	2.56386	0.01267	Yes
# of Bedrooms	128,713.61524	33,335.51115	62,138.00223	195,289.22825	3.86116	0.00026	Yes
# of Cars Garage	135,197.52149	41,549.99056	52,216.46026	218,178.58272	3.25385	0.00181	Yes
Lot Sq Ft Apx	7.00701	3.46421	0.08851	13.92551	2.02269	0.04722	Yes
T (5%)	1.99714						
LCL - Lower value of a reliable interval (LCL)							
UCL - Upper value of a reliable interval (UCL)							

Fig. 8.2 Regression modeling for predictive analytics using significant variables

Mediation: Mediation happens when one or more causes (Xs) lead to an outcome (Y) and the outcome is the cause for another outcome (Z). *Here, Y is a mediator.* For example, a company's R&D expenditure (X) can increase the number of products it has in the market (Y) which in turn can increase revenues (Z). In order to test whether Y is really a mediator, run 4 regressions (i) $Z = a + \beta X + \varepsilon$ (ii) $Y = a + \beta X + \varepsilon$ (iii) $Z = a + \beta Y + \varepsilon$ and (iv) $Z = a + \beta X + \beta Y + \varepsilon$. Assuming that the first 3 regression models are significant, if, in (iv) X is no longer significant when Y is included, it means *full mediation*; if X and Y in (iv) are both significant, it shows *partial mediation*.

Interaction Effects: An Interaction Effect is created when you hypothesize that *two or more predictors, when combined, can impact the outcome*. For example, with the House Price data, suppose you hypothesize that although # of bedrooms and # bathrooms might impact the price of a house, when combined or taken together, they can influence the price of a house. For such a hypothesis, *you would add an interaction effect "# of Bedrooms x # of Bathrooms"* to the model. This model would be represented as $y = a$ (intercept) $+ \beta_1 x_1$ (House Area) $+ \beta_2 x_2$ (# of Bedrooms) $+ \beta_3 x_3$ (# of Bathrooms) $+ \beta_4 x_4$ (# of Cars Garage) $+ \beta_5 x_5$ (Lot Sq. Ft) $+ \beta_6 x_6$ (Yr. Built) $+ \beta_7 x_7$ (# of Bedrooms * # of Bathrooms) $+ \varepsilon$.

Time Series and Autoregression (e.g., ARMA (Auto-Regressive Moving Average): Time Series Analysis is commonly *a univariate (scalar or single variable) technique where the value of a variable changes over regular intervals in time*. Here, the value of a variable in a specific time period (t) is impacted by its value in a previous time period (e.g., $t - 1$). So, the variable serves as the predictor and outcome. The regression is expressed as $X_t = a + {}_1 X_{t-1} + \varepsilon_t$. For example, inventory held by a company in one period can be impacted by the value of the inventory the company help in the previous period. Similarly, a stock price at a specific time can depend on serious stock prices for the same stock based on previous an economic performance such as GDP (Gross Domestic Product which measures the total output of a country's economy). *Popular analysis tests include Box-Jenkins and Box-LJung.* Note that the value in a Time Series can be affected by:

Seasonality (such a specific drop in inventory during holidays or a jump in stock prices during periods of economic upswing). The seasonality can be represented as dummy variables.

	Direct Labor	Direct Materials	Indirect Materials	Logistics	Sales Price	Profit
Product A	500	500	50	5	1505	450
Product B	400	750	50	15	2365	1150
Product C	300	250	100	10	1460	800
Product D	200	500	50	5	1255	500

Fig. 8.3 Optimization and prescriptive analytics for production

Stationarity: A stationary process has the property that the *mean, variance and autocorrelation in the data do not change over time*. The run-sequence plot of the variable over time should be flat and should not show a specific trend. If there are specific periodic increases and drops, it may indicate seasonality.

Data in time series can be *decomposed* using moving averages and exponential smoothing often using *time or period lags* between the univariate outcome and the predictor/s.

Prescriptive Analytics

Predictive analytics works on estimating and forecasting the future. Prescriptive analytics works on coming up with a decision.

What we focus on is a prescriptive technique called **Optimization**. Optimization, as the name denotes, is about coming up with an optimal decision based on some considerations.

1. What is your or the company's goal or objective? Increasing profit or investment returns Decreasing Costs, Increasing Employee Satisfaction, Lowering Tax Expenses, Reaching a Particular Market Share or Customer Loyalty?
2. What are the things that the company can control, configure, and change in order to achieve the goal or objective? Should they change their product portfolio.
3. What are the constraints or obstacles that have to be considered in order to reach the objective or goal? Companies have time constraints, costs or budget constraints, supply or inventory constraints, regulatory constraints, and many more that have to be

considered before a decision can be made. Think of constraints as feasibility issues. If there are feasibility issues such a political or technological issue that may not get your project off the ground, such issues have to be incorporated in a prescriptive, optimization model.

Optimization basically creates and solves a series of separate simultaneous equations where x variables are the things that can be changed to achieve the objective or goal Here is a quick example.

Using Microsoft Excel's Solver[3] to Optimize Choices based on Goals (in this case, maximizing profits from choosing how many products to produce) (Fig. 8.3).

This is what we will try to optimize. A company has 4 products (A...D). Each product requires certain costs for direct labor, direct materials, indirect costs, and logistics. Each product also has a sales price.

Subtracting the costs from the sales price gives you a general sense of Gross Profit (shown as Profit) (Fig. 8.4).

Next, we create a set we want to optimize, i.e., the number of products in the company's portfolio that should be produced to maximize profit.

To do so, we begin by assuming that the company produces 1 of each unit (you can assign any number but 1 is easier for quick calculation check). So, direct labor costs for 1 unit of Product C would be 1×300. Once you have all the totals, you sum up the profit. This is what you

---

[3]You will find Solver under Tools. If you don't have it there, click on add-ins and make sure that Solver is checked. Else, find it as solver.xla and add it in and then check the box.

| | | | | | | | Totals |
No. of Products		Direct Labor	Direct Materials	Indirect Materials	Logistics	Sales Price	Profit
1		500	500	50	5	1505	450
1		400	750	50	15	2365	1150
1		300	250	100	10	1460	800
1		200	500	50	5	1255	500
	Total	1400	2000	250	35	6585	2900
Available Capacity per Period		29200	60500	5800	740		**Maximize Total Profits**
Unused Capacity		27800	58500	5550	705		

Fig. 8.4 Structuring data for optimization and prescriptive analytics

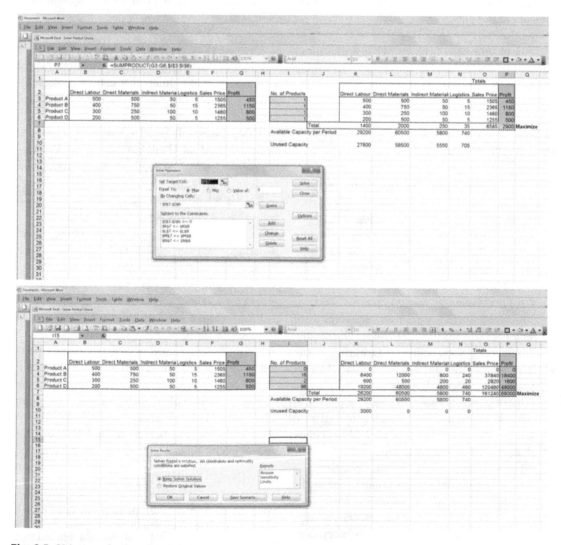

Fig. 8.5 Using excel solver for optimization and prescriptive analytics

want to maximize by changing the numbers in the product portfolio.

The unused capacity cells are just calculated by subtracting the total resources used from the available capacity.

This is a very important screen. When you open Solver, the Target Cell is set to the total profit (P7) from producing 1 unit of each product. Then, you specify that you want the product portfolio optimized by changing the portfolio cells (I3–I6). Next you set the constraints. The first constraint is that you cannot produce less than 0 or each product; the second is that direct labor, direct materials, indirect materials, and logistics costs have to be less than that of available capacity. Therefore, total direct labor costs have to be less than or be equal to $27,800, and so on. Once you assign the constraints, you are ready to solve.

The Optimization results show that, in order to maximize profit, this company should not produce any of A, produce 16 units of B, 2 units of C and 96 units of D, given inventory constraints. Interestingly, the only underutilized capacity is $3000 for labor (which will therefore be deadweight (cannot be used) and will reduce the net profit (Fig. 8.5).

This part covers one of the most pressing aspects of global technology—cybersecurity. As 4IR and COVID-19 digitally pivot businesses and societies, cyberthreats emerge as a dark side of digital transformation, jeopardizing global commerce. The part begins with a brief review of the computing infrastructure. Then, the part covers cyber-attacks and cyber-threats threats, along with a review of espionage, encryption, and cryptography. The part offers cases in support along with post-cyber-attack crisis communication strategies.

Learning Outcomes

By the end of this part, students will be able to:

- Review and Explain the Cybersecurity Infrastructure.
- Examine the Ethics and Outcomes of Hacking and Cybersecurity.
- Assess the roles of human and business process inefficiencies in Cyberattacks.
- Understand how Encryption and Cryptography help protect Data.
- Evaluate various Cyberthreat and Cybersecurity Strategies.
- Develop Leadership Skills to Plan and Conduct Cybersecurity and Cyberattack.

We live in a digital-connected world where our identities, likes, dislikes, eating habits, shopping behavior, financial information, and medical records reside in digital networks deep in the cloud. With the massive growth of connected devices and smart homes (Internet of Things), remote mouse clicks can steal our information, identities, and disrupting the global infrastructure. This module covers one of the most pressing aspects of global technology—cybersecurity. Here, we cover the fundamentals of cyber-attacks and cyber-threats, espionage, encryption, and post-cyber-attack crisis communication strategies.

Cybersecurity—A Tale of Technology, Processes, and People

The pen is mightier that the sword, needless to mention, but the sword protects the freedom of the pen. When things seem to be quiet and prosperous in a country, it is often assumed that the country might be wasting tax dollars on the military. Yet, it may be the military guarding the borders that helps afford the quietude and prosperity. Cyber-security has the same problem. When things are going within a company, cybersecurity invest-ments seem like overkill. In his writings, the famous Roman orator, Cicero, mentions how Romans were complacent about the Hannibal's march across the Alps to destroy Rome. The Romans' panicked utterance *"Hannibal ad*

Portas" (Hannibal at the Gates) happened too late. In the same way, companies often are complacent, only to come to a late realization and a rude awakening after suffering cyber-attacks.

When times are quiet, people often don't care for the military, but when times get tough, when there's an attack, when there's a threat, suddenly the same people find the military crucial. The same person who bemoans why we have a mil-itary and surveillance may end up being the same person willing to sacrifice privacy during times of crisis to feel secure and protected.

A reason why cybersecurity is difficult are because cybersecurity is a three-faced issue. Cybersecurity is more than just a technical problem. Cybersecurity incorporates aspects of economics, human psychology, operational pro-cesses, technology, and culture. Technology is pervasive, and cybersecurity must stay in sync.

Cybersecurity is a multi-billion-dollar industry involving companies and countries themselves. Practicing good and consistent cybersecurity are the only defenses against cyber-attacks. A sophis-ticated cyber-attack can cripple a country's utility or banking infrastructure and thus a country's economy.

Moreover, processes in cyberspace work dif-ferently. None of our traditional physical world mental models work in cyberspace. For example, we hand a credit card over at a restaurant and then it's processed and returned to us and we sign it merrily and go. You wouldn't really handover your credit card in cyberspace or over the

Internet to somebody unless it was secure. But how many times have you thought—well, is the waiter or waitress going to steal my credit card? *Trust is lower in cyberspace*. In cyberspace, there are no physical borders or the protection of walls, fences, or houses. Just like a single drug-dealing house in the safest neighborhood can make the neighborhood unsafe, a single vulnerability in people, processes, or technologies can compromise the entire system and make the system vulnerable.

Your computer might be located within four walls with locked doors but the minute you are linked to the Internet, you're in open space and you're vulnerable. Cyber-attacks are relentless and not bound by time or space. Cyber-attacks occur anywhere and anytime and there are no police or FBI jurisdictions. Cybersecurity and physical security are two very different things.

So, practicing good cybersecurity requires focusing on **People, Processes, and Technology**.

1. **Process**: First, cybersecurity is never merely a technical problem, people who think that it's just a technical problem, only, it's like looking at cybersecurity, like looking at an iceberg you don't see what's beneath the water, you only see what's on top of the water, and you think what's on top the water is just the same as what's beneath the water. How mistaken we'd be once we figure out that only 1/13 of an iceberg floats above water. Such is the issue with assuming that cybersecurity is only a technology problem. At the end of the day, technology tries to mirror a process while reengineering the process for efficiencies.

   Process reengineering is key. If a process is problematic, installing the best technology will not solve anything. If an employee has a terrible work habit, giving that employee an expensive laptop will not make the employee any more productive. You can have the terrible process and the best technology; the terrible process will always win. A hospital might have a problematic process where hospital staff needs to print confidential patient information and pass it around for signatures and approvals. Such a process is likely to create privacy problems because staff might misplace the documents, place the documents in a place where they can be viewed by other patients, visitors, and people. Even if the hospital spent millions of dollars in digitizing documents but still followed a traditionally problematic process of carrying and passing printed documents, digitization investments would be a **sunk cost** (costs that cannot be recovered or wasted costs).

   The best technological intentions without changing the underlying work process can often be a wasted effort. So, anytime a company embarks on cybersecurity, it is prudent to begin by thinking of cybersecurity as a process reengineering problem rather than merely a technological problem. Make sure that the process is fixed before applying a cybersecurity technology. **Corporate culture**, or the long-held beliefs by the company, can also maintain old, decrepit processes that can compromise a company. Make sure that corporate culture evolves with changing times and changing cybersecurity threats.

2. **People**: Second, cybersecurity is a **people** problem. Human beings are emotional creatures and emotion creates variances in what we do and how we act. Moments of weaknesses, rage, frustration, happiness, gloom, all play into our work habits and that can often compromise the most secure systems.

   The rules of cyberspace are different from the physical words, which basically means that, if we're so accustomed to acting in a certain way in the physical world, we can do the same in a cyber-world, assuming a false sense of security. A person, used to discussing one's confidential life to one or few friends, may suddenly blurt out the same on Facebook. Yet, the digital world does not offer the same confines of privacy, as does the physical world. There are ears and eyes everywhere, watching, listening, and sniffing crumbs of information to create a profile and compromise identities for gain. For centuries, warfare has practices **PsyOps** (psychological operations), where war is raged not only between machines of destruction but also by preying on fear in human psychology.

In the thirteenth century, Genghis Khan, the Mongol invader would have each soldier carry three torches to instill fear into enemies who would think that the size of the invading force was three times larger. During the First World War, the British would drop thousands of leaflets over the German trenches to demoralize the German forces. The leaflets said how the German commanders were using German soldiers as cannon fodder. During the Second World War, the Nazi regime is said to broadcast to American soldiers during the 1944 D-Day landings that the *"the Statue of Liberty is kaputt,"* as a way to strike fear and loss of morale on the American soldier's psyche. In cybersecurity, people remain the weakest links, falling prey to social engineers, confidence tricksters, and propagandists that leveraged inherent biases and fears in human psychology. Another issue is employee resistance to change. Employee resistance is a tough thing to manage, especially if the corporate culture does not automatically change in order to reflect changing times. Add to that employee malice, from employees disgruntled from a perception of inequity or unfairness, or perhaps, because they, to a certain degree, have access to the jewels in the crown, they can truly turn against their own company.

3. **Technology**: Third, technology is of course important. Cybersecurity is not just a technical problem. So, technology is necessary, but not sufficient. This next section focuses on the technological and technical aspects of cybersecurity and how they crisscross between people and business processes.

Technology: The Basic Workings

Computers and the Internet work in very interesting ways. A computer simply receives every action you take (moving the mouse, typing a key, typing, clicking, opening, or closing an app or software) and sends your actions as **instructions** to the computer microprocessor. The microprocessor receives every instruction and takes care of every instruction in sequence, like a teller of a cashier. If the teller or cashier is busy with one person, you have to wait till the person is free before you can avail his or her service. A computer's microprocessor behaves in the same way. When overloaded with instructions, it suffers from a backlog and you have to wait for service. That is why you see the dreaded hourglass or Newton wheel when your computer is busy, often a prelude to an application being frozen or a system crashing.

Early on, computers were nothing but display terminals or "**dumb terminals**" that would link to a large mainframe computer that did all the information processing. The mainframe computer was the central system with large tape systems reading data. Computer terminals or **clients** would only send basic requests of queries and read out only what was returned by the mainframe. Over time, computers started carrying their own data and processing power, creating software applications that could be installed and run on each machine. With all the processing power, application content, and graphical interfaces, computers now became **thick clients**. That was until the coming of the Internet.

We are in the 4th Industrial Revolution (4IR) —a bio-physical convergence of technology with every aspect of our lives, from AI and IoTs to Voice Recognition and Metaverses! *But did you know that the origin of 4IR is the story of the origin of databases?*

But the story of databases is a dark tale, starting with the threat of a nuclear war between the US and USSR, and the coming of the Internet.

During the Cold War, the US wanted to protect its military data from a nuclear strike. So, the US military R&D group (DARPA) asked universities to build a digital network (today called the Internet) where military data would be systematically categorized in many places. If a Soviet strike destroyed one military base, the data would be accessible via networked databases by allies across the world. The database became key to the US and NATO's military survival.

A database is a technology that helps organize data, everything from Apple Pay touchless payments, IoT sensors, and Facebook posts to

YouTube, GPS, and Amazon Alexa. With millions of Petabytes of data created and read every minute, databases neatly organize data so that we can search what we need, when we need, and get the most relevant information in milliseconds! Without databases, the 4IR world would cease to exist.

The story of how wired digital networks linked computers and databases to create the Internet is fascinating. Today's 4IR world goes beyond wired networks to include satellite-based wireless (e.g., Elon Musk's Starlink and Iridium) and cellular or mobile broadband such as LTE or 5G.

The problem that networks face is that the wider the network, the slower it is. **Network size is negatively correlated with network bandwidth**. So, we mostly use local, high-speed router-based WLANs (Wireless Local Area Networks) such as the 802.11x networks in our house, airports, and cafes. On an even more smaller network level, we have Bluetooth (such as connecting our wireless earphones) and NFC (Near Field Communication) such as how we use our Smart Watch or Smart Phone for contactless payment while shopping.

But let's get back to how the coming of the Internet tied together the 3 essential technologies: computers, databases, and networks.

The Birth of the Internet

The Internet grew out the fear of nuclear attacks during the Cold War. The **Cold War** was a war that did not see the clash of armies but a lot of defense buildups, rhetorical saber rattling, spy craft, threats of large-scale offensive, and mostly, the threat of nuclear strikes between two superpowers, the US and USSR and their respective allies across the **Iron Curtain**. The Iron Curtain, referring to economic and ideological barriers between the USSR and other communist countries and free-market economies, fell on Europe. The Iron curtain divided Europe into USSR-controlled and US-Western-European NATO (North Atlantic Treaty Organization)-controlled territories, with nuclear missiles pointed at one another. The nuclear threat was real. In 1962, the

Cuban Missile Crisis had brought the US and the USSR on the verge of a nuclear showdown. Schools and cities had nuclear shelters everywhere in the US and Europe. It was the age of **MAD (Mutually Assured Destruction)**, where hundreds of intercontinental ballistic missiles or "birds" would crisscross each other on the verge of space as satellites and early warning systems would automatically fire from nuclear missile silos aimed at strategic targets across the US, Europe, and USSR. It would be nuclear winter.

Did you know that?

Sir Winston Churchill made the phrase "Iron Curtain" popular! Invited by President Truman in 1945 to give a college speech in Missouri, US, Churchill said "From Stettin in the Baltic to Trieste in the Adriatic, an iron curtain has descended across the continent!"

Faced with this impending reality, the US defense asked the Defense Department's Advanced Research Project Agency (ARPA) to create an attack resistant network system that would still allow the US military to maintain its lines of communication, coordination, and control even when facing a large nuclear strike. By 1967, plans had begun for creating **ARPANET** along with two important innovations that would change the world of networked computing.

First, communication between computers was based on something called **circuit switching**. Circuit switching creates a circuit between two computers, much like a telephone connection, to communicate. The problem of circuit switching is that when the circuit is created, the computers can communicate with no one else. Just like a telephone connection that sent a busy signal when someone else was on the line, circuit switched did not allow for simultaneous communications. ARPANET changed communication from circuits to packets. In packet switching, every piece of data is broken into multiple packets and each of the packets could independently travel across the network. Other data packets can also travel through the same network. Suddenly, **packet switching** allowed us to send and receive emails along with streaming videos and voice calls.

The second innovation was built based on creating a "packet-switched" network of nodes where data and information could be served and stored. Instead of relying on a single central server, i.e., a high-powered computer to remotely process and serve multiple clients' requests, to multiple decentralized servers and databases. The idea behind the decentralization was that, if there were a military strike on one central server, it would fail to run, and the US defense assets' command and control would go offline and blind. However, ARPANET's idea of packet switched decentralized servers and databases would maintain business continuity, i.e., the organization's ability to function even after a disaster or attack.

As ARPANET become more and more popular, over the 1970s and 1980s, ARPANET spread across the world as US allies around the globe wanted to use ARPANET to link their defense assets. Like telephone and telegraphs lines, the ARPANET networking infrastructure spread across the globe, underground and undersea, preparing for a Soviet military strike. But then, the strangest thing happened.

In 1989, the **Berlin Wall** that divided Soviet control East Germany (GDR) and US and European ally West Germany (FRG), fell, beginning the end of the Cold War and USSR dominance. USSR (Union of Soviet Socialist Republics), or Soviet Union, formed in December 1922 out of the 1917 Russian revolution with Lenin and Stalin, ceased to exist on December 26, 1991. USSR broke up into 15 countries including the controlling matriarch Russia, Ukraine, Georgia, Kazakhstan, Estonia, Latvia, among many others.

Did you know that?
The beginning of the Iron Curtain was often depicted by Checkpoint Charlie and the Berlin Wall that divided Germany's East and West Berlin!

Suddenly, the Soviet nuclear threat was gone, and the Cold War had ended in a whimper.

No longer facing its nuclear nemesis, the US made a noble and gracious gesture to the world. ARPANET, a military network now spanning across the globe, was handed over the world to use for free, to carry digital, networked traffic at the speed of light across very corner of the world, to usher in a new era of connected peace.

The **Internet** grew out of ARPANET, as a public network that would host the world-wide-web (WWW) application and become the great equalizer and competitive force. Of course, the world paid homage to the US for such as gracious gesture. Companies in the US were not required to specify their country code on websites while everyone else was. This is called **ccTLD** (Country-Code Top Level Domain). For example, Amazon.com will remain Amazon.com in the US but will be Amazon.co.uk in the UK, co.fr in France, co.de in Germany, co.jp in Japan, co.za in South Africa, and so forth. It is a small but meaningful homage to the country that gave us the Internet and changed the world.

Networked Computing

The Internet is based on networked computing. A networked computer such a computer connected to the Internet (or **Cloud**) behaves in a similar way but with more steps or **tiers**. A networked computer has a client (the user's machine such as a laptop or a mobile phone), a server (that hosts the application that will serve you the information you are requesting or querying), and a database (a place and mechanism to store information from which the serves searches, finds the right information and sends it back to the client). In this case, because there are three layers of access, it is called a **Client–Server** three-tier system.

The three-tier client–server system works very much like a restaurant. The client places a request for an order to the server; the server takes it to the kitchen and the pantry to get the requested order, and then brings it to the client or customer.

Today, as long as we are connected to the Internet or the **Cloud** (because network diagrams depict a remote connection such as the Internet as a cloud), we can access information (e.g., Wikipedia, Google) and run applications (e.g., Google Maps, Netflix, Amazon Prime) without have to download all the content. So, our app-driven smartphones and tablets are often called **Thin-Clients** because they are client computers that access servers over the cloud and do not need much storage memory and are, thus, Thin-Clients.

On the web, every data or information, from a text message to a 4k video, is broken into many packets. Each packet is sent separately and independently over the network. Each packet might take a different route to the destination but will eventually arrive at the destination (or **IP address**, an Internet address such as 2a02:26f0:18:494 for www.tesla.com) and be reassembled into the text, image, or video like a jigsaw puzzle by a protocol called **TCP (Transmission Control Protocol)**.

Every web server on the Internet's world-wide-web has a human-readable address called its URL (e.g., www.tesla.com) which hides its actual address or IP address (2a02:26f0:18:494). A Domain Name Server (**DNS**) is used to translate IP addresses into **URL**s so that it can be read and remembered by human beings. A URL is similar to a company's Trademark while the IP address is similar to a company's license number.

Cybersecurity Tenets

So, what is cybersecurity? The International Telecommunication Union (Overview of cybersecurity, 2009) defines it as follows:

Cybersecurity is the collection of tools, policies, security concepts, security safeguards, guidelines, risk management approaches, actions, training, best practices, assurance, and technologies that can be used to protect the cyber environment and organization and user's assets. Organization and user's assets include connected computing devices, personnel, infrastructure, applications, services, telecommunications systems, and the totality of transmitted and/or stored information in the cyber environment. Cybersecurity strives to ensure the attainment and maintenance of the security properties of the organization and user's assets against relevant security risks in the cyber environment.

Cybersecurity deals with protecting the computers, the networks, the information or data packets, and the databases that permeate and define our modern way of life and living.

Three main tenets govern cybersecurity objectives, with the acronym **CIA (Confidentiality, Integrity, Availability)**:

- **Confidentiality**: Confidentiality ensures that certain information be privy only to the people who have the right credentials for accessing it. A company's internal documents, market research, R&D, employee salaries, and performance reports, customer information are example of confidential information. As are your bank information, social security number, credit card information, etc. Confidentiality assures users that companies can be entrusted with safekeeping their information. **Encryption** is the most common and important way to ensure confidentiality. Encryption is a process by which data is scrambled and locked to make it unreadable to anyone but the person that holds the key. Encryption is a splendid way to protect data, and it is important to ensure that a webpage, especially used to enter login information reads *https* before the URL. **HTTPS** (Hypertext Transfer Protocol Secure). Web browsers such as Google Chrome, Safari, and Internet Explorer use encryption to protect communications but it is important to check that any login website uses https.

- **Integrity:** Every day we enter a large amount of information into various apps, websites, and computer systems. Integrity ensures that our information remains unchanged and unaltered unless we specifically approve of the change. Think of it. If a hacker accesses and changes a patient's health information, such as current medications, the integrity of the information is lost, and the effect can be fatal to a patient. Hackers will often times try to intercept or **sniff** information by hiding in the network to steal or alter the information. Sniffing is often done on unencrypted networks such as free coffee shop and airport Wi-Fi connections. This type of attack is also known as **MITM (Man-in-the-Middle)** where a cyber-attacker sniffs information in the network and changes it to serve the attacker's interest. In 2003, Belkin, a manufacturer of networking products such as routers, performed MITM on its own router traffic to send users other Belkin product adverts. Ironically, in 2017, Equifax, an American credit scoring agency that's checks consumer credit records based on their social security numbers, realized that its mobile credit score app credit could be compromised by an MITM attack that could steal customer financial data. Integrity is also paramount for business transactions where buyers and sellers need to be authenticated for a contract to be legally valid and ensure **nonrepudiation** (so that a buyer a seller cannot renege from their contract).

- **Availability**: A computer system that is online, including servers that host websites, should be available for access by the public (e.g., an ecommerce website, an app) or by authorized personnel (e.g., specific file servers, smart home devices, and login-based company websites). The loss of access to a website, app, or network device costs users tremendous inconvenience and large headaches for businesses. Hackers, cyber-criminals, and even cyber-activists will often use an attack called distributed **DoS (Denial of Service) or the Ping-of-Death attack**. Ping of Death is a Distributed DoS attack that occurs when hackers use multiple IP addresses to flood and overwhelm a web server with so many millions of requests that the website will temporarily go out of service and be unavailable to general users. DDoS attacks can cripple a website and webservers. In 2014, the Hong Kong democratic polling site,

PopVote, was bombarded by more than 500 Gigabits of data per second as a Distributed DoS (DDoS) attack. Chinese hackers were the alleged perpetrators intended upon silencing public sentiment in Hong Kong. The most famous DDoS attack was the 2016 **Mirai** Botnet attack that disrupted services of many important sites including Twitter, Netflix, and CNN. The DDoS used a **BotNet**, a network of computers as bots, to bombard and paralyze the servers of Dyn, a network infrastructure company used for DNS (Doman Name System) mapping to map web addresses. More interestingly, the bots in the network were not typical computers but hijacked **IoT** (Internet or Things) devices, i.e., smart networked home and control devices such as Google Nest, Google Home, Amazon Alexa, Smart Refrigerators, Smart Bulbs, and such.

- Another famous DDoS attack was launched by China against Github. Github, the largest public code repository in the world experienced a massive distributed denial of service attack in March 2015. The attack appeared to originate from China and specifically targeted to Github projects, GreatFire, and cn-nytimes (a Chinese version of *New York Times*, both designed to combat censorship in China. This DDoS attack was neither from a person nor from a group but from a country, so it was a state sponsored. In the dramatically changing cyber-attack landscape, players, i.e., cyber attackers, are becoming bigger, larger, and more sophisticated.

Hackers and Cyber-Attacks

The cybersecurity landscape is dramatically changing. In the 1980s, a movie called War Games portrayed a young kid who plays a networked version of some kind of an old arcade game. He inadvertently keys-in some interesting game moves and realizes the old arcade game is nothing but a network link to a war game against the soviets. That was the time when people thought that hacking and cyberwarfare were tales told in movies but now things have changed dramatically.

Hacking is the act of trying to attack and penetrate a vulnerable computer system with an intent to access, steal, or compromise the system for intrinsic motives such as thrills or activism or extrinsic benefits such as subterfuge, theft, of ransom. A hacker with no malintent (such as vulnerability testers) is a **white-hat hacker**; a hacker with malevolent intent of disruption, sabotage, subterfuge, theft, or ransom is a **black-hat hacker**.

Cyberwarfare is the act of conducting *state-sponsored* belligerence via computer networks against another state with an explicit intention to sabotage, disrupt, and destroy another country's networked infrastructure such as power grids, defense systems, land, and air traffic, among many others. In an age where everything is computerized and connected via and over digital networks, every connected device is prey!

Cyberwarfare can be much more debilitating than conventional warfare because cyberwarfare can impact our daily lives. Today, hacking has become a more profitable, unscrupulously, enterprising venture and we move from being amateur hackers to cyber-criminals funded by billion-dollar corporations and nation-states.

Previously, an amateur "white-hat" hacker's main motive was trying to either impress or trying to gain some kind of notoriety by trying and cracking software or penetrating different sites as a way to outwit companies. Companies protected their sites with **intrusion detection systems (IDS)**, a set of hardware and/or software that try and detect if somebody is trying to access your network. IDS look for strange behavior called **exceptions** such as a flurry of unknown requests from one or more websites, access from and to suspicious websites, sudden software downloads, copying of files, attempts to access remotely, among many other actions.

Once IDS sense an issue, it tries to shut down access and then tries to trace the source of the suspicious behavior. While amateur hackers, once detected, are more likely to leave and go, cyber-criminals are not deterred by IDS defenses and figure out backdoors to circumvent the IDS. Not only do black-hat hackers (cyber-criminals)

try to infiltrate and sabotage systems or steal information but also disrupt access to computer systems and steal files containing sensitive information held for ransom.

Did you know that?

Cybersecurity is war between and defenders trying to protect their territories from perpetrators searching for vulnerabilities, aimed at disruption (e.g., malware) and/or profit (e.g., ransomware).

Ransomware: The AIDS Info Disk

Ransomware is nothing but injecting malicious software code used to access and steal information and then hold it for ransom till companies cough up money to resume access and ensure that sensitive information did not get sold or published on the Dark Net or **Dark Web**.

Relying on Process and Human Fallibilities

Ransomware relies on ruses. Ruses have been hallmarks of history, within and beyond the confines of war.

At the 1988 4th International AIDs conference, when 5.25 floppy disks were in vogue, attendees received an innocuous floppy disk titled "AIDS Info Disk." The "AIDS Info Disk" also relied on human fallibility and process efficiencies. The disk label was a ruse but allowed for easy circulation within the conference without raising any eyebrows. The label also enticed attendees to open the file in expectation of something informative. In fact, the floppy contained one of the earliest Trojan ransomware.

Once inserted, the AIDS Info Disk, developed by Dr. Joseph Popp, an evolutionary Biologist, would rewrite the PC boot file, AUTOEXEC. BAT, with its own. The rewritten file would count the number of PC boots. Once the number of boots reached 90, the Trojan would hide and encrypt boot directories and activate a message.

The message asked the user to pay $189 to a PC Cyborg Corporation in Panama as a prerequisite to rebooting and regaining access to the users' PC. Dr. Popp was arrested and claimed that the ransomware was a crusade on behalf of AIDS victims and research.

The commonality between Drake and Popp is the role of ruse de guerre (malicious deception) as an attack vector. While Drake's furled flags and Popp's AIDS info disk, highlight how even robust technical defenses can fall prey to process and human vulnerabilities. In short, the new ruse de guerre lies in deceiving technologies, processes, and humans—a modus operandi that has emerged as a frontline cyberwarfare tactic.

Protecting Cybergates in the Cyberwarfare Age

The 3 Horsemen of Cybersecurity: Technologies, Processes, and People

Cyberwarfare has leveraged on society overarching proclivity to treat cybersecurity as a siloed activity. It is commonplace to find companies and established cybersecurity of ICT professionals relegating cybersecurity as purely an IT activity. Cybersecurity is much more than that.

It is common to think of cybersecurity as a siloed technological solution. However, relegating cybersecurity to merely a technological solution without reengineering business processes and training people to be continuously vigilant opens the cybergates to malicious actors and their ruses.

Technologies are often a binary solution, sold on features and resilience. But even the best technologies can fall prey to a faulty process.

In industry, it is acknowledged that "if you have a bad process and a good technology, the bad process wins." The same holds for cybersecurity and the need for a greater emphasis on "cyber-secure process reengineering." This emphasis would have added benefits on cyber and risk-auditing, cyber-analytics, design, training, among others. Collaborating to create Cybersecurity process reengineering, Cybersecurity analytics, business, and training policies, would add to our rich and existing program set.

The said cases illustrate how a seemingly smaller state-sponsored actors can cripple technological foe by leveraging standard operating procedures (SOPs), human shortcomings, and taking advantage of reactive rather than proactive operational cultures that adopt an attitude of "if it is not broken, do not fix it."

The Dark Web is a nefarious part of the Internet, specifically the world-wide-web, that uses special access such as Tor or I2P protocols. The Dark Web is not searchable using existing search engines such as Google but requires special illegitimate access. The Dark Web is an illegal Internet replete with dangerous information for distribution or sales, such as child pornography, prostitution, drugs, extremist videos, drug transaction, terrorism instructions and videos, hacking software, and even assassins for hire. For example, **Silk Road**, one of the first Dark Webs, was a popular site for drug-related transactions.

The Dark Web is a dangerous place full of hackers waiting to exploit and hack various users of the dark net by injecting dreadful software. Often, amateur hackers called **script-kiddies** can end up downloading deadly hacking code that can hijack their own systems and use their computers as **zombies**, i.e., computers that are secretly controlled by remote hackers to hack other machines. Unbeknownst to the computer owner, hackers can wake up and control other infected "zombie" computers and use them to their advantage, like an inadvertent stooge. Hackers use zombies for hacking attacks because IDS will trace it to the hacked computer rather than the real hacker.

Hackers are ingeniously nefarious and scheming. **Target** was hacked in December 2013. The hackers actually didn't try to directly access the main customer database that was securely hidden and protected by IDS. Instead, the hackers accessed Target's information portal through the digital HVAC (heating, ventilation, and AC) system that was managed by some third-party contractor with much less protection. The HVAC system could be remotely controlled and was linked to the main Target customer information database.

Target had one single network that combined multiple access points, such as access from credit card payment agencies, distributors, logistics companies, among many. Generally segmenting networks is a good idea because, if one network segment is affected or goes down, the other parts of the network aren't affected. Target hadn't segmented its networks that meant that once they enter through the HVAC system, Target's databases were compromised. Hackers could then easily access other databases within Target compromised such as point-of-sale (checkout) systems and ended up stealing 17 million customer records.

In 2014, **Sony Pictures** suffered a setback from a North Korean hack. It was an intellectual property theft—something called **spear phishing**. In a **phishing** attack, a cyber-criminal tries to mimic a popular site, e.g., a bank site, with a false website that looks like a legitimate bank with login fields to steal your bank login information. Spear phishing is a more sophisticated variant of a phishing attack where hackers use spoofed emails that look like they are from a trusted source such as an employer or a bank with a specific, custom message that appears very credible and relatable to the receiver. Spear phishing will target specific individuals rather than a shotgun approach used in phishing where a large swathe of individuals receives emails.

A cyber-criminal would design a false website that looks like a real website and host the site on some foreign server. They might then send millions of false "spoofed" emails to millions of email addresses saying, "We think you misplaced your password, or somebody tried to access your account! Please click here to replace your ID and password!" Below will be a link. If you don't pay close attention to the site address or URL, you may be tricked to click on the link that leads to the false website where you enter your ID and password for the hackers to steal the information and then use the same information to access and compromise your bank and financial information.

While phishing and spear phishing are meant to spoof (trick) users into downloading dangerous malware such as viruses and worms, ransomware, meant to extort money from companies as a hedge against further harm, is rapidly gaining ground. In 2017, a ransomware called **WannaCry** was first detected in Asia that infected computers running Windows XP via the **SMB (Service Message Block)** port, a connection protocol used to chare files and other

© PiaDura LTD 2022
P. Datta, *Global Technology Management 4.0*,
https://doi.org/10.1007/978-3-030-96929-5_10

resources such as printers on a network. Nearly 230,000 computers were infected.

It is assumed that WannaCry originated in China or North Korea. WannaCry spread around the world, and it ended up targeting public utilities and large corporations. WannaCry infected computers with a **worm** (a type of virus that moves across files and computers) that encrypts user files that users cannot open unless a ransom of $300 was paid in 3 days or $600 was paid in 7 days to decrypt user files. **Encryption** is a way to digitally scramble and lock information as a cipher. **Decryption** is a way to digitally unlock, unscramble, and decipher information so that it can be read.

WannaCry even temporarily crippled the British NHS (National Health Service) which is the main universal healthcare service in the UK. NHS hospitals suddenly realized that patient data wasn't available and pathological tests were missing. NHS are asked to pay a ransom to maintain **business continuity** (i.e., keeping all company operations and services running as before). In the 1980s, terrorists used to hijack planes; today, cyber-criminals hijack systems.

Microsoft quickly figured out a security solution against the WaanaCry ransomware and released a **Patch or Update**, a piece of software meant to stop a computer security or performance flaw by fixing the vulnerability or problem. Sadly, a lot of companies running Windows XP disregarded installing the security patch which left their computers vulnerable. *It is imperative to install all latest security patches as auto-updates.*

Between 2016 and 2017, there was another ransomware attack called **Petya**. Petya was a very interesting ransomware. The way it worked was as follows. The ransomware would infect Windows computers (PCs) by infecting the MBR (Master Boot Record) which is a set of sequence instructions and files used to start Windows on a PC. The Petya virus, downloaded as an email PDF file attachment, infected the MBR and forced the computer the restart, except that the computer would never restart. Suddenly, a message would pop-up, demanding a ransom payment in Bitcoin (a cryptocurrency or digital currency network).

In 2017, Russia used a variation of Petya called **NotPetya** as a Russian state-sponsored virus attack against Ukraine prior to the Russia's invasion of Crimea via cities such Donetsk. When Ukraine protested about Russia's actions did not sit well with Moscow. So, on the eve of Ukraine's national holiday, Constitution Day on June 27, Russia infected Ukrainian energy companies, gas lines, banks, and public utilities with NotPetya. The malware attack hit the Ukrainian infrastructure particularly hard - disrupting utilities like power companies, airports, public transit, and the central bank, with a series of cyber assaults against the country and basically crippled Ukraine in just a matter of days. NotPetya used a Ukrainian Tax Preparation company called M.E.Doc's computers as zombies to spread the virus. The NotPetya virus was so effective that its Chernobyl Nuclear Power Plant's Radiation Monitoring System went offline and disrupted services not only in Ukrainian government agencies, banks, and utilities but also in international companies such as the multinational Maersk shipping line (Denmark), Merck pharmaceuticals (US), WOO advertising (UK), JNPT port (India), Cadbury Chocolates (Australia), Saint Gobain Construction (France), and agencies in Germany. NotPetya is assumed to be the most destructive and disruptive attack, costing Ukraine and other international companies upwards of $10 billion.

The power of cyberwarfare is such that you neither need a standing army nor need to fire a single volley; instead all Russia did was create a ransomware, virus that basically brought a country to or the country's utilities to its knees. In the James Bond movie, Skyfall, Q, the young R&D head, quite rightly says *"I'll hazard I can do more damage on my laptop sitting in my pyjamas before my first cup of Earl Grey than you can do in a year in the field."*

There is little exaggeration there.

Malware

Malware has evolved ever so very dangerously. Malware has moved from being relatively innocuous to something debilitating to the user and the infrastructure. So, what is malware? **Malware** (from *mal* for harmful or bad and *ware* for software) is nothing but a malicious piece of software or code that typically damages, disables, takes control of, or steals information from a computer.

A malware can automatically use your network to relay their information back to the cyber-hacker. Malware will often times force some ads onto you with links that might open a **backdoor**, a network port connection that can be quietly used without your knowledge to access your computer, steal your files and logins, or install software that will make your computer behave like a hacking zombie. **Spyware** is a type of malware that spies on a user's computer and tracks user behavior.

Did you know that?

In war, even the best technologies can fall prey to weak processes and human shortcomings.

In the 1580 s, Spanish and French navies amassed a vast Armada of 100 + ships in the Bay of Cadizmto strike England, their arch enemy! Cadiz was immensely fortified. A series of sandbanks, lookout stations, and a large battery of shore guns served as firewalls and intrusion detection systems (IDS)—all trained to spot predefined enemy incursions.

But Francis Drake, the British privateer, used a ruse de guerre (deception of war) to fool the mighty Armada by exploiting process inefficiencies and human fallibility. On April 26, 1587, Drake's 24 ships furled their flags and disguised themselves as merchant vessels, entered the bay, and set fire to the Armada.

Malware Types

Malware has multiple variations. Some of them are:

1. **System Monitors** are spyware that logs or records user behavior. For example, if the user visits a bank website, the spyware will monitor and record every keystroke that can later be used to steal identity and disrupt access.

2. **Cookies** are small pieces of software code used to track what and how we browse the Internet. While cookies from trustworthy and legitimate sites can increase user experience like Amazon remembering what products a user looked at the last time the user visited Amazon's website, spyware tracking cookies can hide in the background and try and steal information and user website visits and interactions and relay the information back to cyber-criminals. A recent European Union (EU) law requires users to provide "informed consent" before a website can install a cookie. The law is meant to reduce threats of spyware tracking cookies.

3. **Trojans** are a type of malware that deceptively install malicious code disguised as a harmless file or document. Trojans are named after the Trojan Horse from Homer's *The Iliad*. In the famous mythology, the Greeks, under Agamemnon, sailed a thousand ships to Troy to punish Prince Paris who had stolen Helen, Agamemnon's brother Menelaus's wife, and had fled to Troy. After 10 years of siege and the loss of famous warriors, the Greeks pretended to depart the Trojan shores and left Troy a very large wooden Trojan horse as a sign of tribute. The Trojans were elated, and they pulled the wooden horse inside the impregnable Trojan fortress. But little did the Trojans realize that inside the belly of the Trojan horse were hidden all the famous fighters including Achilles, Odysseus, and Agamemnon. While Troy was reveling the end of the 10-year Greek siege, Greek

warriors quietly existed the Trojan horse in the dark and burned Troy. A **Virus**, is a software pieces of code whose main job is to infect and modify a software program by injecting its own code and making the software program behave the way the virus wants. A **Worm** is different from a virus because a worm crawls or propagates across computers networks from one system to another, often creating and opening a backdoor for hackers and cyber-criminal to access the computer to steal data or disrupt systems and networks. Worms are often packaged as email attachments, which, when opened, will quietly deliver the malicious code or **Payload**.

4. **Virus**: Similar to how a biological virus requires a host in order to replicate and spread, so too does a computer virus. The computer virus code attaches itself to a host file or program, which may make its way onto a victim's device by way of email attachments, file or application downloads, or malicious links. The virus may remain dormant until the user opens and runs the host file or program. Damages caused by a virus vary, depending on what kind of virus has infected the host. There are six broad categories of viruses, classified by how the spread from device to device. **Boot sector viruses** target and damage the boot processes. **File infection viruses** attach themselves to a variety of file types. **Multipartite viruses** combine the effects of those two previous types. **Network viruses** spread through a LAN by way of shared drives. **Macro viruses** affect files using macros. Email viruses spread through contacts in an email address book. Regardless of what type of virus infects the device, the end goal is consistent with other types of malware, which is to steal sensitive and personal information, destroy files, and slow down operations of a device or network.

The main difference between a Trojan horse and a virus is that Trojans do not have the ability to replicate themselves into other applications or areas of the device. They still can cause damage though in the form of stealing data, installing other malware (such as viruses), and **keyloggers** (a malware used to record a user's keystrokes to figure out logins and passwords).

5. **Worms** are very similar to viruses and Trojan horses regarding the damages they can cause. They differ in the way they are spread though. Whereas viruses need to attach to another file in order to become active and spread, a worm does not. A worm stands alone, entering a system through vulnerabilities; it does not need to be attached to another file that is opened and executed. Therefore, worms can travel all by themselves.

Using vulnerabilities in a system, worms are written to detect files in which the worm can change the permissions or unsecured system functions. Once these files are identified, the worm can spread and complete its intended task. This may be to create a **backdoor** for other malware, collect data, or delete files.

A worm may be written to replicate to other hosts but remain dormant for a period of time while it spreads across the other hosts, and then activate the malicious activity in all the hosts at once. Since the worm can travel alone, once it has infiltrated one host, it can potentially access all the devices on a local area network that do not have sufficient protections rather quickly. This could potentially lead to an entire business, network, government agency, etc., being compromised and at risk for data deletion, stealing, or manipulation—all at once.

6. **Ransomware** is a malware that essentially takes a victim's files hostage until the victim pays a ransom to the attacker in exchange for the release of the files. If the victim does not pay, the ransom may increase, or the attacker may permanently destroy the files.

There are *several types of ransomware* which all have the same goal in mind, which is to force the victim to pay for the use of their own files or devices. One kind of ransomware will completely lock up a device and display only a screen with payment instructions on how to unlock it. The device will be rendered useless until the ransom is paid. The lock screen may make false claims that it originated from a government agency, advising that the user has been fined for suspicious activity on the device. Other ransomware may still allow you to use the device but will encrypt your files until you pay. A third type called scareware may also allow the victim to use the device but will make claims that it is an anti-virus program and has detected issues that it will clean up for a cost. This malware may overload the device with pop-ups until the victim pays the ransom.

Did you know that?

Ransomware criminals are using Ransomware as a Service (RaaS) as a business model to lease their services and giving people without any technical knowledge the ability to launch Ransomware attacks for a flat fee or a commission!

Ransomware has some characteristics that differ from other types of malware. For example, malware will target all kinds of files on the device, encrypting them or scrambling their names. The victim will have to pay a ransom, usually within a specific time frame, and often using difficult to trace **Bitcoins**. Another large difference between ransomware and others is that ransomware is purposely making itself known to the victim, whereas other malwares try to go undetected. The victim can't pay a ransom if they aren't aware of it in the first place.

Ransomware malware can be spread similar to other malware, such as email scams, finding vulnerabilities in software, spreading to and from devices connected on the same network, website traffic redirects, and SMS messages for mobile devices, among others. Commonly though, targets may fall victim to seemingly legitimate software updates, installing files disguised as Adobe Acrobat, Java, and Flash Player updates which pop-up on the device.

The use of ransomware has dramatically increased in recent years, especially with the rise of Bitcoin in 2009 which allowed payments to attackers to remain untraceable. There are several other factors leading to this though. For one, an attack can be carried out on a large number of targets, and even a small success rate can yield high returns for the attacker. Another reason is that any individual person, business, or public institution can be targeted.

While businesses may seem ideal due to not wanting to disrupt operations and the fact that they likely would have more access to funds than individuals, the more concerning attacks are those on our public institutions, specifically hospitals and law enforcement agencies. The information stolen from them is likely going to be much more sensitive and crucial to operations than a private business would have. Aside from bad PR or lost profits for a business, in comparison the effects on a hospital or police department losing files on patient care or criminal cases could easily have devastating effects on the health and well-being of industry and society.

7. **Ghostware** is similar to most other malwares in the sense that its goal is to sneak into a device or network undetected. It is differentiated by the fact that once it is able to complete its task (stealing or manipulating information), it will also attempt to sneak back out undetected. Ideally, the victim is never aware their data has been compromised. Often ghostware will be accompanied by **blastware**.

   In the event a breach is discovered by the victim, blastware essentially self-destructs, destroying itself and the system it has infected. For these reasons, it is very difficult to investigate the use of ghostware and blastware. Either it is successful, and the victim never knows about it, therefore, can't report its activity, or it is unsuccessful and there is nothing left of the system or the malware to inspect to see what kind of data loss there has been. There would also be no way to trace from where the malware originated.

Ghostware is able to remain undetected is by hiding its own files, Window Registry entries, processes, and loaded modules from the operating system utilities. They do this through a process called "hooking." This means that any kernel functionality requests in the operating system are diverted to the ghostware. The ghostware is able to filter out any information that can reveal its existence. The biggest concern with ghostware is that it allows the cyber-criminal constant access to use the device to obtain sensitive information or send out large amounts of spam emails without the user or anti-virus software being aware. Since no one is aware of its existence, it is difficult to track the usage or prevalence of ghostware.

8. **Spyware** is a type of software typically installed unknowingly by a user. It is usually attached to other software that the user is actually trying to install, and it tags along during the installation process. It may be disclosed that the spyware is coming, perhaps buried deep in the terms and conditions that the user may glance over. Once installed, spyware may perform a variety of functions, such as collecting personal information, changing the configurations on the device, or display targeted advertisements to the user. Not always necessarily malicious, this last function is often described as "adware." **Adware** is a type of malware that triggers popping up of unwanted ads, often linking to suspicious and malicious websites, pop-up every time the user uses the computer system. Adware is often installed as a tradeoff for a free or discounted service provided by the desired software. Sometimes, there will be an option to purchase a version of the desired software without the adware. Both are ways that allow the developer to realize income from their programs.

Besides tagging along with a desirable and intentionally installed software, spyware can also work its way into a device by enticing the user to click on a pop-up by offering prizes or essential software that are really spyware. Also, emails or other forms of

messaging may contain links to spyware downloads. In some instances, the spyware may be able to install itself simply by the user viewing an email or website, without even clicking on a link. This is called a **drive-by download**.

Once the spyware has been installed, the user may experience frequent pop-ups, changes in default settings, changes in system operating speed, or issues with running security software. While all of this is happening, the spyware will be collecting sensitive financial information (possibly for future identity theft) or may be tracking browsing habits, which can be sold or used for marketing purposes.

9. **Two-Faced Malware**: To understand how two-faced malware operates, it is important to understand the concept of **sandbox testing**. A sandbox, in the world of cybersecurity, is an environment created on a device, either by a program itself or by the user. The sandbox environment limits what a piece of code in a program or application can do or can have access to within the device. This line of defense prevents a program from tampering with or doing damage to other programs or files on the device. Or it would at least require the program or application to request or declare permissions to access certain features.

10. While many default programs and web browsers installed on a device already operate within a sandbox, not all of them do, nor does software that may be installed. A **sandbox** is a testing environment, often located in a sub-network separated from the main network to try out cyber-attack scenarios and untested software codes to check for system vulnerabilities. In order to ensure the software is secure, the user would have to run the program within a sandbox using programs such as *Sandboxie* or virtual machine programs which allow the user to create a sandbox in which to test software, to see if it initiates any malicious activity.

This led to the inception of **two-faced malware**. As cybercrime becomes more advanced, code is able to be written that appears to be benign and completes tasks as expected while it is under the inspection of the sandbox. However, once the sandbox is no longer restricting the program, it changes its behavior to cause damage or steal data and files. This could even avoid detection from anti-virus software that puts the malware in sandbox for testing. The malware is able to revert back to the "safe" activity while it is under inspection in the sandbox, and then it will resume its malicious activity when it senses the sandbox is no longer being monitored. It is then flagged as safe by the anti-virus, thus helping it avoid further detection in future.

Human and Process Threats in Cybersecurity: Delivering Malware and Initiating Cyber-Attacks

While technical malware carries the payload, **business processes**, i.e., the sequence of tasks and activities, often called workflow, that businesses follow for everyday operations, becomes a testbed for hackers to utilize their cyber-attack strategy and deliver the malware.

A lot of malware (including spyware) attacks install rootkits. A **Rootkit** is a harmful or malicious software that is installed at the **root-level** (highest level of compute control) so that anytime you start your computer, unknown to you, the rootkit malware is also activated. In 2004–2005, US intelligence agencies allegedly installed a rootkit to wiretap more than a 100 Greek government officials' Ericsson mobile phones. The rootkit was installed as a hidden piece of software in the Ericsson phone exchange. Whenever someone used the mobile phone, the rootkit relayed the conversation to 14 prepaid mobile phones registered to anonymous entities. Rootkits, even when not used as malware, can create privacy problems. **Privacy** is the ability of a person or company to maintain control over one's personal information and behavior and not have one's information and behavior shared without explicit permission. Sony invaded its customer's privacy by installing a rootkit in their CDs so that people couldn't copy songs. Sony never mentioned that to its customers. Anytime a customer played a CD on their computer, the CD would quietly install the anti-copying rootkit software without the user's permission. This became a huge privacy issue.

Malware does not merely originate from hackers outside an organization. There are **Insider threats**. Sometimes, malware can originate from employees within the company intended to steal, disrupt, or sabotage the corporation. One type of insider threat is a **Logic Bomb**. A logic bomb is nothing but a piece of software that doesn't look like malware, but it creates a devastating impact on your entire system. For example, in 2006, an UBS bank employee installed a logic bomb that would sabotage UBS's servers and disrupt services, thus dropping UBS stock prices and allowing the employee to make money from shorting (betting that the stock will go down) the UBS stock. Similarly, a disgruntled Fannie Mae (a US mortgage insurer) programmer, knowing that he would be terminated, wrote a piece of software code meant to disrupt Fannie Mae's servers as vindication. Luckily, he was apprehended before he could inflict damage.

Password policies are another point of weakness, both on the human side as well as on the process side. Companies create **password policies** or rules to ensure that cyber-criminals will not be able to guess employee and customer passwords and compromise the organization as well as steal identities. However, password policies are a balancing act. If a password policy is too relaxed, users tend to choose extremely simple and weak passwords. Different polls and studies show users creating weak passwords such as "123,456," "qwerty," "111,111," and "password." Having weak passwords makes it all the easier for cyber-criminals to steal your password, and thus, important personal, financial, or business-related information. Cyber-criminals capitalize on weak passwords a variety of technical or non-technical processes.

Some technical attacks can be carried out to steal passwords via a **MITM** or wire-sniffing attack, which involves placing a wiretap to a network, which analyzes all of the traffic passing through the network. There are different methods of password guessing, such as the **brute force attach**, which uses mathematical algorithms repeatedly to crack the code on someone's password, or dictionary attacks. Other attacks might include keylogging or **keyboard sniffing**, which occurs certain wireless keyboards transmit the keystrokes. An attacker may be able to intercept the unencrypted transmissions from the keyboard to the device. This is more common in low-cost wireless keyboards. By intercepting keystrokes, an attacker would be obtaining the victim's password. While the strength of the password may not matter in this case, a user can strengthen their password by changing it frequently. This way, even if the attacker gains access, perhaps they won't maintain access.

However, frequent password changes and/or having very complicated passwords can also have their disadvantages. A **strong password** is a moderately long combination of hard-to-guess; non-dictionary word-based passwords with a combination of letters, numbers, and special characters, and changed on a regular basis.

However, strong passwords create their own security risks. The risk is not from the policy side but on the people side of the puzzle. We often have a root password based on a combination of numbers and words and names that mean something to us. Often, we will create variations based on the root password by adding symbols or numbers that we can remember. This creates opportunities for cyber-criminals and hackers. Given that we use a version of our passwords at various sites, some secure sites, and some insecure sites, it allows cyber-criminals to test out password combinations in insecure sites. **Insecure sites** are the ones that do not automatically lock us out and log our behavior when trying multiple login attempts. **Secure sites**, such as financial websites, will not only have an HTTPS secure shell encryption but will lock the account after three missed login attempts and send a notification email to the actual account holder that someone is trying to the access the account. However, because we tend to recycle our passwords across secure and insecure sites, it becomes easier for hackers to try and hack passwords at insecure sites to figure out the mnemonic. We, human beings are creatures of convenience and habit and use mnemonics. **Mnemonics** are ways and patterns by which we try to remember things, including our passwords. Think of our own passwords. Our passwords tend to follow a pattern.

Another human and process threat is **password-sharing**. Password sharing is when many individuals use the same passwords for a variety of different systems. There may be some overlap between professional and personal uses too.

For example, one might think sharing a password with a co-worker for a database at work won't pose any threat. If you're at the same company, one might ask what harm could come from letting him or her sign in with your credentials. However, considering the likelihood that the user also uses that same or similar password for their personal banking or social media accounts, they may not consider the ramifications of letting someone else know the exact or perhaps root of all of their passwords. Another risk is that even at the same company, two employees may not be privy to the same level of access to certain customer or financial information about the company (such as employees' personal and salary information).

Did you know that?

It is easier to phish and exploit human psychology and inefficient processes than hack a system. That is what hackers use in more than 80% of cases!

Password sharing can lead to Credential Stuffing. Essentially, when cyber-criminals steal login usernames and passwords from sites and sell them on the **Dark Web**, other criminals purchase these credentials for **credential stuffing**. Credential stuffing happens when cyber-criminals use purchased login usernames and passwords (called credentials) and try to use them in a variety of other sites to gain access.

Given that we tend to reuse usernames and password combinations, credential stuffing is often quite successful and can end up compromising us and our cybersecurity. So, make sure you visit Google Chrome's security and privacy notification to check which of your passwords may have been compromised and sold on the Dark Web. Immediately, revisit any site where you may have used the username/password combination and reset your passwords.

So, when faced with complicated and changing passwords that they can't pattern or remember easily, we, human beings, tend to take dangerous shortcuts—often written out on sticky notes and stuck to the back of computer monitors or under keyboards, for the world to see. We, as human beings, are often the **weakest link** in cybersecurity.

Cyber Espionage or Cyber Spying

While many cyber-threats involve stealing or altering data and files for financial gain of the attacker or to bog down operations of the victim, **Cyber Espionage** or Cyber Spying is meant to illicit or steal secret or confidential information from countries and companies in order to sabotage exiting business gains or secure some competitive advantage over the other.

Cyber espionage may be a business trying to steal a competitor's intellectual property, not for the purpose of bringing down the competitor, but for elevating the attacking business' own product or processes. Or it could perhaps be a business stealing salary information from a rival firm not because they are trying to gain access to the employees' finances or accounts, but because they are trying to remain competitive in their benefits structure. It may also be completely unrelated to any area of commerce, such as a government stealing tactical plans of an enemy state.

In 1998, Russia was accused of using Moonlight Maze, a malware cyber-attack that infiltrated Wright Patterson Air Force Base and stole hundreds of sensitive military research documents. Around 2010, during the height of ALCOA's (Aluminum Corporation of America)

negotiations with Chinese businesses, Chinese hackers, allegedly, sponsored by large Chinese state-owned Steel and Aluminum companies hacked Alcoa's email servers and stole 2,900 emails with more than 860 attachments. In 2011, a Chinese cyber-espionage attack against Renault, the French car manufacturer, stole Renault's secret electric car research and development documents.

So how does an organization spy on competitors? It used to be that they would simply send a fake employee who would try to gain access to critical areas of the target's records or research areas. With the advent of cybercrimes, those fake employees are instead looking for an unoccupied workstation into which they can quickly upload malware to gain access to the system or network. Another method may be to purchase information or access from real employees. A recent survey revealed that one in seven employees would sell their password credentials for as little as $150. Another popular method is something called **Dumpster Diving**. Dumpster diving is a type of **industrial espionage** method by which companies or countries hire people to pick documents from company office rubbish or trash bins or from rubbish bins the homes of government officials and company executives. The documents are then used to check for sensitive government or corporate information as well as used to stitch together a composite to guess your password and/or to conduct social engineering as a preface to a cyber-attack.

Social Engineering

Hackers and cyber-criminals try to compromise and cajole user identity and users' systems using social engineering. **Social engineering** is a way by which cyber-criminals and hackers lure a user into trusting the attacker by preying on the user's psychology. Social engineering is a way by which you use people's emotion and psychology and sense of distress to lure them into confidence before stealing their information or having them download malware.

Most of the time, the human being is the weakest link in the cybersecurity chain. So, cyber attackers often use confidence trickster tactics to get the use to click a link, reveal information, or download software that the user would not have done otherwise. In the 1990s, three blind "Badir" brothers in Israel used voice impersonation and braille-computer displays to social engineer and defraud people of nearly $2 million. They would phone company secretaries impersonating repairmen asking for login and passwords. When the secretary entered the access PIN on the phone, the brothers could figure out the number from the touch-tine sound.

A confidence trickster first gains the target's confidence and then sends a volley of malware or phishing attacks as the first line of cyber-attacks and cyberwarfare. Often, confidence tricksters might set themselves up as a handsome guy or a pretty girl on a social network site wanting to be your friend. Else, they might use monetary incentives or fear (such as "you have a police warrant issued against you" or "you are under tax investigation."

Once you buy into the "con," the social engineer will try to have you reveal some important personal information from you that the attacker can use to create your identity or guess your passwords. In addition, in social engineering, an attacker will often try to send you a link to pictures or file downloads or phished via email or social media with a preface such as "Hey, by the way, if you want to see some more pictures, or if you want to I know a little bit about where I live, or if you want to know a few things about the money that I want to send to you, click here." Once you click, voila, you might be lured to a phished website meant to look legitimate that will steal your information or quietly download some malware, hidden in a document or a picture onto your computer.

So, do not download attachments and especially zipped files from unknown sources. They are often malware payloads.

Social engineering is often the first wave of a cyber-attack. Social engineering includes, often time in combination:

1. **Vishing** or Voice Phishing: In vishing, a computerized automated system will often make a phone call impersonating a bank or government agency (like the Tax department). Vishing typically scares or worries the call receiver into divulging information that can compromise one's finances or identity.

2. **Phishing and Spear Phishing**: Phishing and spear phishing are used to create fake sites that spoof users into believing they are legitimate bank or company website. Spear phishing is a more targeted or focused attack on specific people.

3. **Water Holing**: Like spear phishing, attackers will use social engineering to gather information on the websites a user likes and then try to hack any of those vulnerable websites to install malware. Like animals who return to specific water holes, when users visit one or more of their favorite websites already infected by the attacker, the malware is installed.

4. **Baiting** is another tactic used by social engineers. In baiting, the social engineer gathers information on what interests the target. For example, the target might be the VP of Sales at company X. The social engineer might post or drop an USB device marked "Latest Product Sales of Company Y," company X's rival, to the VP's house or office. When the target uses the USB devices and/or opens the files, the malware infects the targets computer.

Social engineering relies on **Targeted Intrusions**. A Targeted Intrusion is a very focused penetration attack on as system trying to find a trying to breach the system and trying to find vulnerabilities or weaknesses within the person, the process, the technology, and the network. Advanced malware is a key component of targeted sophisticated and ongoing attacks it can be customized to compromise specific high-value systems in the target network.

Targeted intrusion uses a sophisticated combination of stealth and social engineering to either understand the weakness in a system or the weakness in a person in a very strong system. Finding weaknesses in a system can often be more difficult than finding weaknesses in a person. So, it's easier to find weaknesses in a person who is accessing a strong system rather than it is finding weaknesses in a strong system itself.

Similarly, it is easier to guess your access pattern or password on your phone rather than access your phone's technology security. You can have the most secure phone in the world but if your password is compromised, nothing really matters.

Then of course, our false sense of privacy and security often gets the best of us. When do we even care about if somebody's eavesdropping when we are entering passwords? Yet, **shoulder surfers** abound, especially in crowded areas like bars, clubs, events, concerts, airports, and the like. Shoulder surfers will often peek into your phone or computer while you are entering your password or logging into you accounts.

Often, shoulder surfers will work in groups, facing away from you as if making an important phone call. Even though you might feel secure that the person isn't look at your phone or laptop, his or her phone-camera (with lenses on the back of phones) might be recording every password, login, and key entry.

Advanced Persistent Threats (APT)

APTs (Advanced Persistent Threats) are threats that combine malware and botnets to create a multi-pronged cyber-attack, which gives cyber attackers many avenues to bring down a system. It's called APT because off because it's advanced, persistent, and carries a threat. APTs are advanced because they use additional sophisticated equipment such as human intelligence such as social engineering.

APTs are persistent because the malware runs over long periods with low-and-slow approach to avoid detection. Unlike DoS attacks that are overwhelming but quicker to trace and mitigate, persistent attacks are quiet and slow attempts at infiltrating a system. APTs are a threat because they are focused toward creating real damage such as disrupting infrastructure, communications, and markets.

Stuxnet, allegedly created by the US and Israel, was an APT worm that slowed down Iran's nuclear ambition by years. The worm initially infected endpoints running Microsoft Windows and then targeted programmable logic controllers or PLC's, running Siemens Step7 software used to control nuclear fuel refinement.

The APT entered the Iranian nuclear facility in Natanz, Iran, via an USB stick carried by an Iranian employee, unaware that it was loaded with the deadly Stuxnet malware worm. It is guessed that the nuclear plant employee was social-engineered and may have downloaded the malware from a porn site or from some social network female "friend" promising access to some "pictures" online. Although thousands of other users may have downloaded the same malware, the Stuxnet APT worm was sophisticated and advanced. Stuxnet would be harmless unless the user's computer was running Siemen's Step 7 software, used to control high-speed centrifuges used to refine 'weapons-grade' uranium. If Stuxnet found the software, it would automatically download latest version of the malware from the Internet. Once ready with the latest malware, Stuxnet would attack the systems logic controllers by exploiting **Zero-Day attack** vulnerabilities.

A Zero-Day attack vulnerability is a system weakness that has not yet been discovered and thus cannot be detected by anti-virus software. Stuxnet would persistently monitor the operations of the centrifuge and relay the information base to the attack base. Once Stuxnet figured out the operations pattern, the APT would take control of the centrifuges and spin them in a way that would make them fail. Stuxnet would deceptively provide false feedback to external controller readouts being monitored by nuclear plant employees and it would seem that the centrifuges are behaving properly. By the time the employees knew what was going on, it was too late. Stuxnet is believed to have destroyed 20% of Iran's nuclear centrifuges without even firing a shot. As an APT, Stuxnet's objective was directed at attacking supervisory control and data acquisition (**SCADA**) systems in industrial control systems (**ICS**), using infectious malware sent by programmable logic controllers (**PLCs**). Yet, to enter the system, the APT accessed and capitalized on system vulnerability *through a person*.

APT (Advanced Persistent Threat) Malware Characteristics

Stealth: Malware is stealthy. APTs are so advanced that detecting them takes a long time, during while the malware can wreak serious damage. It takes an average of 188 days from infection to detection of malware. It's called being-in-the-wild with a very low catch-rate. So, think of it, 188 days, which basically means little bit longer than over six months between infecting a machine and detecting the malware. Malware target not only human weaknesses but system vulnerabilities.

A **Vulnerability** is a bug or a flaw that exists in hardware or software that creates a security risk and may be exploited by an attacker just like the Siemens Step 7's PLC (programmable logic controller). An **Exploit** is software that takes advantage of vulnerable systems, essentially fooling the vulnerable system software into performing functions and running code of the attacker's choice. While early types of malware were more or less a swarm of independent agents simply infected and replicated themselves with little intention of bringing down large systems or infrastructure, malware today has become a centrally coordinated network application in a very real sense. So now the new generation of malware works as a network-set or as botnets, everything working together, centrally controlled with countries as nations-states sponsoring, coordinating, and controlling such attacks.

Did you know that?

Cyber-criminals look for the right attack surface (the target and level of damage) and then choose the appropriate attack vector (type of cyber-attack). It might be a Zero-Day attack vector for a technology bit it is commonly a phishing attack to easier human targets as a way to breach their systems!

Attack Vector and Attack Surface: In December 2020, hundreds of companies, and government agencies, including US Departments of Justice and Homeland Security, discovered an APT malware that was hiding under plain sight and relaying sensitive information from their computers back to the malware command and control servers. The APT attack as so sophisticated that it was identified as being a part of Russian cyberwarfare.

The APT attack disguised itself as a harmless piece of Solarwinds' infrastructure management software update that would be downloaded and it would quietly move across programs, machines, and systems, communicating back to the mothership (Russian servers distributed around the world). But why choose Solarwinds? The answer lies in attack surfaces and attack vectors.

Solarwinds was a popular software used by multiple organizations and companies around the world, which made Solarwinds an attractive target and a great attack vector. The idea behind an APT target is choosing the largest impact based on greatest "target density."

Ask yourself the question, why were there more aircraft carriers in the Pacific compared while nearly none in the Atlantic?

An aircraft carrier offers a large: "attack surface" and submarines (using torpedoes, etc.) are "attack vectors."

An attack vector has a greater probability of success when the attack vector has a greater density (more and lucrative targets).

During WWII, Japan had 169 submarines spread over the Pacific, South China Sea, and the Indian Ocean while Germany had 1,162 Unterseeboots (785 destroyed).

The Pacific Ocean is 63.8 million mi^2 while the Atlantic Ocean is 41.1 million mi^2. Considering only the Pacific (the Japanese had to cover all of the Pacific in addition to the Indian Ocean), that would create an attack density of 1 submarine every $\sim 378,000$ square miles. On the other hand, the Submarine Density in the Atlantic would be 1 submarine for every ~ 35.000 square miles.

If we were to consider the North Atlantic, the density would more than double to 1 submarine every ~ 14,000 square miles).

The North Atlantic had a higher attack vector density that the Pacific (nearly 1:27).

A low attack density can be assumed to a safer area to bring in large attack vectors such as Aircraft Carriers, compounded by the fact that the US had the courageous UK as its base close to the continent and she was the Queen of the Seas (despite the unfortunate indent with HMS Hood).

Ipso facto, using battle formation logic, it would be less important to carry large attack-surface Aircraft Carries in a dense attack-vector zone such as the North Atlantic, especially when the UK was an ally! Neither Australia nor South China had that proximal and formidable privilege in the Pacific war.

Choosing the Attack Vector: An attack vector is the mechanism by which cyber-threats find their way into a network or system. GitHub, a popular cloud-based software project repository used by companies to collaboratively develop software, automate workflows often serves as a code warehouse.

With so much activity and configurations in play, perpetrators behind the Sunburst hack may have found GitHub to be a fertile ground for capitalizing on a misconfigured code release. The perpetrators may have used the misconfigured public code release along with Solarwinds' in-secure update server credentials to inject malicious code into a component .dll (a shared software code library). The perpetrators then packaged the malware as a harmless-looking regular software patch update.

Increasing the Attack Surface: An attack surface is the amount and area that a cyber-threat can damage via an attack. Organizations need to reduce their attack surface to the minimal while cyber-threats seek to increase the attack surface to a maximum. In the Sunburst hack, the choice of the attack surface seemed predicated by two important assumptions.

First, Solarwinds' Orion infrastructure monitoring software had multiple client organizations, from government to companies, thus making Solarwinds *a valuable common denominator for a hacking gateway into multiple organizations*.

Fault Tolerant Architecture: Malware has a distributed fault tolerant architecture (blueprint for design and operations). Malware is distributed across multiple sources and targets and fault tolerant, i.e., it can function even if other parts of a computer system or network has a problem.

Advanced Malware takes full advantage of the resiliency built into the Internet itself, which means that if one bit goes down the other piece still stays active. So, if one malware goes down it'll find another place to infect and automatically take over that bit. Advanced malware can have multiple control-servers distributed all over the world with multiple fallback options. So, if malware in one system fails or gets detected, another copy of the malware goes active and can also potentially leverage other infected **end-points** (target computers). Malware can even change the communication channels if detected and automatically open a new communication channel to relay information to the attacker.

Multi-functionality: Advanced malware is multifunctional, i.e., the malware can work or morph itself with more than one threat or change communication channels. APT malware will often receive multifunctional updates from **CNC** or **command and control server** run by cyber attackers. So, an APT malware is set up as follows:

The malware CNC server reaches out to multiple malware it has distributed and infected across various systems all over the world. The Malware CNC server constantly sends messages over the Internet to each malware updating their software to create the most damage based on which computer system they have infected. Such over the cloud instructions can completely change the functionality of advanced malware. This multifunctional capability enables an attacker to use various endpoints strategically in order to accomplish desired damage such as stealing credit card numbers, sending spam, or connecting to websites or downloading files containing other malware payloads, such as ransomware. Because of malfunctionality, APT Malware is also **polymorphic**.

Polymorphism is the ability of software to change itself. Polymorphism makes the malware behave like the Roman God Janus with multiple faces or like Aria or the faceless man in Braavos whereby you can change your face if detected. Using polymorphism, APT malware can change a single character or bit within the source code that completely changes the hash signature. A **hash** signature is very much like an ID card for software. A hash is mathematical function used as a signature. Similar to how our signature is a shorter version of our name, hash functions are used to determine a software, database, or message. So, polymorphism is used to avoid hash-based signature detection by anti-virus and anti-malware software.

The way anti-virus and anti-malware works is very much the way WHO (World Health Organization) and CDC (center for disease control) detect new bacteria and virus and create antibacterial and antiviral medicine. The WHO and CDC first try to detect the virus signature such as its chemical composition, how it attaches itself to a protein or to a sort of DNA structure. Then, based on identifying the signature, the WHO and CDC create anti-virus mechanisms or antidotes. The antidotes work when they detect specific virus signatures or markers. Anti-virus and anti-malware work the same way, where they try and detect malware and virus hash signatures, however, if the virus and the malware can morph or change itself, it makes detection enormously difficult. So, APT malware, by mutating its code, can polymorph and change its identity to avoid detection and hide in the system or pass through the network even when its previous identity has been detected.

Obfuscation: Finally, APT malware use obfuscation, which is hiding in plain sight to remain undetected. Advanced malware often uses common obfuscation techniques to hide certain binary strings that are characteristically used in most malware and therefore avoid being detected by anti-malware software trained to search for and detect malware.

Cyber-Criminals and Cyber-Attack Strategies

Cyber-criminals, ranging from a lone hacker to an international agency or even the government, are entities that perpetrate system for financial benefits, terrorism, or disruption and sabotage. The Internet operates across murky waters and, as in international waters, like Somali pirates, cyber-criminals roam in wild abandon and go around hijacking things. That's exactly what cyber-criminals do. However, cyber-criminals often use the façade of legitimate businesses or are sponsored by large corporations and governments motivated by financial or strategic gain.

Cyber-war has evolved to become the next Cold War (like the animosity between the US and the erstwhile Soviet Union) but with costlier consequences. Cyber-criminals today, with large sponsors trying to steal company secrets, disable critical infrastructure, or even spread fake news to sway elections, have far more resources available to facilitate an attack with greater technical depth.

Cyber-criminals employ various cyber-attack strategies. Some of them are:

Reconnaissance: Like criminals in the physical world, cyber-criminals will reconnoiter or carefully study their victims and plan their attacks using social engineering, hacking, or phishing. During reconnaissance, cyber-criminals practice email address harvesting addresses, a way by which a large amount of emails are obtained using various methods to research, identify, and select targets for cyber-attacks.

Weaponization: Weaponization is the way cyber-criminals decide on choosing the malware or hack based on weaknesses in the target/s. Once cyber-criminals have found the right target or targets, cyber-criminals decide on creating the right weapon (malware payload, DoS, which software to infect) and mode of delivery (social engineering, system hack, web attack, DoS/DDoS). For example, cyber-criminals will often identify and infect data files or web pages that the target visits. The cyber-criminal then uses exploits aimed at the target's vulnerable software and delivered as a drive-by download. A **drive-by download** is a cyber-criminal mode of delivery technique where an advanced malware is secretly downloaded to the target's computer while visiting a website.

Cyber-attack strategies rely on **exploitation**, or a way to get the system or the person to trust in the malware. The cyber-attacker has two options for exploitation. The first one is social engineering, which is a relatively simple technique used to lure a human being into clicking a malicious link or opening a malicious executable file, or software exploit.

A software exploit requires technical prowess because the exploit has to essentially trick the operating system, web browser, or application software into running an attacker's code. Now, software exploits are more difficult because it's easier to patch or upgrade and fix software with known vulnerabilities. So, cyber-criminals often try **Zero-Day Attacks** when software is newly released, and all vulnerabilities have not yet been identified and patched. **Patching** is a way to remedy a software problem or vulnerability by installing a fix or update.

Cyber-criminals often times will use zero-day attack strategies for software exploits used to deliver some kind of malware. However, software companies try to identify zero-day attack vulnerabilities and patch them quickly to control cyber-attack threats. So, cyber-criminals still rely on social engineering as the first line of attack. As human beings, we're still running hundreds of millennia-old software in our own brains. We're still prone to emotions, anxiety, fear, distress, and depression and cyber-criminals can use these emotions and others to lay the trap. For sophisticated cyber-attacks, social engineering remains a cyber-criminal's most prolific toolkit.

Next is **installation**. Once the target and the endpoint have been infiltrated, cyber attackers install malware that can deliver its threat payload, avoid detection, and communicate with the cyber-attacker servers.

So cyber attackers often install malware as rootkits that provide privileged root-level access to computers. The malware is activated right when the computer starts. **Bootkits** are kernel mode variants of rootkits. Bootkits are malware used to infect computers that are protected by full disk encryption. A bootkit malware starts even before the computer encryption can even begin at the root-level, allowing it to relay files back to the cyber-criminal or infect the computer and open backdoors.

These backdoors enable a cyber-attacker to bypass normal authentication procedures to gain access to a compromised computer system. The backdoor becomes a secret failover in case the original malware is detected and removed from the system. Bootkit malware can also disable any legitimately installed anti-virus software in the compromised endpoint computer.

With cyber-attack strategies used to install the APT malware, cyber-criminals also create a command and control (CNC) to establish **malware communication** with infected systems and extract stolen data from a target system and network. The attacker can also use CNC to move the malware laterally across the system, targeting other systems on the victim's network, finding vulnerabilities in each and infecting them.

Attackers can further communicate and update an installed malware with encryption. The encrypted malware steals the information, encrypts the stolen information, and sends it back to the server. Company firewalls meant to detect and stop packets containing sensitive data from leaving the company network can be fooled because the packets are now encrypted. For example, cyber-criminals on BitTorrent, a peer-to-peer file-sharing site, are known for using proprietary encryption both for malware infection and command and control. Cyber-criminals further try to bypass proxies to infiltrate remote desktop access tools such as LogMeIn, RDP, or GoToMyPC and inject malware when using remote desktop connection.

Cyber-criminals used RDP vulnerabilities to infect computers with SamSam Ransomware. The 2016 SamSam ransomware used RDP to conduct a brute force attack against JBoss servers, infiltrating and breaching the City of Atlanta's infrastructure control system and the Colorado Department of Transportation. A **brute force attack** is a hacking technique where hackers bombard a system with various login and password combinations until one combination matches and provides the hacker access to the system.

A **proxy** is a computer gateway mechanism used to hide the real network identity of the computer system from intruders and cyber attackers. Cyber-criminals use port evasion using network anonymizers or pot-hopping fool the computer's proxy by tunneling through open and nonstandard ports.

So when your system your firewalls try to protect your computer by blocking certain ports, come command and control advanced malware will evade these ports. These malware also use fast flux or dynamic **DNS** ((domain naming system) used to match a URL to an IP address), to multiple infected hosts, reroute traffic, and make it extremely difficult for any cyber forensic team to figure out where traffic is going. Sometimes, cyber-criminals and black-hat hackers try to reroute the traffic in such a way so as to hide their origin and identity.

Cyber-attack strategies have actions and objectives. Attackers have many different motives including:

1. Data theft and destruction of critical national infrastructure, thus making national infrastructure security a priority. In 2017, a **ransomware** called Bad Rabbit was spread as an Adobe Flash software update. The ransomware paralyzed Ukraine's infrastructure including Kiev (Ukraine's capital) Metro, Ukraine Infrastructure Ministry, and Odessa airport, by encrypting Windows OS file systems and preventing users from accessing and booting Windows. The cyber-criminals demanded ransom to be paid via Bitcoin in order to decrypt files and resume access.

2. **Hacktivism**: **Hacktivism**, a portmanteau of hacking and activism, is a way by which hackers serve as activists to protest or promote a cause or social change. As early as 1989, hacktivists infected the Department of Energy (DOE), High Energy Physics network (HEPNET) and NASA networks with an anti-nuclear WANK worm. During the 2011 Egyptian uprising, Google worked with Twitter and SayNow, a hacktivist group, to rally protestors into simply calling in real-time incidents that were converted into Twitter feed texts. One of the most famous hacktivist groups in the world carries the moniker (pseudonym)—**Anonymous**.

During the 2009 Iranian election, Anonymous, helped protestors circumvent Iranian government's censoring of websites and social media access by creating a protest website with videos of human rights abuses and the protestors video manifesto. In 2011, Anonymous, as a protest against Syrian President Assad's indiscriminate killing of civilians in rebel areas, hacked the Syrian Defense website to create a link to Israel, Syria's mortal enemy. In 2013, Anonymous aided protestors in the Philippines by crashing more than 20 government websites. After the 2015 ISIS (Islamic State of Iraq and Syria) terrorist attack in Saint Denis and the Bataclan night club in Paris that killed 130 people, Anonymous tried identifying ISIS Twitter accounts and taking down ISI propaganda sites. In 2017, Anonymous hacktivists took down multiple websites related to child pornography on the Dark Web.

3. **Cyber-terrorism** is the intentional and premeditated use of cyber-attacks to terrorize people and economies to cause bodily harm or for financial or political motives. While Hacktivists tend to rally around social change, cyber-terrorists want to intimidate.

In 2007, when Estonia, an erstwhile Soviet state and now and independent country, removed a statue of a Russian soldier, Russian practiced cyber-terrorism against Estonia with a large-scale **DDoS** attack that disrupted all Estonian Internet connections leading to lost phone networks, banking, and healthcare information. In June 2017, in relation to the Russian invasion of Crimea in the Ukraine, Russian cyber-terrorism disabled Ukrainian electricity grids, the Chernobyl nuclear plants' Radiation Monitoring Systems, banks, and a host of other services.

Given that technology is our global lifeblood, cyber-threats pose an inordinate risk. Yet there are multiple ways to protect and defend cyber-infrastructures. There are multiple ways to protect **cyber-assets**, i.e., all device hardware, software, networks, and information connected to the Internet or other digital networks. Cybersecurity protection can also help in **BCP (business continuity planning)** and **IRP (incident response planning)**, i.e., the ability of a company to systematically manage an unforeseen incident or event and recover from it with full operational capabilities. They are as follows:

A. Identify and Inventory Cyber-Assets

Cybersecurity protection begins by identifying and inventorying the assets you have to protect. Asset begins with examining the business environment within which the company operates. Primarily, cyber-assets include

1. **Control systems**: Computer and technology systems used to operate various organizational systems for production (e.g., machinery operations, shipping schedule) or services (e.g., check deposit, patient scheduling), etc.

2. **Data and Information Acquisition systems**: Computer and Technology systems are used to collect data and information from inside or from outside the company such as POS (Point-of-Sale data at checkout counters), market research data, credit card information,

etc. Together, the first two cyber-assets are called supervisory control and data acquisition (**SCADA**).

3. Networking systems: Networking systems include hardware and software used to maintain digital communications locally or via the cloud. Networking systems include Gateways, Routers, and Switches. A gateway is often the first line of interface between networks. Network communications will often use routers (a networking hardware that knows the destination or where to send a data packet) and a Switch (a networking hardware that assigns the path to the destination). Data packets are often sent to Servers as gateway nodes. Servers have different functions based on what they serve. For example, a web server serves web pages, a file server serves documents, a media server serves audio and video files, an email server serves emails, a game server serves games, a print server serves printing jobs, and so on.

4. **IoTs (Internet of Things)**: Internet of Things is a name given to non-traditional computing devices that are connected to the Internet. IoTs include emerging connected devices, mainly connected cars, smart home sensors, and actuators such as Nest thermostats, remote garage door openers, voice-controlled devices, baby monitors,

© PiaDura LTD 2022
P. Datta, *Global Technology Management 4.0*,
https://doi.org/10.1007/978-3-030-96929-5_11

smart plugs, smart bulbs, and remote door locks and video doorbells.

IoTs are complex because they can be remotely accessed through a variety of devices including smart phones, smart watches, laptops. Chrysler's in-vehicle connectivity system, **Uconnect**, meant to remotely monitor vehicle functioning information did not require any security passwords or encryption. In 2015, two security researchers or **white hat hackers** (hackers who hack to research or help design security), Charlie Miller and Chris Valasek, wirelessly hacked a Jeep. The white hat hackers changed the Jeep's radio station, turning its windshield wipers and turned the air conditioner on. The security researchers could remotely stop the accelerator from working, stop the engine, and apply or disengage the brakes.

A **DDoS botnet** (a networked set of DoS cyber-attack bots or small pieces of autonomous code), Mirai, bombarded French web host OVH and a DNS server Dyn in 2016 with 1.1 terabits of data per second (Tbps). The botnet accessed the system via smart IoT consumer devices such as IP cameras and routers. The attack stopped access and availability of websites of Amazon, Netflix, Twitter, and The New York Times for hours. Newer Mirai botnet variants such as Hajime, Madura, and Wicked botnet are constantly looking for access weaknesses in IoT devices and technologies.

Even modern medicine is reliant on the convenience of networked remote access. That makes RFID medical devices such as pacemakers and defibrillators are vulnerable to cyber-attacks. **RFID** or Radio Frequency ID is a type of chip embedded in a variety of products and applications that allows dis tance monitoring such as radio tags on endangered species, secure cargo, warehouse freight) medical devices.

5. Secondary supporting systems such as virus scanners, HVAC systems, and uninterruptible power supplies (UPS) are also remotely controlled and vulnerable to attack. The 2014 Target hack that stole millions of credit card information happened through an HVAC system. Large HVAC systems are often connected to the Internet so that 3rd party HVAC vendors can remotely control temperature and monitor energy usage. Because an HVAC system operates across an entire company, the HVAC system can act as a bridge that hackers can use to access company networks. This is called HVAC hacking or **HVACking**.

B. Protect
Protecting cyber-assets focuses on developing and implementing a variety of appropriate safeguards to ensure that computer systems, networks, and databases are available, secure, and trustworthy. Some of the ways to protect Cyber-assets are:

1. **Network Security**: Given that servers are very important, companies try to protect servers using firewalls and proxy servers. A **firewall** is a network security system that monitors and controls access to networked computers and servers based on policies. A firewall is like a bouncer at a club that is instructed on who to let in and who to keep out. A **proxy server** hides the real IP address of a server with a "masked" proxy IP address. Because the proxy hides the real IP address, a cyber-criminal or hacker will have difficulty trying to disrupt service, load malware, or steal information.

2. Network Segmentation, VPNs, and Access Control: **Network segmentation** or Zoning is a protection mechanism that splits a network into multiple subnetworks or subnets, each with its own firewall and proxies for protection.

Network segmentation can not only reduce congestion across the whole network by separating Internet traffic based on specific requests but also increase security by isolating parts of the network from others. Even in the case of an attack, a subnet may be compromised but the rest of the network will remain functional. Companies will often segment the network based on web servers, database servers, file servers, email servers, employee computers, IoT devices, and so on.

Each subnet can act like an isolated network that limits attacks to one rather than to all. Here is an example of basic network segmentation architecture. The access to a company's website will direct traffic through a router with multiple firewalls for each network segment containing servers and computers.

3. A **"perimeter" firewall** filters and monitors public access to the company's Web Server that serves pubic and customer access to products, services, and information. The public access network segment is known as the **DMZ (Demilitarized Zone)** or the zone of open Internet access. Another firewall after the DMZ offers the second line of protection and defense that will filter packets and access before someone can enter the company's internal network segments and servers. Servers must always be behind firewalls.

4. A **VPN (Virtual Private Network)** is a secure tunnel that allows controlled access for authenticated users to access internal corporate networks and servers. A VPN sits on the firewall that users can connect over the Internet. The VPN also provides access control.

5. **Access control** is a way by which companies can control which user can access which system, network segment,

and server. Typically access control is offered via a combination of login user ID and password.

Access control is based on three major premises:

- What "is": What "is" identifies and gives access to the user based on some kind of biometrics such as fingerprints, retinal scan, face scan, voice scan, and even gait scanning.
- What "has": What "has" identifies and gives access to the user based on some that the user carries such as a token ring, credit card, passport, ID, car key, etc.
- What "knows": What "knows" identifies and gives access to the user based on what the user knows such as passwords, PINs, SSN, a code, etc.

Good access control policies use a combination of the three: What "is," What "has," and What "knows." Today, access controls are getting more sophisticated with **2FA (2 Factor Authentication)** and **MFA (multi-factor authentication)**. An ATM or Google and Apple logins use 2FA. An ATM requires a card (what "has") and a PIN (what "knows"). Google and Apple logins will often create an **OTP (One Time Password)** or an authentication code that is sent to another device a user owns such as a smartphone. Access control is achieved by ensuring that the user has both passwords and/or a combination of the password and the phone/device to which an authentication code has been sent.

Access control is critical to **Identity and Access Management (IAM)**. Identity and Access Management is a process by which user identity is used to manage custom-access to various resources with an organization. IAM creates, deletes, and performs changes to user identity and access controls.

Once a user is authenticated, IAM creates various authorizations or the controlled ability of the user to access various organizational information and resources. Authorizations are crucial in organizations, especially in relation to **separation of duties**. A user may be authorized to only write a program or create purchasing order while another user may be authorized to view the program for quality control or approve the purchase order. Proper authorization increases cybersecurity.

When the user provides a right set of credentials, authorizations are often based on **discretionary** or **non-discretionary access controls**. Discretionary authorizations are custom authorizations, allowing users to access one or more system resources within the organization based on ad-hoc clearance.

For example, a consultant hired by a company may need to access some operations documents and employee performance reviews. Based on the need, the IAM group will create a discretionary access to only those documents across one or more servers and subnets. Non-discretionary authorizations are often role-based pre-assigned set of access privileges based on the user's role. For example, a marketing research intern will have a pre-designated authorization for accessing product and market documents as well as access to certain Internet product and market databases. On the other hand, an HR employee will have automatic, role-based access to HR forms, grievance files, and employee schedules and performance logs, etc.

Protecting cyber-assets is a preventative measure. Much like preventative care for a human being that requires vaccinations, inoculations, regular checkups, health monitoring and exercise, protecting cyber-assets requires careful vigilance that can limit chances of cyber-attacks and contain the impact of a potential cyber-attack. For example, **PCI DSS (Payment Card Industry Data Security Standards)** ensures cybersecurity protection of credit cards and user identity. PCI DSS compliance requires that companies follow certain guidelines:

  i. Build and Maintain a Secure Network and Systems
 ii. Protect Cardholder Data
iii. Maintain a Vulnerability Management Program
 iv. Implement Strong Access Control Measures
  v. Regularly Monitor and Test Networks
 vi. Maintain an Information Security Policy

C. Diagnose and Detect

Diagnosis and detection are based on designing, developing, and deploying systems and ways to identify causes and reasons behind any cybersecurity issue or concern. Diagnosis and detection are similar to a medical diagnosis where certain symptoms signal that things may be wrong. The physician, like a cybersecurity teams, diagnoses various symptoms to narrow the issue to some root causes.

In cybersecurity, detection can discover cybersecurity issues on time before an irrecoverable or damaging attack. **Intrusion Detection Systems (IDS)** is a software system to continuously monitor security and detect and stop anomalies and events. IDS can be either **HIDS (Host IDS)** or **NIDS (Network IDS)**.

A HIDS is IDS software that is installed on the user's (host's) computer. The HIDS checks for unexpected changes in user files such as sudden deletion, copying, content changes, attempts to attach files to email, and attempts to access system and boot files, etc.

NIDS is IDS software that monitors the network and network traffic. NIDS safely monitors strange and threatening behavior in the network and can try and trace the issue or, if need be, redirect the threat away from the cyber-assets.

Both HIDS and NIDS follow rules and specifications to monitor cyber-threats. Every instance of threat or strange behavior is flagged and logged for further investigation.

D. Mitigate and Encrypt

Mitigating cyber-assets is a way to reduce or eliminate the impact of a threat by responding in an appropriate manner. Mitigation is similar to receiving a prescription medicine of shot from the physician that is meant to boost your immunity and fight back against the germs.

One of the most important parts of mitigation is planning which also touches upon preventative care. Think of it. The better we take care of our health, the better we can thwart health threats.

Once cyber-threats have been detected, the most common way to mitigate cyber-threats is by creating and applying hardware, software, and **firmware** (hardware and software combination) fixes, patches, and updates. A **fix, patch, or update** is a piece of software that rewrites existing computer systems, software codes, and applications to eliminate existing and future cyber-threats. Fixes, patches, and updates act like prescription medicine meant to cure the ailment and provide the body with antigens and antibodies to mitigate infections. *Ensuring that computer systems have the latest security fixes, patches and updates is a must.*

Even though fixes, patches, and updates can try and remedy cyber-threats, the solution is often more reactive than proactive. Information may have already been stolen. So, how can information be protected so that, even if there were to be a cyber-attack and a breach, information remains private and confidential, unreadable to the cyber-criminals?

Cryptography

Cryptography is the answer. **Cryptography** (crypto = secret and graphy = writing) is the science behind encryption and confidentiality and is fundamental to mitigation planning. A central tenet of response planning is preparation for a cyber-attack where "the loss of possession should not mean a loss of confidentiality." Simply put, while it is improbable that a person or company will never misplace documents or information or never be hacked, the loss of information possession (by someone who finds, hacks into, or steals the information) should not automatically compromise the person or the company. But how do you do that? The answer—encryption. **Encryption** is a way of encoding or secretly scrambling information so that the information would be unreadable and unintelligible to the general person that steals or intercepts it but only readable or "**decrypted**" by "authenticated" users with proper access rights to that information.

Encryption and decryptions act like locks and keys. Encryption uses a key to lock the door, increasing privacy and confidentiality. Decryption can only use the same or another exact key to unlock the door and access its contents. Because the same "privately kept" key can open and close the door (i.e., encrypt and decrypt) the message, this is called **private key** or **symmetric key** encryption. However, if the private key is ever stolen or compromised, the entire encryption logic falls apart.

Private Key Encryption

From countries to companies, cryptography has been popular since the dawn of civilization and war. Around 500 BC, the Spartans used a device called **Scytale**, a cylinder to roll the spiral-cut information parchment. The Spartans would write military directions on the parchment, wrap it around the Scytale, and cut the scroll parchment at an angle. This created a **cipher**, a garbled encrypted message. The cipher would then be sent via a messenger for secret communications. Only the legitimate receiving party would have a Scytale of the same size and width used to create it. Even if the enemy intercepted the messenger, unless the cylinder was exactly the same size to the one that was used to create the message, the message on spirally cut scroll would be unintelligible to the interceptor.

Around 50 BC, Julius Caesar, the Roman general and Triumvirate, created the Caesar cipher to encrypt messages. **Caesar cipher** used a substitution mechanism where each alphabet was substituted by another alphabet *3 spots forwards*. So, a Caesar cipher for the word "Rubicon" (the northeastern river that separated Rome as a republic from the rest of Italy; the river that Julius Caesar crossed with his 13th Gemina legion to begin the civil war, turning into a dictator and then being stabbed to death by his friend Brutus and other senators) would be "*Uxelfrq*" where R is substituted by U, u by x, b by e, and so on.

Around sixteenth century, Blaise Vigenere's **Vigenere square** became the next notable cryptographic encryption. The Vigenere square uses the 26 letters of the alphabet to be arranged in rows and columns to create a 26×26 character square. The alphabet set moves by 1 le tter for each row. The cipher encryption required a message and a key phrase. For example, assume we want to encrypt the same message "rubicon" and we choose a key phrase "caesar." The key phrase has to match the message size. The message "rubicon" has 7 letters and "Caesar" has 6. So, in order to match the message, the 6-letter "caesar" would become the 7-letter "caesarc" by simply repeating the key phrase (or cutting the key phrase if longer than the message) till they match. Using the message "RUBICON" for the columns and the key phrase "CAESARC" for the rows, the intersecting letters would create the cipher. So, the intersection of R in the columns and C in the rows is T; U and A is U; B and E is F, etc. The Vigenere cipher would convert and encrypt "rubicon" into "*tufacfp*."

Moving forward four centuries, the case of the **Zimmerman Telegraph** requires mention. In 1917, at the height of the First World War, the US had assumed a neutral position while the war raged on with Britain, France, Russia on one side and Germany, the Austro-Hungarian Empire, and the Turkish Ottomans on the other. It was a tense time and Britain had severed the German telegraph cables in the Atlantic. The Americans were neutral, and the Germans requested the Americans to allow the Germans to use their telegraph lines under the Atlantic Ocean. In January, a top-level German foreign officer went an encrypted telegram to the German Ambassador to Mexico. The message was one of serious concern and posed a national threat against the US, the same country that had generously allowed Germany to use its telegraph lines. The message instructed and incited Mexico to attack the US' with Germany's assistance in order to reclaim its lost territories of Texas, New Mexico, and Arizona that the US had won or bought from Mexico during and after the Mexican American War of 1846. The revelation of the message prompted the US, under President Woodrow Wilson, to join World War I against Germany (Fig. 11.1).

But how did Britain decrypt the encrypted German telegraph message? The German encryption code was based on German **cipher** code system 0075 made up of 10,000 words and phrases numbered 0000 to 9999. British Intelligence intercepted or sniffed the encrypted message and had decrypted the message. Although the Germans had encrypted its 10,000 word and phrases into military vocabulary into a number cipher, the Germans did not have a word for "Arizona." So, the Germans had to split the word Arizona into a set of phonetic syllables "AR, IZ, ON, A" and created codes for them. The British Naval Intelligence code-breakers used this, along with a German codebook retrieved from a drowned sailor, to reverse engineer and **decrypt** the message.

Private key encryption became more widespread during World War II. The air was rife with espionage and uncertainty about the next big war. World War I was meant to the "war to end all wars" but the World War II was there. The Nazis had taken over Germany, the Russian communists had signed secret agreements with the Nazis, Austria was annexed, and Poland was

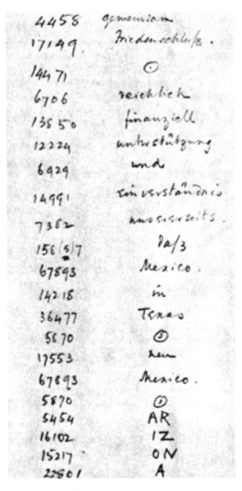

Fig. 11.1 Zimmermann telegram code (Courtesy Wikipedia)

invaded in September 1939. Spies, armed with radio transmitters and codebooks, were spread across every country, collecting information to pass on to their governments. A **codebook** contained private passkeys that encrypted and decrypted a message. A codebook could be as harmless looking as a normal novel or a book of poems whose contents could be used to create passkeys.

For example, a spy codebook could be based on a copy of Longfellow's 1867 translation of Dante's *Divine Comedy* (*Divina Commedia*). Using this version/copy of the book, spy handlers used substitution to create a private key for encryption. The letter "A" might be substituted with the 20th letter "I" in Canto II in Volume III (Paradiso); "B" substituted with the 11th letter "T" in Canto V in Volume III (Paradiso); "C" with the 165th letter "M" in Canto I in Volume II (Purgatario); "D" with the 42nd letter "P" in Canto XI in Volume I (Inferno); "E" with the 2nd letter "H" in Canto XXXIII in Volume III (Paradiso), and so on. The spy would send a communiqué via a small radio transmitter where ABCDE would be encrypted as ITMPH, decodable by the spy handler's HQ. The cat and mouse game between the spies and the spy-catchers was mainly focused on the spy-catchers trying to seize the codebook that could compromise the confidentiality and encryption of the message.

Although private key or symmetric key encryption can be very clever and ingenious, it suffers from one serious and fatal disadvantage. The entire encryption operation in private key encryption relies on the private key to cipher and decipher a message. If the private key is lost, stolen, or compromised, it can defeat the integrity of the entire encryption system.

During World War II, Nazi Germany used the **Enigma** machine that increased encryption sophistication. The Enigma cipher machine looked like a large typewriter and used a complex combination linking a keyboard to a plugboard, multiple rotors, switches, and reflectors. The Enigma machine operated as follows. The numbers in parentheses approximately guide the operation in the circuit diagram (Fig. 11.2).

A. The user decrypting a message would start with a daily key. The daily key would be used to create the daily cipher arrangement. Keys would be changed daily so that the arrangement structure of the cipher operation would become very difficult.

B. The user would start typing in the message (1). The typing would trigger electric flow where each letter would link to a plugboard (2) where it would be substituted based on the daily cipher arrangement.

C. The substituted letter would then touch a contact in a fixed rotor (3) that was linked to scramblers.

D. Scramblers had multiple moving rotors (4, 5) where the contact point in one rotor would touch the contact point of the next rotor that

Fig. 11.2 Enigma cipher and circuit (Courtesy Wikipedia)

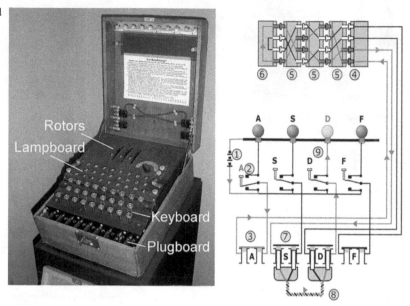

would touch the contact point of the next rotor and so on till more letters and characters were substituted. Once all the contact notches were used, the rotor would move the notch sequence that would make it even more complicated guessing the rotor notch order.

E. The resulting electrical signal from the last rotor would go through one of two reflectors (6) that would reverse the signal flow but with a different combination because the rotors keep shifting.

F. Finally, after the reverse path with new rotor sequences (7), the electrical signal would light up a connected letter via the plugboard (8) onto a lamp board (9). The lamp board letter would be the encrypted letter. The Enigma cipher changed settings each day and there were 159 quintillion (a billion times a billion) combinations.

The Allies' breaking of the Enigma code depended on a multitude of factors. A few Enigma messages and ciphers had been found but the complex wiring and rotor combinations were unknown. Perhaps, the Polish mathematician, **Marian Rejewski**, was key in solving the

permutations to figure out the rotor combinations in 1933, even before the war had begun.

The British also captured Enigma cryptographic documents from German submarines (U-boats) such as U110 and U-559. In Bletchley Park, UK, the British code-breakers used **Alan Turing**'s newly designed Bombe machine, a predecessor of the computer, to intercept German transmissions, use the Polish permutation as the program and use "Wrens" (Women's Royal Naval Service, WRNS) to crack the code before the Germans reset them daily. Women such as **Mavin Batey** became so deft at understanding enemy code operators that she could guess that an operator was using his girlfriend's name "Rosa" as the initial daily key. Mavin Batey was even able to decrypt an *Abwehr* (German Military Intelligence) Enigma message, one of the most difficult to break. Even though most Enigma ciphers were never cracked, the cracking of the German U-boat and Luftwaffe (air force) Enigma ciphers helped end the war by two years, along with the destruction of the German U-boat fleet that was sinking American and British convoys and assistance during the D-Day landings.

Did you know that?

World War II women codebreakers like Marvin Batey were able to crack German Enigma ciphers by understanding human psychology to guess the initial cipher key! Humans are always the weakest link!

In recent years, private key encryption became more sophisticated. IBM designed **Triple DES** (Data Encryption Standard) that used three consecutive 56-bit keys to encrypt the data. A fixed size key (e.g., 56-Bit) is called a **Block Cipher**. **AES** (Advanced Encryption Standard) succeeded DES and used a 128-Bit block size and larger keys (128, 192, and 256-Bits) that made it more difficult to break. Another type of private key cipher is a **stream cipher** where, instead of replacing (substituting) message chunks with a fixed block key, a stream cipher encrypts each message character with a stream of random character keys to create a cipher. **RC4** is a stream cipher named after a famous cryptography researcher, Rivest often uses disposable private keys that are used only once, thus reducing/mitigating chances of compromising the message.

Asymmetric or Public Key Encryption

The Enigma cipher, although based on private (symmetric) key encryption, added a set of changing combinations with moving rotors so that the encryption logic kept changing, making guessing the private key difficult. However, as cryptography evolved, it ushered in a new cryptographic system called an **Asymmetric key** or **Public Key Encryption**.

While a private or symmetric key infrastructure is based on a single codebook to encrypt and decrypt the message, an asymmetric key or Public key encryption is based on the following:

- Public Key Encryption uses a combination of two keys, a **public key** and a **private key** for the sender of the message and a public key and private key for the receiver of the message.

- The private keys of the sender and the receiver are, as the name suggests, private and *known only* by the sender and the receiver, respectively.
- The sender and receiver public keys are open and can be used to encrypt or decrypt messages.
- Certification Authorities (CAs) link public keys to specific identities of people and companies.
- A message encrypted with the sender's public key can only be decrypted using the sender's private key and vice versa (encryption using the sender's private key can only be decrypted using the sender's public key). A message encrypted with the receiver's public key can only be decrypted using the receiver's private key and vice versa.

Suppose a spy is sending a coded message (cipher) from Iraq to the UK's MI-6. The spy can encode the message using the spy's private key (only known to the spy and not MI-6) and send the cipher to MI-6. MI-6 can decrypt the cipher and retrieve the message using the spy's public key (openly available). Alternatively, the spy can encode the message using the MI-6's public key (openly available) and send the cipher to MI-6. MI-6 can decrypt the cipher and retrieve the message using MI-6's private key (only known to the MI-6 and not to the spy).

While this 2-key combination makes compromising the encryption system more difficult, there are certain problems with each of the above combinations. In the first case where the spy encrypts the message with the spy's private key, this makes the message authentic in terms of the sender (only the spy knows the spy's private key) but it makes it difficult to authenticate the receiver. Anyone that has the spy's public key can decrypt the message. Could the spy be certain that only MI-6 decrypted and read the message? No! That creates a chance for a breach.

Similarly, in the case where the spy encrypts the message using MI-6's public key and is decrypted by MI-6's private key, the spy can authenticate that only MI-6 can read the message. However, given that MI-6's public key is open, MI-6 cannot be certain that it was the spy and nobody else that encrypted the message. A sender or receiver denying sending or receiving a message is called **repudiation** and can create a lot of issues, from espionage to business contracts.

With each approach having its own disadvantages, digital signatures are used as a solution. A **Digital signature** is a public key encryption based mathematical schema or model that can authenticate both the sender and the receiver to ensure **non-repudiation**. Digital signatures are used in our mobile bank transactions, emails, online documents signatures, cryptocurrencies such as bitcoins, among many others. Suppose a business S is sending a private contract to another business R for acceptance (Fig. 11.3). A Digital signature works as follows.

1. S takes the original contract and encrypts the contract using R's public key. Nobody but R can decrypt the contract because decryption requires R's private key that only R knows.

2. S runs a cryptographic hash on the original contract to create a message digest (MD). A Hash is a mathematical algorithm that coverts a message into fixed size bit string to ensure message integrity (i.e., ensuring that the content and the accuracy of the message have not been changed or compromised). MD is the resulting product from a hash. A reverse hash can be run on the MD to recover the message and check for integrity.

3. S now takes both the encrypted contract (from Step 1) and the MD and encrypts the combined set S's private key. Nobody else knows S's private key so this encrypted package, ensuring that the sender S is authentic. This is the second layer of encryption.

4. Once R receives the double-layered cipher, R's system works in reverse to decrypt the contract.

5. R uses S's public key to decrypt the first layer of cipher to reveal the encrypted contract and MD. Because S's public key can only be used in correspondence to S's private key, R now knows that S and only S could have sent it. This ensures non-repudiation and confirms that S is the sender.

6. The double-layered cipher includes the encrypted contract and MD. First, R uses R's private key to decrypt the encrypted contract. The contract was encrypted by S using R's public key and can only be opened by R's private key, known only to R. If the contract is decrypted, S is assured that R and only R received the contract and cannot be repudiated.

7. Finally, R uses a reverse hash to convert the MD back into the contract. The contract from the MD is compared with the decrypted contract that was originally encrypted (in step

Fig. 11.3 Example of a cryptographic hash and message digest (Courtesy Wikipedia)

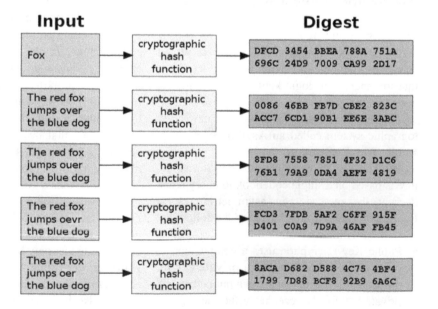

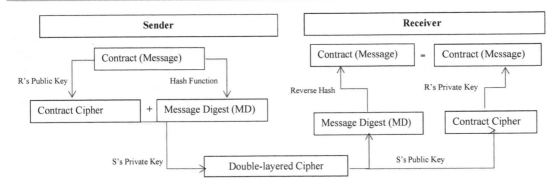

Fig. 11.4 Digital Signature for Authentication and Non-Repudiation

1) with R's private key. If both contracts match, both S and R know that nobody tampered with the integrity of the contract. Now, R can accept the contract. Both S and R know that the contract wasn't tampered with. R is assured that S is the one that sent it and S is assured that R is the only one that received the contract (Fig. 11.4).

Public and private keys used in a public key encryption are based on very large **prime numbers** (numbers that are divisible only by 1 and by themselves, e.g., 3, 7, 11, 23, 37, 997). **RSA** (Rivest Shamir and Adelman) and **DSA** (Diffie-Hellman) are two popular public key encryption standards. DSA is faster at signing, slow at verifying. RSA is faster at verifying, slow at signing. So, RSA is used for encryption while DSA is used for digital signatures.

Cryptocurrency and Blockchains

Public Key Encryption is the essence of Cryptocurrency. The idea of cryptocurrency has been floating around for a decade, trying to create a single global currency without exchange rates, currency manipulations, and country borders. Just like a currency note carries a number, an issuing agency (e.g., Bank of England, US Treasury), and a value, cryptocurrency is an encrypted data string that represents a currency unit with an ID. **Blockchains**, a global peer-to-peer network, monitors the flow of every

cryptocurrency ID, maintaining a secure log of every transaction as each cryptocurrency changes hands from buying, selling, and transferring. Therefore, unlike paper currency, the path of every cryptocurrency can be traced or audited. Unlike paper currency, cryptocurrencies are decentralized and not issued by a country or bank. **Bitcoin** and **Ethereum** are two of the more popular cryptocurrencies.

Cryptocurrencies are digital: Traditional currency is defined by pegging (linking) it to another well-respected global currency such as the US Dollar or by pegging it to gold reserves. Cryptocurrency is completely digital. Cryptocurrencies are stored in people's and companies' digital wallets and transferred digitally to other peoples' digital wallets. No physical currency exists.

Cryptocurrencies are verifiable: Cryptocurrencies use something called **Proof-of-work** to verify that the cryptocurrency is authentic and not counterfeit. A proof-of-work is a system of "hard-to-compute" but "easy-to-verify" computational puzzle that ensures the integrity and authenticity of the cryptocurrency. Proof-of-work also limits cryptocurrency production (called crypto currency mining). After all, too much production lowers the value of a currency.

Cryptocurrencies are maintained by Public Ledgers: From creation to transaction, the movement of every cryptocurrency is confirmed and stored in a public ledger or a log book across a globally distributed digital network called blockchain. Cryptocurrency transactions use public key encryption to encrypt identities of cryptocurrency owners and very transaction. A cryptocurrency transaction is made using an encrypted digital signature confirmation to ensure and authenticate both the sender and receiver.

E. Respond, Communicate, and Recover

Even when companies have a splendid framework to identify cyber-assets, protect them, diagnose and detect cyber-threats, and mitigate cyber-attacks using cryptography, the ability to respond, communicate, and recover is essential.

Response to a cyber-attack is a company's ability to react to a cyber-threat systematically and effectively. A company's cybersecurity **IRP** (Incident Response Plan) is its response guideline and process triggered by a cybersecurity incident. **Communication** is the way a company should articulate, report, and reach out to various stakeholders such as customers, employees, market analysts, and regulators. **Recovery** is the way by which companies can speedily resume and restore normal operations after a cybersecurity event.

An IRP is a very systematic document that is a combination of a set of checklists and formal processes that include:

- Identify all cyber-assets, services, and processes required to keep the company operational. With your security team, take inventory of your data assets and potential risks, and conduct an impact assessment. So, understand what your data assets are, what are the things that are likely to be vulnerable, what are the most critical parts of your infrastructure, of your software that is really going to impact your brand reputation. Purchase cyber-insurance, if possible.
- Identify all personnel resources responsible for managing all assets, services, and processes. Train personnel on how to react to a cyber-attack or cyber-event. Know what kind of attacks make you the most vulnerable, anticipating potential goals of an attack, and running simulations like military drills within the working group.

- Denote the scope of each incident in terms of severity and how to **flag** a cyber-event. Cyber events are often flagged based on how much the event, e.g., number of queries to a data server per second, falls outside of acceptable limits.
- Create scenarios based on severity and response plans for each scenario. Ensure that every cyber-event is logged and analyzed.
- Create specific maps and plans for Subject-Matter-Experts—whom to contact for forensics, legal counsel, technology vendors for investigation, communication, and recovery. For example, it might be more prudent to call the FBI after a cyber-event because data flow is a cross-border issue. Wait for the FBI, in tandem with the legal counsel, to guide the communication and investigation.
- Regularly conduct IRP drills based on various scenarios and combinations. Revise IRP based on drill results.
- Integrate IRP and Communication strategies as a part of your recovery or **Business Continuity Planning (BCP)**.
- Communicate to customers from a dedicated, secure site that is easily identifiable and cannot be easily spoofed or create confusion.

As a part of IRP and BCP, companies need to create **SOP**s (**Standard Operating Practices**). An SOP is a best practice that is used as a standard operational template for an organization, across departments, divisions, and functions. Sadly, IRP is often times lacking in companies. The 2017 massive Equifax cybersecurity hack revealed Equifax's dreadful response planning. Equifax set us a site for victims called "equifaxsecurity2017.com" but failed to communicate the exact address to its own social media support employees. Equifax's Twitter responses ended forwarding victims to different website called "securityequifax2017.com." The site "securityequifax2017.com" was a fake "phishing" site, luckily set up by a developer that was trying to highlight Equifax's IRP failings. Similarly, the November 2018 Marriott hotel chain data breach exposed 500,000 of its customer data. As an IRP, Marriott used a third-part contractor, CSC, to send emails to victims using an email address "email-mariott.com." Wary victims were slow to act because the email address looked like it was a spoofed email. The victims thought that they were being scammed by criminals, much like looters after a riot or protest, trying to spoof and phish to steal data after an attack. The confusion led to a recovery slowdown.

With 2.4 billion Internet users and over 30 billion devices connected to the Internet by 2020, the probability of new attack vectors and attack surfaces is increasing every day. The more and varied the devices on the network, the greater the asset management complexity. That increases the attack surface for cyber-criminals. While it may be impossible to stop an attack, good IRP can somehow contain the fallout and maintain continuity. In this section, let's explore additional cybersecurity SOPs.

- **Stop Malware Communication**: Firstly, communication is the lifeblood of an attack. If a company can stop the threat from communicating, it can protect itself, quarantine, and neutralize the attack.
- **Analyze Cybersecurity Logs**: Second, numerous opportunities exist to detect and correlate. A cyber-attack is a process. Here, cybersecurity analytics becomes useful to detect and correlate the multiple steps involved in the advanced attack life cycle to trace/find the cyber-attack pattern. There are multiple chances to identify and counter various cyber-threats—so don't just focus on infection, focus on everything from social engineering to how it communicates—to find multiple different areas where you can nip the cyber-attack in the bud.
- **Focus on the Process Reengineering**: Often, the company's process, rather than technical functionality, is the threat. Response requires understanding the cyber-threat. It's not what the malware does but how a malware operates. Processes are important but understanding the process by which the malware operates can neutralize future malware attacks. In order to

respond, and recover, treat the threat as an extensible framework, not simply the functionality of the specific payload.

- While it is imperative to know what and where a malware wants to steal information, it is even more important to understand the process by which the malware tries to steal the information. If you can understand the process, then you can rectify the whole system. Similarly, if a company wanted to change how it communicates with its employees and customers, the best strategy is to change or reengineering the communication process, rather than trying to fix separate miscommunications. Realize that the problem lies in the process; if you can rectify the process you find the problem and you can take care of the problem altogether.
- **Practice Defense-in-Depth**. Defense-in-Depth refers to separating multiple security solutions so that, if a cyber-attack compromises one cybersecurity device, it will not automatically crash all cybersecurity devices. Understand that cyber-threats exist across multiple points; so must cybersecurity. Firewalls whose main job is to create a wall between the outside environment and a company's internal systems. Intrusion prevention using makes sure that companies have proper anti-virus and encryption and IDS can trace and prevent intrusions.
- Advanced endpoint protection ensures that devices are properly protected. Content filtering ensures that access to critical data is limited. Encryption systems ensure that confidentiality and privacy are maintained even if systems are compromised. These security solutions are separated to provide defense in-depth. A Defense-in-Depth strategy makes it difficult, if not impossible, to identify, correlate, and counter complex coordinated attacks that take advantage of multiple attack vendors.
- **Determine Attack Vectors**: Focus on the growing multitude of attack vectors, including applications, URLs, and websites, they can host and enable threats exploits they can create command-line shell access to targets with

escalated privileges. Realize that cybersecurity must expand beyond the perimeter to include network endpoint and cloud environments. You can have the best security in your phone but if you're using an unsecure Wi-Fi network your phone data can be compromised. So, practice using secure networks and secure devices or endpoints when communicating.

- **Ask Policy and Legislative Questions**: Think forward about cybersecurity policy and legislative aspects and frameworks. We still don't have clear answers to many a question. For example, what is the right division of responsibilities between governments and private sector in terms of defense? For example, look at the division of responsibilities between governments and private sector. For example, when Equifax, the credit rating agency, has a breach that compromised 113 million Social Security Numbers (SSNs), including perhaps you and me, the same individuals also work for other companies. Some of these individuals may work for defense firms like Boeing or Lockheed Martin; they could even be members of the FBI, CIA. Could a consumer credit agency breach also compromise other companies and agencies? Could cyber-criminals be able to stitch together identities and use them to gain access into other company and agency systems? If such a multi-agency compromise were to happen, who bears what responsibility? What is a private sector breach such as the breaches in Equifax or Marriott divulged identities of government employees paid by taxpayer dollars? What is the responsibility of the private sector and what is the responsibility of the government in securing data and IRP? How should regulators approach cybersecurity in their industries?
So how do you create cyber policies for different industries? If you have different cyber policies for different industries, what happens if your company is a part of more than one industry, for example, Google or Amazon? Which cybersecurity regulation do you end up using? What actions are acceptable for

governments, companies, and individuals to take and what actions are not? Who is responsible for software flaws? What happens if there is a software flaw, is it the software designer or is it the software implementer and integrator? In a global reality, who bears accountability when individuals, companies, and data reside and flow across different countries and different organizations, connected via different networks to the ubiquitous Internet?

- **Have a Crisis Management Plan**: In September 2017, Equifax had a data breach that lost 113 million Social Security numbers. The thing is, it took Equifax about two to three months to even realize that the breach had even occurred. The question is, it takes a long time to even know that there's somebody who's invading your privacy and violating your entire structure, or entity, but once you know that, what do you do? Data breaches affect brand reputation and require crisis management. And central to a crisis management is a communication plan. If you don't control communications proactively, the media and the Internet will overwhelm you with irrational doom.

- **Practice Cybersecurity Communications**: Having defined steps in the communication protocol is an imperative. First, create a cross-functional breach response team, comprising of PR, marketing, and technology. Get your marketing people to maintain product and brand reputation. Decide who is best suited to handle what part of the crisis communication. Create a responsibility and accountability matrix across the cross-functional group.
Determine and document exactly what you're legally obligated to disclose. If you don't know what you're obligated to disclose, call the FBI. Do realize that cyberspace is an international phenomenon; it's not a local phenomenon, which means that your local police has no jurisdiction, the only one that has jurisdiction is the FBI or the Interpol. If dealing with classified information, communicate with defense partners, the government

and law enforcement, possibly the FBI and follow their advice. Go step by step. Don't try and communicate things based on hunches but based on legal counsel and FBI guidance.

- **Create Relationships and Communicate Prudently**: Invest in relationships with external security professionals, bloggers, and the traditional media and use them as your advocates.
  - Handle communication sensitively, make sure your communications relay pertinent information, and quell rumors and assumptions.
  - Make certain your crisis and communications response team have qualified experts in each of the technical and functional areas of your business, so that they can communicate using proper terms and the proper jargon. Your software engineering response team member might be best equipped to respond to a technical media publication while your marketing response team member may be the best person to field questions about the brand.
  - Proactively initiate a press meeting, upon confirmation by general counsel, rather than reacting. Don't guess anything. No comment is better than a misconstrued comment. As a breach unfolds over hours, days, weeks, and months as more facts become available, and you may not want to jump the gun and presume what happened. Seek FBI, cybersecurity experts', and general counsels' guidance. Don't take a shot in the dark. Remember, every time you disclose information, you're held liable for that disclosure, which basically means that can be brought up in court.
  - As time passes, communicate to your employees and customers what was learned and what was done to improve security as a result. Don't forget to dust off and periodically revisit your IRP. Cybersecurity response is a cycle, not just a single reaction. As mousetraps get better,

mice get smarter. Even as you fix your existing security, hackers will once again try and break through your system by preying on social engineering, process problems, and technology vulnerabilities.

The next page shows how the dangerous Sunburst cybersecurity hack compromised large companies and government agencies, all of them using the Solarwinds software (Fig. 11.5).

Transition Exercise: Strategizing and Modeling Global Cybersecurity

Purpose

Globalization and strategic use of technology are mainstream concepts today. Yet, with emerging technologies and digitization comes a new generation of unknown, uncertain cyber-threats that can lay the "best laid plans of mice and men" to waste. With company operations stretched across the globe, every country's culture creates a premise that can serve to be a cyber-opportunity or a cyber-threat. So, understanding how global culture affects a company's cybersecurity strategy is paramount to survival. Can you use your knowledge to add to this imperative?

From Amazon Alexa listening to you in the background while helping you order your Camera and groceries via Amazon Prime to Google's Nest Thermostat figuring out when you're not at home, choose one IoT device that you would be comfortable with and one that you would not. Explain why using the bases of security and privacy.

Assignment:

1. It is generally accepted that companies and countries need to have defensive policies and store data more securely. But cybersecurity is both a cultural and psychological game as it is technical. In that regard, you have been asked to join in as a consultant for a company with global divisions in Brazil and Russia. Based

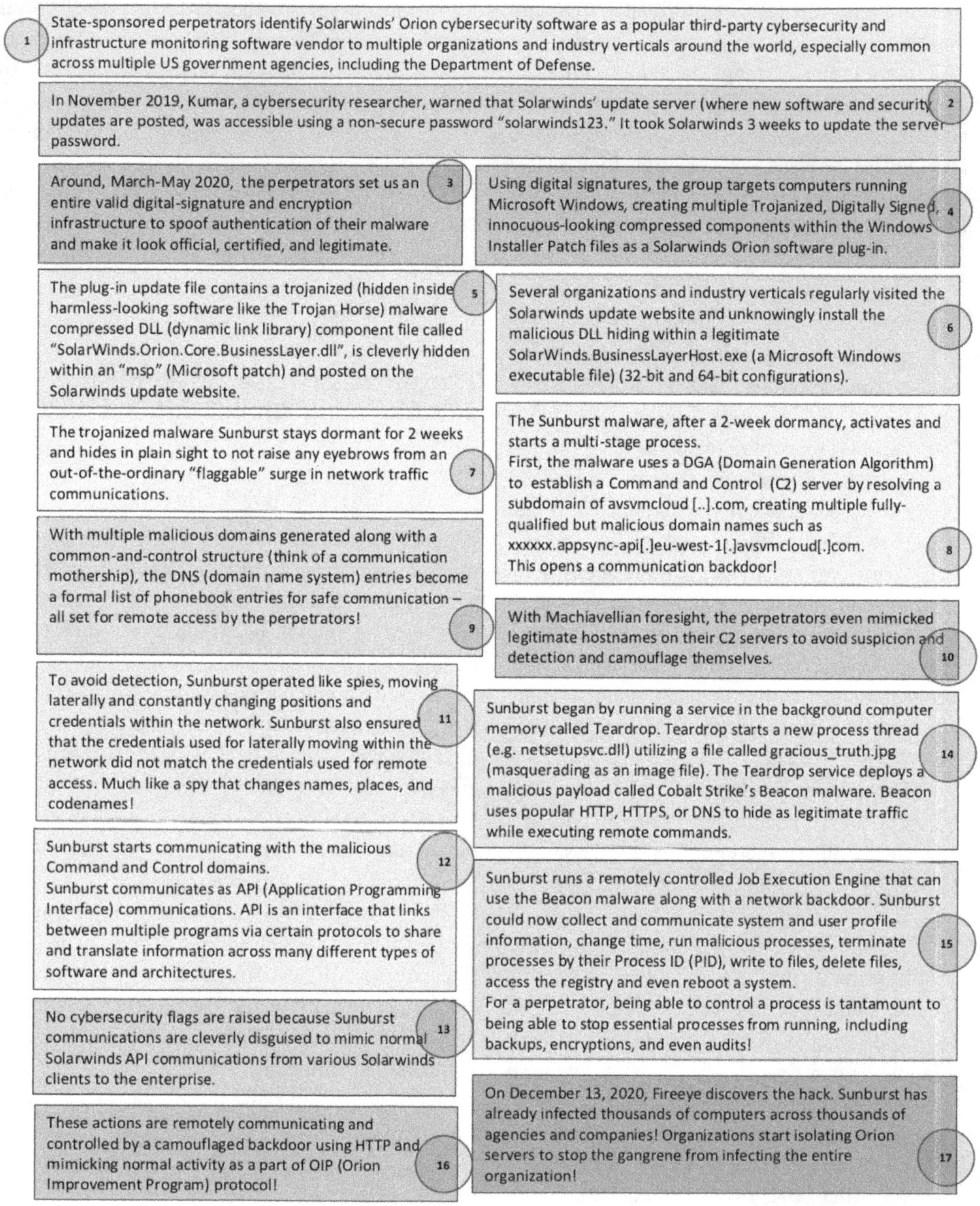

1. State-sponsored perpetrators identify Solarwinds' Orion cybersecurity software as a popular third-party cybersecurity and infrastructure monitoring software vendor to multiple organizations and industry verticals around the world, especially common across multiple US government agencies, including the Department of Defense.

2. In November 2019, Kumar, a cybersecurity researcher, warned that Solarwinds' update server (where new software and security updates are posted, was accessible using a non-secure password "solarwinds123." It took Solarwinds 3 weeks to update the server password.

3. Around, March-May 2020, the perpetrators set us an entire valid digital-signature and encryption infrastructure to spoof authentication of their malware and make it look official, certified, and legitimate.

4. Using digital signatures, the group targets computers running Microsoft Windows, creating multiple Trojanized, Digitally Signed, innocuous-looking compressed components within the Windows Installer Patch files as a Solarwinds Orion software plug-in.

5. The plug-in update file contains a trojanized (hidden inside harmless-looking software like the Trojan Horse) malware compressed DLL (dynamic link library) component file called "SolarWinds.Orion.Core.BusinessLayer.dll", is cleverly hidden within an "msp" (Microsoft patch) and posted on the Solarwinds update website.

6. Several organizations and industry verticals regularly visited the Solarwinds update website and unknowingly install the malicious DLL hiding within a legitimate SolarWinds.BusinessLayerHost.exe (a Microsoft Windows executable file) (32-bit and 64-bit configurations).

7. The trojanized malware Sunburst stays dormant for 2 weeks and hides in plain sight to not raise any eyebrows from an out-of-the-ordinary "flaggable" surge in network traffic communications.

8. The Sunburst malware, after a 2-week dormancy, activates and starts a multi-stage process.
First, the malware uses a DGA (Domain Generation Algorithm) to establish a Command and Control (C2) server by resolving a subdomain of avsvmcloud [..].com, creating multiple fully-qualified but malicious domain names such as xxxxxx.appsync-api[.]eu-west-1[.]avsvmcloud[.]com. This opens a communication backdoor!

9. With multiple malicious domains generated along with a common-and-control structure (think of a communication mothership), the DNS (domain name system) entries become a formal list of phonebook entries for safe communication – all set for remote access by the perpetrators!

10. With Machiavellian foresight, the perpetrators even mimicked legitimate hostnames on their C2 servers to avoid suspicion and detection and camouflage themselves.

11. To avoid detection, Sunburst operated like spies, moving laterally and constantly changing positions and credentials within the network. Sunburst also ensured that the credentials used for laterally moving within the network did not match the credentials used for remote access. Much like a spy that changes names, places, and codenames!

12. Sunburst starts communicating with the malicious Command and Control domains.
Sunburst communicates as API (Application Programming Interface) communications. API is an interface that links between multiple programs via certain protocols to share and translate information across many different types of software and architectures.

13. No cybersecurity flags are raised because Sunburst communications are cleverly disguised to mimic normal Solarwinds API communications from various Solarwinds clients to the enterprise.

14. Sunburst began by running a service in the background computer memory called Teardrop. Teardrop starts a new process thread (e.g. netsetupsvc.dll) utilizing a file called gracious_truth.jpg (masquerading as an image file). The Teardrop service deploys a malicious payload called Cobalt Strike's Beacon malware. Beacon uses popular HTTP, HTTPS, or DNS to hide as legitimate traffic while executing remote commands.

15. Sunburst runs a remotely controlled Job Execution Engine that can use the Beacon malware along with a network backdoor. Sunburst could now collect and communicate system and user profile information, change time, run malicious processes, terminate processes by their Process ID (PID), write to files, delete files, access the registry and even reboot a system.
For a perpetrator, being able to control a process is tantamount to being able to stop essential processes from running, including backups, encryptions, and even audits!

16. These actions are remotely communicating and controlled by a camouflaged backdoor using HTTP and mimicking normal activity as a part of OIP (Orion Improvement Program) protocol!

17. On December 13, 2020, Fireeye discovers the hack. Sunburst has already infected thousands of computers across thousands of agencies and companies! Organizations start isolating Orion servers to stop the gangrene from infecting the entire organization!

Fig. 11.5 The 2020 Sunburst [Solorigate] Hack Campaign Sequence

on cultural differences in those countries, *assess two cybersecurity threats and offer two strategic recommendations on how to defend against the threats.*

2. Based on the Sunburst hack model and diagram shown above, think of 3 managerial and policy strategies you would try and use to secure a company/organization.

This part ties together the various aspects of global technology management with a guide for managing global operation and projects, digital transformation, and the role of sustainability. Managing global operations and projects with an eye on sustainable operations and digital transformation remain highly in-demand skills for all students across various careers. The part begins with building a case for digital transformation and sustainability in operations. Next, in this part, students learn useful project concepts and modeling, from outsourcing strategies to calculate project valuation using NPV and ROI as well as PERT process modeling. The part ends with understanding 4IR digital transformation fundamentals and inherent challenges, highlighted by important concepts and global cases.

Learning Outcomes

By the end of this part, students will be able to:

- Investigate how companies around the world practice digital transformation and use technologies to achieve Sustainable Development Goals.
- Evaluate outsourcing ad offshoring conditions and considerations.
- Examine how emerging technologies and technology innovations impact sustainable operations.
- Evaluate how project management techniques can be used to manage global operations and projects.

- Examine the promises and challenges of digital transformation projects in light of politics, strategy, and economics.
- Apply leadership qualities to leading global operations, strategy, and security within an automated world.

Global Projects, Sustainability, & Digital Transformation

As a manager, one of your crucial jobs is to understand the interweaving of various operational, particularly sustainable operational, decisions in this post-COVID-19 world. This book focuses on operations in a technology-centric, globalized world. We look at the structure and problems of outsourcing and offshoring from social and economic perspectives. Knowing that globalization underscores our everyday lives and markets, we look at how to assess and manage projects where work is globally distributed.

The new world seems a fragile normal. But the new normal is more global, more interconnected, and more sustainable. 4IR is rapidly ushering in a new economy, quietly under the covers. 4IR is rapidly making digital transformation a reality and you need to be prepared to manage this digital transformation.

The final piece touches upon the highlights of offshoring and outsourcing, managing, and leading global projects and understanding the basic functioning of global supply chains that connects markets, and us, together.

4IR Operations, Technology, and Sustainability

The 4IR world is a world of convergence—convergence across global boundaries, across industries, and across politics. The 4IR world is supply chain dream and a nightmare, raising and dashing projects and sustainability opportunities and hopes.

A company might design something in using a 3D wireframe in Ohio, US, send the software specifications to India and manufacturing specs to China. Bits and bytes fire up and fly at the speed of light, communicating specifications, needs, and real-time changes. The packaging team might be in the Malaysia and the Software quality control might be done in the Netherlands. The final product might be packaged and shipped from Hong Kong to the UK—ready for the Christmas market.

COVID-19 and Global Operations

When the world woke up to the COVID-19 pandemic, countries and companies thought that it would be another market crash. The market certainly crashed over a few weeks but suddenly technology came to the rescue. Companies could use automation to keep factories running, Teams and Zoom meetings would ensure collaboration, companies like Amazon and Alibaba would feed our remote shopping, and Uber Eats and Doordash would deliver food from restaurants!

COVID-19: China's Gilded Opportunity

Once governments lowered interest rates and handed large unemployment benefits, a lot of people suddenly wanted to spend the surplus. Chinese factories, already at the manufacturing forefront, received hundreds of millions of orders to satisfy unprecedented online orders.

The world wanted technology and consumer products and China was happy to serve! People suddenly forewent public transport because of social distancing guidelines and wanted cars. People wanted more IoT technologies to manage the new houses they were purchasing with cheap credit. People wanted more consumer goods and companies purchased more industrial machines to satisfy demand.

This created supply chain problems.

With so much demand, global shipping lanes from China to the rest of the world were simply overwhelmed. The same container that cost about $1500 to ship suddenly hit a peak of nearly $20,000 by September 2021. China could produce fast enough but there weren't enough ships or dock capacity to load and unload them. Even ships carrying container cargo were just sitting offshore because docks did not have capacity to unload cargo.

The other supply chain problem originated from out growing technology appetite. With just about every complex product using technology,

© PiaDura LTD 2022
P. Datta, *Global Technology Management 4.0*,
https://doi.org/10.1007/978-3-030-96929-5_12

microchip demand has gone through the roof! Especially cars! People purchased cars to avoid the pandemic and avail cheap credit. But latest cars use nearly 3000 matchbox-sized microchips. The 4IR world is microchip-famished.

Therein lies the problem!

First, there are only two Asian major chip manufacturers, Taiwan's TSMC and South Korea's Samsung, both already overwhelmed!

First, China mainly controls most metals that are used in technology hardware. China's saber-rattling with the west left China petulant and jaw-boning the flow of microchip raw materials. China invested heavily into its own national microchip fabs.

COVID-19 became China's passport to its gilded age. US political isolationism meant China's economic globalism. Knowing that technology is tomorrow's zeitgeist, the red dragon invested on building its own technological and socio-political portfolios and propaganda.

China's technological propaganda emphasized how the US bullied the world by preventing China's rise. US' ban on importing Huawei 5G hardware had sowed economic acrimony. With the world closing their travel doors, China had a captive national audience. Chinese propaganda swept the mainland, calling for greater technological independence from "capricious western sanctions." China invested its gains on its "Made in China" strategy, showcasing quality Chinese innovations in AI, robotics, and space exploration. At the height of the pandemic, when global streets fell silent, China showcased its normalcy, with running factories, open markets, travel and lively streets, all run by Artificial Intelligence (AI) tracking individual movements. Chinese citizens were jubilant, with China landing rockets on the dark side of the moon and on the red Martian soil.

On the social front, China's propaganda machines roared to life, extolling the Chinese Communist Party's virtues over US democracy's vice. Documentaries and videos attenuated democratic philosophies. In recurrent news clips, run over and over again, the Chinese media pumped out footage of apoplectic MAGA supporters storming the sacrosanct Capitol and of US' human rights violations and the BLM movement. Chinese media leveraged American mask-wearing divisiveness as the talking point, telling its own people how people in the US refused to wear masks and let their neighbors die.

Suddenly Hong Kong's umbrella revolution and extradition laws, the Xinjiang province's Uighurs, or its Tiananmen Square student deaths faded into distant memory.

US' isolationism, first under President Trump, followed in-step by President Biden, lent China the opportunity to take global center stage, mimicking US' approach after WW II.

In this globally connected, technology-driven world, an isolationist approach can backfire and shift control to another strategic international competitor. Whenever there is a vacuum, someone will step in to fill in and control the gap. With US global engagement in retreat, China used US' isolationist approach to fill the vacuum, offering flexible credit to global governments often sanctioned for human rights by the west. China had finessed the practice in Africa and was now rolling it out in Afghanistan after the hasty US pullout.

COVID-19 and Global Supply Chains

During COVID-19, when manufacturing and physical presence came to a halt, companies had to keep running. So, COVID-19 became a fulcrum to invest in 4IR automation and robotics as a way to keep factories operational without people.

Interim, China filled in the demand–supply gap! In 4IR, the world relies on efficient global supply chains of metals that are crucial to 4IR technological hardware. With countries such as China controlling mining rights to precious metals such as Chromium in South Africa and Cobalt in Congo, for semiconductor supply chain and the electric vehicle battery supply chain. The race for controlling the technological supply chain is on!

4IR has accelerated the need for rare earth elements (REE). There are 17 rare earth elements that drive and will keep driving the 4IR. REEs are essential for multiple 4IR technologies, from lasers and 5G to smartphone displays. These metals belie technological hardware, from sensor and other digital micro-electronics to green energy and electric vehicle battery tech.

Over the past decade, China realized the global technological growth and cleverly invested in Africa, securing large-scale mining rights precious metals required for the 4IR economy. Today, China controls more than 80% REE production, lifeblood of the 4IR industry.

Rare Earth Elements

Rare Earth Elements (REE) are not necessarily rare. Rather their mining is often dirty and environmentally degrading. But a shortage of these precious metals and REE can grind the 4IR supply chain to a halt.

Most of these metals and REE are used to produce semiconductors or microchips that process everything from car acceleration and battery consumption to IoTs (Internet of Things) and 3D printing in 4IR.

In 2021, smartphone, computer, and car manufacturers had to slow down or stop production because of a microchip shortage.

A Modicum of Microchips

Microchips defined the 3IR computing age. But microchips are incredibly difficult to design and manufacture. The semiconductor manufacturing process is incredibly complex.

From a business standpoint, microchips have two main players:

i. Chip designers that design the chips. Companies around the world, from ARM's smartphone chips, Apple's M1 chip (based on ARM's chip architecture), or Nvidia's video game GPUs just focus on designing remarkably sophisticated microprocessor circuits. Their proprietary designs are then sent to microchip manufacturers. Smarter chip innovatively designs and packs more and more circuits into a single chip (such as Quad-core).

ii. Chip manufacturers or foundries that produce, package, and ship the microchips. There are three very powerful chip foundries in the world. US' Intel, South Korea's Samsung, and Taiwan's TSMC (Taiwan Semiconductor Manufacturing Company). Among them, TSMC is, by far, the most productive and perhaps the global chip foundry leader, innovating faster and better and more reliable production processes and technologies.

Microchips have essential components. Essential components needed to make a product are known as **BOM (Bill of Materials)**.

1. This 99.99%+ pure crystallized silicon wafer that makes the microchip base. Typical wafers are about 8″ in diameter (they vary from 2″ to 10+″) and about 750 μm (micrometer or 1 millionth of a meter) thick. That is about the thickness of 6 hair strands. The cool thing about silicon is that it can be a great electricity conductor and sometimes an insulator. The silicon wafer is doped based on where we decide to conduct and where to insulate. That creates a circuit.

2. A doping agent is then added as an impurity to increase microchip conductivity. Boron, phosphorus, arsenic, antimony, inter alia, popular microchip doping agents.

Once the BOM is ready, it's time to start the microchip manufacturing process. The basic microchip process steps are as follows:

1. **Wafer Creation:** A silicon chunk is cut into wafers, similar to cutting a thin slice of prosciutto!

2. **Masking:** Because wafers are sensitive, wafers are coated or masked with silicon dioxide to protect them from light-sensitivity.

3. **Fabrication**: Once a microchip circuit design is uploaded, the design needs to be etched on to the silicon chip. It all starts with light, called **Photolithography**. Think of photolithography as using light to etch a circuit just the way we use light to create a high definition photograph. Photolithography etches circuits on top a silicon wafer.

4. **Testing**: Wafers are tested to check if their circuits are working properly. After all, these circuits run all our 4IR devices and we don't want them to fail, do we?

5. **Sawing/Separating**: These 8″ silicon wafers have many chips and circuits, and they have to be cut into small chip-size pieces, known as sawing or separating. After sawing, each chip is tested again and again for quality, then packaged, and shipped to various client companies that will use them to power on our 4IR devices.

Did you know that?

A US F-35 fighter jet needs about 427 kg (941 pounds) of rare earths, and each Virginia-class nuclear submarine, about 4.2 metric tons of REE.

A Brief Take on US Manufacturing

During COVID-19, the overall US manufacturing sector underwent a V-shaped recovery. But this positive momentum is more concentrated in technology and financial services, rather than in manufacturing. In facts, services comprised on 39% of deals in 2019 and 35% of deals at the end of 2020 Q3 (a 14% drop, pressured by commercial and consumer services).

In 2019, there were 223 deals (about 6.1% of total M&A [Mergers and Acquisitions] deals). But in Q3 2020, the manufacturing sector only had 156 deals (5.3%) compared to last year, a 12.6% drop.

Industrial Production fell by 3% in 2019. However, the manufacturing index has bounced back to 59.3 (beating the 56.4 estimate), up more than 25% from 47.2 in December 2019.

Still, manufacturing M&A is facing a lot of uncertainty, pressed by COVID-19 and China's industrial position (along with the industrial saber rattling).

Manufacturing's future is a 4IR-driven manufacturing Perestroika where manufacturing restructuring needs to align its sector with the future world order.

With the changing nature of work and the workplace, the new order of it is a harbinger of three trends:

i. Gobbling up weaker manufacturers
ii. Divesting non-value added divisions.
iii. More 4IR technology and automation-focused M&As

Eaton selling off Hydraulics and plastic and rubber hose divisions to Danfoss and keeping and active M&A pipeline for data-center services, electrical, aerospace, and electro-mobility. GE went the same route, trimming its non-value-added fat:

GE divested (sold off) its transportation unit to Wabtec for $11 billion and its BioPharma business to Danaher Corp for $21 billion (along with divesting its Baker Hughes stake with a $2.7 billion transaction), and (iii) a more automated future driven by AI, robotics, and IoTs.

On that basis, manufacturing is waiting out the storm—fiscal stimulus, China trades, post-election uncertainty. With easier access to cheap credit but massively high P/E valuations among in horizontal and verticals to gobble up, valuations are riding the crest. With access to cheap credit and the changing nature of work, marked by high digital transformation, newer business models (more modular BTO rather than build to forecast, BTC), we see manufacturing M&A deals raiding the 4IR wave, focusing on advanced manufacturing tech and tech-services to increase integration and consolidation.

The line between traditional manufacturing and 4IR will blur even further with more focus toward heavy automation and lights-out factories such as Japan's FANUC, Amazon Kivas, and Tesla's factory automation (that uses Fanuc robots). The primary focus is shifting the operational model to reduce fixed and variable costs of labor. Skills shortages will remain a headwind.

If manufacturing does not automate and consolidate on its own, Private Equity will become a stronger presence in forcing consolidation and streamlining with greater automation.

Technology and Sustainability in Global Supply Chains

Supply chains are one of the major areas where technology is changing competitiveness. With more far-flung and diverse supply chains all over the world, coordinating such supply chains becomes crucial. Even more so, with longer and wider supply chains, it is important to keep an eye out for the impact of such supply chains on sustainability and the environment.

UPS trucks never turn left in right-lane driving countries such as the US, Germany, France and never turn right in left-lane driving countries such as the UK, Australia, and South Africa? Turning left in a right-lane driving country can cause accidents and more fuel. So, UPS uses technology to optimize its delivery routes in a way that allows UPS to deliver packages without turning left. UPS's route optimization helps it save 6–8 miles per route. That amounts to savings of 10 million gallons of fuel every year and 100,000 metric tons of CO_2, equivalent of 21,000 cars every year.

Sustainability is key to conserving resources and our planet. Technology and operations have to be managed in correspondence with sustainability goals. In fact, the new world order is using technology to create sustainability. Technology, as we have learned, can reengineer processes to reduce costs and create efficiencies. Technology also increases transparency by helping log (record) every change and movement in a process. Sustainability is built of the premises of reengineering and transparency and that is where technology is reshaping supply chains and operations.

Did you know that?

UPS optimizes its driving with right-turn only or left-turn only routes (based on right-hand or left-hand drive) to save 10 million gallons of fuel every year and 100,000 metric tons of CO_2, equivalent of 21,000 cars every year!

Sustainability, Kaizen, and Process Reengineering

Sustainability begins by reducing waste. That is where Kaizen's process improvement becomes an imperative.

Kaizen is a Japanese term that means continuous improvement or "change for the better." A company that practices kaizen is a philosophy of constant review and reengineering of existing processes to make it better. As a supply chain manager, you will have to review the supply chain to find out the **value-added costs** (costs that provide greater value of your product or service to the customer) and **non-value-added costs** (costs that are liabilities for your company and the customer and lead to a lack of fulfillment and eventually, a loss of sales and customer satisfaction). For example, it takes about 42 days between the ordering of a new car and the delivery of the car to the customer. Can you believe that, out of these 42 days, approximately 4 days are spent on production, 7 days on shipping, and 3 days for testing and order-handling while the other 28 days are spent on paperwork? Yet, the supply chain spans all 42 days. 90 percent of the time spent on paperwork is a non-value-added cost where the customer waits in anticipation while the car is on a lot somewhere. If you could reengineer the supply chain, wouldn't you begin by reengineering the part where time is wasted on non-value-added paperwork? If a company is truly practicing *kaizen*, every employee from the shop floor worker to the CEO is working to eliminate waste on a daily basis.

Efficiencies, sustainability, and transparency are hallmarks of competitiveness in a global world. Now that we have a fundamental understanding of how technology and reengineering can drive competitiveness, we can embark on creating operational value by using TPS (Toyota Production System) best practices to build a competitive edge.

Did you know that?

The Chinese government preaches "Stomach Wars" as a way to promote ordering less food in restaurants to reduce food waste!

Global Kaizen Best Practices: The Toyota Production System

The Core Tenets of TPS

Competitiveness drives our world economy and technology is the poster-child for leading the competitiveness with more efficiencies and greater transparency.

Tire companies in the US were once very famous and dominated the globe. However, with Japanese competitors in the market, US tire manufacturers simply decided to change their machines and technologies but not their culture. Culture governs processes and without a change in culture, the best technologies did not add any value. Over time, the famous tire manufacturing cities such as Akron in Ohio fell prey to competition and the tire plants closed and thousands of jobs were lost.

The Toyota Production System (TPS), originating from Japan, is both a philosophy and operational planning procedure that organizes technological and human resources in its own operations but with a keen eye on suppliers and customers.

TPS is known as "lean," mainly because TPS was designed to remove excess fat that would slow down a company. With the advent of digitization and technology, it became easier to automate and reengineer to reduce wasteful, non-value-added steps in any process. Reducing waste or "muda" is the primary goal of TPS.

In order to eliminate waste, companies need to figure out what waste is and where it exists in existing processes. Even though companies may offer different services, waste is often a common phenomenon found in repetitive activities and arcane ways of doing things. Once companies identify waste, they can often use technology to reduce or eliminate waste in a company thus improving performance and quality.

TPS's central theme is based on getting only resources needed. In short, TPS's central theme is on-demand resource use. That is where technology comes in. Technology, combined with robotics, automation, analytics, and software, has therefore become the centerpiece of a TPS philosophy.

TPS Objectives

These are the 6 key objectives underpinning TPS's central theme:

1. **Modular**—Modularity is the ability to build small, independent pieces and components that can later be integrated to form a larger product of service. Think of modularity as Lego pieces. Each Lego piece is independent and works but you can combine various Lego pieces to build different structures. Technology offers modularity where software can be built in pieces that can then call other software code over the network when needed. Optimize each individual step of the system. In other words, make each part as efficient as possible to get the most from the least.

2. **Quality**—In order to reduce flaws or defects, an operation must be modular that will allow quality checks to be conducted at every module level. This ensures that each part of the operation will perform well. If an operation has three processes with each process running at 90% performance, the total system reliability is not the average but the product of three processes, which is $90\% \times 90\% \times 90\% = 72.9\%$!

3. **Costs**—Reduce costs. Technology and on-demand modular systems only call and use resources when needed (think of Uber as calling a taxi when needed).

4. **Postponement**—Build a product or service that the market needs. Modularity allows companies to practice something called "postponement" where the final product is assembled not at the manufacturer but closer to the market. If a customer wants slight changes

to the product or service, postponement allows companies to do so by combining the right pieces at the end rather than building the final product early on that will not sell. Think of cloud computing where you can choose what software features you want and having the software offer you personalized service over the network without you having to pay a premium for features you did not need or want. Make a product that is demanded by consumers. If there is no demand, all products and services are sunk costs.

5. **Flexibility**—Operations must be flexible so that if there is a need for change, the change can be easily implemented. Technology such as robotics can be easily reprogrammed to work in a different way to manage flexibility (such as changing the angle of a bolt installation) compared to human beings that have a steeper learning curve. The system must be flexible enough that it can be modified easily.

6. **Just-in-Time**—The ecosystem and the relationship between customers and suppliers must be reliable. To access and get resources Just-In-Time (JIT), the ecosystem must be well integrated so that a product or service will be delivered on time and right when needed without concerns or uncertainties.

7. **Kaizen**—Kaizen or continuous improvement is based on well-defined standard operating procedures, good measures of performance, and empowering people involved in operations to innovate and constantly improve at the grassroots level. Technology allows better and finer monitoring with less variance and when combined with people with a kaizen culture, the operation can be continuously improved over time.

Reducing the Seven Wastes for Sustainability

TPS categorizes waste into seven categorizes. The seven wastes are:

1. **Overproduction**—Overproduction is when companies tend to build volumes without knowing if they will sell. Overproduction is a common in production and even services (having too many waiters and waitresses at a restaurant without knowing how many customers might be present). Overproduction is a costly problem because it increases costs from storing excess products and having to get rid of them at a discount or at a loss if they don't sell. Toyota Production System tries to eliminate overproduction by practicing a "Just-In-Time" approach where products and services are offered only when they are ordered. With technology, analytics is being used to accurately predict what customers might order later. Amazon is supposed to use its analytics technologies to be able to predict what we are likely to purchase a year before we even purchase it. Amazon can even track how quickly you use household necessities such as detergents and shampoos to predict when you might want the next delivery before you actually decide to order them.

2. **Waiting**—Whenever a component or a person is not doing anything at an assembly line or a company, companies waste time and money from waiting. Every employee, resource, and component must be utilized and put in action. Else, anytime that a resource is unutilized, waste from waiting happens. If a taxi is waiting for a passenger, a food court buffet is prepared and waiting for patrons, a server or a teller is waiting to serve, or a nurse or physician is waiting for a patient, it signals waste, underutilized, or unutilized capacity. Technology has dramatically saved such costs with the emergence of on-demand services such as Uber to provide taxi service only when needed, Airbnb utilizing unused housing capacity to offer hotel services, or on-call nurses and physicians—all to reduce waste.

3. **Transporting**—Transporting products between processes is a cost and adds no value to the product. Instead of having warehouse workers waste time from moving across tens of thousands of warehouse shelves, Amazon's Kiva robots pick up shelves and bring them to the order fulfillment operator that picks the right products to fulfill an order.

4. **Inappropriate Processing**—Many organizations use expensive high precision equipment where simpler tools would be sufficient. Toyota is famous for its use of low-cost automation, combined with immaculately maintained machines. Investing in smaller, more flexible equipment where possible reduce the waste from inappropriate processing.

5. **Unnecessary Inventory**—Excess inventory increases lead times and consumes productive floor space. Technology is being used to stow (stock) and order inventory for the next process on when it is needed. Technologies such as predictive analytics and machine learning are used to better assess what is need when and by how much.

6. **Unnecessary/Excess Motion**—This waste is related to ergonomics and is seen in all instances of bending, stretching, walking, lifting, and reaching, leading to more litigations. Companies are therefore using robotic technologies to reduce unnecessary movement and repetitive motions that could lead to injuries and workplace safety.

7. **Defects**—Rework or scrap have a direct impact to the financial and operational bottom lines. The longer a defect is left in place, the greater the chance of a larger problem. Technology is being used to quicker and continuous monitoring as well as methods such as Agile are being used to increase more modular designs in smaller sections to be integrated later.

TPS taps into the knowledge and insights of team members while providing them with a lot of training and responsibility. It is only by capitalizing on employees' creativity that Toyota can continuously improve and "reduce difficult jobs by practicing modularity to simplify them. In TPS, jobs are ranked in three categories—green, yellow, and red. The goal is to improve jobs to the green category which means the difficulty has been eliminated.

Some of these kaizens (improvements) have been achieved through simple process improvements, such as moving assembly tools and

materials to accessible locations. Robotics are used for loading heavy materials and working at complex angles that could hurt a human being, thus eliminating a difficult job altogether.

In summary, advanced flexible manufacturing is having a workforce that's trained and able to compete in a high-technology economy, using "flexible manufacturing" techniques that take advantage of computer and robotics technology to respond instantly to changing needs and increasing sustainability goals.

Did you know that?
Nuclear power is one of the most sustainable yet feared energy sources. France used nuclear power to generate 70% of its energy.

Here are some examples of how various companies are practicing supply chain sustainability (Table 12.1):

Blockchains: Reengineering for Sustainability

Reengineering for sustainability is one of the most important issues companies face today. However, in order to know how reengineering is improving sustainability, companies need to transparently track and trace their operational and supply chain processes. That's why blockchains are becoming the next big technology in operations and supply chains.

Blockchains are increasing supply chain transparency with digitally shared, incorruptible, distributed ledgers. It is a key technology for next generation operations. As discussed previously, blockchains create a record of every activity within a process, allowing transparent monitoring of any product or service at any given point of time. So, blockchains add to sustainability because blockchains increase traceability.

Cradle to Grave transparency: Blockchains can trace a product from its cradle to grave. Take for example the travels of a diamond. The

Table 12.1 Supply chain sustainability practices

Supply chain activities/practices	Sourcing	Forward logistics	Operations	Reverse logistics
Reengineering	Coca Cola and Pepsi Co. farms use crushed coconut, a waste by-product of the extraction of coconut water, as ground cover on the farms. In addition to providing nutrients, this reduces weeds and prevents excessive water evaporation	Align warehouses close to suppliers, reducing miles traveled	Sortation devices are used to ready packages for distribution to point-of-sale with 12.5% less energy is used to do the same job than was done in 1998	Use conveyor and sortation systems to automate the sortation and disposition stages of the return process for like products
Resource management	Pepsi Co. extends resource conservation with set quantifiable goals for energy, greenhouse gas, water, agriculture, and forestry resource conservation	Utilizing the Voluntary Interindustry Commerce Solutions (VICS) program to reduce fuel consumption and air pollution in the trucking industry	Internal lighting system, "energy management and retrofit program for its internal lighting needs" that saves electricity costs	Samsung Take-back And Recycle (S.T.A.R.) toner recycling program, uses pre-paid Smart Label for returns that Samsung can refill, reprocess and reuse component resources
Reduction	Unilever and Pepsi Co. have zero tolerance for illegal activities in our supply chain and zero tolerance to reduce land displacements of any legitimate landholders	Eliminate unneeded items from the shipment, right-size the packaging, and sustain packaging	Precision bearings also reduce wear and tear on the equipment, which means lower repair and replacement costs for sortation system	GENCO, a Pittsburgh, Pa.-based 3PL pharmaceutical uses returns to an incineration plant that converts the waste to reduce energy waste. The plant creates two million kilowatt hours of electricity annually from this process, enough to light 220 homes for one year
Recovery & recycling	Pepsi Co. recovers beetroot water to irrigate plants for biomass generation	Paper mills using polycoated paper for recycling. The plastic coating on the polycoated paper gets burned off and can now be recycled	Switch to lightweight, recyclable plastic packing material, and recycling of pallets	Energized Eco Batteries with 30% recycled materials from reverse logistics

Diamond might be mined in Sierra Leone, sent to India for cleaning and cutting, shipped to Antwerp in Belgium for final quality control, and then to London in the UK to be retailed at an expensive outlet. We might purchase a diamond, but how can we ensure that the diamond was not a "conflict diamond," i.e., a diamond mined in a civil war zone rife with atrocities and brutalities? A blockchain associated with a piece of diamond could change the equation and add transparency to every transaction. Who mined it, where, and when? Who purchased it next? A warlord or a legitimate dealer? Where was it sent to next? With blockchains maintaining a real-time ledger of operations, every transaction would be transparent, therefore creating an entire audit chain that can be monitored for any discrepancy. Is that 82% dark chocolate from Colombia that reads "fair trade" truly practicing "fair trade?" Fair trade is one of the **sustainability development goals (SDGs)**. As a part of the SDG that required sustainable living wages and reduction of poverty, blockchains can verify whether a piece of chocolate was truly "fair trade."

Think of the sustainable supply chain for "organic" tomatoes. When you purchase a tomato, how do you know where it came from, how it was stored (temperature, time), and who really produced them? Blockchains could potentially improve the Tomato Supply Chain by facilitating the exchange of information in the process. More specifically knowing where the product is going and where it has been. Keeping track of these things is extremely important in order to be a successful business. Certain information would include evaluations of the food as well as assertations in regard to the manufactured products. By also asking certain agencies of certification to reinforce these assertations will fully stress the importance of these specific guidelines to follow. This would significantly impact the production of tomatoes in a positive way. Validating the quality of results in an increase of efficiency during the order fulfillment cycle. Which is described as the amount of time from customer authorization of sale orders to the customer receipt of product.

Blockchains can also improve food security. With blockchains, you can trace the digital ledgers to trace every movement of a good. The Blockchain allows the tomato grower and seller to share information with another privately and securely but also has the supply chain validate this information without necessarily violating individual entity trust. It has become a trending technique for companies to publish assertions about the quality of the food produced. However, not all information on the Blockchain is available to the public. Proprietary information, methods, measures, recipes, and other sensitive data can be shared securely with selected participants. This keeps a very discrete line of communication thus reducing the risk of food contamination.

Exercise

Companies and startups around the world practice digital transformation and use technologies to practice SDG goals (1, 3, 4, 6–8). Choose 2–3 technologies from around the world to critically examine how those technologies address specific SDGs. Now, offer 1–2 ways of improving/innovating the technology for the host country as well as if they planned on using the technology in their own country (allowing yourself to personalize your innovative thinking to what matters to you).

We've always outsourced some form of production. **Outsourcing**, i.e., the activity of letting a third party produce a good or service for your consumption, is nothing new in organized society. We rarely bake all our bread and instead outsource it to a fresh bakery down the street for croissants and scones; we outsource our dining to restaurants and chefs, our libations to vineyards, distilleries, and breweries; our home additions to contractors; and our vehicles to car manufacturers. Coming to think of it, we outsource most of our activities to other people and companies.

While outsourcing has been a part of human organization from the days of bartering for the past 500 generations, **offshoring** has always been a bit of a foster child. Offshoring includes **near-sourcing** and **offshoring**. Near-sourcing is where countries offshore to another country that is geographically very close (such as Nike in the US offshoring shoe fabrication/production to Mexico, Dole offshoring banana production to Central America, or Cadbury's offshoring chocolate production to Belgium). Offshoring is a process by which companies outsource production and servicing farther across country boundaries. Globalization, armed with the Internet that simplified and sped up communications at the speed of light, suddenly made offshoring popular. Offshoring allowed companies to lower their production costs and become more competitive across global markets. Walmart and Tesco could offer cheaper goods, more options, and better competition, leading more a win for

customers. Yet, offshoring in a globalized world is not always a rosy proposition; it comes with its own thorns.

Did You Know That?

In 2014, 45% of US manufacturing workers were offshored in China! While a large part of the offshored goods were imported back to the US, a lot of the same products were sold in Chinese markets because of Chinese demand for Western brands!

Managing the Outsourcing and Offshoring Process

Companies constantly decide on whether to build (produce on their own, in-house) or to buy (outsource or offshore to a vendor). In the age of globalization, companies often try to focus more on the R&D, innovation, and design and offshore other operations, particularly IT Operations (**IT Offshoring** or **ITO**) such as managing old running systems (also called **legacy systems**) such as mainframes as well as older programs and systems with programming environments such as COBOL, C, Pascal, etc.). Another popular area of offshoring is business processes (**Business Process Outsourcing** or **BPO**) such as HR processes (payroll and compensation; scheduling; HR training;

recruitment), Financial and Accounting processes (such as Accounts Receivables (money that a company is waiting to collect from sales) and Accounts Payables (money that companies need to pay to other companies and suppliers) management; investment and market research). Another offshoring area is **Operations and Back-Office Processing Offshoring** such as offshoring call centers, supply chain, and logistics, etc. In recent years, with newer global market opportunities, companies are practicing **KPO (Knowledge Process Outsourcing)** such as R&D for local markets (e.g., GM's China R&D to design Buick cars for Chinese roads and Chinese customers).

The Offshoring Process

Outsourcing is a difficult task. Offshoring, even more so, owing to greater distance, different country laws, labor supply, capital markets, and of course, cultures of operation.

A Basic Overview of the Offshoring Process

1. **Decide what to Offshore**: A company planning offshoring its IT, business processes, production, or any other activity must begin by assessing which of its processes it wants to offshore. The client firms must be willing to take the risk of losing control over the activities it wants to offshore as well as be willing to deal with the time and costs of selecting and monitoring the offshoring vendor as well as dealing with offshoring uncertainties such as currency fluctuations, logistical and cultural uncertainties, among others. Below is a brief offshoring decision guide.

   In deciding on what processes to offshore, companies generally conduct a Needs Assessment. In the Needs Assessment, companies try to figure out **what** activities or processes they want offshored, **why** they want them outsourced (the corresponding costs of offshoring and the benefits (savings) from offshoring) over the long term. Then subtract the costs from the benefits to calculate the

value of the offshoring decision. Once the value is positive over the long term, companies need to decide on **when** to initiate offshoring search and when to actually begin offshoring. One way to decide on a **timeline** is via **reverse engineering the project timeline**. **Reverse engineering** is a process by which individuals and companies can retrace the way something was built by taking apart the final product or the final proposed timeline. Reverse Engineering helps companies schedule on when to embark on each stage of their offshoring puzzle. For example, if a company decides to begin its offshore production by December 2010, the company can start reverse engineering the schedule using something like a **Gantt Chart**, a diagram describing a schedule, in this case, the offshoring project schedule.

2. **Identify and Select Countries**: A company planning offshoring, i.e., the client firm, begins by selecting appropriate countries and specific cities as offshoring locations. Chengdu in south-central China is an auto manufacturing and pharmaceutical hub; Shanghai is a better R&D and technology hub; while Guangzhou in the southeast is a good general production hub. New Delhi in northwest India is a good back-office processing hub while Chennai in southeast India is a good programming and financial research hub. There are several factors client firms need to consider when choosing an offshoring venue (country). Some of the **offshoring country selection factors** are:

   a. **Educational Institutions**: The offshoring country must have a proper educational system to ensure that companies to which clients plan to offshore can recruit a quality labor force. Apprenticeship centers (community colleges) and universities create graduates that join the work force and offshoring countries must be able to promise not only a consistent supply of labor but also the right type of labor required for what offshoring clients want. That is why Chinese universities focus a lot on production and operations engineering training and Indian universities focus a lot on information technologies and programming.

b. **Internet and Telecommunications**: The offshoring country must have a robust Internet and telecommunications network that allows swift and secure information flow and communication between clients and vendors. Globalization is spurred by information circumnavigating the glove in seconds, allowing clients to "chase the sun." Therefore, offshoring countries need to host a robust and reliable telecommunications infrastructure such as high-speed Internet, ubiquitous Wi-Fi connections, and high-speed cellular networks.

c. **Banking and Capital Markets**: The offshoring country requires must have a good banking infrastructure, preferably a reliable capital markets infrastructure. Banking refers to activities related to managing money flow in an economy by offering deposits and lending. Capital markets refer to activities related to the buying and selling of investment products such as bonds and stocks. The offshoring country's banking system can increase trust in clients that clients can safely transfer money and vendors are be able to get loans to keep their operations running, from investing in new machines and facilities to paying employees without worrying about shutting down their operations from a **credit shortage or credit squeeze**, i.e., not being able to get a loan to meet payments. Capital markets can add further value if companies can fairly trade stocks and bonds in the market to diversify risk and issue bonds in addition to or as a substitute for bank loans.

d. **Political Climate**: The offshoring country must have a stable political climate. The stability of a political climate lends faith to offshoring clients that laws and regulations will remain in place and will not radically change with successive governments. That is why Moody's, Standard and Poor's (S&P), and Fitch demerits a country's ratings whenever there is political turmoil or uncertainty, with AAA as the highest (safest) and SD as the lowest (riskiest). According to S&P's 2017 ratings, the US is AA + , the UK AA. The PIIGS' 2017 ratings are as follows: Portugal BBB−, Ireland A + , Italy BBB, Greece B−, and Spain A−. S&P rated the BRICS as follows: Brazil BB−, Russia BBB-, India BBB−, China A + , and South Africa BB.

e. **Local Market**: With incomes rising around the world, the offshoring philosophy is evolving to "**Think Global, Act Local.**" In 2019, Chinese customers purchased nearly a third of all global cars manufactured. For example, the US' General Motors makes more profit from selling cars in China than it does in the US. With 25% import tariffs and such a large car market, GM, Ford, Volkswagen, BMW, have billions in Greenfield Investments (investing in overseas factories to sell in local overseas markets) to escape import tariffs.

3. **Initiate Offshoring Search**: Once offshoring clients have selected an offshoring destination country; they narrow their search to specific offshoring vendors or suppliers with their selected country. Offshoring clients begin by issuing an **RFP (Request for Proposal)** that is similar to a position announcement but instead advertises its need for specific production or services from multiple vendors based on formal specifications and expectations, with quotes and to be submitted by a specific deadline. Offshoring clients commonly require **closed bids**, i.e., sealed vendor bids where price quotes and service specifications are not revealed to competing vendors.

4. **Identify and Select Companies**: Once the offshoring client has received bids from various offshoring vendors by a prespecified deadline, the offshoring client begins evaluating each offshoring bid. *Price is never the only criterion for choosing a vendor.* Offshoring is a critical matter and has to handle

with all due diligence and due care. There are **SLAs (Service Level Agreements)** that refer to contractual specifications of the services the vendor is expected to provide and perform under client guidelines. In addition, offshoring clients need to take into consideration **non-SLAs**, other aspects of the offshoring vendor that can make or break the deal and lead to offshoring success of failure. Some of the criteria used are as follows:

a. **Vendor Company Age**: The age of the offshoring vendor matters. If the offshoring vendor has been in business for a while, it signals that the vendor must be offering satisfactory offshored products and services to clients.

b. **Vendor Company Size and Capacity**: Company size is measured by the sales volume (number of units produced or serviced), sales revenues ($ sales), and number of employees. A larger company may not always be the best choice. A large company can look lucrative but might have multiple clients, some with larger accounts than your company. That could lead to treated with a lower priority. That could lead to being treated with a lower priority. On the other hand, a smaller vendor might offer your company more specialized service and higher priority. But, the smaller vendor might not enough resources on hand to tackle unexpected problems or issues!

c. **Vendor Company Reputation**: Vendor reputation is a reference and a testament to how well a vendor operates and meets its client obligations. Offshoring clients must research vendor reputation from client references. Clients need to check vendor reputation across many different facets, particularly in relation to (i) how well does the offshoring vendor protect the client's IP (intellectual property)? (ii) what % of time have the vendors missed production, delivery, or service schedules? (iii) what is the vendors **uptime** (when vendor services and systems are running) and **downtime** (when vendor services and systems are not

running due to internal operational errors or maintenance). Downtime is costly for clients because it can slow down the vendor's ability to fulfill their obligations to the client; (iv) what are the vendor certifications such as Capability Maturity Model (CMM) for project management expertise and/or ISO certifications such as ISO 9000 for production excellence? (v) how swiftly and how well does the vendor respond to issues that might arise? (vi) how good is the vendor's management team to ensure smooth operations? and (vii) does the vendor take care of all contractual operations by themselves or do they sub-contract to cheaper vendors? This latter can be particularly vexing because the vendor might use its reputation to win the offshoring contract only to divvy up the contract and hand it as sub-contracts to cheaper local vendors with questionable reliability.

d. **Vendor Company Cash Flows**: Vendor cash flows, especially cash flow from operations, is a good yardstick of how well the offshoring vendor practices cost control. **Cash Flows from Operations (CFO)** are useful because they can tell you the revenue the vendor generates from its core offshoring operations and how it spends the cash. Offshoring clients are always looking for vendors with a good cash flow because it assures clients that the vendor will stay in business.

5. **Negotiate and Ratify Contracts**: Once offshoring clients have selected the country and the vendor, contract negotiations begin. Contract negotiations are crucial to long-term well-being of an offshoring relationship. Often contract negotiations are like a chess game. The offshoring client, being the brand owner, is closer to the market and needs to be more flexible in offering product revisions as market and consumer preferences change. So, the offshoring client may try to negotiate for a **shorter-term, flexible contract** so that, every time there is a change in the market, they can revise their specifications

for the offshoring vendor. The story is different for the offshoring vendor. An offshoring vendor, in order to make the best off its infrastructure and distribute its fixed costs, needs to produce more of the same product. The more they produce using the same machines and production lines in larger batches, the lower their fixed costs per unit produced. Fixed costs per unit are calculated as Fixed Costs/Number of Units. The more units they produce, the lower the fixed cost per unit. With that in mind, offshoring vendors want a **longer-term, less-flexible contract** that will allow them to produce the same product over a very long time without having to setup new production runs, molding or requiring different specifications. At the end of the day, both the client and the vendor typically settle on a compromise. Be prepared for that.

Offshoring clients also need to pay close attention to vendor price quotes. Often, a cheaper vendor price quote might seem enticing at first, but clients need to make sure that there are no hidden fees. Offshoring clients should ask vendors to provide **fully loaded cost estimates** to prevent costs later on. Similarly, it is often useful to offshoring clients to ensure that legal matters be settled in the offshoring clients' country. Often, offshoring vendor countries may not have the most equitable judicial system and settling legal matters may take too long and may be biased. It may be prudent for offshoring clients to require that all legal arbitration and issues be handled by courts in the offshoring client's home country.

6. **Audit for Quality Assurance**: Once contracts are signed and agreements ratified, offshoring clients need to maintain multiple formal lines of communication to monitor and audit the offshoring vendors performance for quality assurance constantly and periodically. Errors, if not correctly early on, tend to magnify. One error becomes the input into another process and amplifies the error. If an error is not detected early on and the company waits till later, the error propagates and amplifies. This creates a **bullwhip effect** where a small issue amplifies itself over the long term. Another effect to note is the **Pareto effect**, which states that 20% of issues create 80% of problems. It is important that errors are detected early on and corrective actions are taken immediately.

In order for offshoring clients to limit their risk to quality issues and errors that, because of complex linkages, can erode their brand credibility and reputation and decrease their competitive advantages, offshoring clients must periodically audit their offshoring vendors. This should be stipulated in the contract. An **audit** is a thorough examination of a process, activity, or company to ensure that the process, activity, or company is following prespecified criteria. It is common for offshoring clients to set up operational audits of their offshore vendors to check whether the vendors are following regulations, guidelines, and specifications while maintaining labor laws and ethical practices. For example, Apple has a strict Supplier Conduct that states: "Apple is committed to the highest standards of social and environmental responsibility and ethical conduct. Apple's suppliers are required to provide safe working conditions, treat workers with dignity and respect, act fairly and ethically, and use environmentally responsible practices wherever they make products or perform services for Apple. Apple requires its suppliers to operate in accordance with the principles in this Apple Supplier Code of Conduct ("Code") and in full compliance with all applicable laws and regulations."

As production and services get offshored, they attract a unique set of benefits as well as, often, intractable problems from globalization.

Offshoring Benefits

Companies love offshoring because it is profitable. Executives and managers love offshoring because of the **front-loaded** (at the onset) capital benefits that add to bonuses. Capital benefits come from getting rid of fixed costs. An executive or manager running HR payroll, or a call center (customer support) has to worry about multiple fixed costs. Real estate costs of the office property that amount to thousands of dollars per month. Then add in utilities from heating, electricity, water, to coffee. Tens of employees working across multiple shifts. Add employee benefits such as vacation days and healthcare and costs keep going up. One of the major reasons why executives and managers like offshoring is to wash their hands-off fixed costs of operations. Offshoring HR Payroll or Call Centers means the companies can sell or repurpose their real estate meant for HR Payroll or Call Centers, save employee salaries and benefits at US or UK prices, not worry about things like absences, sick leaves, and vacation time and the loss of productivity, Instead, companies will contract with offshore firms as third-parties to staff and produce/service HR Payroll or Call-Center support and pay them a local wage that is considerably lower than US or UK labor wages and salaries. This frees up a lot of cash for executives and managers and often leads to receiving big bonuses.

Often, if companies feel that they need to better control offshored quality or do not trust the quality of work that will be provided by a vendor (supplier), companies will rather invest in building a **Captive Center** in an offshore location that is managed by the client (company) rather than an offshore 3rd party vendor. That still allows the company to lower its costs by hiring offshore labor while monitoring its work quality.

Similar to a captive center, companies also invest in **Greenfield Projects** where companies build foreign operations from scratch to access the local market and often secure some tax advantages.

Did You Know That?

China, in order to secure better trade relations with the US, spent more than $8.5 billion in Greenfield projects in the US between 2000 and 2014.

Investors love offshoring because offshoring to low-cost countries increases profits. Offshoring props up **employee productivity** and **earnings per share (EPS)**. Productivity appears to increase because companies can now earn the same or higher revenues with fewer employees (offshoring allows companies divest business segments such as IT support, HR, etc. and have fewer employees). So, even if the company is earning the same revenues, it has fewer employees). Employee productivity is output/input, i.e., revenues/employee costs. With fewer employees on the company payroll, productivity looks much better. **Earnings Per Share (EPS)** is calculated as the ratio of Net Income and the Number of Shares Outstanding, i.e., the number of shares traded on the open market. With fewer fixed costs from offshored labor and real estate costs, Net Income often rises while the Number of Shares Outstanding remains the same, therefore pushing up the EPS ratio—something that market investors and analysts welcome with open arms.

Employees hate offshoring because it is a business prelude to giving you the sack and passing you a pink slip. Sorry mate, but you lost at musical chair.

How paradoxically rational would it then be if you were to hedge your potential sacking by buying more equities in your firm? The greater the probability of your sacking, the more you would buy stocks in your firm. If you knew that your function would be shipped as a part of a BPO (Business Process Outsourcing), you would buy even more because EPS in the next few quarters would shoot up…the more you offshore, the more you buy, till, of course, your firm goes belly up—then, sell!

For **vendors** (companies to whom we outsource or offshore), offshoring benefits come from **back-loaded** (later on) profits. While **client** firms (the ones that outsource or offshore their work) reap benefits of offshoring early on from cost savings, vendor firms reap benefits later. Vendors have to invest heavily at the onset to build the right operational infrastructure for production or services for the clients, find and train workers for the job, find banks or investors to loan them capital, among other things. Once they build the operational infrastructure, they need to market themselves to get contracts from client firms willing to outsource to them. Vendors need to reach **critical mass**. Critical mass refers to the number of contracts, number of clients, and the amount of revenue required to break-even or reach a level of profit. However, once vendors reach the critical mass and build the trust that makes clients **buy-in** (accepting the deal) and outsource to the vendors, vendors try to **lock-in** clients by making clients dependent on vendors with promised deals and long-term contracts.

Offshoring Costs

Offshoring is considered one of the major underpinnings of globalization, further underscored by information and communication technologies. Yet, behind the cost savings are issues that are murkier, both for the client firm that offshores and the vendor firm that receives the offshoring contracts. It is important for companies to understand that as they get more and more dependent on vendors, the convenience from someone else taking care of their activities increases, but their control over quality, management, and culture decreases.

The idea of offshoring production and services appears to be a splendid cost-saver at first until companies realize that their competitors are also outsourcing and choosing the right supplier/vendor cannot be done at a mere whim. *Vendors have to be vetted extremely carefully because of* **complex linkages**. If you choose the wrong vendor that supplies a faulty product, your brand is what will suffer because the market holds the brand responsible rather than the vendors that manufacture, produce or service the brand. In 2016–2017, Samsung Galaxy phones were exploding. Samsung outsourced its battery production to third-party vendors. These batteries were defective because of creased connections and welding that made the wires touch each other and create a fire hazard. In 2017, Toyota, Mercedes, Volkswagen, and GM had to recall millions of cars, costing them over a $1 billion from lawsuit settlements and servicing, because of a faulty airbag manufactured by a common supplier, Takata. The defective airbags could deploy improperly and shoot out shards of metal that could kill the driver and passengers. Similarly, if your company offers a good product or service but its offshored call-center support is dismal, the market and consumers would blame the country for choosing the wrong outsourced or offshored call-center support vendor. That means companies need to ensure that they choose the vendor truly fit for the task.

The offshoring vendor, while benefiting from offshoring in the short term, has to deal with long-term consequences. This creates a **moral hazard**, where a short-term benefit can be offset by long-term costs. The term **moral hazard** is an economics concept that refers to a condition where people, companies, or countries take more risk than needed because they feel that they will be saved or bailed out. The case of the PIIGS squandering money and then being bailed out is an example of moral hazard. The fact that having an insurance on a house can prompt a homeowner to be less cautious about taking good care of the house, knowing that in the event of disrepair or robbery, the homeowner will be fully reimbursed. During hurricane Katrina in the US, hurricane victims were usurping millions of taxpayer dollars knowing that FEMA (Federal Emergency Management Agency) would bail them out for more than what they had lost. This issue of moral hazard plagues decision-making because creating something that seems to be *good from far can end up being far from good*. For example, the fact that countries offer welfare (an apparently moral way to help the poor in living with some dignity) can turn hazardous is people abuse welfare as a way to evade working or earning and education, thus hurting the country's economy in the long term. Unemployment benefits, disability benefits, universal healthcare, all offer aspects of moral hazards where they, seemingly moral choices at face value, can end up being abused.

And it is this moral hazard that is such a prickly affair. Moral hazard, as the term signifies, is the confounding act of morality that appears wonderfully apt for the short term but adds to socio-economic and often murderous woes in the long term.

Communism was the most recent moral hazard. Who does not like the idea of an ideal world, an egalitarian society devoid of the oppression of the classes, a reminiscence of John Lennon's lines, "Imagine no possessions"? But the practice of communism was far removed from the once-idealized utopia. To save an ideal of equality, they slaughtered, imprisoned, confiscated, and controlled. Protection of the ideal was more important that the protection of the people. After all, the people served the ideal rather than the other way around. What begins as idealized morality migrates, in the long term, to a menacing leviathan scorching the population to deify the ideal. From Taliban fundamentalists to North Korean communists, an assumption of an infallible ideal that will flower the earth often scorches an otherwise fertile ground.

The Obama administration's healthcare initiative was an interesting case in point. A fractured economy needs jobs that drive up individual income rather than drive up market uncertainty about an impending legislation. An uncertain market drives corporation to assume a deflationary position, posting profits without committing to labor investments. Rather than directing profits toward capital investments in labor and equipment, corporations find it more prudent to tighten their belts for unforeseen contractions from over regulation.

Governments should focus more on creating opportunities, not bureaucratic regulations.

Regulations are necessary only when market forces are confusing or monopolizing. Else, too much government intervention such as **nationalization** (government purchases of private companies) can erode free market efficiencies. In a free market, customers decide which company survives and which does not. In a nationalized economy with tremendous government interventions, the government uses public tax dollars to subsidize poor performing companies and industries. Since 2007, Venezuela nationalized its oil, cement, and steel industries, and even food distribution, leading to an even poorer performance and one of the worst economic crises in modern times. In five years from 2012

to 2017, the Venezuelan currency, Bolivares, lost 1/10,000 of its value.

Countries such as China and India that host offshoring vendors often face similar morally hazardous behavior. While offshoring adds short-term gains to the economy, the long-term costs can be hazardous. In China, thousands of factories spewing toxic fumes such as carbon monoxide and Sulfur Dioxide, so much so that Beijing residents are often asked to stay indoors because of the toxic pollutants in the smog, especially during the winter months when the heavy cold air settles close to earth, carrying with it all the air pollutants. Most of China's major cities are covered in a toxic gray shroud of polluted air. In China, soil and water are contaminated with heavy metals such as mercury, lead, cadmium, copper, nickel, chromium, and zinc, making cancer one of major causes of death and leaving more than 500 million Chinese without clean, drinking water.

The story is no different in India. India, although largely an offshore destination of IT services, has seen a massive rise in goods production for the local market, where rising incomes create a greater demand for more consumer goods and staples. With very few environmental regulations in place, corruption is rampant, leading to mass abuse of pollutant and waste disposal. In 2017, Indian cities were so enveloped by pollution that flights had to be canceled and, good grief, even the white marble of the Taj Mahal turned green.

Therein lies the moral hazard. The practices that often build an economy can, over, time destroy life that economic development was meant to uplift in the first place. Knowing that economic growth is venerated, offshoring vendors will often operate with wantonness and without scruples that can destroy the environment.

VCs Going VCs

The once communist Viet Congs are now Venture Capitalists. If you see Vietnam today, you will immediately agree with the statement that the Vietcong are becoming venture capitalists. Nationalists suddenly becoming internationalists

—adding the Ho-Chi-Minh trail to its logistical infrastructure. Offshoring has been the newfound development strategy for Vietnam trying to seek a piece of the lucrative pie off China and India. Ever since the 17th parallel ceased to exist as political boundary and north and South Vietnam merged, Vietnam crept out of the communist closet to realize that a good rate of return is quite a fab alternative to reading Mao or Marx. The party has tasted the blood of capitalism and become a maneater. As The Economist magazine puts it, quite aptly, Vietnam is now the domicile of "ardently capitalist communists." After all, capital is still dear even when you are not formally practicing capitalism.

And that is exactly what China fears in the offshoring puzzle. The shadow from Vietnam looms long and dark on the Chinese coast. It is a gathering storm with all the markings of the Chinese checkmate. The same industrious might, a strong central party governance that can get things done in a flash and the structural assurances of finance (money supply), sound labor supply, and infrastructure are Vietnam's selling point. Adding to that is the fact that it has less of political baggage and is barely a menacing compared to China. The new threat is from the contribution margins (revenues—costs of goods sold) from production rather than from ideas.

Did You Know That?

During the Vietnam War, Vietnam's Ho Chi Minh was one of China's acolytes. Today, Vietnam distrusts China and is one of the up and coming manufacturing venture capital investment region directly competing against China!

Managing Global Operations: Supply Chains

Outsourcing and Offshoring are strategic and cost-based decisions regarding "to make or to buy." Such decisions are converted into action via creating and managing global projects.

Finally, getting products in on time for fulfillment is critical. This is where understanding global supply chains becomes important.

Supply Chains Connect Global Operations

Like it or not, the world is flattening. Stop by and step into a Target, Wal-Mart, Best Buy, or Home Depot store and you will find goods made in China, India, Philippines, Turkey, or El Salvador. Look up your Dell Express Service Tag and call the 1-800 number and, within a few key presses, you are talking to a call center in Mumbai or Bangalore, India. Be it goods or services, your everyday world is closely intertwined with the global community- all by virtue of a supply chain. And supply chains are mostly global.

Let us begin with a definition as a first step toward understanding the global supply chain. A **supply chain** is a complex global network of various companies, technologies, and infrastructure resources (facilities, ports, airports, roads, etc.) that have to work together in coordination to ensure end-to-end fulfillment of goods, services, and information for providing the highest value to customers. Supply chains affect every part of a company- from marketing to accounting. It is a fun and exciting world or managing people and processes around the globe. Know it and get ready for it because you are in it.

Did You Know That?

During the 2nd Industrial Revolution when steamships ruled the waves, large ships would empty their coal reserves in 5 days! Britain dominated global trade by building a coal supply infrastructure across the world, from Jamaica to India, to Australia!

Basic Pieces of a Global Supply Chain

To visualize the global supply chain, think of it as a process broken into multiple stages and activities.

- **Procuring/Sourcing raw materials** (process of getting parts, materials, components from multiple suppliers)
- **Inventory** (process of storage and accounting prior to production, materials management, and sales)
- **Ordering** (assuming demand-based, process of ordering is the process by which the customer places and orders online or offline and is processed by the company)
- **Production, assembly, and packaging** (process of getting the finished product ready for shipment to the downstream supply chain)
- **Shipment** (logistical process of delivery to distribution centers)
- **Warehousing** (process of receiving finished products and managing them to be shipped out at a moment's notice)
- **Distribution** (process of moving products from a distribution center to other distributers, wholesalers, retailers, and resellers)
- **Retailing** (process of online and/or offline display, cataloguing, and order taking)
- **Delivery** (process of shipping the product to the consumer on-site or off-site)
- **Fulfillment** (process of ascertaining the proper (timely, accurate, not DOA (dead-on-arrival)) receipt of the ordered product by the customer)
- **After-sales servicing** (process of ensuring support and service provisioning in case of defects and malfunctions)
- **Reverse logistics** and disposal (process of streamlining returns, removals, and disposal of products) for reuse and sustainability

Global supply chains are the new paradigm of the flat world. We live in world run by competition and innovation. Providing a quality product or service to customers at the right time is essential. If the supply chain stalls, millions of dollars of sales are lost forever. Here are some of the famous **supply chain disasters** and their effects on the market[1]:

Foxmeyer's 1996 Distribution Disaster: New order management and warehouse automation systems led to inability to ship product and failure to achieve expected savings; bankruptcy and sale of the company.

Adidas 1996 Warehouse Meltdown: Adidas couldn't get a first and then a second warehouse system and its automation to work. Adidas' inability to ship leads to market share losses that persist for a long time

Toys R Us.com 1999 Christmas: Toys R Us' online retail division could not make Christmas delivery commitments to thousands, leading to the infamous "We're sorry" emails on Dec. 23. Eventually, Amazon took over fulfillment and Toys R Us is not merely a shadow.

Hershey's Halloween Nightmare 1999: New order management and shipping systems didn't start off correctly and Hershey missed critical Halloween orders, leading to $150 million in lost revenue and a 30% stock drop.

Cisco's 2001 Inventory Disaster: Cisco faced a lack of demand and inventory visibility from a market slowdown leading to $2.2 billion inventory write-off and Cisco's stock price cut in half.

Apple's 2010 iPhone 4.0 Debacle: Apple's products are designed in California but assembled in Shenzhen, China. The 600,000 iPhone preorders on day one overwhelmed the assembly, inventory, distribution, and overall supply chain, leading Apple to randomly cancel preorders and delaying the original delivery date.

KFC's 2018 UK Chicken shortage: In 2018, KFC changed its chicken supplier that created order discrepancies, leading to chicken supply shortage, and forcing KFC to close half of its 900 UK stores. Such is the complex linkages between suppliers and importance of fine-tuning order integration.

ASOS 2019 Warehouse Debacle: ASOS, a high-turnover, fast fashion company with more than 85,000 SKUs, had a warehouse management system (WMS) programming fault. ASOS' WMS wasn't updating an SKUs received from suppliers or customer returns but updating orders shipped. This created a false sense of SKU shortage even though supplies piled up internally and clogged up its operations, costing ASOS $30 million.

2021 Ever Given Container Ship Grounding: In March 2021, Ever Given, one of the largest container ships, 1,300 feet long and 220,000 tonnage, got grounded in the Suez Canal from high winds and a sandstorm. Ever Given was traveling from Malaysia to the Netherlands. Stuck for 6 days, the grounding delayed 300 ships, with an alternate route via the Cape of Good Hope costing a ship $26,000 in fuel, per day, in addition to the costs and delays of adding another 13 days to the route.

7 Global Supply Chains Facts

Global supply chains impact all the above aspects of business. *Global supply chain management requires companies to focus coordinating companies, people, technologies, and processes for timely, customer-centered fulfillment while reducing risk, uncertainty, and cost.* Here are some of the important takeaways.

1. **Supply chains exist for every product or service**: Whether you are purchasing a Kinder Bueno in Gourdon, a tiny hamlet in the south of France, or an M&M in a city like Shanghai, every product, regardless of whether it is sold at a metropolis or at. A tiny rural village in the world, has a supply chain, even when locally produced. Supply chains not only exist for products such as the Calabrese salami you eat of the iPhone that you carry but also for services. **Product and services supply chains** leverage technology and span the globalized world of business across products, **services** (your call-center support or your laptop repair under warranty), and **information** (your international ATM transaction). The flow of goods, services, or information can be **downstream** (from the manufacturer to the consumer) or **upstream** (from the consumer back to the manufacturer).

Product or goods supply chains are the most common version of a service chain that we imagine. Supply chains for products include multiple vendors (suppliers or sellers) who manufacture or source various components for the client (the buyer). For example, let's look at the global supply chain for a Dell PC. In order to assemble a PC, Dell (as a client) sources (purchases) components from different vendors around the world. A typical Dell PC sources memory chips (RAM) and optical drives (CD-RWs, DVD-RWs) from Japan, network cards (for Wi-Fi or Ethernet), monitors, and cooling fans from Taiwan, hard drives from Singapore, video cards from Hong Kong, sound cards from France, microprocessors from the US, keyboards from Mexico, as well as from other global vendors. Once the components have been sourced and added to inventory, the Dell plant in Austin, Texas assembles them to ship them out to you, the customer.

Group Exercise

As a team, research the Internet to find a set of shipping ports for each of these countries. Now, assuming the role of a supply chain coordinator, choose two alternative routes to ship the parts to the Dell's Austin facility. Which of the two alternative routes would you choose and why? Explain.

1. **Supply Chains are Bi-directional**

When materials and information flow one way, acknowledgments, and cash flow the other way. Therefore, if you really need to trace a supply chain, trace the money flow—it will reveal the connections! That is why you find the FBI or MI-5 constantly say when they try to unravel a plot: "follow the money." That is why every supply chain manager needs to understand the cash flow. So, pay particular attention to **cash flows from operations** in your cash flow statement. *Operations activities include the production, sales, and delivery of the company's product as well as collecting payment from its customers. This could include purchasing raw materials, building inventory, advertising, and shipping the product.*

2. **Supply Chains are more than Transportation and Logistics**

a. The Service Supply Chain

If you have ever returned a product to a store or received an Return Merchandise Authorization (RMA) from a store to ship an item back to the retailer or manufacturer, you have already used the service supply chain. A service supply chain includes parts of a supply chain that exist to provide important value-added services to consumers before and after the sales of a product. *Service supply chains can be forward or reverse.* A forward service supply chain includes parts forecasting and planning as well as forward logistics. The forward service supply chain's objective is to ensure that the shelves are stocked with products that consumers demand. A lot of important forecasting and planning goes on in the background so that the milk is fresh, and the latest DVDs stocked. A reverse service supply chain includes reverse logistics (including product/part return), repair and refurbishment, and warranty management. When your laptop malfunctions under warranty and you call the support center, the reverse service supply chain is put into action. If the call (support) center cannot fix your problem, they will ask you to ship back the laptop. An RMA will be issued for your case that will be transferred to a shipper who will send you a prepaid shipping carton to pack your laptop for pickup. The laptop will be sent to a repair facility where it will be refurbished or exchanged for a new laptop and shipped back to you. However, reverse service supply chains also include recycling your old refrigerator (that Home Depot picks up for you when you buy a new refrigerator from the store) or other environmentally degradable or non-degradable products (we will discuss them later under green supply chains).

b. The Information Supply Chain

The Information Supply Chain (ISC), in contrast with goods and services supply chains, focuses on the movement of information across global supply chains. The ISC runs parallel to the physical supply chain and collects data from every single process of the supply chain and integrates the data so that companies can view what is going on in every part of their global supply chain. Data and information from every part of the supply chain are fed forward and made available virtually for review and inspection by various companies and governmental agencies. Think of the ISC as an information grid on a dashboard that shows how goods are flowing across the supply chain. A bottleneck or a disruption is immediately notified. The Fig. 13.1 shows a Supply Chain information dashboard that tracks a part of the supply chain. Starting clockwise from the top left, the first indicator shows how much of the forecast margin has been met; Ending-On-Hand (EOH) inventory displays the number of Stock Keeping Units (SKUs) on hand at different centers; Order fill rate looks at the percentage of orders fulfilled by suppliers.

Revenue and cost show SKU procurement financials; total supplier speed shows how fast the suppliers are fulfilling orders (too fast in the red zone will add to inventory costs and too slow will end up in missed sales); and the demand–supply mismatch displays the difference between the quantity demanded by the market and the quantity supplied (once again, there needs to be a balance).

Did You Know That?

Amazon's warehouse operations and logistical systems are so good at routing and delivery that Amazon Prime deliveries threated the US Postal Service. Facing such competition, USPS now does weekend deliveries! Competition always benefits the customer!

If you have ever withdrawn cash or charged your plastic internationally, you have used the ISC. The minute you put your debit card into a foreign machine, information from your machine is sent to the processing bank that electronically communicates with your bank (turn your card and you will find international communication

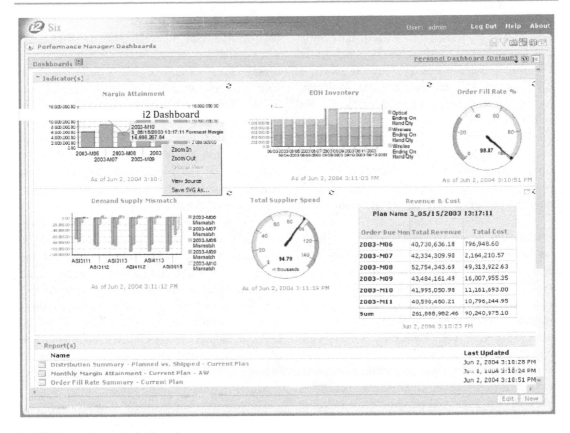

Fig. 13.1 Supply chain dashboard

vendors such as Star, NYCE, Cirrus, Maestro). The international connections allow the local bank to check your account to see if the funds are available. Once it is confirmed, the local bank processes the transaction with an international clearing house (like a half-way house vouchsafes for you and your bank) and you hear the flutter of local currency ready for you. Now, isn't that amazing? Behind the scenes are complex information networks that use technologies such as Electronic Data Interchange (EDI) to communicate across the world. Nowadays, with large scale digitization, Electronic Document Handling (EDH) and Electronic Content Management (ECM) are being used to scan, store, and transfer large volumes of documents at every part of the supply chain (from shipping manifests to Bills-of-Lading (BOL or B/L)). Enterprise Resource Planning (ERP) systems are increasing ICS transparency by making the information visible across different parts of the organization and the supply chain.

3. Supply Chains are Global

Supply chains span the global and are the veins and capillaries of international business. So, supply chains include various countries and their politics. When Venezuela elected Hugo Chavez in 1998, his socialist position worried the rest of the world. Venezuela is the fifth largest oil-exporting nation in the world and oil revenues sustain more than half of its earnings. Moreover, Venezuelan oil supplies cater to 13% of US demand. Even though Hugo Chavez vocally opposes the US, Venezuela has been maintaining oil supplies to the US because of the much-needed revenues. Still, the politics of Venezuela is becoming worrisome as the Venezuelan government is rapidly nationalizing oil, passing them to the Russians as a show of solidarity, and renegotiating contracts with western oil companies. A political rift can create dry a part of the oil supply chain and create severe oil shortages for US energy demand. Similar issues exist with Iran. Because the supply chain is global and requires managing many different companies from various cultures and political views, supply chains are sensitive to changes in the political climate and/or the mismatch of cultures.

4. Supply Chains Rely on Infrastructures

A robust and secure supply chain requires public (governmental) and private (non-governmental) infrastructure investments. A supply chain has to rely on a series of public and private infrastructures- from transportation networks and climate-controlled warehouses to national and local regulations. Think of how problematic it would be if an exotic fishery did not have a proper transportation infrastructure (e.g., an airport) to deliver the catch on time. Often times, perishable goods sit in ill-managed warehouses or in transit before they have to be discarded. Sadly, supply chains often suffer from a **last-mile problem**. The last-mile problem relates to a lack of or prohibitively expensive infrastructure between a manufacturing facility to the closest transportation network or between the last warehouse and the customer (downstream last-mile problem). Even if there is an excellent supply chain infrastructure, most supply chains suffer from the last-mile problem. For example, while the supply chain is extremely well-oiled between Europe and the US eastern seaboard, once the goods are delivered to warehouses in New Jersey, delivering the goods to a retailer in Manhattan (a few miles away) becomes prohibitively expensive and often a nightmare.

5. Supply Chains need Coordination

Because the supply chain spans across multiple points in the globe (we will discuss political and cultural issues later), you, as a supply chain manager, will coordinate across people and companies around the world to review and reengineer the processes to provide the biggest bang for the buck. According to a 2004 research by two Harvard professors, Oliva and Watson, a supply chain consists of multiple moving parts. As a result, planning global supply chains require a lot of negotiating, hand-wringing, capacity planning, and network configuration of warehouses, distributors, and retail stores. Each supply chain activity is controlled by a different company and each company acts in its best interest. Therefore, as Oliva and Watson explain, "it is necessary to overlay a coordination system: an explicit definition of processes, responsibilities, and structures to bring together multiple functions and organizations. The design of the coordinating system expands the supply chain problem space to include, among other things, the assignment of roles and decision rights among the coordinating partners, the selection of partners, the design of incentives, and the design of processes to monitor performance, set goals and solve problems.[2]" Thus, *coordination is essential in global supply chains*.

Coordination is essential to solving the global supply chain puzzle. As a manufacturer, you will be interested to know whether the different suppliers have delivered your raw materials before you can schedule your production on time and in the correct batch or quantity. As a shipper, you would like to coordinate with the manufacturer to see what form of transportation they require and how many items need to be delivered within a certain time and cost; as a retailer, you would like to coordinate with the shipper and the manufacturer to check when the items would arrive at the store for your customers; as an individual customer, you would like to know when the supplier delivers the materials that you have ordered. In real life, companies must write **extensive contracts** or provide some form of **revenue-sharing incentives** to motivate supply chain coordination. Technology is providing another means to supply chain coordination. New advances in technology, including EDI and ERP systems are creating large **Inter-Organizational Systems (IOS)** where organizations electronically communicate (using EDI or the Internet) with each other across the supply chain—sharing information from start to finish. If you buy a product on Amazon.com, it immediately notifies a shipper electronically and the shipper issues a tracking number for your product. The tracking number allows you and Amazon to check the status of supply chain fulfillment from Amazon.com's warehouse to your doorstep. **Technology is adding a new degree of automated coordination in global supply chains**.

Did You Know That?

Tesla uses the Japanese Robot manufacturer FANUC's robots, named Wolverine and Iceman, to build a car in 3–5 days—its operational assembly line purring away at 5 cms/second.

Transparency is a key aspect of every supply chain, regardless of whether you are managing a product, service, and information supply chain. Transparency is an ability of a person or organization to *verify* (ensure and authenticate that the transaction really did happen, and the right person accessed it), and *audit* (create a trace and trail for an item or information as it moves across the supply chain and transacted across various people or organizations) every transaction.

6. Global Supply Chains must address complexity and risk

Supply chain complexity is defined as the state of supply chain operations caused by the intertwining of multiple global supply chain partners involved in different financial regulations, markets, politics, and activities to create a challenging state of volatility, uncertainty, and risk. Increased globalization increases complexity. The SARS virus in Hong Kong and SE Asia created unintended risks in the supply chain. The financial meltdown in 2009 created a ripple effect- bankrupting financial institutions and creating reneging problems with vendors and letters of credit. The events surrounding 9/11 caused problems with shutdowns at Motorola, TI, and others. Because of complexity some companies have tried to manage the supply chain independently by division. Take IBM, for example.[3] In order to reduce complexity, each IBM division—PCs, servers, storage devices and others—operated its own supply chain. Every division ran distinct manufacturing lines, negotiating its own deals with components suppliers and using its own billing systems and ways of naming parts and products. By standardizing across divisions, IBM was able to reduce supply chain costs by over $3 billion, which did not count an additional $2.6 billion in price reductions occurring in component markets, for a total of $5.6 billion in savings. However, division leaders had to relinquish control of sourcing, manufacturing, and even design of some products. Moreover, because every division operated as an independent supply chain, they were unable to gain economies of scale (from collective bargaining and large-volume based discounts).

7. **Supply chains follow a push or pull strategy**. Activities in a global supply chain span the life cycle of the product or service. Supply chains follow a **push or pull supply chain strategy** and sometimes a combination of the two. A push supply chain follows a producer or supply-centric philosophy where a product is designed and built and sent to the customers. Push strategies are popular when goods in a supply chain are channeled based on predetermined forecasts and large production batches. Push strategies are very common and are found in most consumer products—from designer clothes to LED LCD TVs. A pull supply chain is a consumer or demand-centric supply chain. A music CD at a retail store with a set of tracks is a push strategy while your downloading of specific tracks that you want from iTunes is a pull strategy.
A pull supply chain follows a Build-to-Order (BTO) philosophy that is driven by customer demand. The pull supply chain is gaining popularity as companies are competing on customization. Dell's online customization is an example of a BTO philosophy where you choose within a (limited) set of option to

create a customized PC based on your demands. Once you send the order, the PC is built to your specifications and delivered to you. Similar customization strategies are also becoming popular in the automobile industry.

Push and Pull Supply Chains

A **Push vs. Pull** Supply Chain strategy is best applicable for the following situations:

A portion of the supply chain where demand uncertainty is low: A push strategy relies on forecasting and produces a fixed number of items. If uncertainty is high, demand for the items fluctuates heavily and a forecasting becomes a problem. When uncertainty is low because demand is somewhat stable (for example, for milk, bread), it is easier for producers and manufacturers to plan ahead with their orders and follow a push strategy.

In a "pull" system the consumer requests the product and "pulls" it through the delivery channel. An example of this is the build-to-replenish strategy followed by Maytag where they manufacture washers and dries only when bought by a customer. Similarly, Ford Australia only produces cars when they have been ordered by the customers.

In a push strategy, current orders based on historical order records from retailer: A push strategy is appropriate when the upstream supply chain maintains stock (inventory) on hand based on the history of stock records of the down-stream entity (individual or company). A supplier will rely on historical orders from the manufacturer; the manufacturer from the distributer; the distributer from the retailer; the retailer from the customer. **Links from supplier to customer are downstream while customer to supplier is upstream**. Now here is a problem, famously known as the Bullwhip effect. The retailer looks at its history of customer buying patterns and maintains a stock (and some extra "buffer" (or surplus) stock or inventory called safety stock). The distributor to the retailer knows that the retailer may need some extra inventory from time to time and prepares itself with its own surplus inventory or safety stock. As a simple example, if you consider that each upstream entity maintains a 10% safety stock, can you calculate how much the safety stock is inflated as you move 4 entities upstream (Hint: compounding effect)? This is the bullwhip effect where the upstream stock inflates like a ripple from the crack of a bullwhip.

A push strategy is useful when there are issues with demand patterns and production batches: A large part of any supply chain is assessing capacity. Companies invest heavily into their infrastructure and these infrastructures bear fixed costs (costs that must be met regardless of how much of the infrastructure is used). On the other hand, companies often do not have the resources at their disposal to take care of specific orders. Therefore, companies are often limited (constrained) by their resources. A company's capacity refers to its ability to handle scale and scope of orders. Therefore, if there is a sudden change in orders, the company may fail to meet them because it may require resources to be over-committed (for example, producing 3000 components from a single die press when the machinery can fabricate 1200 from a single die press) or under-committed (for example, when a machinery requires a minimum of 1000 pieces in a batch to be run but there is an order of 200 pieces). In such cases, companies work off their existing capacities, produce a certain number of pieces, and use a push strategy in their supply chain. Remember that a push strategy uses existing capacity and is therefore less expensive than a pull strategy.

Comparing Push vs. Pull Supply Chain Strategies

At this point, it is useful to understand that *a pure form of pull strategy or push strategy is often infeasible*. Therefore, supply chains often use a compromise of a push and pull strategy where it is a pull strategy to a certain point upstream and push strategy after that. A **decoupling point** is where pull and push strategies interface (Table 13.1).

Table 13.1 Push vs pull (on-demand) supply chains

Push strategy for supply chains	Pull strategy for supply chains
Triggered (initiated) downstream by manufacturers	Triggered (initiated) upstream by customers
Used for low demand uncertainty	Used for high demand uncertainty
Used in stable markets	Used in unstable markets
Production and distribution are supply driven	Production and distribution are demand driven
Easy to implement	Difficult to implement
Excess inventory due to bullwhip effect	Little excess inventory
Less expensive	More expensive

Global Supply Chain Mini-Cases

Supply Chains Matter: From Fashion to Terrorism to Software

Whether it is H&M or Al Qaeda and ISIS, supply chains are the lifeblood of any global operation. Let's look at how their supply chains are similar yet radically different.

Welcome to the digitally transformed world of Fast Fashion! H&M (along with Zara, Shein, ASOS, and Uniqlo) is famous for visiting famous fashion shows and taking pictures of the latest fashion highlights from *haute-couture* companies such as Gucci and Chanel. H&M designers pore through these designs, use 3D models for perfect-pattern cuts to reduce cloth waste and tweak these designs ever so slightly to make them more functional, and create *haute-couture*-inspired design specs!

Once the design is tweaked to ensure that there are no *haute-couture* design claims, H&M designers upload these 3D digital specs from the latest season and to multiple **contract vendors** and fabricators around the world, from China to Bangladesh. Some provide a particular button; some the thread; some the zipper, some the fabric- and someone else puts together (or fabricates) the apparel in some distant corner of the world. Digital cloud monitoring systems record every piece of the sourcing and fabrication process, starting from where a thread originated to who did which stich and cut. Once the finished apparel goes through quality control, the final product is ready to be shipped to H&M.

Depending on the season and the **service contract**, the vendor either moves the clothing to a distributer or decides on a shipper to deliver H&M's fashion line for the season. These shipping routes can be over land, air, or water or a combination (called multi-modal)- crossing different countries around the world to reach H&M warehouses. These are a part of the H&M's **supply chain logistics**. At every point in this supply puzzle, H&M tracks information on the movement of its goods from start to finish (also called **end-to-end** and **order-to-fulfillment** in supply chain parlance). These distribution centers ship different styles to different retail stores based on specific style and size demands. That's why you find slightly different apparel selection between the H&M store in London and the store in Beverly Hills.

Did You Know That?

By digitally transforming the fashion supply chain, Fast Fashion companies like H&M and Zara can copy, tweak, and sell runway designs in a 3–4 weeks compared 9–12 months for a high-end fashion brand such as Chanel or Gucci!

Now, let's visit Al Qaeda's supply chain. Al Qaeda's supply chain works on the sales of drugs, mainly cocaine and heroin, to fund its terrorist operations. Anwar al-Awaki, Al Qaeda's operations chief residing in Yemen is its supply chain planner. Columbian cocaine is flown into Guinea Bissau, a West African country run by corrupt military commanders. Drugs from Afghanistan are delivered by trucks to northeast Iran. The Persian Gulf and North African ports are the **main distribution centers** from which drugs are smuggled into the Europe via boats and trucks by local smugglers. The drugs are then sold dearly in the European markets where drugs and Euros change hands to fund terrorist recruitments and attacks.

ISIL/S (Islamic State of Iraq and the Levant/Syria) or Daesh, the brutal Islamic state terrorist group, instead relied on invading regions to control lucrative petroleum reserves. Exploiting the internal strife and power vacuum created after the fall of Iraq's Saddam Hussein, Libya's Muammar Gaddafi, and the Syrian civil war, ISIS began by invading petroleum-rich regions to control the oil supply chain and extricate revenues.

The Wired magazine interviewed Thomas Friedman, the foreign affair columnist for The New York Times and the international best-selling author of books such as *The Lexus and the Olive Tree, The World is Flat,* and *Hot, Flat, and Crowded.* In the 2005 interview, Mr. Friedman mentions that the **world is a gigantic supply chain** that terrorists are trying to bring down. He specifically mentions how a terrorist group is *"...is nothing more than a mutant supply chain. They're playing off the same platform as Wal-Mart and Dell. They're just not restrained by it. ... It's an open source religious political movement that works off the global supply chain. That's what we're up against in Iraq. We're up against a suicide supply chain. You take one bomber and deploy him in Baghdad, and another is manufactured in Riyadh the next day. It's exactly like when you take the toy off the shelf at Wal-Mart and another is made in Shen Zhen the next day"*.[4]

Did You Know That?

When Interpol or MI6 audits global terrorist supply chains, they follow the reverse flow of money. In supply chains, money, and goods (including terror) flow in opposite directions!

Securing Software Supply Chains

Even software has a supply chain. The software supply chain carries data packets and code from vendors to clients with the network as the logistics infrastructure. These data packets and codes originate from all across the world, hopping across nodes and warehouses around the globe. Some roads are safe; some are not. Some warehouses are legitimate; some are not. A packet can be hijacked, warehouses can be infiltrated, malicious code can be injected into a legitimate-looking packet like a legitimate lorry hiding a terrorist.

The ability of the perpetrators to create a digital signature and certification infrastructure and implant and trojanize the 2020 Solarwinds Orion update and perpetrate a global Solarwinds' Orion infrastructure hack underlines the need for revising authentication processes and protocols. The newfound cyber-attack wisdom lies in evasion rather than the shock of awe of DoS attacks. APIs, that serve as logistics connectors across various software and system in the global network, are particularly vulnerability in the software supply chain.

With an ever-spreading software supply chain, code integrity is critical. Therefore, ensuring the integrity of code repositories where vulnerabilities might be disclosed and malicious lookalikes could be injected.

We have to realize that supply chains are what controls every part of our lives. For centuries, **supply chains have been the circulatory system in any economy. Control and constrict the blood flow and the part of the body goes numb and perishes.** In history, sieges were planned to isolate a city or an economy from its supply chain. Without a supply chain, there would be no energy, no food, no ammunition, and the city under siege would be starved into submission—it was a bloodless form of forced surrender. Stories on sieges and attacks on supply chains are always on the newswire today.

- Somali pirates attacking cargo freighters in the Gulf of Aden in the Horn of Africa to disrupt international supply chains for ransom or terrorism.
- The German U-boat's naval blockade siege of the Atlantic to sink and destroy US and British ships to completely disrupt UK's supply chain during World War II and force it into submission.
- The German army (Wehrmacht) also practiced a supply chain siege on Stalingrad during World War II to defeat the city and force it to surrender.
- Israel's siege of and embargo against Gaza was a way to limit Hamas' access to weapons to inflict harm on Israel. Embargoes are a form of siege and are aimed at choking the supply chain.
- In the 1990's, Iraq was under siege by a naval blockade under an international embargo.
- If you listen to the news, you will hear about the UN (United Nations) decision on supply chain embargoes on Iran to deter its nuclear plans.

Group Exercise

Research the Internet to find any two famous sieges in history. Read them and briefly explain how the siege used a supply chain strategy to isolate their enemies into submission.

Supply Chain Coordination: Li and Fung, a Supply Chain Matchmaker

With the emergence of global supply chains, supply chain consultants have emerged. In fact, supply chain consultants are middlemen. Such is the case of Li and Fung, a century-old trader in Hong Kong that has become one of the most prominent middlemen and supply chain consultants for companies sourcing from South-East Asia. Li and Fung began as a trading company and used their experience and contacts to create a network of quality suppliers and producers. For the buyer, Li and Fung provides quality materials on time and within cost. For the supplier, Li and Fung provide sales and revenue opportunities, timely payment, and limits reneging (backing off from a contract). Over time, Li and Fung have become experts in matchmaking, while masking their buyers and suppliers.

Li and Fung, in the analog world of the 1990s, practiced global supply chain matchmaking, just the way Alibaba and Amazon.com do today.

The predominant adage in global outsourcing, supply chains, or digital transformation is based on reducing their **Cost of Sales (COS)** or **Costs of Goods Sold (COGS)**.

Look at any P&L (Profit and Loss) or Income Statement (Fig. 13.2).

The P&L statement above shows that the company's COS is 46.23% in 2019, 47.47% in 2020, and 54.57% in 2021. Whatever is left is called the **Gross Profit Margin** or **Gross Margin**, one of the most important operational financial ratios that analysts take heed, mainly because companies have control over their internal operations but not over their customers. A company that with lower COGS signifies better operational and supply chain management. In the above example, the company's gross profit is decreasing i.e., from 53.67% in 2019 to 45.43% in 2021. Obviously, this company needs to lower its COS or COGS.

There can be two approaches toward lowering COGS. First, you can scout for lower prices around the world to source every component from a variety of vendors. Now that is a cumbersome affair. You have to look for best quotes, convince yourself that these vendors are reputable and quality suppliers who will deliver the right product on time. You have to visit multiple facilities to ensure operational excellence; negotiate pricing and

```
                        INCOME STATEMENTS
                          (in millions)

Year Ended March 31,                 2019          2020          2021
------------------------------------------------------------------------
Revenue                          £14,580.2     £11,900.4      £8,290.3
Cost of sales                     (6,740.2)     (5,650.1)     (4,524.2)
                                 -----------   -----------   -----------
Gross profit                       7,840.0       6,250.3       3,766.1
                                 -----------   -----------   -----------

SGA expenses                      (3,624.6)     (3,296.3)     (3,034.0)
                                 -----------   -----------   -----------
Operating profit                   4,215.4       2,954.0         732.1
                                 -----------   -----------   -----------

Gains from disposal of fixed assets   46.3           -             -
Interest expense                    (119.7)       (124.1)       (142.8)
                                 -----------   -----------   -----------
Profit before tax                  4,142.0       2,829.9         589.3
                                 -----------   -----------   -----------

Income tax expense                (1,656.8)     (1,132.0)       (235.7)
                                 -----------   -----------   -----------
Profit (or loss) for the year    £  2,485.2    £  1,697.9    £    353.6
```

Fig. 13.2 An example Profit & Loss (P&L) or income statement

create contracts; set up delivery dates for each component so that the pieces are there on time for production.

Alternatively, the company can contract with a company such as Li and Fung or Alibaba who will be the matchmaker and manage the global supply chain for that product. Of course, Li and Fung will charge a fee or premium for their services. But their operational and supply chain differentiation comes from their long-standing expertise in choosing the right component suppliers from their vast network.

Suppose a company wants to design and sell a speaking teddy bear. The company will upload a 3D specs and voice recognition requirements, along with quality, cost, and lead-time information to Lui and Fung's digital platform. Once uploaded, the platform will use the specs to create a comprehensive BOM (Bill of Materials) that specifies every component and material need to build the speaking teddy bear. The platform will internally query its vast supplier-network for each

BOM part. The plastic body might be sourced from a vendor in Vietnam. The microfiber coat from a vendor in China, the eyes, wiring, motors, transistors, and speakers from China. The plastic legs, voice recognition and IC chips from Japan, and packaging from Hong Kong. The digital platform can then ship all components and materials to an assembler or fabricator in Shenzhen in China, with different quantities with various labeling requirements shipped to different markets around the world.

Of course, digital matchmakers and platforms, from Alibaba to Paypal and eBay, charge their users and clients a premium for managing the uncertainty of dealing with hundreds of global buyers and suppliers to lower their COGS (costs of goods sold).

What is evident from the above examples of supply chain coordination is the how Li and Fung and Alibaba use **Digital Transformation** to manage millions of global clients and vendors to reduce COGS.

Modeling Global Project Operations

Implementing most business decisions requires creating and managing them as business projects. Every business project is a juggle between the three pieces of the **Iron Triangle**: **Project Cost**, **Project Time**, and **Project Scope**. The reason why it is called an iron triangle is because cost, item, and scope are correlated. Project scope is the complexity of the project in terms of what it wants to accomplish. Projects with a larger scope will increase project time because more complicated projects will take longer to complete. That is one reason why, during project planning, managing scope creep is imperative. **Scope creep** is when a project ends up adding unneeded complexities because of constantly adding more and more features and trying to do too much too soon. Complexity is a project curse. More complexity requires more coordination and coordination is a costly affair, requiring more resources and more time commitments. Time, of course, is highly correlated with costs. The longer it takes to accomplish project tasks, activities, processes, deliverables, and milestones, the more expensive it gets. Every resource costs money. The longer a resource is used, the more it costs. Therefore, to tame the project iron triangle, begin by taming

project scope. That is the basis for project control. Here is a basic view of the corporate project control hierarchy.

But how do good project managers reduce project crept and manage complexity? One of the most important ways to manage complexity is by practicing modularity. **Modularity** is the practice of breaking down a product, task, or activity into small, manageable, and measurable pieces. For example, building a car can be broken down into multiple modular parts and assemblies. Each module can be at the component level (e.g., fuel injector, dashboard GPS module) and at the assembly level (engine assembly, dashboard assembly). A key advantage of modularity is lowering complexity. The longer you wait on the project, the more the chances of errors. It's easier to correct an error early than late. If things are beginning to go off scope, off budget, or off schedule, you want to detect them and correct them quickly rather than wait till later and have the errors magnified (Fig. 13.3).

Uncertainty is the bane of business decision-making. While risk is based on the estimated probability of something untoward happening, risk can be hedged (such as buying insurance against it). However, uncertainty is the worry that something that was not known, considered, or

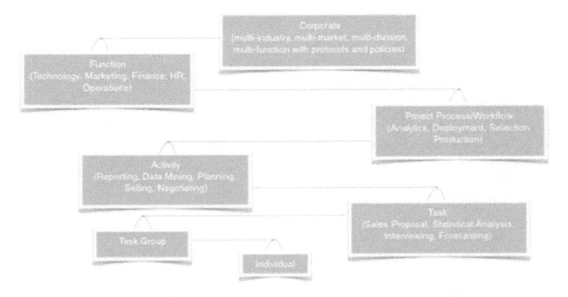

Fig. 13.3 Project, process, and tasks within a company

thought about might happen and that would thwart operations. So, uncertainty is the unknown chance of something an unknown event. Risk has a pattern (thus a probability). Uncertainty does not have a pattern.

PERT and Project Scheduling

Anytime you have uncertainty, all your project dimensions; from resource allocation, to quality fluctuation, to risk, to cost, to scope, to time, they're always likely to go up. The best way to reduce uncertainty is through better project planning. **PERT** (Program Evaluation and Review Technique) is an invaluable project planning tool/technique that can be used to mitigate uncertainties in project costs, schedules, and scope.

A global company is planning on entering a new international market. It has the following phases and timeline chalked out in weeks. The way companies calculate activity duration is based on a combination of optimistic, average, and pessimistic estimates gathered from historical data or surveying/brainstorming. Typically, **Activity or Task duration is calculated** as a weighted average of the average of Pessimistic time (P) + Optimistic time (O) + 4*Average time (A) or (P + O + 4A)/6. *Note that if your activity has more uncertainty, assign a higher weight to the pessimistic time.*

Table 13.2 shows how each new international market entry depends on other activities. **Key Performance Indicators (KPIs)** need to be defined (Activity 4) to gauge international market performance. However, KPIs can only be established only after Gap and Feasibility Analysis (Activity 2) and Market Opportunity Assessment (e.g., the size of the market and purchasing power of local customers) and Partnering Options (e.g., direct business, local partnering). Baseline Project Plan and Budget (Activity 5) and Beachhead Team and Executive Allocation (Activity 6) can be conducted in parallel (simultaneously) once KPIs have been defined.

Once the activity sequence has been established, the PERT model can diagram the flow of activities. Typically, each activity in the PERT model includes the following information.

Once the project timeline is mapped, a few basic calculations highlight some important project concepts.

Every activity has an **Early Start** (ES), **Late Start** (LS), **Early Finish** (EF), and **Late Finish** (LF) times. ES refers to when an activity can start at the earliest and LS refers the latest an activity can start. LS refers to when an activity can start without holding up the entire project at the latest and LF is the latest that an activity can finish (Fig. 13.4).

The International Market Entry Project begins with Activity 1. Activity 1 is the first

Table 13.2 PERT modeling task breakdown for an international market entry project

New International Market Entry Activities	Depends on	Time (in weeks)
1. Due Diligence Market Segmentation Analysis	-	4
2. Due Diligence Gap Analysis and Feasibilities	1	3
3. Due Diligence Market Opportunity and Partnering Options	1	4
4. Define KPIs (Key Performance Measures)	2, 3	2
5. Baseline Project Plan and Budget	4	2
6. Establish Beachhead Team and Allocate Executive	4	1
7. Begin Recruiting Market Team	5,6	2
8. Review Product/Service Readiness and Create Localized Features	7	3
9. Patent Review to Deter Copying of Idea	8	2
10. Choose Price and Channel	9	2
11. Promote and Pilot	10	3

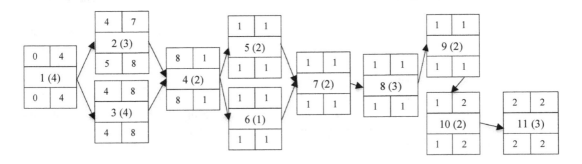

Fig. 13.4 PERT Model for an International Market Entry Project

activity, and its ES is therefore Week 0. It takes 4 weeks to complete and the EF is Week 4. Activities 2 and 3 can begin only after Activity 1 has ended. So, ES for 2 and 3 is Week 4. It takes 3 days for activity 2 to complete and 4 days for activity 4 to complete. Activity 4 depends on activities 2 and 3. The earliest activity 4 can start is week 8. While activity 2 can finish by week 7 at the earliest, activity 3 can only finish by week 8. Because activity 2 is being conducted simultaneously with activity 3, activity 2 has an extra day. Activity 2 can begin a day late and still end on time for activity 4 to begin on time. This extra time available on a project schedule is called **Slack**. When calculating ES and EF, ES times will always take the value of the longest of the previous activities. That's because the next activity cannot begin unless the longest of the previous activities is complete.

Calculating the latest start (LS) and latest finish (LF) happen in reverse. Once the earliest finish (EF) for the final activity has been calculated (If there are more than one final activity, choose the one with the longest duration because that activity requires completion before the project can be closed), the EF for the final activity

becomes the LF. In this case, activity 11's EF of 24 weeks is also the LS. Subtract the activity duration of 3 weeks and the LS is 21 weeks. The key is to realize that when reverse calculating LS and LF for cases where there are multiple activities, choose the lower of the LS values from the activities as the LF of the previous activity. That is because preceding activities need to be completed on time for the next activity to begin at the earliest.

The series of activities that have no slack need to be completed right on time and without any delay. That series of activities that have no slack is called a **Critical Path**. In this case, the CP is based on Activities 1 – 3 – 4 – 5 – 7 – 8 – 9 – 10 – 11 with a total of 24 weeks (in our example, the LF for activity 11).

Did You Know That?

The PERT chart became a critical project modeling during the Cold War between the US and the Soviet Union. The US Navy invented the PERT chart to collaborate with NATO countries to build its Polaris missiles faster than the Soviets!

Steps in Project Decision-Making

Project decision-making is a sequence of activities from initiating a project to closing a project.

1. You create the **project charter** and identify a list of assets needed. A charter also requires a champion, called project champions, typically an upper level manager or executive that will champion the project and push change management as well as can iron out internal creases. *The Project Charter should define the project scope and identify relevant assets and resources required.* Then you create your **WBS (Work Breakdown Schedule)**. WBS is a modular way to create piecemeal project deliverables. A WBS breaks down a project into a hierarchy of processes, activities, and tasks, each with its own measurement, deliverable, and control objectives. Set up as a tree structure, a WBS uses modularity to build a project structure around a small unit or product or service rather than just focusing on labor or machine hours. It is quite common at international auto companies' service departments to create global WBS for auto services. Previously, a battery replacement task would be billed based on number of hours of labor and the amount of materials assigned to the replacement. Today, it is common for international service departments to have a single global database based on WBS. Battery Replacement would be a separate WBS with pre-designates labor hours, machine hours, and materials. Regardless of whether it takes the dealership longer or shorter to replace the battery, the customer would receive a fixed charge across the globe.

2. Identify your stakeholders as a part of good project governance—that's an initiation project. It is important to consider stakeholders as people who are both going to be directly as well as indirectly involved with the project. Not all stakeholders have direct project involvement, but it is a splendid idea to keep them informed in the process.

3. Start the project with a baseline plan in terms of project scope, resource costs and schedules, deliverables, and milestones. Here, modularity is key. Modularity increases interchangeability and integration with a better chance to catch and fix errors early on.

   a. Determine project life cycle and shelf life: Focus on Module reuse.

   b. Modular Approach: While a project may have a shorter shelf life, specific project modules can be left in play and have a longer shelf life. E.g., 70% of the modules may be reused because of their scalability or portability. Thus, earned value potential remains for the modules.

   c. Assign initial planning and creating/ building for (i) initial outlays and (ii) on-going costs (TCO) over the life of each project module.

   d. Translate and assign $ value benefits (including cost savings) over each module's life cycle.

   e. Link benefits to Return on Asset (ROA) and Cash flows from Operations

   f. Breakdown multiple benefits for each project module over time. E.g.,

      i. Scalability benefits over next 7 years; UX benefits for 4 years; security benefits for 3 years.

      ii. Allows you to create a reconfiguration timeline and preempt resource and asset allocation.

   g. Estimate the IRR (hurdle rate) from historical projects. Else, use the inflation rate.

   h. Calculate the Present Value (*PV*) for each project module: PV = Module Value per period module/$(1 + IRR)^{periods}$.

   i. Create a Project Module Value-Multiplier: Divide the *PV* by the initial capital outlay to calculate profitability.

NPV and ROI

Here is an example. Suppose a multinational business is creating a Micro-services project such as a bank account transfer that will record customer UX (user experience) over the network

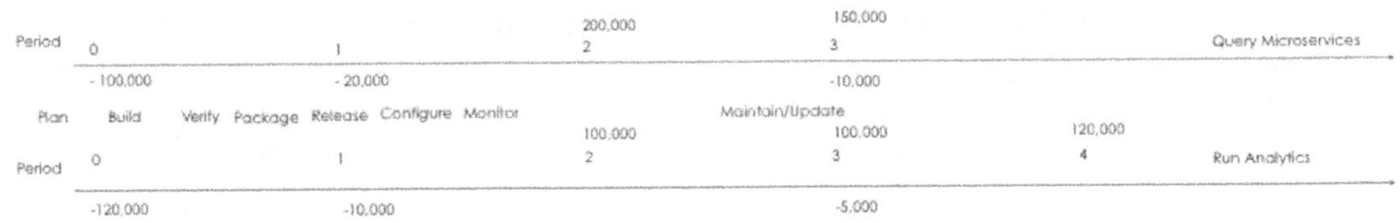

Fig. 13.5 NPV and ROI Assessment for a Micro-services Technology Project

and update a database to trace points of improvements and bottlenecks.

Let's break the project into only two modules: (i) Query micro-services and (ii) Run Analytics.

Let's choose two modules and plot them over time in Fig. 13.5:

Module "Query Micro-Services" has the following resource and cash flow requirements. At the beginning of the project module, there is an initial $100,000 budgeted investment at the beginning of the year followed by a $20,000 and $10,000 investment in the first and third year for WBS micro-services resource allocations. The micro-services project starts paying back with more bank users using the online account transfer micro-services rather than physical bank clerks and tellers, amounting to $200,000 and 150,000 savings (thus positive operational cash flows) in years 2 and 3.

The international bank also plans to assess user interactions strategically and analytically with its banking applications around the world by investing in an analytics application that would create customer behavior profiles. The module, "Run Analytics," requires three WBS investments: $120,000 initially to jumpstart the project, $10,000 in the first year, and $5,000 in the third year. The analytics micro-services project, by creating more personalized services for customers, increases engagement and retention, leading to positive cash flows of $100,000 each in years 2 and 3 and $120,000 during year 4.

With both micro-services being developed for international customers, which module offers the best **Return on Investment (ROI)** and by how much?

A quick, initial estimate might be based on subtracting all project module cash outflows from project module cash inflows. The Micro-Services Query module has $350,000 cash inflows and $130,000 cash outflows, apparently leading to a $220,000 cash flow. The Analytics module has $320,000 in cash inflows and $135,000 in cash outflows, apparently leading to a $185,000 cash flow. Yet, something is lost in translation.

The previous section on inflation shows how money loses value over time. For projects to budget efficiently, projects must budget all cash inflow and outflow estimates over time and compare them to a single period of time. *All project ROIs (returns of investments) must be calculated as their **Net Present Value (NPV)**.* NPV is value of all future cash inflows and outflows related to a module, activity, life cycle, or project that incorporates the time value of money. NPV therefore considers the reality that investments in projects could have been invested somewhere else for a better return. The expected ROI that a company expects from a project has to be higher than the inflation rate; else, the company could have just purchased some US Treasuries to protect itself from the value of money eroding from inflation. Companies often will, unless they have their own internal rates of return (IRR) (typically more than the inflation rate) that they use to benchmark project performance, use inflation rate as the **Hurdle Rate** (the rate past which a project has to deliver in order to be considered).

This is particularly important in international business because each country has different inflation rates or the rate at which its currency loses value. If your global business had divisions in Turkey, Ukraine, US, and France, each country's inflation rate would have different effect on the NPV. In 2017, Turkey's inflation rate was 11%, Ukraine's inflation rate was

14.5%, US's inflation rate was 2.1% and France's inflation rate was 1%.

As noted earlier when discussing compounding, calculating the future value of an investment is based on the formula where Future Value (FV) = Present Value (PV) multiplies by $(1 + \text{discount or hurdle rate } i)^{\text{time periods } n}$.

$$FV = PV \cdot (1 + i)^n$$

Using the same formula, a Net Present Value is nothing the PV of all future net cost inflows and outflows shown as (k stands for each specific time period):

$$NPV = \sum \frac{FV_k}{1 + i^{n_k}}$$

Using the calculation, NPV for the micro-service query project in Turkey would be is:

$$NPV = \frac{-100,000}{(1+0.11)^0} + \frac{-20,000}{(1+0.11)^1} + \frac{300,000}{(1+0.11)^2} + \frac{150,000 - 10,000}{(1+0.11)^3}$$

So, for the micro-service query project in Turkey, $NPV = -100,000 - 18,018.02 + 243,486.73 + 102,366.79 = \$227,835.51$, \$205,254.56 in Ukraine, 299,793.30 in the US, and \$310,169.46 in France.

On the other hand, for the Analytics project, NPV is \$99,932.94 in Turkey, \$80,513.59 in Ukraine, US \$160,884.42 in the US, and \$174.681.73 in France.

The higher the inflation rate or hurdle rate (or IRR), the lower the NPV and therefore the ROI. So, based on the inflation rate or the hurdle rate (or IRR), the same project, even within the same company, may be greenlighted in one country and discontinued in another.

1. Assess project performance like a business: Increase Accountability, Transparency, Causality, Resilience, and Productivity.
   a. Accountability: ability to assign and measure governance.
   b. Transparency: ability to audit and trace performance and pitfalls.
   c. Causality: ability to identify root causes and fix them. Remember the Pareto rule that 20% issues create 80% of problems.
   d. Resilience: ability to respond to incidents and maintain continuity.
   e. Productivity: ability to benchmark and trace output/input over time.
   f. Reduce resource input costs and Reduce variance = Increase savings and consistency.

2. Organize and prepare resources to carry out all the project work (you control scope, and you control resources, you control various degrees of risk), and then you finally close the project.

3. The primary documents require to begin a project are the project charter including the project management plan and deliverables (scope) acceptable by the customer, followed by creating internal project documents.

4. Projects begin with a lot uncertainty that requires cost and time buffers in case things go wrong. As the project progressed and modules are delivered, and milestones achieved, uncertainty decreases as does the influence of initial stakeholders. What increases, on the other hand, is the cost of changes. It's very important to realize that, as a project moves forward or matures, changing the project scope becomes very expensive because it impacts everything else that has been previously done. Changing one thing later might require changing 50 other things. This basically means that a project should plan ahead. Project costs and staffing level are serious concerns. Any changes from the initial project create more and more complexities and deliverables. In the process the project institutes more resource, dedicates more time, and assumes more cost, jeopardizing the iron triangle. It is important to realize that as you move forward, cost increases, especially at the point where you're delivering a lot of project specifications and modular outcomes. *The cost of a project goes up as if trying to implement something new at the end of the project.*

5. Under scenarios of risk, which often times is a very interesting piece of the puzzle, companies might find it beneficial to consider quality and risk as paired combinations, which basically means projects want to increase quality while decreasing risk. Risk is not just quantitative (the impact of a risky scenario on costs or time) but also qualitative. Companies often perform qualitative risk analysis that tries to analyze issues that are mostly subjective in nature: Who are the people creating problems? Are there motivational or cultural issues at the root of the risks? Are there certain cultural or socioeconomic issues that may suddenly stall an international project? How can the company deal with corruption and bribery in managing its projects across borders? Internally, could there be some people who will be absolutely resistant to any changes and create various problems that could throw the project at risk? The quantitative components of risk are much more objective in nature, such as currency headwinds, leveraging or losing arbitrage opportunities, tax areas, new regulations and tariffs that are coming into play, specific increases in labor costs that could impact your project, among many others.

6. As projects progress and move through project activities, it is very important to stay modular because the smaller the work packages, the quicker it is to notice problems or certain issues and immediately create solutions or create better exception plans or **IRP**s. As the project is ready to be deployed, it is important to **pilot** it first and practice a **phased transition**. It is not a good idea to practice a large scale go-to-live where a single issue might stop all operations. Instead, it is more prudent to pilot the project and practice phased transition by introducing modular project components in small pasts of business operations while checking for glitches and preparing fixes. Keep the original system running as a redundant fallback as the new project deploys smoothly.

Notes

1. Worst Supply Chain Disasters, John Gilmore, Supply Chain Digest, 2006 (http://www.scdigest.com/assets/FirstThoughts/06-01-26.cfm?cid=57&ctype=content).
2. http://hbswk.hbs.edu/item/4170.html.
3. http://scm.ncsu.edu/public/hot/hot040623.html.
4. http://www.wired.com/wired/archive/13.05/friedman.html?pg=2&topic=friedman&topic_set=Image 1.4: https://www.flickr.com/photos/76074333@N00/3062305870.

http://fortune.com/2012/07/30/amazons-recommendation-secret/.

https://nextbillion.net/from-smart-meters-to-water-atms-innovative-solutions-to-bring-water-services-to-rural-africa/.

https://www.treehugger.com/natural-sciences/new-shark-repellent-fishing-hook-will-minimize-accidental-shark-catches.html.

http://www.sharkdefense.com/other-research/smart-hooks/.

https://www.worldwildlife.org/stories/wwf-develops-a-new-technology-to-stop-poachers-in-their-tracks.

https://medicalfuturist.com/ten-ways-technology-changing-healthcare.

https://mashable.com/2014/01/21/amazon-anticipatory-shipping-patent/#wMg3yR2b9iqp.

https://www.theguardian.com/sustainable-business/2014/dec/18/technology-prevent-waste-food-developing-countries.

https://vcsolutions.com/4-ways-successful-companies-leverage-technology/.

https://www.cnbc.com/2018/06/25/how-one-mining-giant-is-using-technology-to-revolutionize-operations.html.

Nwankpa, J. K. & Datta, P. (2022). Leapfrogging Healthcare Service Quality in Sub-Saharan Africa: The Utility-Trust Rationale of Mobile Payment Platforms, *European Journal of Information Systems*, Vol. 31(1), https://doi.org/10.1080/0960085X.2021.1978339.

Nwankpa, JK, Roumani, Y. & Datta, P. (2021) The Role of Digital Business Intensity and Knowledge Management *Journal of Knowledge Management* (https://doi.org/10.1108/JKM-04–2021-0277). August 14th.

Datta. P. (2021). Cyberruse at the Cybergates: Technology, People and Processe. *ISACA Journal*, Vol. 6 (4), pp. 51–58.

Datta, P. (2021). Hannibal at the gates: Cyberwarfare & the Solarwinds sunburst hack. *Journal of Information Technology Teaching Cases*. https://doi.org/10.1177/2043886921993126.

Datta, P. & Nwankpa, J. Digital Transformation and Pandemic Crisis Continuity Planning during COVID-19, *Journal of Information Technology Teaching Cases*, Accepted.

Datta, P., Whitmore, M. & Nwankpa, J. (2021) A Perfect Storm: Psychological and AI (Technological) Antecedents to Information Bias Anchoring (IBA) in Social Media News, *ACM journal: Digital Threats: Research and Practice*. In Print.

Datta P, Walker L. & Amarilli F. (2020). Digital Transformation: Learning from Italy's Public Administration. *Journal of Information Technology Teaching Cases*, Vol. 10 (2), pp. 54–71. https://doi.org/10.1177/2043886920910437.

Datta, P. (2020). Digital Transformation of the Italian Public Administration: A Case Study. *Communications of the Association for Information Systems*, 46. https://doi.org/10.17705/1CAIS.04611.

Datta, P. & Diffee, E. (2020). Measuring Sustainability Performance: A Green Supply Chain Index. *Transportation Journal*, Vol. 59 (1), pp. 73–96. https://trid.trb.org/view/1682851.

Datta, P. & Hill, G. (2020). Antecedent Effects of Info Content on User Attitudes Toward Radical Technology-Brand-Extension: Info Content on User Attitudes of Brand Extensions. *Journal of Electronic Commerce in Organizations (JECO)*, Vol. 18 (1), pp. 36–58. https://www.igi-global.com/article/antecedent-effects-of-info-content-on-user-attitudes-toward-radical-technology-brand-extension/241247.

Datta, P., Peck, J., Koparan, I. & Nieuwenhuizen, C. (2018) Entrepreneurial Continuance Logic: The Interplay between Climate, Commitment, and Entrepreneurial Responsiveness, *Management Decision*. https://doi.org/10.1108/MD-05-2017-0537.

Rickett, L. & Datta, P. (2018), Beauty-Contests in the Age of Financialization: Information Activism and Retail Investor Behavior, *Journal of Information Technology*, Vol. 33 (1), pp. 31–49.

Diffee, E. & Datta, P. (2018), Cybersecurity: The Three-Headed Janus, *Journal of Information Technology Teaching Cases* (*Journal of Information Technology* sister Journal), Vol. 8 (1), pp. 161–171. https://doi.org/10.1057/s41266-018-0037-7.

Digital Transformation is different from **Digitization**.

Digitalization or Digitization is converting a product or a service from a physical product or service into a digital format based on bits and bytes that are stored in a computer, a server, or on a network such as the Internet. A physical book can be digitized into a PDF or an eBook format. Music from a record, tape, or CD can be digitized into an MP3 or AAC format. Photos can be digitized into JPG, PNG, TIFF, or other formats. Movies can be digitized into formats such as MP4. Digital formats offer multiple advantages over physical formats.

1. When products and services are digitized, there are no, in fact, negligible, **stocking or inventory costs**. A store has a limited shelf space to stock items. However, when the items are digitized, storing infinite items is the same as storing one item. Netflix can have one digital copy of Rogue One that can be streamed to a million different viewers on-demand without having to worry about stocking a million physical DVDs.

2. Digital products and services, because of their negligible costs, increase **profit margins**.

Profit margin is the percentage of sales that a company can earn as a profit. **Gross Profit Margin** is the percentage of profit on sales revenues once you deduct the cost of producing the product or service for sale. A DVD or Blu-ray costs much more to manufacture, ship, and stock compared to a digital version of the movie stored on a server. A Blu-ray disk might cost $2.50 to purchase, $0.50 to package, and $1 to ship and store for a total of $4.00. The Blu-ray might be sold for $16. Suppose the company sells 1000 movies. Therefore, the gross margin is equal to the (Sales Revenue—Costs of Goods Sold)/Sales Revenue or $12,000/$16,000 = 75%.

In comparison, storing a digital copy of the movie may cost $100 for storing a single copy that can be used millions of times without requiring repeated manufacturing and be sold for $16 for each digital download. Suppose the company sells 1000 digital copies. In this case, the gross margin is $15,900/$16,000 = 99.375% compared to 75% for the physical media. If marketing and other administrative expenses are the same, then the **net profit margin**, i.e., the percentage of net profit (after subtracting expenses, interests, taxes, and depreciation from gross profit), would be the same too. Digitization increases profitability because production and delivery costs are nearly zero while allowing more revenues.

3. Digitization allows companies unbundle. **Bundling** is a way by which multiple

Supplementary Information: The online version contains supplementary material available at (https://doi.org/10.1007/978-3-030-96929-5_14). The videos can be accessed individually by clicking the DOI link in the accompanying figure caption or by scanning this link with the SN More Media App.

products or services are combined together to be sold as a single piece. From bundling TV + Internet + Phone to bundling songs together into a single CD, bundling has been a popular strategy as a way to reduce fixed costs by combining multiple items. How many times have we purchased a CD album for 2 or 3 songs out of the 10 songs we paid for in the album? Digitization makes **unbundling** simple by allowing collections to be separated and sold per piece. iTunes or Google Play unbundle albums and sell songs and TV episodes priced and sold individually. Suddenly, a previously bundled CD album can be unbundled into single songs priced separately, thereby increasing customers' ability to purchase single songs for $0.99 on impulse rather than thinking about purchasing an album for $12. Moreover, digitization reduces and often eliminates chances of customers changing their minds and returning products. Once you have downloaded an eBook, song, or movie on sites like Amazon or purchased a subscription to Netflix, you cannot return the product as you might have for a physical good.

Digital transformation, on the other hand, is converting entire organizational processes into a digital process using various types of digitization For example, a library digitizing its books or a company digitizing its documents is an example of digitization but not digital transformation. Digital transformation is not just piecemeal digitization but reengineering and transforming an entire process.

So, digital transformation for the library would be reengineering and transforming the entire library book checkout process where a customer/user would be able to remotely login, find books in various formats (readable formats such as EPUB, PDF, mobi, audiobooks), digitally checkout the books on their computer or mobile device, and digitally borrow the book for a certain period, after which the books would be automatically returned to the server and the user would have to borrow them again. No more fees, lugging around multiple books, or waiting in checkout queues.

Digital Transformation was key to Netflix's success.

Netflix's Digital Transformation was not just digitizing movies and TV series but also creating a digitally transformed process where a user could subscribe to become a Netflix customer, digitally search through Netflix's entire catalog, and create preferences and receive recommendations. A subscriber can then create watch-lists based on personal preferences, watch media by streaming them across different devices such as Apple TV, Roku, smartphones, and computers, pause the media in one device and carry on another. Even more so, Netflix's streaming algorithms can modulate streaming media quality based on network speeds. When network speeds are slow, media is streamed at lower quality. So, Netflix has simply digitally transformed the entire movie-watching process and experience that is more than simply digitizing media.

COVID-19 and the Digital Transformation Pivot

COVID-19 Pandemic: The Genesis

The beginning of 2020 saw a gathering storm—Coronavirus. The Coronavirus (technically called SARS-CoV-2 and its infection is called COVID-19) is a mutant variety of the 2003 SARS-CoV (Severe Acute Respiratory Syndrome) and the 2012 Middle East Respiratory Syndrome (MERS).

By April 24, 2020, COVID-19 had infected more than 2.79 million people worldwide and killed 196,000 people across 218 countries.

COVID-19, a locally transmitted infection, particularly debilitating and fatal for people with immune disorders and the elderly with existing respiratory illnesses and pneumonia, has brought the entire world economy to its knees in a matter of weeks.

The Coronavirus name is based on the shape of the virus looking like a prickly crown. Coronavirus is highly contagious and, because, it is a novel virus, there is no herd immunity (herd immunity is our ability to build immunity through generations of exposure and vaccinations).

Coronavirus is typically transmitted from particles in the air and touch, especially from droplets from sneezes, coughs, and residual viral particles on surfaces and objects (there is still research going on in terms of how long the SARS-CoV-2 virus stays active on plastic, metal, and clothing). If a person touches a contaminated surface and then touches one's mouth or nose, the virus can be transmitted via mucous membranes, requiring face masks, gloves, ventilators, and respirators to reduce viral spread. The virus incubates in 6–8 days and then, if the carrier is vulnerable, displays symptoms, primarily high fever (>102 °F), fatigue, breathing difficulties, diarrhea, among others. Not all infected individuals show symptoms but can carry and spread the contagion like wildfire. Controlling the virus requires sweeping testing to identify infected carriers, regardless of symptoms.

With the new Coronavirus immune to existing antibiotics and analgesics, the search for a vaccination is still ongoing, given the unique, novel nature of the SARS-CoV-2. Each new virus, just like a computer virus, has a distinct and unique signature. Finding the signature requires using specialized test kits that require DNA and blood serum tests. With a sudden and unprecedented contagion, the number of cases rapidly surpassed the number of available test kits.

With the desperate need to control the virus and the improbability of being able to evaluate the entire population, countries around the globe are instituting and necessitating quarantines, public closures, and social distancing (maintaining a 6-feet distance to reduce susceptibility to the pathogen even if others carry it) as the only ways to reduce the contagion spread.

It is presumed that SARS-CoV-2 originated from consuming wild animals (that's why meat products meant for human consumption are treated with antibiotics to kill harmful pathogens) and is said to have originated in the Wuhan province in China (the epicenter) sometime in November 2019. With China being the epicenter of global trade, the virus spread fast, across every corner of the world. In an age of unfettered travel and open borders, tourists and company employees traveling and conducting business in China became infected and carried the SARS-COV-2 virus with them on planes and trains around the world, innocently interacting with many others as the virus transmitted itself through surfaces, sneezes, coughs, and physical contacts (e.g., handshakes). Prevention required quarantining, washing hands, using sanitizers, wearing masks, avoiding gatherings, and not touching high traffic surfaces. But none knew and none was any wiser!

One hundred years ago, the 1918 Spanish Flu infected 500 million and killing 50 million people worldwide, including 675,000 people in the US, 228,000 people in the UK, 5 million and 12 million in China and India, respectively. At that time, trains, a rapidly emerging transportation technology, were carrying hundreds of thousands of soldiers from World War I trenches in northern France to countries all across the globe, from returning US army soldiers in installations linked by rail to steamships carrying soldiers to south Asia and the orient.

Today, global trade carries contagion around the world!

Did you know that?

Wildlife and environmental conservation are critical in reducing future chances of another pandemic! A Zoonotic virus transfer from wildlife to humans was culpable for Europe's Plague, Africa's AIDS, and East Asia's SARS-CoV-2!

In December, Dr. Zhang, a Wuhan physician reported a viral pneumonia sample from a patient to the Chinese CDC (Center for Disease Control). The Chinese CDC reported the virus to be a novel (new) Coronavirus. However, the Chinese government decided to investigate the new outbreak at a seafood market thought to be the origin of the virus by suddenly closing the market down for "environmental improvement." The Chinese public was not warned of any outbreaks and people kept going about their businesses while infecting one another. On 19 January, more than 40,000 Wuhan residents attended an annual potluck, unaware that a silent virus was lurking among them.

On December 30, Dr. Li, a young Wuhan physician, turned into a whistleblower and posted on WeChat (a Chinese version of Facebook) that an unidentified Coronavirus infection was spreading. The Chinese government censured Dr. Li for rumormongering and spreading lies online. He contracted the virus and eventually died on February 7, 2020.

By 20 January, Beijing and Shenzhen started reporting COVID-19 infections. On February 2nd, 2020, COVID-19 had infected more than 40,000 people in China. By March 19, only six weeks later, China reported nearly 81,000 COVID-19 infections (pointing at a doubling effect every 6 weeks). With infections reaching the capital city and all around the country, China started massive quarantine efforts. China set up command for epidemic control (CEC) centers across cities. The Chinese Ministry of Education canceled physical school classes and postponed the entire semester. Tourists sites were closed, and travel curtailed. The primary focus was pandemic CCP by flattening the curve ("flattening" the curve refers to a plateauing effect on total number of COVID-19 infection cases, equating to a zero marginal increase). March 19, 2020, was the first day that China did not report any new COVID-19 cases.

In the face of the ongoing Coronavirus (COVID-19) pandemic, China's draconian response sealed off entire cities and halted all flow of goods and services. China employed technologies such as AI (artificial intelligence) facial recognition to monitor movements of people in and out of cities and public places. China used Internet filters to block any kind of fearmongering and hoarding of supplies. As draconian as that sounds, China's reasoning was based on its own existential crisis. If the virus spread, the world would stop purchasing and trading with China. It had to control the contagion and control it, fast. In the west, such a decision seemed bizarrely authoritarian.

China's instituting a severe quarantine and lockdown for 2 months was both necessary and severe, particularly for its own and the global

economy. With China's economy dependent on supplying raw materials and products around the world and worldwide economies in thrall of cheaper Chinese materials and goods, the Chinese Wuhan Coronavirus quarantine revealed the strange beginning of a tear in the globalization fabric.

The 2 months of the draconian but imperative Chinese quarantine is estimated to cost the Chinese economy a 10–20% drop in GDP. Chinese companies depend on exports and a quarantine forced all production to grind to a standstill.

As the Coronavirus endemic in Wuhan turned into an epidemic and then a pandemic by mid-March 2020, COVID-19 cases and deaths began surfacing beyond China in Japan, South Korea, Iran, and Italy.

COVID-19 infections sent shockwaves across the globe. The initial response was that of complacence—feeling that COVID-19 was an endemic contained within a region (e.g., SARS in South-East Asia and MERS in the Middle East). However, as SARS-CoV-2 spread to Iran and Italy with mounting infections and death counts, complacency turned into panic. Lombardy, Italy's most economically dynamic region and home to Milan, became the European Coronavirus epicenter. Italy followed China's quarantine policies and began a gradual quarantine, curfew, and economic shutdown to contain the contagion. France, Germany, Spain, and the rest of Europe, gripped by a fear of rapid contagion escalation, followed suit. Tourist sites were closed, travel bans were instituted, and cities, shops, restaurants, and bars turned into ghost towns.[1] In early March, the US and Europe began closing their borders, businesses, and travel.

---

[1](part of discussion) *There were interesting positive environmental effects from the economic shutdowns. At the beginning of the pandemic, China's manufacturing slowdown turned to be a blessing in disguise. China's pollution haze that commonly enveloped its large manufacturing regions such as Shenzhen, Beijing, and Guangzhou, slowly started dissipating, and air quality improved significantly! In Venice, where residents had long bemoaned the cost of tourism on its dwindling infrastructure and ecological damage, the shutdown suddenly saw its polluted water clearing with instances of dolphins returning to the lagoons. An economic slowdown became an environmental boon. Such are the fragility of the quality of life and the quality of living.*

The news of COVID-19 labeled as a pandemic, border closures, and economic shutdowns severely impacted the financial markets. Countries and regions with high economic activities and economic progress were also the ones hit the most by the contagion. The image points toward a shuddering reality—contagion follows trade.

The news of business closures and quarantine advice meant fewer people going out to shop, eat, and work. With more than 36% of US workers working in a gig-economy estimated at over $4.5 Trillion globally, the shock would be spellbinding. In a gig-economy, workers work ad-hoc contract jobs such as taxi drivers or driving for Uber or Lyft, perform service deliveries for companies such as DoorDash, Instacart, and Uber Eats, or work for hourly wages in retail stores, restaurants, and tourism, the estimated quarantine impact was simply reeling. Quarantine meant no earnings, no healthcare or sick-pay, and no income buffer. Thus, pandemic CCP is an imperative.

Social quarantine is equated to economic quarantine. With travel restrictions, the same airline companies that were posting record profits were suddenly flying empty planes and laying off employees. Hotels, casinos, movie theaters, tourist sites, and restaurants were deserted. Factories were closed from contagion fears. Less production meant less energy demand and oil prices plummeted to around $30 per barrel, igniting a price war with Saudi Arabia trying to undercut Russia. The US airline industry requested $50 billion as a government bailout with hotels and casinos in line for help. Face masks and hand sanitizers were in shortage, increasing the probability for contagion spread. Unscrupulous individuals started hoarding sanitizers and toilet paper supplies, extorting and profiteering from concerned and vulnerable people.

The stock market reacted ominously and spiraled into the sharpest economic downturn. By mid-February 2020, the Dow Jones index, S&P 500 index, and NASDAQ (sample indicators of the overall US Stock Market. Dow Jones tracks 30 representative stocks, S&P 500 tracks a weighted set of 500 representative stocks and NASDAQ tracks technology stocks) had reached records at 29.551 points, 3386 points, and 9817 points, respectively. Fears from an impending economic downturn from SARS-CoV-2 pummeled the indices and brought down the indices by nearly 40% in a matter of 3 weeks, pushing world economies into a bear market territory and signaling a recession.

In order to practice pandemic CCP, global governments had to step in. China, Europe, and the US have all pumped hundreds of billions in stimulus for helping pay for sick leave, quarantines, and business credit that can help businesses weather the downturn without massive employee layoffs and bankruptcies. By mid-March, Europe and the US Federal Reserve cut interest rates to nearly 0% to ease borrowing and lending.

Did you know that?

Even though global stock markets dropped precipitously after COVID-19 was declared a pandemic in 2020, technology firms and their digital transformation promises rebounded markets in a V-shaped recovery!

Digital Transformation for Crisis Management: Examples from the 2003 SARS Epidemic

During a crisis, multiple actors and stakeholders, from technology firms and governments agencies to general businesses and individual entrepreneurs, embark of providing public health technology solutions for CCP. For instance, during the 2003 SARS (Severe Acute Respiratory Syndrome) epidemic in China:

1. Sunday Communications, a Hong Kong mobile phone operator, used cellular tower location-information and SMS to alert subscribers if they were near areas with prevalent infections.

2. The World Health Organization (WHO) created collaborative GPHIN (Global Public Health Intelligence Network) for research collaboration across 11 laboratories in 9 countries. The GPHIN network used email and a secure WHO Web site to share investigation and clinical-trial outcomes along with

electron-microscope virus images, genetic material sequences, and SARS patient tissues from fatalities in real time.

3. Singapore public hospitals used RFID tags and hidden sensors to electronically monitor movements and interactions of every person in the building. All interaction data were stored in a database for 20 days (twice that of the 2003 SARS incubation period) for any contact-tracing all individual encounters with infected patients and personnel for rapid quarantining.

4. Alibaba launched a B2C marketplace for online shopping of much-needed items for the millions under self-quarantine. Since then, Alibaba has burgeoned to become the Asian equivalent of Amazon.com along with one of the largest FinTech (Financial Technology) firms in the world, with a market capitalization of more than $500 billion.

Thus, digital transformation during a crisis underscores a unique set of characteristics: (i) Modular, (ii) Collaborative, (iii) Secure, and (iv) Transparent.

1. **Integrate Modularity**: The COVID-19 pandemic highlights the decentralized and independent nature of solutions development and delivery all across the world. Various companies are fabricating their own versions of ventilators; global research centers and pharmaceutical firms are attempting their own SARS-COV-2 antigen testing and vaccines; organizations, agencies, and companies are offering independent "virtual" telemedicine and teleconsulting services; companies are using proprietary AI and machine learning algorithms for contact tracing, fever, and facial recognition; companies are creating their own digital content and platforms for digital delivery of education and entertainment. Yet, without modularity, each independent solution, however marvelous in its own right, is difficult to integrate to offer a single concerted approach.

   During World War II, independent technological innovations, such as radar and codebreaking, became truly impactful when they were integrated. This led to the Allied decryption of Luftwaffe sorties into the British Isles along with radar information to track and deter air attacks. Driven by the need to arrive at solutions swiftly and competitively during a crisis, governments and organizations need to use, reuse, invest, divest, consolidate, outsource, and integrate various independently crafted solutions.

   Modularity relies on integrating independent solutions by allowing *decentralization at the periphery and centralization at the core*. During crises, innovations and solutions occur independently, from pharmaceutical drug discoveries and ventilators to AI, machine learning, and E-commerce solutions. Each solution is modular, developed independently. In order for societies to harness these distributed modular solutions, countries and international agencies must be able to *dynamically scale their capabilities and integrate various modular solutions* to digitally transform a society for continuity during a crisis.

2. **Practice Synchronous Collaboration and Accessibility**: With multiple sources of data, modular innovation, and technologies at the periphery, there has to be an established mechanism to *synchronously access and collaborate across a globally distributed and decentralized model*.

   During the 2003 Severe Acute Respiratory Syndrome (SARS) epidemic in China, Sunday Communications, a Hong Kong mobile phone operator, used cellular tower location-information and SMS to alert subscribers if they were near areas with prevalent infections. The World Health Organization (WHO) created a collaborative COVAX (Collaborative Vaccine) during COVID-19 and the Global Public Health Intelligence Network (GPHIN) for the 2003 SARS. Both COVAX and GPHIN built research collaboration across multiple laboratories across many countries. Also, Singapore public hospitals used RFID tags and hidden sensors to electronically monitor movements and interactions of every person in the building. All interaction data were stored in a database for 20 days (twice that of the 2003 SARS incubation period) for any contact-tracing all individual encounters with infected patients and personnel for rapid quarantining. During the same period, Alibaba launched a B2C marketplace for online shopping of much-needed items for the millions under self-quarantine.

3. **Enhance Security and Reliability** to combat the epidemiology of fear: While collaboration and accessibility are crucial during a crisis, the need for rapid escalation and scalability requires a secure and reliable digital infrastructure. Security and reliability are exceedingly important to *maintain information integrity and deter any epidemiology of fear*, from cybersecurity threats (e.g., Zoom bombing) and fake news to runs on hand sanitizers, toilet paper, and essential PPE and groceries.

In China, residents are required to scan a mandatory QR "health code" on smartphones prior to using the subway or entering shopping centers to prove they are at low risk of having COVID-19. The QR health code combined with personal health data creates a reading that is either green (likely COVID-19 free), yellow (at risk of COVID-19), or red (likely COVID-19 positive). In Taiwan, the government "geo-fences" people under quarantine at home and in hospitals by continuously tracking their cellphone "location-data" signals and police enforcement.

4. **Balance Transparency and Privacy**: Crises create social idiosyncrasies, none more so than that of society's willingness to temporarily forego privacy for the sake of prevention and continuity. The proliferation of AI software embedded in location-services and contact-tracing apps along with CCTV (closed circuit televisions), thermal camera hardware can erode privacy. While society is willing to relinquish its privacy for safety, the opportunity costs are high unless managed

transparently. Pandemic CCP has to *ensure resilience by balancing transparency and privacy.*

Managing Digital Transformation: A 4IR Answer to the Future

The ominous emergence of SARS-COV-2 (COVID-19 hereafter) pandemic intensified society's needs for digital transformation. While digital transformation has been a growing industry and research catchphrase, with a plethora of definitions, strategy, and structure of digital transformations (refer to Vial, 2019 for a comprehensive literature review), lacunae remain in understanding unique digital transformation attributes during crisis continuity planning (CCP, hereafter).

A crisis is a phenomenon involving unexpected threats and uncertainty related to existing economic and operational structures including industry, health, labor, government, and society.

In recent years, societies and organizations have preemptively "digitally transformed" themselves to become industry and social trailblazers. Microsoft has dramatically reshaped its offerings using its "Azure" cloud platform. Amazon has built entire ecosystems based on its "Alexa" cloud-based voice recognition platform and its "AWS" web-storage and computing services. Even economies, such as Estonia, Norway, and Italy, have digitally transformed their government services. In 2019, Italy prototyped "IO" as a mobile-first digital transformation of their entire government services portfolio to increase access and reduce transaction costs from physical interactions.

How Asia Used 4IR to Manage COVID-19

In China, all residents during the COVID-19 crisis were required to scan a mandatory QR "health code" on smartphones prior to using the subway or entering shopping centers to prove they're at low risk of having COVID-19. The QR health code combined with personal health data, create a reading that is either green (likely COVID-19 free), yellow (at risk of COVID-19), or red (likely COVID-19 positive). In Taiwan, the government "geo-fences" people under quarantine at home and in hospitals by continuously tracking their cellphone "location-data" signals and police enforcement.

South Korea (formally, Republic of Korea) is the most connected country in the world (McCurry, 2020) and has used technology to balance transparency and privacy. With an area of 38,750 square miles home to 51.7 million inhabitants, South Korea has a relatively high population density of 1313 inhabitants every square mile. South Korea is affluent and industrialized with $46,451 per capita GDP (purchasing power parity) (2020).

Located in the south of the Korean peninsula, South Korea and China are dominant trading partners with more than $268 billion in mutual trade. In 2018, South Korea exports to China amounted to more than $162 billion and imports from China amounted to more than $106 billion (Global Edge 2020). With China as South Korea's largest trading partner, South Korea closely monitored the spread of the Wuhan virus.

South Korea (formally, Republic of Korea) is the most connected country in the world (McCurry, 2020) and has used technology to balance transparency and privacy. With an area of 38,750 square miles home to 51.7 million inhabitants, South Korea has a relatively high population density of 1313 inhabitants every square mile—compounding contagion dangers.

South Korea reported its first case in January 2020. Yet, South Korea has been able to manage the pandemic much better than its industrialized peers (Table 14.1).

South Korea received international praise for its handling of the pandemic based on process transparency. South Korea used 4IR mobile technology to converge multiple data points to tackle the outbreak with contact tracing. People who tested positive were asked to describe their recent movements, aided by GPS phone tracking, surveillance camera records, and credit card transactions. The government created two mobile phone applications to follow and monitor potential patients.

South Korea's process transparency was so well documented and openly communicated across the country that South Korea was the only country to hold an election in the middle of the COVID-19 crisis. Figure 14.3 depicts the South Korean government's process workflow for electoral voting under COVID-19.

Maintaining process transparency and establishing a culture of open communication about the transparency is central to digital transformation for successful CCP. Process transparency creates a culture of openness and trust, rather than suspicion and rancor. For example, the US government's initial perspective of COVID-19 as a partisan play against the incumbent president created a rift that summarily deepened partisanship and distrust, leading to unneeded, disruptive protests and an abounding of conspiracy theories. On the other hand, countries such as South Korea, New Zealand, Italy, the UK, and South Africa established a single, open line of communication that reiterated the need for testing and self-disciplined isolation, leading to lower partisanship, even amidst economic hardships and recessionary pressures (Fig. 14.1).

Table 14.1 COVID-19 Data at the height of the pandemic (Data from WHO as of May 7, 2020)

	Confirmed cases	Recovered	Deaths
Italy	215,858	96,276	29,958
Singapore	20,939	1712	20
South Korea	10,810	9419	256
Worldwide	3,388,936	1,076,390	238,937

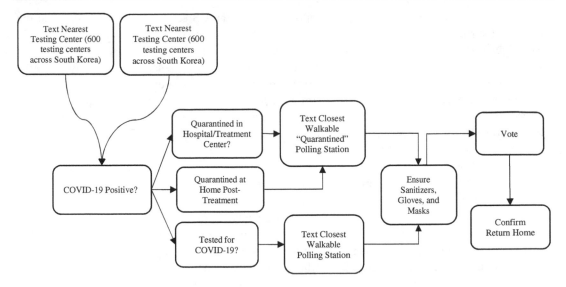

Fig. 14.1 South Korea's Electoral Voting process workflow during COVID-19

Singapore's COVID-19 responses also offer a case-in-point in modularity, collaboration, reliability, and process transparency. Singapore, a small island of 5.7 million people and 280 sq. miles, needed to take drastic measures. As the world's 3rd largest financial center, the 2nd largest gambling center, and one of the largest logistics hubs, Singapore economy relies on continuous traffic flow. More than 20% of Singapore's population of 5.7 million people are foreign workers with a vast majority been low-wage laborer with work permits.

Singapore recorded its first COVID-19 case on January 23, 2020. Immediately the country embarked on extensive tracing of contacts of each person infected and released detailed information about clusters of cases. Government websites shared the age, sex occupation as well as travel details and when the patient sought medical assistance. As a result, the country was able to limit the spread of the virus while maintaining a sense of normalcy on its streets. It was touted as an early success story and blueprint in containing the spread of COVID-19. Even the director-general of WHO Tedro Adhanom Ghebreyesus recognized Singapore's effective COVID-19 response when he notes that Singapore is "leaving no stone unturned." Yet, in a crisis of this nature where collaboration and integration across every segment of the society are vital to controlling the pandemic, Singapore's superior digitally enabled trace and track operations ignored certain segment of its community.

Did you know that?
Combining GPS locations and real-time threat data, countries use "Geo-Fencing" to highlight and caution areas of threats, warning people not to visit specific areas because of impending dangers, from terrorism to contagion!

The Business Side of Digital Transformation

The digital transformation pivot is not only reshaping society but also business. COVID-19 has pivoted digital transformation in society, from individuals to institutions to businesses. What is remarkable about this crisis is that it is a front-loaded health crisis and a back-loaded economic crisis.

E-commerce is one of the primary pieces of this "forced" digital transformation- from virtual meetings, virtual education, virtual business, and even virtual life. The digital generation is simply basking in their prescience.

But does this benefit everyone? The answer, of course, is a solid No. Overall, the impact for the entire economy may be Yes in the long term but remains a depressing. No in the short term.

Revenue generation is replaced by revenue sequestration! Digital transformation is driving revenues and monetization. There are two evolutionary categories: platform and channel. The question is, how quickly can companies pivot from a traditional to an alternative revenue model?

Businesses are rapidly switching channels to digital platform: Santana, an Angolan and South African production moved directly to Netflix which is rapidly moving in with its platform to compete and disrupt existing movie businesses. Disney's release of Mulan on Disney plus will serve as a precedent for movie production firms on whether developing a digital platform is more lucrative than the physical model! Other block-busters such as Christopher Nolan's Tenet were released in parallel, on both HBO Max, the online streaming channel, as well as in movie theaters.

Banks and Insurance are digitally transforming into FinTech setups! Companies like Robinhood are changing day trading and companies like Betterment are changing the way we invest long term in various mutual funds.

Digital fulfillment is becoming the channel of choice. Restaurants and newspapers are getting particularly involved in these areas. Restaurants are considering the opportunity costs of reducing inventory and fixed personnel and real estate costs and moving closer to online channels such as Uber eats! Media outlets are relying more on podcasts for news delivery with greater control of advertising choices—rekindling the retro love for radio! Only digitally!

Central to this evolutionary shift is the growth of a subscription model! Amazon wardrobe is challenging high street! Hello fresh is challenging restaurants! Even WSJ has a wine subscription model threatening bars and wine retail! Yoga studios are going online as is education.

But why?

First, the US economy, particularly, most the world economy is often service-heavy. Not E-commerce type technology services but more traditional services such as retail, travel, F&B, entertainment, and tourism. While those services often used to provide respite as quick employment, the same services were the first to be tossed by the wayside to protect life over the economy. In April 2020, at the height of pandemic fears, BLS reported nearly 38% unemployment in hotels and food service workers. Statistics are even more dire for Lyft and Uber drivers. Globally, approximately 100 million workers were unemployed in these high-risk travels and tourism-related services, with a $1 Trillion drop in global GDP.

However, during the same period, Uber Uber's food delivery service experienced a sales growth of 54% and Uber's revenue grew 14% year-on-year. This highlights how food service can maintain continuity using E-commerce as the digital switch. In the long term, food service industries might use this crisis as a way to trim their employee and other operational fixed costs and lean more toward a pickup and delivery-model rather than a physical-service setup (much like what Starbucks has been doing with more drive-throughs and online orders in lieu of seating spaces). With more viral work and binge-worthy streaming TV shows, eating ins are looking more enticing. Of course, as the weather cools, patio seating will become more of an issue and interior-renovation operational costs might put-off a lot of restauranteurs from traditional dining and look toward more virtual delivery channels. After all, restauranteurs still need to cover their costs. So, restaurant might use E-commerce to pivot in the long term, but service industry workers are likely to pay, interim.

Second, physical retail is the hardest sector hit by the pandemic. With High-street deemed as high-risk, online retail, driven largely by Amazon Prime, has completely upended the status quo. The already languishing mall stores with frightfully high fixed costs, are now in their death throes with empty isles and higher per-head operational costs (more COVID-19 distancing-based costs with fewer customers). It is but natural that Amazon.com is contemplating buying out the once-giants JC Penney and Sears stores and converting them into fulfillment warehouses.

There, the die is cast. Whatever post-COVID-19 normalcy looks like, traditional mall stores and their services will have to bury their pride, and perhaps their existence.

But demographics and cultures can create challenges. Consider Italy and Iran. Italy is an interesting case because Italy has one of the world's oldest population distribution with more than 23% aged 65+ . Coronavirus is particularly debilitating for older people and Italy has fallen prey to this very phenomenon. More than 40% of Italian deaths are for Italians aged 80+ and more than 30+ for Italians aged 70–80. Moreover, winters in Italy, especially with an older residential infrastructure (lacking central heating and airflow), there is a greater probability for fevers, colds, and respiratory/bronchial issues, thus compounding the situation. It is quite likely that, as summer sets in, cases will fall.

Iran is a slightly different case. There are certain similarities with Italy such as greater incidences of fevers, colds, and respiratory/bronchial issues owing to an under-developed residential infrastructure. Certain Iranian idiosyncrasies add to the debacle, including (i) a lack of well-developed healthcare infrastructure (including testing infrastructure such as test kits, isolation facilities) (some Iranians might argue that sanctions have denied them access to medicine) and (ii) political ignorance and a general disdain for logic under the existing regime that seem to taint every negative occurrence as a foreign conspiracy and scourge, notwithstanding practicing religious norms such as mosque attendance where thousands rub shoulders in close proximity.

Transition Exercise

How will Technology shape Globalization?

Purpose The purpose of this exercise is to help you apply your understanding the intersection and confluence of globalization and technology. The assignment will help you examine bottlenecks and roadblocks related to implementing emerging technologies across the world while paying close attention to issues and concerns that differentiate efficient versus effective strategies.

Assignment: Globalization was driven by cheap labor and technology, but technology, particularly AI and robotic automation, is creating a new world order where the same cheap human labor in China and India may be left for naught. Assume you, as a think-tank analyst, have been asked to assess the impact of technology on globalization. *Come up with two opportunities where technology can make globalization blossom and two threats where technology can make globalization wither.* Explain your choices.

Managing a Large-Scale Digital Transformation: An Italian Case Study

Companies and governments have embraced digital transformation as the elixir of the twenty-first century. But what impedes digital transformation? This case study article is based on data gathered from field research with the Italian Parliament and the Digital Transformation High Commissioner's Office in the Ministry of the Interior. The case surfaces the context, challenges, and solutions for large-scale Public Administration (PA) digital transformation. The case study highlights how PA digital transformation in a large democracy is never a technical but a socio-technical solution. Successful digital transformation needs to understand, address, and change socio-political and socio-technical mores that often define the culture.

Underscoring this research is an analysis of digital transformation within the Italian Public Administration. Public administration (PA) encompasses all governmental and public services including services provided by federal, regional (e.g., states and provinces), municipalities, and local agencies. The Italian PA, with 60 million people, 8000 municipalities, and 22,000 local administrations, highlights how a digital renaissance is a preface for innovative disruption challenges. The digital transformation case uses Italy as the backdrop and *Team Digitale*, a team of talented individuals embarked on building public administration (PA) efficiencies and rebooting Italy's digital innovation footprint, as the protagonist. For granularity, the case focuses on two digital transformation projects, *ANPR*, a unified public registry for all Italian residents, and *PagoPA*, a universal digital payment platform for public administration.

This case shows best practices and challenges faced when trying to tackle a mega-project across an entire economy. The case offers digital transformation recommendations, generalizable across any global democracy. The case analysis and recommendations bring to light how, contrary to private organizations, institutionalizing a disruptive innovation in a democratic country at a time of fiscal austerity highlights interesting decision-making issues and facets.

A .Genesis

Risorgimento (Resurgence)

The spring dawn over Rome seeped through its baroque splendors like a resplendent cloak, unveiling 28 centuries of architecture, art, and history. Rome was once *Caput Mundi*, the capital of the world, a host to the Caesars, the Popes, artists, and architects and innovators, such as Bernini, Bramante, Michelangelo, Vitruvius, and Galen.

Italy was experiencing growing numbers of Ricarica and Tesla EV (electric vehicle) charging stations facing historic facades and architecture. Modernity and antiquity side by side, sometimes in harmony and sometimes in discordance.

Italy's history has long been one of wonder and woe. Modern Italy is a new-found country. Italy was primarily a patchwork of independent feudal nation-states (see Fig. 14.1) vassals to and ruled by Spanish, followed by Austrian monarchs. It was Napoleon that created the first albeit short-lived Italian Republic (Repubblica Italiana) in 1802, consisting of northern Italian regions (called Cisalpine) with Milan as the Capital.

After the fall of Napoleon in 1814, divisive feudalism returned with various kings and the papal states entrenching regionalism (Fig. 14.2).

The *Risorgimento* (resurgence) unified Italy as a single territory in 1848 and turned a nation state in 1861. Since 1946, after World War II and the fall of Mussolini, Italy became a parliamentary, constitutional, multi-party democratic republic where the President is de jure or largely ceremonial and the de facto powers are vested in the Prime Minister. Executive power is vested in the Council of Ministers and the Prime Minister is referred to as the President of the Council of Ministers.

Fragmentation

Yet, Italy's multi-party system is fragmented. Since World War II, there have been 61 governments (recent government turnovers in Appendix). The sheer number of political parties has often led to policy fragmentation and stalemates, plagued by shifting coalitions, constant compromises, and deal-making. There are active center-right and center-left coalitions with more than 10% votes, 5 major parties each with more than 4% votes, more than 25 minor parties with 1% or more votes, and more than 35 regional parties. Recently, there have even been calls by parties such as Lega Nord (Northern League) (once Lega Nord per l'Indipendenza della Padania (Northern League for the Independence of Padania)), to secede northern Italy. Although Lega Nord currently renamed itself Lega in 2018 to appeal to all Italian voters, its origin and secessionist philosophy highlights the intrinsic divisions within Italian regions spread across communes, incomes, and urban/rural differences.

Politics often plagued Italy's Public Administration governance. A typical Italian approach for managers of public bodies, and also of private companies, is to sweep away the initiatives of previous management and start again. Since transformation initiatives are likely to require a timeframe which is longer than the duration of the appointment of managers, the result is either a set of ambitious projects which are not

Fig. 14.2 Historical Italian Feudal States (Wikipedia)

completed or small, not sufficiently ambitious initiatives pursued with a tactical approach.

Although Italian had long been the language across the Italian (Apennine) peninsula and one can read Dante and Petrarch written around the thirteenth century, local dialects, practices, and customs have prevailed for centuries. The coming of the television in the 1960s made the present-day Italian language the lingua franca. Yet, differences remain. Some southern Italians view northern Italians as cold-hearted, mechanical people only interested in money. Similarly,

some northern Italians view southern Italians as poor and lazy with no interest in progress. During the period of Italian stagnation from 2001 to 2008, southern Italy faced a 7% drop in GDP while northern Italy clawed itself out of stagnation with a 2% GDP growth. This sharp contrast in fortunes across the peninsula led to a migration of southern Italians into northern Italy. The impact was multifaceted. First of all, southern Italy, already impoverished and agrarian, lost a large part of its population and its associated tax revenues. Southern Italians, facing economic

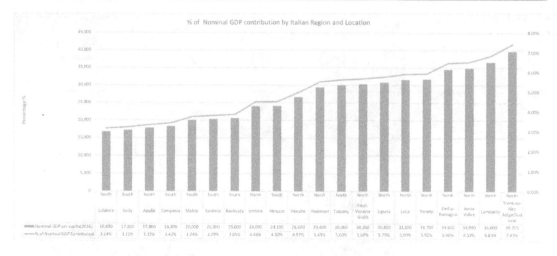

Fig. 14.3 GDP Contribution by Northern and Southern Italian regions

hardships and high unemployment, started having fewer children, compounding the population crisis. At the same time, northern Italians felt that the influx of southern Italians in their midst threatened their livelihoods and their lifestyles (Fig. 14.3).

Eurozone and the Sovereign Debt Crisis

The arrival of the twenty-first century and the establishment of the Euro ushered in a world of change. Italy was being forced to reconcile with a competitive world marked by technology and globalization. Italy traded in its 142-year old currency (1861–2002), the Italian Lira, and adopted the Euro. As a part of the Eurozone, Italy would enjoy less currency fluctuations and currency risks, more transparency and greater access to its markets, allowing for more lucrative trading opportunities.

But there was one catch. The Euro, by itself, would not bring economic stability and prosperity. Countries would need sound management, adhering to Economic and Monetary Union (EMU) rules and reducing anticompetitive labor and legal practices. The

Maastricht Treaty required Eurozone members to control gross government debt (the accumulation of previous government deficits) to GDP ratio to remain under 60%.

Then came the 2008–2012 European sovereign debt crisis. The European sovereign debt crisis compounded the malaise of the Italian Economy. Since 2008, globalization and cheap credit had turned Italy, along with Iceland, Portugal, Greece, Spain, and Ireland, profligate. Italy, Greece, and Ireland were each carrying government debts more than 120% of their GDP.

The Euro, by itself, would not bring economic stability and prosperity. Countries would need sound management, adhering to Economic and Monetary Union (EMU) rules and reducing anticompetitive labor and legal practices. The Maastricht Treaty required Eurozone members to control their "gross government debt (the accumulation of previous government deficits) to GDP ratio" to remain under 60%. Both rules required reining in government spending and increasing revenues from productivity and taxes (Datta, 2019).

However, in Italy, governments started getting larger and more inefficient, funding overgenerous pensions, while foregoing competitive technology and resource investments in an age of

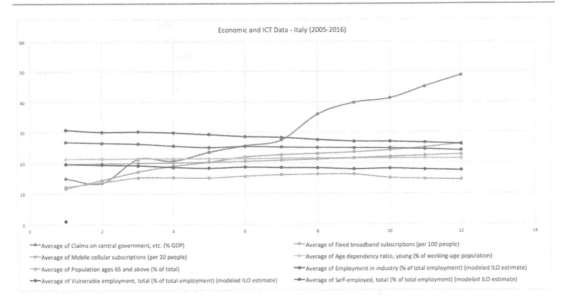

Fig. 14.4 Italy economic data based on OECD data

global competition. Productivity was low and tax evasions became rampant.

By the time the 2012 European debt crisis waned, the Syrian war began. Italy saw itself right at the center of a mass-migration doldrum. Millions of undocumented immigrants, some fleeing the Syrian war and some stowaways from other areas, poured over the borders into southern Italy, trying to find a way into Europe. The fragile southern Italian economy further felt the pinch as migrant refugees overwhelmed the already-strained economy and infrastructures.

By 2019, Italy's public debt was 132% of its GDP, more than 30% of Italian youth was unemployed, 5 million Italians (more than 8%) were living in poverty, and more than 22% of the population was aging. The situation was getting worse. High unemployment and low birth-rate along with an aging population that was living longer required more pension and welfare spending, adding more to the public debt burden. In 2019, the government rolled Italy's 2011 pension reform retirement age from 67 years back to 62 years, further tipping an already unsustainable pension and welfare system that is second highest in the Eurozone, after Greece (Fig. 14.4).

The Social-Political Landscape

While historical and economic matters were troublesome, the most pressing issues stymying public income and economic inflows even in the face of growing public debt were sociological. The two primary sociological issues were a flagrant eschewing of taxes and corruption.

Tax Evasion

In addition to such external upheavals is the internal Italian culture of tax evasion and a culture of PA opacity leading to corruption. Between Napoleon's fall and exile in 1814 until the end of World War II, the hostility between the Catholic Church and the state created an atmosphere where states' taxing of people was derided, creating a culture of rampant tax evasions. In 1814, Italians mobbed, beat, and killed Giuseppe Prina, Italy's finance minister and first tax collector under Napoleon's unified Italian Republic. Nearly two centuries later, in 2012, after the new Prime Minister Mario Monti announced a crackdown on tax evasions, mobs attacked and bombed tax agencies (Hein, 2018).

To date, tax evasion remains frightfully commonplace, underscored by a culture of "only fools pay" (Plumer, 2011).

Gig-economies that revolve around temporary or short-term work are particularly rife for tax evasion. From street vendors peddling wares to laborers hired off the street, evening entertainers or bands booked for a restaurant gig—all contribute to the tax evasion malaise.

Tourism largely involves a multitude of gig-based businesses. The gig-economics of the Italian tourism sector are often based on quick, small cash transactions that are very difficult to trace and audit, creating a shadow economy where millions of euros exchange hands in cafes, restaurants, hotels, and street peddlers without being reported as revenues. Gig-economies often rely on peer-to-peer transactions that are exceedingly difficult to audit and trace. Transactional opacity accentuates the shadow economy, creating a deadweight economic loss in terms of formal unemployment statistics, and eventually tax revenues.

As a result, the shadow economy, with under-the-table cash exchanges and people driving Ferraris and Porsches without declaring any income, dearly costs the Italian economy. In 2011, the Washington Post (Plumer, 2011) reported that the Italian government was losing €300 billion per year to tax cheats, a sum that could pay off Italy's €2.2 trillion debt in less than eight years (Datta, 2019). It was imperative that Italy build a mechanism to deter income obfuscation.

Did you know that?

Tax evasion is a culture among many corrupt regions, from India to Italy, where it is believed that "Only fools Pay!" In these regions, cash transactions are more common, from bribes to payoffs, because cash cannot be traced while digital transactions can. In 2011, the Italian government lost €300 billion per year to tax cheats!

Corruption is connected to fragmentation and bureaucracy. The complexity of delivering some services, e.g., think of some important authorizations, gives power to public officers to streamline or block processes, providing ground for corruption.

Corruption and a Lack of Trust

Corruption costs Italy around €80 billion, amounting to nearly 4% of Italy's GDP, each year (Transparency International 2017). Out of 180 countries, Transparency International (2018) ranked Italian corruption 52—a dismal rank at par with Grenada and Oman.

The 1992 *Mani Pulite* (clean hands) pointed fingers at widespread PA corruption investigations, referred to as *Tangentopoli* (bribe city). It started with Judge Di Pietro finding Mario Chiesa, a member of the Italian Socialist Party, guilty, with Chiesa's party chastising him as a villain. Chiesa felt the chastisement a betrayal and turned whistleblower, beginning the *mani pulite* investigation that implicated more than 500 politicians and thousands of PA officials in indiscriminate bribery and fraud charges across everyday transactions, financing, and government-run energy utilities such as Eni. The *Mani Pulite* investigation led to the dramatic electoral defeats and disappearance of four major political parties and sent a shockwave across Italy. With more and more politicians and PA officials fearing indictment, the 1994 Silvio Berlusconi government relaxed corruption scrutiny in Italian companies and converted criminal charges into administrative misdoings. Even Berlusconi's brother, Paolo, had admitted to corruption crimes. Upon taking office, Berlusconi relaxed anti-corruption and accounting fraud laws, leading to widespread money-laundering, scams, and fraud schemes across the country. In 2012, Berlusconi himself was convicted of and voted out of the Senate because of Tax Fraud, banning him from seeking political office of four years.

Fig. 14.5 Italian Society: Trust in Institutions (*Data* Demos [2011–2018])

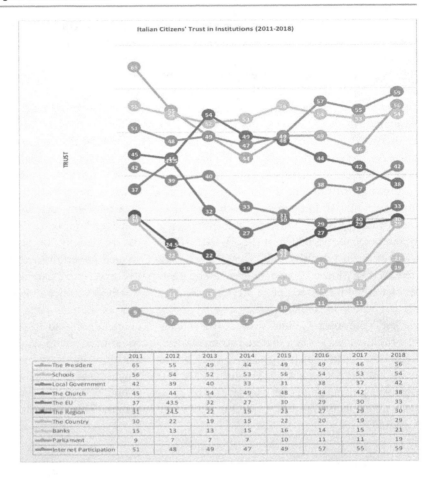

Italian Citizens' Trust in Institutions (2011-2018)

	2011	2012	2013	2014	2015	2016	2017	2018
The President	65	55	49	44	49	49	46	56
Schools	56	54	52	53	56	54	53	54
Local Government	42	39	40	33	31	38	37	42
The Church	45	44	54	49	48	44	42	38
The EU	37	43.5	32	27	30	29	30	33
The Region	31	24.5	22	19	23	27	29	30
The Country	30	22	19	15	22	20	19	29
Banks	15	13	13	15	16	14	15	21
Parliament	9	7	7	7	10	11	11	19
Internet Participation	51	48	49	47	49	57	55	59

Italians signaled low trust in political parties, the Italian PA, and the Parliament. Italian public sector projects take nearly six years to complete and cost four4 times more than that of the rest of Europe. Corruption drains public funds (Scaglia, 2010) and increases profligacy. It comes as no surprise that two-thirds of Italians do not believe that anti-corruption measures work, perhaps a subliminal reason for tax evasions (Fig. 14.5).

B. Digital Transformation: Transparency & Combating Corruption

Tax evasion and corruption were costing the Italian government billions and austerity was knocking hard at Italy's doors. In the past two decades, Italy's per capita income growth has been nearly zero. Yet, Italy's population is aging and Italy's Age Dependency Ratio (ratio of 64 + to 15–64 working age population) is more than 56% (World Bank, 2018), reflecting pension costs surpassing working age contributions.

Digitally transforming Italy's PA would present the only way out of the continuing and upcoming doldrums.

In 2010, the EU proposed digital transformation across all EU member states as a way to combat internal inefficiencies and promote PA transparency. The digital transformation plan built upon the 2009 German Digital Agenda, the European Commission forwarded the Europe 2020 agenda based on "smart, sustainable, inclusive growth" by raising employment, R&D, energy efficiency, education, and income.

The fragmentation of the Italian Public Administration system added to existing PA inefficiencies. Italy's PA system is composed of a complex hierarchy of intertwined bodies and at times has unclear and overlapping competences. As a result, services for citizens are sometimes based on processes not fully integrated and supported by automation, personal data are replicated in several, frequently inconsistent, databases. It comes as no surprise that the Italian PA hosts nearly 160,000 databases and 11,000 data centers across the peninsula.

Smart growth needed a knowledge and innovation economy. Economic growth via digital transformation was at the heart of it. Invigorated by the positive evaluation of the EU 2011–2015 e-Government Action Plan that highlighted increased sharing of best practices across member states and increased public service access, the EU proposed the creation of a "Digital Single Market" (European Commission, 2010). A Digital Single Market was estimated to create hundreds of thousands of jobs and over €415 billion to the EU (European Commission, 2017). EU members independently set their national strategies and plans for the "Digital European Agenda."

Digital Transformation and a Digital Single Market could transform an economy in several ways.

Transparency and Accountability

Digital transformation creates a two-way street of transparency between government and taxpayers alike. The government's new-found ability to uncover more tax information utilizing a central data platform magnifies not only their view of taxpayer information, but in turn, magnifies taxpayers' ability to access public data and to receive government reports with added reliability, frequency, and depth. Government reports which were once impossible to assemble due to lack of human computing bandwidth or were unreliable due to lost paper trails, suddenly can come to life with digital tools. A nimble digital platform also possesses the capability to rearrange existing data with timely answers as the public asks new questions regarding the tax system. This contributes further toward enhancing system transparency and trust with fewer

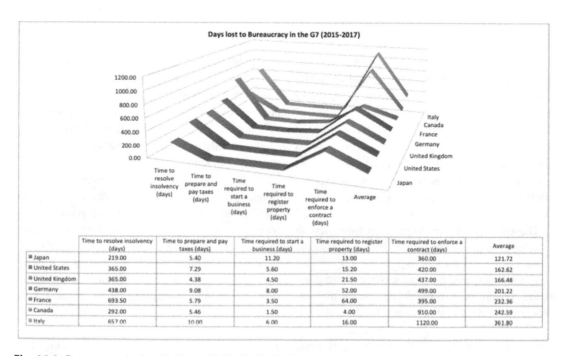

	Time to resolve insolvency (days)	Time to prepare and pay taxes (days)	Time required to start a business (days)	Time required to register property (days)	Time required to enforce a contract (days)	Average
▦ Japan	219.00	5.40	11.20	13.00	360.00	121.72
▦ United States	365.00	7.29	5.60	15.20	420.00	162.62
▦ United Kingdom	365.00	4.38	4.50	21.50	437.00	166.48
▦ Germany	438.00	9.08	8.00	52.00	499.00	201.22
▦ France	693.50	5.79	3.50	64.00	395.00	232.36
▦ Canada	292.00	5.46	1.50	4.00	910.00	242.59
▦ Italy	657.00	10.00	6.00	16.00	1120.00	361.80

Fig. 14.6 Bureaucracy in the G7 (*Data* OECD [2015–2017])

hidden corners in a tax collection system (Fig. 14.6).

Greater transparency in reporting of tax revenue collection is accompanied by greater government accountability to the population. This accountability based on the use of access to a trusted central data platform can take many forms including more informed conversations regarding subjects such as the share of tax burden borne by specific taxpayer groups. This type of dialogue shines brighter light on the often-elusive subject of creating a fair tax system. It can also mitigate the effect of "fake news" when the same trusted data source can be referenced by all, rather than leaving reliance to a variety of other untested sources. A well-respected data source has the potential to calm the viral Internet storms to a large degree. In effect, transparency encourages higher participation of taxpayers in both the tax system design as well as spending of tax revenue.

Digital transformation also increases privacy, security, and accountability. Consider EU's GDPR (General Data Protection Regulation) dealing with consumer data privacy. Digital transformation allows for an easier and simpler way to manage consumer data privacy, often impossible if paper-based. Given that it is much more difficult and costly to manage the privacy of a piece of paper compared to digital information that is cheaper and easier to offer secure access, thereby increasing reliability, transparency, and trust. Paper-based transactions are vulnerable to pilferage, misplacement, or loss, opening up vulnerabilities and compromising consumer privacy. A digital trail is relatively more secure and transparent than a paper trail. While digital information might be vulnerable to cybersecurity breaches from a single point of access, paper-based information is much more vulnerable to multiple points of access. In short, digital transformation increases privacy, reliability, and transparency in comparison with traditional paper-based systems, therefore increasing consumer trust.

PA Revenues

Public sector digital transformation carries with it an implicit expectation that it produces a broader tax base, predicated upon its capability to identify additional income sources more readily. This capability allows it to carve major inroads into tax evasion from previously hidden income sources. In specific, self-reported income arising from a self-employment typically has a lower reporting incidence compared to other forms of business. Digitization can also enable quick account cross referencing and simpler access to additional corporate income data on self-employed individuals, as well as on VAT revenues.

Digital transformation also addresses concerns related to the growing gig-economy. While gig-economies can exacerbate the incidence of income under-reporting, the growing digitization of the gig-economy is remedying issues surrounding income obfuscation and tax evasion. Digital transformation of a gig-economy forces transparency thus increases income reporting. For example, instead of taxi drivers dealing in off-meter cash transactions, rooms being let off the books, or cash exchanging hands for goods and services, digital gig-platforms such as Uber, Airbnb, and M-Pesa have forced transactional transparency on an otherwise opaque culture. Over the past decade, digital gig-economy business models (e.g., Airbnb, Uber, Doordash, M-Pesa) use digitization to easily integrate peer-to-peer incomes with federal tax agencies that simplifies tax reporting and adds transparency to an otherwise set of opaque shadow transactions that have plagued tax agencies in the past.

Did you know that?

Threatened that digital transformation increases transparency and competition, Rome's taxi union posts misleading placards reading "It is illegal to use Uber in Rome!" when it isn't true!

This expanding model of income generation is best captured by a powerful combination of a central company that digitizes multitudes of small transactions and transmits them to a public sector tax agency that possesses the digital ability to record the income. In contrast a traditional government reporting system would more haltingly identify these small digitized bases of employment revenue.

However, such digital transformation efficiencies disrupt the status quo. For governments that are overly entrenched in traditional workflows, such disruptive innovations are often threatening to both the government and the public, leading to eschewing digital transformation. For example, it is quite common in Rome to find placards reading "It is illegal to use Uber in Rome." The placard bears no semblance of truth (Uber is legal in Rome). Instead, the placard signals resistance by the Taxi drivers' union, fearful of Uber's disruptive innovation. Similarly, in Beirut, Lebanon's capital, hailing a taxi is a particularly convoluted process involving a series of hand gestures, timing, and customary haggling. Such a convoluted process is so tied into the fabric of the culture that Uber has had a difficult time establishing itself, owing to entrenched cultural norms as a protectionist veil against the increased transparency that Uber brings.

Yet, countries that can successfully adopt digital transformation to punctuate its traditional and bureaucratic entrenchments find the change most welcome. Governments that can change their own operational culture stand to win from digital transformation.

For example, Estonia's digital X-road platform coordinates across the private and public sectors to transmit and share information at no cost which alleviates many reporting issues. An Estonian Uber driver's individual earnings can be electronically registered by Uber Technologies and in turn, automatically recorded by the Estonian government's tax platform. Hence digital transformation encourages a rise in levels of income reporting by self-employed individuals. This capability allows a government to increase its tax base through reporting simplification for

the taxpayer while it also introduces "digital enforcement."

Digital transformation begets "digital enforcement"—resulting in higher tax revenues without the need to institute time draining and possibly unneeded tax policy changes (Gupta, 2018). India, facing decades of PA inefficiencies and tax evasion, implemented a series of reforms via PA digital transformation and demonetization, leading to an increase of 80% in tax returns over the four-year period from FY 2013–2014 to FY 2017–2018 (Chandrasekhar, 2019).

The capabilities of digital transformation extend beyond just income tax revenue increases to VAT revenue. Multiple types of VAT digital projects have already produced remarkable results. According to the Intra-European Organisation of Tax Administrations, the gradual installation of New Generation Fiscal Machines (NGFM) from 2008 through 2012 in Armenia saw fiscal revenue growth from approximately ֏550,00 dram in 2012 to ֏825,000 dram in 2015 (Pashayan, 2018). Other countries have experienced similar gains in VAT collections with digital transformation. The Federal Tax Service of Russia (FTS) found that their VAT collections grew from ₽2.45, ₽ 2.66 to ₽3.07 in billions of rubles from 2015 to 2017 after instituting mandatory digital VAT reporting. This amount increased despite economic fluctuations that may have predicted otherwise (Volvach, 2018).

Reduce Inefficiencies

Greater efficiency through digital transformation travels in from many avenues on the roadmap of government systems. There is time savings for existing work and quicker communication, both stemming from digitization of mundane tasks. In the UK, Her Majesty's Revenue and Customs (HMRC) began their digital journey in 2013. As of 2018 automation of tasks had taken place for 56 processes and 14 million transactions had been completed by these "robotized" processors (Collard, 2018).

Thanks to increased processing capability, AI, and machine learning, a more accurate and encompassing tax database leads to efficiencies in the audit function. The benefits of increased efficiency will continue as Big Data comes into play. Large sources of accumulated data will empower greater use of data analytics as tools to predict expected incomes and identify discrepancies.

The taxpayer realizes added efficiencies as well through time saving filing methods, a quicker response time from government, and perhaps most important, quicker refunds.

Estimated savings for developing countries reveals vast benefits, as they have been projected at 1 percent of GDP or $220–$320 billion on an annual basis. The share translating to government would be approximately 0.5% of GDP or $105–$155 billion with the remaining going to businesses or individuals (Gupta, 2017).

In the case of Estonia's X-road platform, it was reported in 2016 that increased efficiencies from the platform would save 820 traditionally defined (nondigital) work years. In addition, a single occurrence savings is projected at 2% of GDP resulted from the introduction of digital signatures (Gupta, 2018). For Estonia, a 2% savings on its 2018 GDP of $26 billion amounts to approximately $520 million in yearly savings.

However, in Italy, bureaucratic encumbrances have further maligned Italian PA digital transformation initiatives, often to officers' and citizens' disappointment and chagrin. As a consequence of the inefficiency of public bodies and of the misalignment between the timeframe needed to successfully implement a transformation project and the timeframe needed for existing schedules, end users have often been disappointed by the digital initiatives and do not push for transformations and public officers lose confidence on digital transformation. This condition results in a self-reinforcement, where it becomes more and more difficult to change. It is a phenomenon commonplace in manufacturing companies where misalignment between the technology adoption timeline and existing manufacturing contract fulfillment timeline leads to disillusionment about technological transformation. Thus, when one or more digital initiatives fail, companies lose confidence in the technology and refuse to participate in further technological

initiatives, thus contributing to the overall's company's failure in keeping up with the changing times.

Increase social and environmental sustainability: Inclusivity (social) and Sustainability (environmental).

The Internet has been hailed as the "great equalizer" and Internet-based access underscores digital transformation. Digital transformation is an involved process based on tenets of access, reliability, transparency, and trust—tenets that engender social and environmental sustainability. Access is offered via an Internet-based networked economy accessible by anyone, anywhere, and anytime via a networked, mobile device (e.g., a smartphone, tablet, or laptop). Reliability stems from the network maintaining connectivity (or uptime) and consistency of content over time and space (e.g., when traveling). Transparency is rooted in the ability of the user to trace a transaction (e.g., a query, a process, a payment) from start to finish. Finally, trust refers to a users' sense of security that allows the user to participate and contribute, often an aftereffect of transparency and a sense of security.

Digital transformation is inherently inclusive, allowing anyone with a connected device to access and transact anywhere and anytime. With 24/7, location-independent, and demographic-independent access, digital transformation bridges socio-political, economic, rural–urban, communal, and even gender-based divides, increasing social sustainability.

Digital transformation also ushers in environmental sustainability by replacing traditional, predominantly paper-based resources and transactions with digital transfers. Digital transformation offers paperless transactions. The US federal government spends $440 million on paper printing, of which one-third are never used (Ende, 2018). Traditional bureaucratic processes are replete with non-value added activities (e.g., having a paper form printed, being signed in triplicate, photocopied, stamped, and restamped, visits to multiple agencies) and corresponding resources needed to staff these activities. Non-value added activities increase wastes and thus increase costs. Five decades ago, the New Yorker

Magazine (1970), in discussing Italian bureaucracy, remarked that the cumbersome Italian state machinery needed as many as 50 signatures from different officeholders prior to making a simple decision. Half a century later, the bureaucratic shadow still envelops many Italian public administrations. Collecting 50 signatures requires resources, travel, and emissions. Converting archaic physical activities to digitized processes can vastly reduce environmental footprints while adding transparency and speeding up the entire process. For example, the use of digital signatures to replace physical signatures not only increase environmental sustainability but also increase efficiencies, transparency, and trust.

For Italy, digital transformation was a likely solution to rebuild trust in the government—trust that was sorely lacking. In the process, Italy's PA digital transformation would increase transparency, tax revenues, efficiencies, sustainability, and serve as an equalizer to usher in a digital renaissance.

C. Italy Digital Transformation: The Birth of Team Digitale

Despite earlier attempts to advance a digital transformation agenda to address and mitigate Italy's problems of tax evasion, corruption, and lack of PA transparency, there had not been much progress.

Beginning in 2016, under the auspices of Prime Minister Matteo Renzi, *Team Digitale*, a newly formed team of talented individuals embarked on rebooting Italy's public administration efficiencies and the country's digital innovation footprint.

Team Digitale was led by Diego Piacentini, one of Amazon.com's top executives, *pro bono*. Piacentini began by recruiting top talent from the private sector unencumbered by deep political entrenchments. He called them "missionaries" whose job would be to deliver a series of digital transformation solutions effectively and efficiently for the Italian public and the Italian public administration.

Team Digitale, with Piacentini and his "missionaries," launched a series of digital transformation initiatives. Their Mobile-First approach decided that the smartphone would be the device of choice and the cloud the venue of choice. With a once-only principle, no redundant system would be built, saving the government millions of dollars. Team Digitale's systems development followed an Agile development philosophy that was quick, modular, and interoperable. All government systems would transparently connect and talk to each other using open-source APIs. Data and information would be analyzed and freely shared. Collaboration would be paramount.

Scale and Scope

The new-found team, Team Digitale, would sow the seeds of digital transformation that would positively affect the lives of Italy's 61 million people across 8000 municipalities and 22,000 local administrations.

The scale and complexity of the digital transformation project were overwhelming. The Italian PA had 25,000 government websites, 160,000 databases, and 11,000 data centers spread through 8000 municipalities and 23,000 local agencies. The government employed 32,000 IT workers with 18,000 in central public administration (PAC) and 14,000 in local public administrations (PAL). Another 10,000 IT contract workers were spread across local and central governments, altogether amounting to a €5.7 billion yearly IT budget. However, with such complexity and distributed, autonomous IT projects carry the burden of burgeoning cost and resource redundancies and waste.

ANPR and PagoPA Projects

Team Digitale started redesigning and relaunching ANPR, PagoPA, SPID, and CIE. ANPR, the national digital resident registry; PagoPA, the single payment system; SPID, the digital identity system; and CIE, an electronic ID card—all built a common and secure data platform and standards with transparency and interoperability.

ANPR was the national resident population registry that was a part of the digital transformation operating system. ANPR would create a single, unified Italian resident identity by stitching together information across multiple, often redundant, identities spread across 8000 municipality databases, and tens of thousands of PA forms. ANPR started off with 1 municipality that had migrated their resident data in September 2017. Beginning with only one registered municipality, ANPR expected 4000 of Italy's 8000 municipalities and 45 million of Italy's 60 million citizens digitally registered by 2019 (Medium, 2019).

PagoPA was the centralized financial platform meant for every form of PA payments and disbursements. Any Italian could use PagoPA to pay for everything from traffic fines to taxes, licenses, and utility bills. The platform would also allow any Italian to receive any disbursements from the government including tax returns and pensions. The PagoPA platform was convenient and secure. PagoPA had built an ecosystem consisting of all major credit cards, banks, payment networks (e.g., Visa), and payment providers (e.g., PayPal). Accessing PagoPA required a secure email credentialing and authentication process that PagoPA would use to validate identity prior to financial access. PagoPA transactions had grown from a mere 150,000 digital government transactions by 2015 to 3.5 million transactions by the first four months of 2018, with more than 430 payment service providers covering 90% of Italy's banking system (Team Digitale, 2019d).

The SPID project had issued 4.9 million digital identities since September 2016 and 94% of municipalities had issued 5.5 million CIEs (electronic ID cards). For SPID, the annual growth rate in released identities from 2016 to 2017 was 422%. (Team Digitale, 2019a) and 12 million CIE cards (2019b).

Even more interestingly, Team Digitale had achieved their ambitious undertakings using merely 63.2% (€9.3 million) out of their €14.7 million allocated budget. This was exceptional in a country where projects were often rigged, mismanaged, and over-budgets.

Team Digitale had integrated their PA digital transformation solutions into a single e-Government platform called *io* (Italian for *me*) as a mobile-first one stop government services platform (Fig. 14.7).

On October 30, 2018, Team Digitale received a vote of confidence from Italy's political stakeholders in the form of a vote affirming that its existence would remain constant until December 31, 2019, despite party leadership changes. Previously Team Digitale had operated as *prorogatio*, but the October 30, 2018, vote secured a mandate for more than a year of continuity.

In a country which has had sixty-one governments since World War II, this mandate stands out as no small feat. The mandate's significance demonstrated itself in August 2019 when Team Digitale carried on despite a government upheaval which led to revisions in party alliances and almost to a snap election after just fourteen months of a coalition in power. The coalition split up but Prime Minister Conte survived.

In spite of the political flux, the government deemed Team Digitale's contribution important enough to be scheduled for absorption as a permanent department within the Prime Minister's office, regardless of political colors and succession. Italy had realized that PA digital transformation could save Italy's financial distress and increase transparency and accountability to battle corruption and raise trust in the public sector.

With the digital solutions designed and put into production, coordination, awareness, and adoption were the next stages for successful PA digital transformation. The results were laudable thus far. The next push was based on comprehensive adoption and implementation.

Team Digitale was helping a new renaissance take shape, meant to unify Italy via digital transformation of its public administration.

D. **Challenges**

Digital transformation of an entire country's public administration is not a smooth ride. Emerging technology is rapidly changing society's operations. Phone taps are replacing mouse clicks and users demanded simplicity,

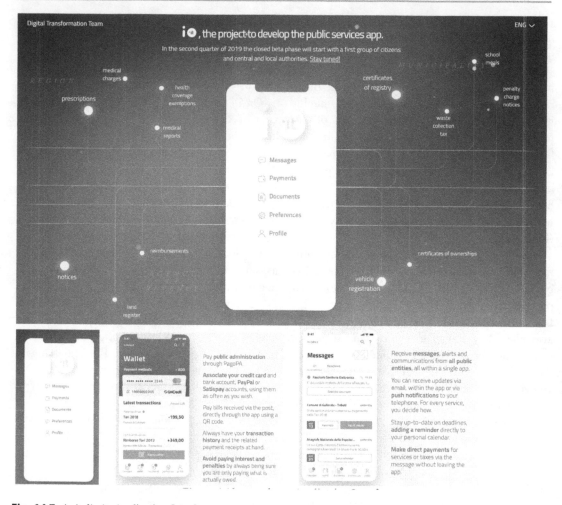

Fig. 14.7 *io.italia.it*: Application Interface

availability, and access. Successful PA digital transformation needs to be simple, available, and accessible in order to spur public awareness and interest. But, how does a country build public awareness and interest in digital transformation? Lessons learned from such a digital transformation highlights how digital renaissance is a preface for innovative disruption challenges and ways to overcome them.

Socio-Cultural Disruption

Digital transformation, while ushering in tremendous efficiencies, is a disruptive innovation that challenges precedents and the status quo, compounded by the scale and complexity of the PA digital transformation project. The Italian PA digital transformation encompasses 60.5 million Italians across 8000 municipalities and more than 20,000 communes. Complexity stems from a variety of political loyalties, cultural mores, and traditions existing in a democracy where every person, region, and culture has a voice. With a diversity of voices entrenched in deep historical differences and traditions, the Italian PA is a complex tapestry of conflicting opinions and beliefs. Even today, there are deep divisions between the *mezzogiorno* (8 southern Italian states) and northern Italian states owing to historical alliances and acrimonies. The disruptive effects of digital transformation are more

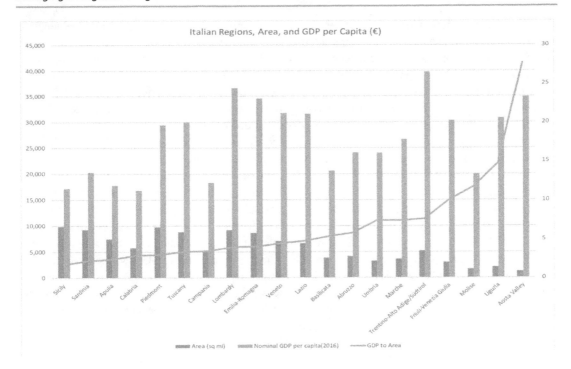

Fig. 14.8 Italian regions, area, and GDP per capita

pronounced in certain regions, cultures, industries, and people. While a difference in digital transformation in industries is a preface to the digitally transformed company or industry holding a competitive edge over its slower rivals, the issue is much more precarious for the PA. In PA, digital transformation sinks or swims with the entire country in tandem. Digital transformation in the PA is a failure unless all Italian regions, all communes, and the entire Italian population adopt the digital transformation (Fig. 14.8).

Political Upheaval

An added challenge associated with government related projects lies in successfully navigating an often-changing political landscape. The required continuity involved in a large multi-year project risks buffeting winds if political leaders and parties change frequently and choose to install either new project goals, policies, or personnel. Italy had a bitter history of PA leadership turnover and political infighting. Between 1945 and

2019, Italy has had 61 different Prime Ministers leading the government. With a slew of coalitions vying to gain power, the EIU (2017) referred to Italy as a "flawed democracy" because of "a high degree of fragmentation and instability" that precipitates "short-lived coalition governments." As shown in Fig. 14.7, it is not surprising that Italians had the lowest trust in the Italian Parliament (11% in 2017 and 19% in 2018) and Italian banks (15% in 2017 and 21% in 2018). A challenge for the Italian PA's digital transformation is engendering the Italian population's long-lost trust in the PA apparatus that is seen as promoting digital transformation.

Digital Literacy

The third challenge lies in the Italian population's lackluster digital literacy and engagement. Italy suffers from a digital skills gap touching both end users and civil servants. The Italian population is getting older and with limited digital competences. On the other hand, public officers, both managers and employees, are not capable of promoting and supporting the adoption of digital solutions. As a consequence, some offices are crowded by citizens requesting documents or asking for services that could be easily delivered online. This picture is not homogeneous across Italy and is left to the initiatives of local public bodies.

According to the 2018 e-Government Benchmark Report, Italy had medium levels of overall government digitization (around 58%), slightly below the EU average. Italy's Open Data and Private Sector Digitization are very close to the EU almost in line with European average. But, in Italy, digital skills, technology usage, network quality, and connectivity were low, issues that could inhibit adoption and effective use of digital PA services by citizens. Italy had the lowest adoption of e-Government digital services (less than 18%) in the EU28 (28 EU countries), with only 22% of Italians interacting online with the public administration, compared to the EU average of 53% (Fig. 14.9).

The Digital Economy and Society Index (DESI) data offers some interesting insights. Italy surpassed the EU in its open data platforms and fixed broadband coverage, with tremendous improvements over the EU in 5G readiness. With PA digital transformation focusing on a mobile-first philosophy, Italy's 5G readiness is tremendously useful, notwithstanding Italy's relatively lower ultrafast broadband coverage. Italy has more document digitization (pre-filled forms) and more access to more e-health services than the EU.

However, looking beyond Italy's excellent technological infrastructure, challenges emerge. Italian users appear to be keener on using mobile devices to watch videos rather than for Internet search, shopping, or banking, revealing greater interest in entertainment over utilitarian outcomes. In terms of e-Government users, EU surpasses Italy by nearly 73%. Further, with 30% fewer Italian ICT (Information and Communication Technologies) specialists and nearly 35% fewer female ICT specialists compared to the EU, the data signals undertones that hint of a lack of digital workforce preparedness and a lack of adoption, despite a strong ICT infrastructure and service and data services. In short, the 2019 DESI figures point toward Italy's robust technology infrastructure but tepid technology adoption and use.

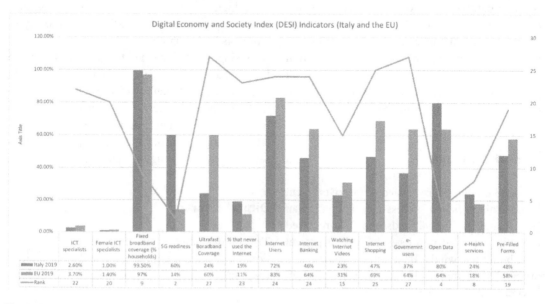

Fig. 14.9 Digital Economy across Italy and the EU

Did you know that?
Around the world, countries need policies and socio-cultural innovations to increase female participation in 4IR technology areas!

E. Recommendations

What is interesting is that Public Administration is, in some respects, similar to a private sector multinational. Italy, a part of the EU, is required to follow EU mandates, one of which is digital transformation. Yet Italy is a sovereign democracy in its own right, open to public discourse changing politics. A similar thread runs in a multinational company where each international division holds a certain level of dependence and some level of autonomy and in some cases, corporate fiefdoms. This interesting tension of dependence and autonomy, similar to an EU country, creates a more complicated tapestry of technology, governance, and society that must be understood and addressed for digital transformation to succeed.

1. Strategic Flexibility: Manage Deep and Broad Change

Two clients, together, define the success of Italy's digital transformation. Focus on the two client groups as two distinct customer segments: the PA and the Italian Public. However, each client needs a slightly different approach for awareness and adoption.

PA digital transformation requires managing deep and broad changes, awareness and access across politics, society, economy, and technology.

Countries such as Estonia had made major leaps in PA digital transformation. However, the character of Estonia as a country was vastly different compared to that of Italy. Estonia, once a part of the Soviet bloc, is considerably homogenous and its sense of arising as a nation-state owes from its independence from Soviet control after the fall of the iron curtain. Estonia is a small country with 1.3 million people and minimal administrative, cultural, historical, or regional complexities. There is a greater sense of commonality and unity in history and tradition across all Estonians compared to Italy, once patchwork of independent kingdoms forced to unify under a banner.

Digital transformation depth refers to ensuring that digital transformation buy-ins cover all PA levels and layers, from the federal government in Rome to regions, provinces, municipalities, down to the smallest Italian commune (*communi*). Every PA level and layer, from the largest municipalities to the smallest commune, must be committed to the philosophy and action of digital transformation.

Digital transformation breadth refers to ensuring that digital transformation covers the wide range of population across every demographic, sociological, and cultural divides. Even if a small part of the population fails to join the digital transformation, the digital transformation has failed. In a country, public administration services are public goods and must be accessible to every member of the population. Even if a small part of the population cannot access or use PA digital transformation services, the government, and thus taxpayers, will have to bear the costs of supporting and maintaining a parallel set of services.

Italy was facing both promises and pitfalls. Italy's Open Fiber broadband provider was using Nokia to bring 1 Gbps (Gigabit per second) fiber-to-the-home (FTTH) connections to Clusters C and D (Italy's demarcation of small towns and rural areas). Mobile phone subscriptions in Italy were high but a digital divide remained. Digital divide refers to the difference between population that have Internet availability and access compared to the population that is deprived of Internet availability and access. In 2017, Italy had one of the highest levels of digital divide in Europe with only 69.5% Internet access (ISTAT, 2018), perhaps owing to the fact that nearly 55% of Italians live in towns of less than 50,000 people and 18% living in towns of less than 5000 people. Italy also suffered from one of the lowest university education rates in Europe. Moreover, after the European sovereign debt crisis, nearly 4.7 million Italians were living below the poverty line.

Italy is on the cusp of a digital reunification. The key to unification is the ability to renovate thinking and the way of doing things. The PA's flexibility needs to be dynamic. The local population trusts its local government the most—the local government has its fingers on the pulse and can be the agent of change. Every locale is different, epitomized by decades, often centuries of beliefs and traditions. PA can't simply ask them to suddenly substitute their tradition in the name of progress. That can destroy trust.

If local governments feel that central government is simply going to dictate canons, they might suppose that digital transformation is dictatorial, rather than democratic, even with our elemental philosophies of openness, transparency, and sharing. So, I suppose, we need to standardize at the core and customize at the periphery! In democracies, successful PA digital transformation needs buy-ins from both the public and the PA officials.

2. Maintain an Apolitical Stance

Public administration digital transformation governance and championship require a more cautious approach than private companies (Fig. 14.10). While, in the private sector, close ties between projects and top executives as project champions are applauded and encouraged, such close ties can become burdensome in the public sector. For PA, a strong and direct link between PA projects and politicians (akin to executives) as project champions can be perilous. Especially in democracies where administrations come with an expiry term, strong project affiliations often come with a cost. If an administration is presumed to be too closely associated with a project, the demise of an administration may equate to the demise of the corresponding project (talk about Obamacare).

Team Digitale members established an apolitical stance as a result several key factors. One factor lies in the fact that a large portion of its members are not politicians and come to the group from work in the private sector. It is not unusual for them to express an interest in returning to the private sector after a period of service. This sends a strong signal which indicates they do not plan to stay in the political arena and potentially compete for positions with career politicians.

Diego Piacentini, the first High Commissioner for Italy's digital transformation, served as a notable example of these practices. Diego's 2016 appointment as High Commissioner of newly founded Team Digitale sent a strong signal. In specific, his work was pro bono with a self-imposed two-year "term limit" meant to signal

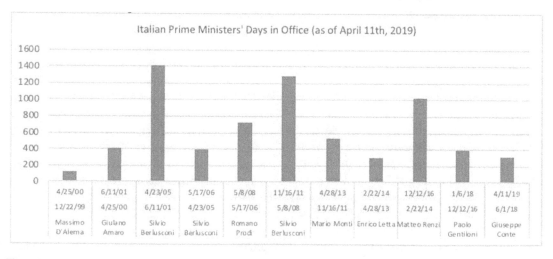

Fig. 14.10 Italian Prime Minister Turnover (*Source* Britannica [2018])

his interest in improving Italy rather than nurturing a political ambition.

Another signal that those with Team Digitale are not seeking political gain is their willingness to sacrifice and work alongside other government departments for the betterment of Italy. Many members showed this commitment as they took pay cuts when they moved from private to public sector positions.

3. Phase in PA Digital Transformation

When implementing a solution, a go-to-live approach is often mired in too much complexity implemented too soon without a buffer. Returning to the ACA (Affordable Care Act or Obamacare) analogy, the US launch of ACA was a go-to-live initiative without any underlying buffers or fallbacks. Complexity of the go-to-live project pushed project costs 1600% over budget, from an anticipated $100 million to $1.7 billion. Upon launch of the ACA's healthcare.gov platform with no phased transition, healthcare.gov was fraught with issues and service interruptions, leading to backlash toward the system. It is estimated that only 1% of interested users were able to sign up for the government-mandated health insurance in the first week. Of the 1% that could access the site and sign-up, it was reported that a part of the users' sign-up information was incomplete.

Team Digitale was prudently phasing in Italian PA's digital transformation.

Technology implementation has to be conducted with the culture and context of the deployment in mind. The priorities of people in Milan or Florence may not be the same priorities of people in Cortina, Aosta, Rimini, or Lecce. Technology, per se, is meant to reengineer for efficiencies. Yet, efficiencies may not matter to many parts of the population where time has a different meaning and connotation.

There are many small towns and provinces where people enjoy their old way of life. They go to a post office or a government agency to sign or deposit a paper because that is where they find community. The post office or the government agency is the community's waterhole. There, they meet with their friends, talk about their lives and living, exchange pleasantries, and renew their social connections. There, efficiency is secondary, and community is primary. Using digitization to remove that tradition can be viewed as tantamount to the destruction of the social fabric!

In such a culture and context, how should you practice digital transformation without threatening the social fabric? One way is to practice **phased transitioning**. Instead of trying to radically change the culture and the ways of life in these communities, *Team Digitale* practiced incremental adoption. Instead of a go-to-live approach that would require every municipality and every individual to change over to the digital platform on a specified date, Team Digitale allowed PAs to gradually transition over to ANPR and PagoPA. To ease the transition, Team Digitale embarked on creating technical and social conduits to phase in the transition.

On the technical front, Team Digitale began by creating SDKs (software development kits) and APIs (Application Programming Interfaces) for the ANPR and PagoPA platforms. SDKs (or devklts) are complete software packages including libraries, code, documentation that other developers can use to customize software to meet their requirements. Team Digitale's SDKs were made available to every PA so that each PA could install the software and customize the software to integrate it with their existing PA software and services. APIs are code that allow one program to access and update another program without needing to read each other's code or write any code from scratch. Team Digitale's APIs allowed any PA to link its own data (independent of the program it was written in originally) to the ANPR and PagoPA platforms.

On the social front, Team Digitale tried to ensure that digitization did not radically change the way people socially interacted. If a person felt more comfortable going to the post office or the tobacconist to pay for government and public services, Team Digitale made sure that such an "analog" process was not disrupted for the person. Instead, the post office or the tobacconist would be the intermediary that would help set-up and link the person's account and payment (e.g., check routing and account, credit cards) to the PagoPA platform.

Team Digitale's phased transition was working.

ANPR started off with 1 municipality that had migrated their resident data in September 2017. But, by March 2019, of the 8.000 municipalities in the country, we have 1765 transitioning to ANPR. From 1 to 1765 municipalities in 18 months. As of mid-October 2019, 31 million of Italy's citizens and 3600 municipalities had migrated to ANPR, with an open-access SDK (software development kit) and an API for easy municipal connectivity to the central ANPR registry (Team Digitale, 2019). ANPR expected 4000 of Italy's 8000 municipalities and 45-million of Italy's 60 million citizens digitally registered by the end of 2019 (Medium, 2019).

PagoPA transactions had grown from a mere 150,000 digital government transactions by 2015 to 3.5 million transactions by the first four months of 2018, with more than 430 payment service providers covering 90% of Italy's banking system. Growth has continued progressively, with the number of total transactions up to 59 million as of mid-2019 and transactions during the first months of 2019 up over 466% compared to the same time period in 2018.

In addition to *Team Digitale's* awareness and adoption initiatives, *Team Digitale* considered leveraging existing data collected from two specific sources: one for the Italian public and one for the Italian PA.

Since 2011, Italy had successfully launched its National Health Information System (NSIS) as the national information framework for Italian patients. The NSIS database carried a lot of patient information. Instead of asking people and PA to refill the data from scratch, Team Digitale could reduce redundancies. Team Digitale could leverage and build upon the existing NSIS information and work with healthcare clinics and hospitals to collect the rest of the data that was needed and was not already in the NSIS system.

Similarly, for Italian PA and businesses, PagoPA could leverage the e-invoicing database and infrastructure, especially given that, since January 2019, e-invoicing was mandated for all Italian government contracts.

Successful digital transformation should leverage existing adoption and digital infrastructure.

4. Create and Incentivize Digital Literacy Vocational Education

Italy had been steadily reforming its digital infrastructure. Italian digital services' mobile friendliness grew by 88% in 2018 from 2017. Italy was proactively building ultrafast, yet affordable Internet access. Data protection laws are at par with EU's GDPR. What Italy lacked was a digital workforce.

Digital literacy is the preface to building a digital workforce. Education is the first step! The digital divide is on the front of digital literacy, not digital device ownership. Italy has a lot of smartphone subscribers and is still in need of digital literacy.

Digital literacy and education were central to success. The Italian government was trying to spur digital transformation. Italy needed to elevate its technology education, Diego Piacentini had once recommended moving *Team Digitale* from Rome to Milan because of Rome's lack of good IT talent. Italy needed more technological skills. Italy had been graduating a paltry 14 out 1000 students in STEM (Science, Technology, Engineering, and Mathematics) and there seemed to be a very low appeal of vocational education in these areas.

Digital transformation needs access to a labor force trained in technology and medicine. If demand for digital services grows but not the supply of a qualified labor force, labor costs will rise. Italy needed to produce more students that know how to design and build technologies. Not just digital natives but digital visionaries, designers, and developers.

Did you know that?

One of Southern Europe's biggest struggles is creating a digitally proficient workforce that can break away from tradition and embrace innovation!

A 2018 OECD report says that salary satisfaction for digital and IT skills in Italy is less than in other countries. Italy offers a 1.7% hourly wage premium for digital skills compared to a 3% premium in the OECD. That makes attracting top IT talent more difficult and decreases student interest in joining the digital workforce.

The OECD report remarked on how 30% of Italians use E-commerce compared to 50% in the OECD. Higher education increases digital participation (The Economist Intelligence Unit, 2019) and Italy needed more "skilled" digital natives and more digital inclusion in Italy's current population. Digital literacy education and vocational training were paramount.

The Italian government had realized the issue and was trying to address this problem. The 2015 National Plan for Digital Schools (*Piano Nazionale Scuola Digitale*) had begun teaching students digital skills at primary school. The Ministry of Education has started this reform called "La Buona Scuola" to impart digital and computer science skills to prepare them for a digital future and contribute to Italy's digital performance. But there were two issues. First, the program was in its nascency and too early to observe results. Secondly, Italy urgently needed a digital workforce and time was a luxury. Italy needed more vocational education to bridge the gap between supply and demand. Moreover, Italian women lagged 12% behind Italian men in digital participation. Italy needed more women in STEM education.

Bridging the gap is more difficult in practice than in theory. Italy's education system is highly unionized and bureaucratic, making it resistant to quick changes. A digital workforce is needed to keep Italy competitive in the digital world where every footprint is digital. But, in order to achieve that objective, Italy needed quicker solutions.

Not everybody in the workforce could afford to return to University. There was a need for on-demand education over the Internet that could be offered in small digestible modules, starting from the fundamentals of digital literacy to more advanced training to prepare people in various aspects of digital literacy.

But how should the Italian government spur both digital literacy and adoption? One way could be to use the €60 billion in estimated savings to incentivize Italians. €60 billion for 60 million Italians amounts to $1000 of savings per person. With $1000 in potential savings, offer €300 to each Italian in two parts: €150 in value of basic digital literacy education credits for each Italian. Even with a €300 incentive, the government will be saving €700 per person.

Additionally, Italy is the second biggest beneficiary of European Investment and Structural Funds in the 2014–2020 period, with €44 billion injected to spur Italy's economy. 70% of the funds are allocated to the less-developed southern regions of Campania, Puglia, Basilicata, Calabria, and Sicilia. There are bank loans available to local governments for digitization. Beginning in 2019, *Cassa Depositi e Prestiti*, an investment bank, will offer loans to local governments to speed up digital transformation.

The Italian PA could use digital transformation savings with the EU Cohesion fund of €40 billion to "bundle" vocational digital literacy training, available as a free educational credit.

There was not just an extrinsic "financial" incentive but an intrinsic incentive beyond educational benefits. With a changing world and society becoming more environmentally conscious, digital transformation can be promoted as a case for **environmental sustainability**. Less paper use means fewer wood being used. Less physical visits, commuting, shipping, and mailing documents mean less emissions and greenhouse gases.

The Italian PA could engage the younger Italian millennial and environmentally conscious parts of population to adopt and promote digital transformation as not only increasing efficiency and transparency but also reduce environmental damage.

5. Build Trust and Transparency across Government and Grassroots

Vox populi, vox Dei (the voice of the people is the voice of God). But, in a democracy where people's voices matter, if the "voice of the people" does not trust the government's digital transformation, all is lost. Trust in has to begin at the grassroots. All change management begins with trust.

User Experience

Digital transformation's ultimate aim is benefiting the public, increasing efficiencies in their daily dealings with the government, and putting their tax dollars to use. If the general population find digital transformation useful and the user experience simple, the grassroots population will buy into the digital transformation philosophy.

Team Digitale began by writing articles and having academics research on how ANPR, PagoPA, and SPID can reduce the customary bureaucratic maze of paperwork and government office visits, thus aiding PA efficiencies, transparency, and tax allocation toward non-bureaucratic matters. Research by venerable, august Italian universities, could increase awareness trust about PA digital transformation among the population. But how many people would actually read these findings? Team Digitale needed to choose the appropriate delivery channel such as newspapers for a certain population segment, social media for another population segment. Reach was essential to building trust.

Bureaucratic Friction

Trust in PA digital transformation also requires simplifying bureaucratic friction. Bureaucracy decreases efficiency, increases complexity, and costs and reduces trust. Italian PA digital transformation, meant to reduce bureaucracy, still relied on too many agencies.

Along with education, digital transformation needs political stability and regulatory flexibility. Italy's *Digital Administration Code (DAC)* is adding rigidity when we need flexibility. Some rules are good but too many laws are tantamount to micromanaging.

The Italian government, based on the provisions of Article 52, paragraph 6, of the Digital Administration Code (Codice dell'Administrazione Digitale, CAD), establishes digital regulation in a world where technology changes faster than policymaking. Agency for Digital Italy (AgID or L'Agenzia per l'Italia Digitale) then uses CAD and guidance from the Prime Minister's office to set the national digital transformation agenda. AgID, in addition to the Italian Government's 2014–2020 Strategy for Digital Growth, also tries to increase digital literacy and participation among the elderly, immigrants, small businesses, and disabled citizens. Team Digitale would then try to design and deliver digital transformation solutions. Each effort takes time and adds more to the already burdened bureaucracy. Some of the efforts were redundant rather than complementing. Italy's PA digital transformation governance model needed restructuring for trust and transparency.

DAC was coming up with technical rules and regulations that were quickly becoming obsolete. DAC needs to be flexible and neutral to keep pace with fast-paced technological change. DAC needed to focus more on open-citizen communication and data-integration rather than regulating the unknown. Successful digital transformation needs to eliminate data silos and create a single data platform.

Transparency

Transparency is a preface to building trust, especially for traditionally profligate governments famous for engaging in closed-door decisions. Team Digitale approached every aspect of their development with a keen eye toward transparency. Team Digitale followed an open-source philosophy. Instead of choosing a large and prominent vendor such as Microsoft Azure or AWS (Amazon Web Services) to build their projects, Team Digitale assembled their solutions from scratch using open-source solutions (e.g., the LAMP stack (Linux, Apache, MySQL, and

Python, PHP, and Perl)). Moreover, every piece of software that Team Digitale built upon the open-source platform was made available to the public on GitHub for added clarity and scrutiny. Transparency was a rare phenomenon in a country often plagued by traditions of black-box decisions and closed-door negotiations. Companies, such as Ferrari, Lamborghini, Prada, Ferragamo, are still privately held with little to no transparency of their finances or operations. In such a landscape, a transparent digital transformation is a breath of fresh air. Between 2016 and 2019, the Italian government has changed hands four times, but Team Digitale's transformation has consistently stayed on in every government's ledger books. That is an attestation for transparency.

Team Digitale reduced complexity by making processes more modular, and therefore, more manageable. Here, modularity is key. Large and complex projects have high costs of failures, unless noted early on. But how can an issue be traced before it blows out of control and costs? Team Digitale broke large projects into small, understandable, and manageable chunks—a centerpiece towards building agility, figuring out problematic instances at the onset, and keeping an eye on both time and costs. After all, time is money and errors tend to magnify themselves unless nipped in the bud. Modularity makes finding the bud easier and identifying root causes early on. Team Digitale's developments followed such a modular agenda in order to contain costs and deliver their digital transformation projects on time and under budget (Fig. 14.11).

Building more local participation is an imperative. 42% of Italians trust their local government compared to 19% trust in the Italian Parliament. Only 59% of Italians participate via the Internet in some way. Less than 25% of Italians use the Internet to interface with the government and less than 10% use the Internet to complete government forms online. Although participation grew from previous years, the numbers are dismal. The numbers are lower in southern Italy compared to the north. However, southern Italians trust their local governments more, perhaps because of entrenched and long-standing practices and culture. Enlisting local government to help and engage with and can help change local culture! After all, Italians trusted their local PA (42% in 2018) much more than the Italian parliament (19%) decreeing PA digital transformation.

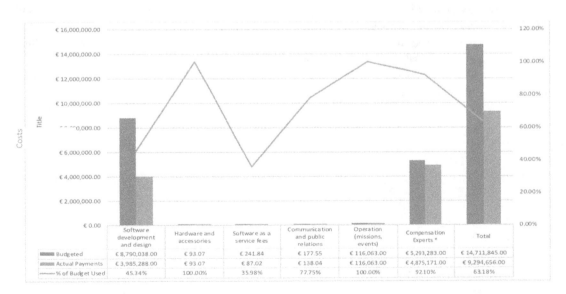

	Software development and design	Hardware and accessories	Software as a service fees	Communication and public relations	Operation (missions, events)	Compensation Experts *	Total
Budgeted	€ 8,790,038.00	€ 93.07	€ 241.84	€ 177.55	€ 116,063.00	€ 5,293,283.00	€ 14,711,845.00
Actual Payments	€ 3,985,288.00	€ 93.07	€ 87.02	€ 138.04	€ 116,063.00	€ 4,875,171.00	€ 9,294,656.00
% of Budget Used	45.34%	100.00%	35.98%	77.75%	100.00%	92.10%	63.18%

Fig. 14.11 *Team Digitale* budget utilization (since establishment of Team Digitale until 01/25/2019) (*Data* Team Digitale)

Did you know that?

The biggest digital transformation challenge is building trust around 4IR technologies, especially when the Internet and Social Media are rife with rumour-mongering that sows division and discrepancies!

That's where technology and improved design can change attitudes. Team Digitale built their PA digital transformation projects offering the best user experience (UX) based on accessibility and transaction simplicity (reminders, notifications, easy linking to payments). Italians may be wary of dealing with government but might welcome interacting with an independent solution from *Team Digitale*, uninfluenced by political parties and agendas. Once Italians realize that *Team Digitale* does not carry a partisan agenda but focused on building efficiencies for all citizens with a simple and smooth user experience, Italians will adopt the change.

Team Digitale was continuously expanding the ecosystem. More than 90% of Italian banks and payment service providers were on the platform, following strict PCI (payment card industry) security standards. Any public administration can use Team Digitale's PA APIs to link onto ANPR registry and the PagoPA digital payment platform. Team Digitale was increasing types and quality of PA services, integrating a multitude of public services such as water and sewage, school fees, health expenses, and car licenses.

Silver Lining and a Cloud

Change management requires simplified governance. For Italy, restructuring AgID and creating a single permanent body that eliminates bureaucracy is important, especially when PA digital transformation underscores a simplified, frictionless government. The new permanent digital transformation body liaise with local governments for nationwide execution. It can also help local governments transition and digitize its existing infrastructure and processes. Paired with local governments can increase social inclusion and participation. Together, they can increase trust and transparency—necessary for nationwide PA digital transformation adoption.

On December 14, 2018, Italy had passed Legislative Decree no. 135. This decree granted legal authority and transferred the governance of Team Digitale's projects to the Prime Minister's office. Team Digitale was set to be a part of the Ministry of the Interior, a permanent cabinet office. That was a deliberate and strong signal of support and continuity from the government. Team Digitale could now follow UK's GDS (Government Digital Services) model to remove redundancies and consolidate resources to build a stronger, more visionary digital body.

In a digital age, *vox digitalis, vox populi* (the digital voice is the voice of people).

References

Datta, P. (2020). Digital transformation of the Italian public administration: A case study. *Communications of the Association for Information Systems, 46.* https://doi.org/10.17705/1CAIS.04611

Datta, P. (2021a). Hannibal at the gates: Cyberwarfare & the Solarwinds sunburst hack. *Journal of Information Technology Teaching Cases.* https://doi.org/10.1177/2043886921993126

Datta. P. (2021b). Cyberruse at the cybergates: Technology, people and processes. *ISACA Journal, 6*(4), 51–58.

Datta, P., & Diffee, E. (2020). Measuring sustainability performance: A green supply chain index. *Transportation Journal, 59*(1), 73–96. https://trid.trb.org/view/1682851

Datta, P., & Hill, G. (2020). Antecedent effects of info content on user attitudes toward radical technology-brand-extension: Info content on user attitudes of brand extensions. *Journal of Electronic Commerce in Organizations (JECO), 18*(1), 36–58. https://www.igi-global.com/article/antecedent-effects-of-info-content-on-user-attitudes-toward-radical-technology-brand-extension/241247

Datta, P., & Nwankpa, J. Digital transformation and pandemic crisis continuity planning during COVID-19. *Journal of Information Technology Teaching Cases,* Accepted.

Datta, P., Peck, J., Koparan, I., & Nieuwenhuizen, C. (2018). Entrepreneurial continuance logic: The interplay between climate, commitment, and entrepreneurial responsiveness. *Management Decision.* https://doi.org/10.1108/MD-05-2017-0537

Datta, P., Walker, L., & Amarilli, F. (2020). Digital transformation: Learning from Italy's public administration. *Journal of Information Technology Teaching Cases, 10*(2), 54–71. https://doi:10.1177/2043886920910437

Datta, P., Whitmore, M., & Nwankpa, J. (2021). A perfect storm: Psychological and AI (technological) antecedents to information bias anchoring (IBA) in social media news. *ACM Journal: Digital Threats: Research and Practice* (In Print).

Diffee, E., & Datta, P. (2018). Cybersecurity: The three-headed Janus. *Journal of Information Technology Teaching Cases (Journal of Information Technology* sister Journal), *8*(1), 161–171. https://doi.org/10.1057/s41266-018-0037-7

Nwankpa, J. K., & Datta, P. (2022). Leapfrogging healthcare service quality in Sub-Saharan Africa: The utility-trust rationale of mobile payment platforms. *European Journal of Information Systems, 31* (1). https://doi.org/10.1080/0960085X.2021.1978339

Nwankpa, J. K., Roumani, Y., & Datta, P. (2021, August 14). The role of digital business intensity and knowledge management. *Journal of Knowledge Management.* https://doi.org/10.1108/JKM-04-2021-0277

Rickett, L., & Datta, P. (2018). Beauty-contests in the age of financialization: Information activism and retail investor behavior. *Journal of Information Technology, 33*(1), 31–49.

Index

© PiaDura LTD 2022
P. Datta, *Global Technology Management 4.0*,
https://doi.org/10.1007/978-3-030-96929-5